INSURANCE PLANNING

James F. Dalton
Michael A. Dalton
Thomas P. Langdon
Joseph M. Gillice

4th Edition

MONEY EDUCATION
115 JAMES DRIVE WEST
SUITE 140
ST. ROSE, LA 70087
888-295-6023

Printed in the U.S.A.

ISBN-13: 978-1-936602-21-6

ABOUT THE AUTHORS

James F. Dalton, MBA, MS, CPA/PFS, CFA®, CFP®

- Adjunct professor at George Mason University (2014 - present)
- Adjunct professor at Georgetown University (2002 - 2014)
- Former Executive Vice President, Assessment Technologies Institute LLC
- Former Senior Vice President, Kaplan Professional
- Former President, Dalton Publications LLC
- Former Senior Manager of KPMG, LLP, concentrating in personal financial planning, investment planning, and litigation consulting
- MBA from Loyola University New Orleans
- Master of Accounting in Taxation from the University of New Orleans
- BS in accounting from Florida State University in Tallahassee, Florida
- Member of the CFP Board of Standards July 1996, Comprehensive CFP® Exam Pass Score Committee
- Member of the AICPA and the Louisiana Society of CPAs
- Member of the Financial Planning Association
- Member of the *Journal of Financial Planning* Editorial Review Board
- Author of *Money Education's Quick Sheets*
- Co-author of *Cases in Financial Planning: Analysis and Presentation* (1st - 2nd Editions)
- Co-author of *Retirement Planning* (1st - 11th Editions)
- Co-Author of *Fundamentals of Financial Planning* (1st - 4th Editions)
- Contributing Author of *Insurance Planning* (1st - 4th Editions)
- Contributing Author of *Estate Planning* (1st - 8th Editions)
- Author of Kaplan Schweser's Personal Financial Planning Understanding Your Financial Calculator
- Author of Kaplan Schweser's Understanding Your Financial Calculator for the CFA® Exam
- Co-author of BISYS CFA® Study Notes Volumes I and II
- Co-author of Kaplan Schweser's Personal Financial Planning Cases and Applications
- Co-author of the Kaplan Schweser Review for the CFP® Certification Examination, Volumes I–VIII and Kaplan Schweser's Financial Planning Flashcards

MICHAEL A. DALTON, PH.D., JD, CFP®

- Former Chair of the Board of Dalton Publications, L.L.C.
- Associate professor of Accounting and Taxation at Loyola University in New Orleans, Louisiana (retired)
- Adjunct professor at George Mason University (2014 - present)
- Adjunct professor at Georgetown University (2002 - 2014)
- Former Senior Vice President, Education at BISYS Group
- Ph.D. in Accounting from Georgia State University
- J.D. from Louisiana State University in Baton Rouge, Louisiana
- MBA and BBA in Management and Accounting from Georgia State University
- Former board member of the CFP Board's Board of Examiners, Board of Standards, and Board of Governors
- Former member (and chair) of the CFP Board's Board of Examiners
- Member of the Financial Planning Association
- Member of the *Journal of Financial Planning* Editorial Advisory Board
- Member of the *Journal of Financial Planning* Editorial Review Board
- Member of the LSU Law School Board of Trustees (2000 - 2006)
- Author of *Dalton Review for the CFP® Certification Examination: Volume I – Outlines and Study Guides, Volume II – Problems and Solutions, Volume III - Case Exam Book, Mock Exams A-1 and A-2* (1st - 8th Editions)
- Author of *Retirement Planning and Employee Benefits* (1st - 11th Editions)
- Author of *Estate Planning* (1st - 8th Editions)
- Author of *Fundamentals of Financial Planning* (1st - 4th Editions)
- Author of *Insurance Planning* (1st - 4th Editions)
- Co-author of *Income Tax Planning* (1st - 8th Editions)
- Co-author of *Cases in Financial Planning: Analysis and Presentation* (1st - 2nd Editions)
- Co-author of *Dalton CFA® Study Notes Volumes I and II* (1st - 2nd Editions)
- Co-author of *Dalton's Personal Financial Planning Series – Personal Financial Planning Theory and Practice* (1st - 3rd Editions)
- Co-author of *Dalton's Personal Financial Planning Series – Personal Financial Planning Cases and Applications* (1st - 4th Editions)
- Co-author of *Cost Accounting: Traditions and Innovations* published by West Publishing Company
- Co-author of the *ABCs of Managing Your Money* published by National Endowment for Financial Education (NEFE)

Joseph M. Gillice, MBA, CPA, CFP®

- President, Dalton Education, L.L.C.
- Former Director of University Programs for BISYS Education Services
- Former adjunct instructor in financial planning at Georgetown University in Washington, D.C.
- Former adjunct instructor in financial planning at Duke University in Durham, NC
- Instructor in live online financial planning programs for Rice University, New York University, and Northwestern University
- Author of *Financial Calculator Essentials*
- Co-author of *Fundamentals of Financial Planning* (1st - 4th Editions)
- Co-author of *Insurance Planning* (1st - 4th Editions)
- Co-author of *The Dalton Review® Pre-Study Materials in Fundamentals of Financial Planning and Insurance*
- Co-author of *The Dalton Review® Pre-Study Materials in Investment Planning*
- Developed the Online Executive Certificate in Financial Planning program for New York University and Northwestern University
- MBA from Georgia State University
- BS in finance from Florida State University

Thomas P. Langdon, JD, LL.M.

- Professor of Business Law, Gabelli School of Business, Roger Williams University, Bristol, RI
- Principal, Langdon & Langdon Financial Services, LLC (Connecticut-based tax planning & preparation firm)
- Former Professor of Taxation at The American College, Bryn Mawr, PA.
- Former Adjunct Professor of Insurance and Economics at The University of Connecticut Center for Professional Development
- Former Member (and Chair) of the CFP Board's Board of Examiners
- Master of Laws (LL.M.) in Taxation from Villanova University School of Law
- Juris Doctor, from Western New England College School of Law
- Master of Science in Financial Services from The American College
- Master of Business Administration from The University of Connecticut
- Bachelor of Science in Finance from The University of Connecticut, Storrs, CT.
- Chartered Financial Analyst (CFA), Certified Financial Planner (CFP), Chartered Life Underwriter (CLU), Chartered Financial Consultant (ChFC), Accredited Estate Planner (AEP), Chartered Advisor in Philanthropy (CAP), Certified Employee Benefits Specialist (CEBS), Chartered Advisor in Senior Living (CASL), Registered Employee Benefits Consultant (REBC), Registered Health Underwriter (RHU), Associate in Life & Health Claims (ALHC), and Fellow of the Life Management Institute (FLMI)
- Associate Editor of the *Journal of Financial Services Professionals*
- Co-author of *Estate Planning* (1st - 8th Editions)
- Co-author of *Income Tax Planning* (1st - 8th Editions)
- Contributing of *Insurance Planning* (1st - 4th Editions)
- Faculty member for National Tax Institute

ABOUT THE CONTRIBUTING AUTHOR

RANDAL R. CANGELOSI, JD, MBA

- Practicing litigator throughout Louisiana, in business/commercial law and litigation, products liability litigation, wills and trust litigation, environmental law and litigation, medical malpractice defense, and insurance law and litigation
- Has successfully defended numerous corporations, businesses, and doctors in jury and judge trials
- Juris Doctorate from Loyola University New Orleans
- Masters of Business Administration from Loyola University New Orleans
- BS in Finance from Louisiana State University
- Member of the American & Federal Bar Associations
- Member of the Bar of the State of Louisiana
- Member of the New Orleans and Baton Rouge Bar Associations
- Board Member of La Lupus Foundation
- Board Member of Baton Rouge Chamber of Commerce
- Former Board Member of the Baton Rouge Area Chapter of the American Red Cross
- Admitted to practice before US District Courts, Western, Eastern & Middle Districts of Louisiana
- Admitted to practice before the Federal 5th Circuit Court of Appeals
- Admitted to practice in USDC, Southern District of Iowa (Pro Hac Vice)
- Admitted to practice in Circuit Court of Wayne County, Mississippi (Pro Hac Vice)
- Admitted to practice in Circuit Court of Barbour County, Alabama (Pro Hac Vice)
- Admitted to practice in Court of Common Pleas, Darlington County, South Carolina (Pro Hac Vice)
- Admitted to practice in Los Angeles County Superior Court, California (Pro Hac Vice)
- Admitted to practice in Superior Court of New Jersey: Morris County (Pro Hac Vice)
- Admitted to practice in 17th Judicial Court, Broward County, Florida (Pro Hac Vice)
- Former Chairman of New Orleans Bar Association, Community Service Committee
- Former Chairman of New Orleans Bar Association, Food and Clothing Drives
- Co-author of *Personal Financial Planning: Theory and Practice* (1st - 3rd Editions)
- Co-author of *Professional Ethics for Financial Planners*

ABOUT THE REVIEWERS & CONTRIBUTORS

We owe a special thanks to several key professionals for their significant contribution of time and effort with this text. These reviewers provided meticulous editing, detailed calculation reviews, helpful suggestions for additional content, and other valuable comments, all of which have improved this edition

Dr. James Coleman has over 15 years teaching experience, including undergraduate, graduate, and Executive MBA programs at Troy University, Mercer University, and Dalton State College. In addition, as Vice President of Market Results, a financial planning training and consulting firm, he has helped hundreds of candidates pass the Certified Financial Planner™ exam over the last decade. Prior to his academic career, Jim spent over a decade in public accounting and corporate management, concluding with the position of Managing Director of Public Relations at Federal Express, where he was responsible for the company's global public and investor relations activities. His degrees include a MS and Ph.D. from University of Alabama as well as BBA in accountancy from University of Mississippi.

Donna Dalton made a significant contribution to this textbook by her thoughtful and meticulous editing throughout the book. She provided many valuable improvements to both the textbook and instructor materials. We are extremely grateful for her contributions.This book would not have been possible without her extraordinary dedication, skill, and knowledge.

Barbara Gavitt is currently the Vice President of Product Development for A.D. Banker & Company ITP. Barb has worked in the insurance and financial services industry and as educator and trainer since 1991. She has developed curriculum and facilitated training for insurance and securities licensing programs, continuing education, insurance designation programs, and professional development. Barb completed the Certificate in Distance Education program from Indiana University in 2011 and holds a BS in Education from Eastern Michigan University. She is also a Certified Distance Education Instructor, CDEI™, through the International Distance Education Certification Center (IDECC®).

Andrew J. Head, MA, CFP® brings 14 years of financial services experience to his position as the Director of the Western Kentucky University CFP® Board Registered Financial Planning Programs as well as the WKU Center for Financial Success. He joined the faculty at WKU in 2010 and teaches courses on Estate Planning, Tax Planning, Risk Management & Insurance Planning among others. He is the faculty advisor to the WKU Financial Planning Association (FPA) Student Chapter as well as serving on the Board of Directors for FPA of Kentuckiana. Outside of his duties with WKU, Andrew operates a multi-state fee-based RIA.

Gary J. Knoepfler, Jr., CPCU, FIC has been involved in the insurance industry in Louisiana since 1977. His experience includes Marketing, Underwriting and Management with Southern Insurance Service and several divisions of the American International Group (AIG). From 1990 until February 2011 he was the Branch Supervisor of Reimbursement Consultants, Inc, a company that handles a specialized area of workers' compensation claims, and he is now an independent consultant and a Field Agent with the Knights of Columbus. Gary attended LA Tech University and earned his Chartered Property Casualty Underwriter (CPCU) professional designation in 1993.

Katheleen F. Oakley is the Academic Program Director for classroom and web-based CFP Certification Education programs in the Susanne M. Glasscock, School of Continuing Studies at Rice University. She is co-author of Money Education's Cases in Financial Planning, Analysis and Presentation, 1st edition textbook and instructor manual. Kathy is also former vice president and chief financial planning officer with Kanaly Trust Company

(Houston, Texas), the former director of financial planning for the Houston office of Lincoln Financial Advisors, and a former board member of the Pearland Economic Development Corporation. She is a member of the Financial Planning Association. Kathy received her BS in Finance and an MBA from the University of New Orleans.

Robin Meyer made a significant contribution to this textbook by organizing and directing the entire project. Developing a textbook that is aesthetically pleasing and easy to read is a difficult undertaking. Robin worked diligently with the authors and reviewers to manage the project, performed numerous reviews, and provided invaluable feedback throughout the entire project. This book would not have been possible without her extraordinary dedication, skill, and knowledge.

Dr. Moshe Shmuklarsky has a keen personal interest in the conceptual underpinning and practical knowledge related to business and personal finance as reflected by his Master of Business Administration from the John Hopkins School of Professional Studies and a Certificate in Personal Financial Planning from the Georgetown University. Dr. Shmuklarsky has more than 25 years experience in research and development of drugs and vaccines. Through the application of the Balanced Score Card, Dr. Shmuklarsky has transformed the Department of Clinical Trials at the Walter Reed Army Institute of Research in Washington DC to a center of excellence in clinical research.

Kristi Tafalla is an attorney and personal financial planner specializing in income tax and estate planning. She teaches estate planning, income tax planning and comprehensive case courses through various CFP® Board-Registered Programs as well as comprehensive reviews for the CFP® certification. She is a contributor to Money Education's *Estate Planning for Financial Planners* and *Retirement Planning and Employee Benefits for Financial Planners*.

PREFACE

Insurance Planning is written for graduate and upperdivision undergraduate level students interested in acquiring an understanding of financial planning from a professional financial planning viewpoint. The text is intended to be used in an overall curriculum in financial planning in an Insurance course or in a course that combines Fundamentals of Financial Planning and Insurance.

This text was designed to meet the educational requirements for a Fundamentals Course in a CFP® Board-Registered Program. Therefore, one of our goals is to assure CFP® Board-Registered Program Directors, instructors, students, and financial planners that we have addressed every relevant topic covered by the CFP® Board Exam Topic List and the most recent model curriculum syllabus for this course. The book will be updated, as needed, to keep current with any changes in the law, exam topic list, or model curriculum.

SPECIAL FEATURES

A variety of tools and presentation methods are used throughout this text to assist the reader in the learning process. Some of the features in this text that are designed to enhance your understanding and learning process include:

- **Key Concepts** – At the beginning of each subsection are key concepts, or study objectives, each stated as a question. To be successful in this course, you should be able to answer these questions. So as you read, guide your learning by looking for the answers. When you find the answers, highlight or underline them. It is important that you actually highlight/underline and not just make a mental note, as the action of stopping and writing reinforces your learning. Watch for this symbol:

- **Quick Quizzes** – Following each subsection you will find a Quick Quiz, which checks and reinforces what you read. Circle the answer to each question and then check your answers against the correct answers supplied at the bottom of the quiz. If you missed any questions, flip back to the relevant section and review the material. Watch for this symbol:

- **Examples** – Examples are used frequently to illustrate the concepts being discussed and to help the reader understand and apply the concepts presented. Examples are identified in the margin with the following symbol:

EXAMPLE 1.1

- **Exhibits** – The written text is enhanced and simplified by using exhibits where appropriate to promote learning and application. Exhibits are identified with the following symbol:

EXHIBIT 1.1

- **Key Terms** – Key terms appear in **boldfaced type** throughout the text to assist in the identification of important concepts and terminology. A list of key terms with definitions appears at the end of each chapter.

- **End of Chapter Questions** – Each chapter contains a series of discussion and multiple-choice questions that highlight the major topics covered in the chapter. The questions test retention and understanding of important chapter material and can be used for review and classroom discussion.

- **Quick Quiz Explanations** – Each chapter concludes with the answers to the Quick Quizzes contained in that chapter, as well as explanation to the "false" statements in each Quick Quiz.

- **Glossary** – A compilation of the key terms identified throughout the text is located at the end of the book.

Additional Information Available on Money Education's Website (money-education.com)

- Financial Calculators
- CFP Board Principal Knowledge Topics
- Resourceful Websites

VISIT OUR WEBSITE AT MONEY-EDUCATION.COM FOR UPDATES TO THE TEXTBOOKS

Table of Contents

CHAPTER 1: INTRODUCTION TO INSURANCE

CHAPTER 2: CHARACTERISTICS OF INSURANCE

CHAPTER 3: HEALTH INSURANCE

CHAPTER 4: LIFE INSURANCE

CHAPTER 5: DISABILITY INSURANCE

CHAPTER 6: LONG-TERM CARE INSURANCE

CHAPTER 7: ANNUITIES

CHAPTER 8: PROPERTY & LIABILITY INSURANCE

CHAPTER 9: CREDIT PROTECTION

CHAPTER 10: SOCIAL SECURITY

APPENDICES

CHAPTER

1

INTRODUCTION TO INSURANCE

INTRODUCTION

"Nothing in life and nothing that we do is risk-free."[1] Our everyday life is full of risks and uncertainties. Many of these risks can have overwhelming impacts on our lives. For example, in 2013, a total of 32,719 people died in motor vehicle crashes[2]. In that same year,

- There were 1,240,000 fires reported in the United States. These fires caused 3,240 civilian deaths, 15,925 civilian injuries, and $11.5 billion in property damage.[3]
- There were 4,364 triplet births.[4]
- There were 345,031 robberies in the United States.[5]
- There were 23 lightning fatalities in the United States.
- There were a total of 53 authenticated, unprovoked [6]shark attacks across the United States in 2013[7].

Having your home burned to the ground from a fire is devastating, mentally as well as potentially financially. Having triplets? That may also be devastating, mentally, as well as financially. While extremely unlikely, being struck by lightning is certainly devastating in that it is likely to cause death, which in turn may be financially disastrous to family members.

Some risks are unavoidable. Some are easily avoidable. For example, it is easy to avoid shark attacks by staying out of the ocean. It is also easy to minimize shark attacks by staying in the very shallow waters or swimming in waters that have minimal or no reported shark activity. There are other methods that one might use to minimize shark attacks, such as shark spray.

Most shark attacks do not result in death. However, most are extremely painful, may result in the loss of limbs, and will generally require time in the hospital. Therefore, most shark attacks have a financial cost. This potential cost is not something that most people think about when they step off the sandy beach into the murky waters of the ocean.

For those who are willing to accept the risk of entering the ocean, where sharks reside, they could attempt to jointly lower the severity of any financial cost of a shark attack. They could do this by each voluntarily contributing a small sum of money into a shared pot. With as many people who enter the ocean, contributing even a single dollar could create a massive pot of money to help the victims of shark bites. There may be some ocean goers who choose to not join the group and thus, not be covered by the pool of funds. Some might even argue that surfers and those who frequent the ocean are at greater risk compared to the casual beach vacationer and should therefore contribute two dollars. This concept of pooling risk and pooling resources is the basis of insurance today. The concept that those who are at greater risk, such as the surfers, should be required to pay more in premiums to be covered is also a key part of insurance today.

1. Quote from Ken Salazar, former United States Secretary of the Interior
2. National Highway Traffic Safety Administration. 2014. 2013 motor vehicle crashes: overview. Report no. DOT HS-812-101. Washington, DC: US Department of Transportation.
3. www.nfpa.org/research/reports-and-statistics/fires-in-the-us
4. www.cdc.gov/nchs/fastats/multiple.htm
5. www.fbi.gov/about-us/cjis/ucr/crime-in-the-u.s/2013/crime-in-the-u.s.-2013/violent-crime/robbery-topic-page
6. www.lightningsafety.noaa.gov/fatalities/fatalities13.shtml
7. Shark Research Institute

Insurance, as described in our shark example, is equivalent to paying money into a pot that will pay in the event that someone is hurt, injured, or in need based on the risk that is being insured. However, there are other ways to minimize loss from risks.

Two ways to minimize losses are to avoid the risk and to minimize the risk. For example, it turns out that more than 80 percent of the victims of lightning are male and most strikes occur during the summer months. It also turns out that the largest percentage of lightning strikes occurred while victims were fishing. While the data is clear that males are more likely to be struck by lightning, it is unlikely that lightning picks out the males from the females. It is more likely that it is the activities that males are engaged in that result in being struck by lightning. Given this limited information, it should be easy to reduce the likelihood of being hit by lightning by avoiding fishing, for example. Just by avoiding fishing or avoiding the summer months while fishing will reduce the likelihood of being stuck by lightning.

How would someone avoid risk? In the case of sharks, staying out of the ocean will avoid the risk. In the case of lightning, staying indoors will likely accomplish this avoidance of risk. However, it is often not possible or practical to completely avoid risk. Ocean activities are enjoyable and most people are rightly unconcerned about shark attacks. Likewise, most people are conscious of the risks of lightning strikes and mitigate these risks in various ways, including not holding a 1 iron to the sky in a thunderstorm in the middle of a fairway.[8]

HISTORY OF INSURANCE

Insurance is very common today. We are required to have liability insurance to obtain a drivers license. We are asked if we want insurance when we purchase a vacation or buy electronics that cost more than about $100. However, insurance is not a new financial concept or product. Interestingly enough, the use of "insurance" dates back to thousands of years BC where traders used the principles of insurance to minimize the risk of loss. In addition, the Greeks and the Romans set up guilds or organizations designed to care for the families of members who died. If a member died, the guild provided for the needs of the families that were left behind.

In 1666, the Great Fire of London consumed over 13,000 homes. Out of this devastation was born the need for fire insurance. Many of the early companies that began after the fire had their own fire department to minimize the damage of fire for the members whose property was insured with them. Over time, the idea of a municipal fire department replaced the flawed concept of each company maintaining its own fire department.

The oldest documented insurance company to come out of this tragic event was started back in 1710 and was originally know as Sun Fire Office. Today, it is part of, through various acquisitions, the company known as RSA Insurance Group, which is based in London, England and generates more than $12 billion in annual revenue.[9]

8. Lee Trevino, a very successful professional golfer who competed with Jack Nicklaus, was actually hit by lightning in 1975. His famous quote is that "not even God can hit a 1 iron."
9. www.rsagroup.com

Although the Greeks and Romans set up guilds to care for surviving family members, the first life insurance policy taken out is credited to Richard Martin in 1583. The policy was a one-year term policy on the life of William Gybbon, who was a citizen of London. Initially, the insurer refused to pay when Gybbon died within that year. However, after the case was adjudicated, Martin was awarded the proceeds.[10] Today, life insurance is sold in many forms, from inexpensive term insurance to more expensive permanent policies that are designed to provide coverage for life.

Disability insurance has its beginnings in England with the Railway Passengers Insurance Company of London in 1849. This insurance was to provide protection for the dangerous journeys on the relatively new train system.[11] Disability insurance has expanded significantly from those early days. Today, disability policies insure against sickness and accidents and have numerous definitions of what it means to be disabled. This flexibility in terms of how a disability is defined allows for consumers to acquire the proper type of coverage based on their particular needs.

Germany became the first nation in the world to adopt an old-age social insurance program in 1889, designed by Germany's Chancellor, Otto von Bismarck. The idea was first put forward, at Bismarck's behest, in 1881 by Germany's Emperor, William the First, in a ground-breaking letter to the German Parliament. William wrote: "*. . . those who are disabled from work by age and invalidity have a well-grounded claim to care from the state.*"[12]

By the time America moved to social insurance in 1935 the German system was using age 65 as its retirement age. But this was not the major influence on the Committee on Economic Security (CES) when it proposed age 65 as the retirement age under Social Security. This decision was not based on any philosophical principle or European precedent. It was, in fact, primarily pragmatic, and stemmed from two sources. One was a general observation about prevailing retirement ages in the few private pension systems in existence at the time and, more importantly, the 30 state old-age pension systems then in operation. Roughly half of the state pension systems used age 65 as the retirement age and half used age 70. The new federal Railroad Retirement System passed by Congress earlier in 1934, also used age 65 as its retirement age. Taking all this into account, the CES planners made a rough judgment that age 65 was probably more reasonable than age 70. This judgment was then confirmed by the actuarial studies.[13]

In 1935, there were 7.8 million Americans who were age 65 or older. The average life expectancy for a 65 year old in 1940 was 12.7 years for males and 14.7 years for females. As President Franklin D. Roosevelt said on August 14, 1935, at the signing of the law authorizing Social Security, the intent of the Social Security program is to "give some measure of protection to the average citizen and to his family against the loss of a job and against poverty-ridden old age." At its inception, Social Security was intended to provide retirement benefits only. In 2014, over 59 million Americans will receive almost $863 billion in benefits from The Social Security Administration. The program provides many more benefits that were initially contemplated, including benefits to retired workers, spouses, family members, and disabled workers. In addition, Medicare, which was passed into law in 1954, provides health benefits for those who are age 65 or older.

10. *The Life Insurance Game*, by Ronald Kessler, Holt, Rinehart and Winston, New York, 1985.
11. A. P. Woodward. "The Disability Insurance Policy"
12. SSA.gov/history
13. SSA.gov/history

Social Security Costs 1940 to 2020

EXHIBIT 1.1

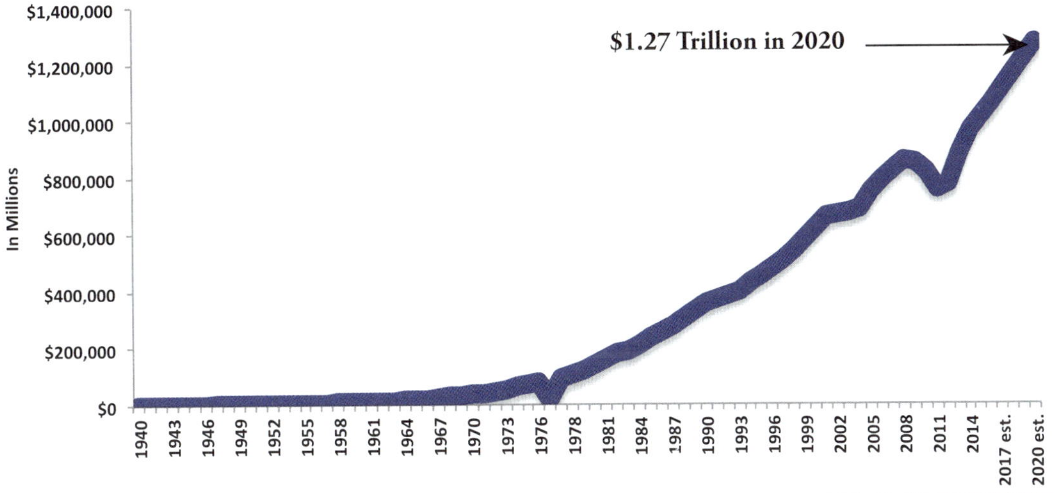

Source: White House Budget Historical Files

In addition to the more common forms of insurance, there are more esoteric types of insurance. Lloyds of London is the most famous insurance company in the world providing unusual types of insurance. Lloyds is an insurance market of members that was founded in a coffee shop in 1688. The company began in marine insurance, but is more famous for the unusual policies it writes. For example, it has written the following unusual insurance policies:

- Ben Turpin, silent film comedian of the 1920s, bought a $25,000 insurance policy with Lloyd's, payable if his trademark crossed eyes ever uncrossed.
- In the 1930s, "Jimmy 'the Schnozzle' Durante's infamously large nose was insured by Lloyd's for $140,000."
- Marlene Dietrich insured her voice for $1,000,000.
- Bruce Springsteen insured his voice for £3.5m.
- Bette Davis insured her tiny waist against weight gain for $28,000.
- Betty Grable insured her legs for $1,000,000.
- In 2006, David Beckham, famous soccer player, insured his legs for £100m.
- Dolly Parton has insured her reputedly breasts for £3.8m.
- Rolling Stones' guitarist Keith Richards' hands are insured for $1.6m.
- James Dean took out a policy on his life for $100,000 just a week before his tragic death at the age of 25.[14]

These are but a few of the famous and unusual policies underwritten by Lloyds, which is known as the world's leading market for specialized insurance. Lloyds is also well known for Kidnap and Ransom (K&R) insurance, which is becoming more important for celebrities and corporate executives around the world.

There are other types of unusual insurance. Athlete's have special needs in terms of insurance in the event of an injury disabling them from playing their sport. In terms of extremely unusual

14. www.lloyds.com/lloyds/about-us/history/innovation-and-unusual-risks/going-out-on-a-limb

insurance, a London based company sold more than 30,000 alien abduction insurance policies throughout Europe, according to Geico's website.

INSURANCE INDUSTRY

Today, the insurance industry is a significant part of the United States economy with U.S. insurance net premiums written totaling over $1 trillion in 2014.[15] The insurance industry employs 2.5 million people as of the end of 2014,[16] and accounts for over 2 percent of the U.S. economy.

Insurers in the United States rank among the largest purchasers of corporate, sovereign, state, and local bonds. Insurer investment portfolios also include short-term commercial paper, asset-backed securities, and other financial instruments. Some U.S. insurers are significant participants in other institutional markets, such as the derivatives and securities lending markets.

Insurers have also been diversifying by expanding into new geographic markets and developing a greater array of insurance product offerings and services. Some insurers and non-insurance affiliates have become more involved with the broader U.S. financial markets, not only as customers or counterparties, but also by engaging in activities such as banking and asset management services. Evidence of this interconnectedness of insurers with the broader financial system was apparent in the financial crisis. Although firms such as American International Group (AIG) represent the most prominent examples, other insurers were also affected by the recent financial crisis.

In Title V of the Dodd-Frank Wall Street Reform and Consumer Protection Act (the Dodd-Frank Act), Congress established the Federal Insurance Office (FIO) within the U.S. Department of the Treasury. In addition to advising the Secretary of the Treasury (Secretary) on major domestic and prudential international insurance policy issues and serving as a non-voting member on the Financial Stability Oversight Council (Council), FIO is authorized, pursuant to the Dodd-Frank Act, to:

- monitor all aspects of the insurance industry, including identifying issues or gaps in the regulation of insurers that could contribute to a systemic crisis in the insurance industry or the U.S. financial system;
- monitor the extent to which traditionally under-served communities and consumers, minorities, and low- and moderate-income persons have access to affordable insurance products;
- recommend to the Council that it designate an insurer as an entity subject to regulation as a nonbank financial company supervised by the Board of Governors of the Federal Reserve System (Federal Reserve);
- coordinate federal efforts and develop federal policy on prudential aspects of international insurance matters, including representing the United States, as appropriate, in the International Association of Insurance Supervisors and assisting the Secretary in negotiating covered agreements; and
- consult with States regarding insurance matters of national importance and prudential insurance matters of international importance.

15. www.naic.org/cipr_topics/industry_snapshots/snapshot_ye_14.htm
16. BLS

PERSPECTIVE OF THE TEXT

The perspective of this text is that of a professional advisor who is providing professional services to clients in the area of risk management and insurance. In order to provide the highest level of service to the client, the advisor must have a thorough knowledge of important areas of risk and the best methods for mitigating those risks.

The advisor must have a working knowledge of risks that can wreak financial havoc on a person's or family's financial situation. Some of these risks are:

- premature death
- disability
- health issues
- liability issues
- property damage
- long-term care needs
- running out of money during retirement

The advisor must also have a thorough understanding of products that can minimize the financial impact of such events. Many of the products are complex and have numerous tradeoffs that the consumer must navigate.

Advisors need a deep understanding of retirement, disability, and survivorship benefits provided by Social Security and the benefits provided by Medicare to properly advise clients of the government sponsored safety net programs and to determine any gaps that need to be filled to meet client goals or needs.

EXHIBIT 1.2

OVERVIEW OF THE TEXT

Chapter(s)	Topic
2	Characteristics of Insurance
3	Health Insurance
4	Life Insurance
5	Disability Insurance
6	Long-Term Care Insurance
7	Annuities
8	Property & Liability
9	Credit Protection
10	Social Security

CHAPTER

2

CHARACTERISTICS OF INSURANCE

LEARNING OBJECTIVES

After reading this chapter, you should be able to:

1. Identify and explain the four categories of risk.
2. Describe and explain the personal risk management process and its seven steps.*
3. Describe how insurers use risk pooling to pay for losses incurred by policyholders.*
4. Determine and select the best risk management alternatives using the risk management decision chart for individuals.
5. Provide examples of the 4 primary risk management techniques available to individuals.*
6. Explain the causes and contributors to losses including perils and hazards.
7. Identify the requisites for an insurable risk.
8. Describe insurance as a legal contract including the elements of a valid contract and the unique characteristics of an insurance contract.
9. Describe law of agency.
10. Differentiate the types of insurance companies.
11. Define and communicate key insurance policy terms, coverage, conditions, & exclusions.*
12. Describe the underwriting process and adverse selection.
13. Calculate co-insurance costs for property.
14. Identify the various valuation methods used in insurance.
15. Explain the factors that affect policyholder premiums and recommend appropriate methods for reducing household insurance costs.*
16. Describe how the insurance industry is regulated and rated.

* CFP Board Resource Document - Student-Centered Learning Objectives based upon CFP Board Principal Topics.

INTRODUCTION

As discussed in Chapter 1, insurance is a product used by individuals and companies to transfer risks and the financial uncertainty regarding those risks to third party insurers. These individuals and companies pay a premium to a third party insurance company, which determines the premiums based upon the expected claims to be paid out during a given time period. The theory behind insurance is that individuals and companies are pooling their premium dollars, so that anyone in the pool of similar risks that suffers a financial loss, will be able to recoup most (if not all) of those financial losses. The third party insurer is providing a convenient way to pool and manage those risks that it insures.

Insurance coverage is usually a critical component of a personal comprehensive financial plan. As a financial advisor, it is important to have an in-depth understanding of various types of risk exposures, appropriate types of insurance, and dollar amounts of appropriate coverage for an individual or family. Most individuals require some or all of the following:

- Life insurance to protect against premature death
- Health insurance to protect against injury or sickness for all family members
- Disability insurance to protect against the loss of income from the inability to work due to sickness or accident
- Property insurance to protect a home, personal property, the personal auto, or other assets
- Long-term care insurance to provide benefits for custodial care and/or skilled nursing care
- Personal liability insurance to protect personal assets and future earnings from potential liability judgments

One of the financial advisor's most important responsibilities is to assist individuals and families in avoiding catastrophic financial losses. This chapter explores types of insurable risks, elements of an insurance contract, legal characteristics of an insurance contract, the risk management process, and risk management techniques.

CATEGORIES OF RISK

KEY CONCEPTS

1. Distinguish between pure risk and speculative risk.
2. Identify the differences between subjective and objective risks.
3. Determine why the law of large numbers is useful for insurance companies.

Insurance is simply a legal contract between the insured and the insurance company (insurer), by which the insured transfers risks to the insurer and the insured pays a premium to the insurer. In return for the premiums, the insured receives a promise from the insurer to pay in the event the insured experiences a covered financial loss. There are certain types of risks that can be transferred to an insurance company, while other risks are not transferable because they are not insurable. These uninsurable risks are discussed later in this chapter. **Risk** is defined as the chance of loss, uncertainty associated with loss, or the possibility of a loss. Risk can be divided into four categories:

- Pure and Speculative Risk
- Subjective and Objective Risk
- Fundamental and Particular Risk
- Nonfinancial and Financial Risk

PURE AND SPECULATIVE RISK

Pure risk is the chance of a loss or no loss occurring. With pure risks, there is no chance of experiencing a gain. An example of a pure risk is, either your car is in an accident and damaged or it is not. Pure risks are insurable, since an insurance company is only going to pay when the insured actually suffers a financial loss. Pure risks include many of the same risks all individuals are exposed to and the types of risk a planner must evaluate and plan for each client. Examples of pure risks include:

- Premature death of a primary wage earner
- A prolonged illness or injury of a client or family member
- The inability of the client to work because of sickness or accident
- Wind damage to the personal residence
- The inability of the client to take care of himself in old age
- A legal judgment against the client

Speculative risk is the chance of loss, no loss, or a profit. Speculative risk is the risk that an investor takes when buying a stock or an entrepreneur takes when starting a business. The investor or entrepreneur makes an investment and takes the risk in the hopes of experiencing a profit. Insurance is not available for speculative risks because most speculative risks are willingly entered into for the purpose of making a profit.

Subjective and Objective Risk

Subjective risk is the risk that an individual perceives based on their prior experiences and the severity of those experiences. Individuals perceive risks differently and their behavior in addressing those risks depends upon that perception. If an individual perceives the subjective risk to be high, then the individual will take appropriate steps to reduce the subjective risk.

EXAMPLE 2.1

Every Friday night, Brandon and Ivan go to their local bar to celebrate the start of a new weekend. They typically have multiple shots of whiskey and wash them down with a few mojitos. One Friday night, while driving home, Brandon is pulled over and arrested for DUI. Brandon serves six months in jail, pays a $10,000 fine, and serves 200 hours of community service. Ivan on the other hand, manages to drive home each Friday night without being stopped. The next time Brandon and Ivan go out, Brandon has one drink and calls a cab to drive him home. Ivan on the other hand, has multiple drinks, gets in his car and drives home. Brandon currently has higher subjective risk than Ivan, because Brandon perceives severe negative consequences of another DUI. Objective risk in this case is measured by blood alcohol level.

Objective risk is the difference between the expected and actual losses. As the number of loss exposures (or the pool of insureds) increases, objective risk is reduced because the actual results are more likely to approximate expected claims. Objective risk varies indirectly with the number of loss exposures in an insured pool. The better an insurer is able to manage its objective risk, the more efficiently they can price premiums.

EXAMPLE 2.2

An insurance company has 50,000 auto policies and expects to pay claims on 10% or 5,000 policies during the year. The actual claims for the year are 4,900 which is 100 fewer claims than the insurance company expected. The variation between expected claims of 5,000 and actual claims of 4,900 is objective risk. Objective risk is generally measurable while subjective risk is a feeling.

Fundamental and Particular Risk

Fundamental risk is a risk that can impact a large number of individuals at one time, such as war or an earthquake. Fundamental risks are difficult for insurers to insure, because they can lead to severe financial consequences for the insurance company. Some fundamental risks, such as war or a nuclear hazard, are uninsurable. Other fundamental risks, such as an earthquake or flood, are insurable but require a separate earthquake or flood insurance policy. Some fundamental risks, such as flood insurance or unemployment insurance, require government support or social insurance programs.

A **particular risk** is a risk that can impact a particular individual, such as death or the inability to work because of a sickness or accident. An important difference between fundamental risk and particular risk is that fundamental risk will impact a large group of individuals simultaneously, whereas a particular risk only impacts one individual.

Nonfinancial and Financial Risk

Nonfinancial risk is a risk that would result in a loss, other than a monetary loss. An example of nonfinancial risk is the emotional distress a family experiences when a loved one dies. **Financial**

risk is a loss of financial value, such as the premature death of a family's primary wage earner. Life insurance can protect against this financial risk, help the family achieve financial goals and provide a lump-sum amount to pay expenses for the family during the grieving process.

Understanding Risk

EXHIBIT 2.1

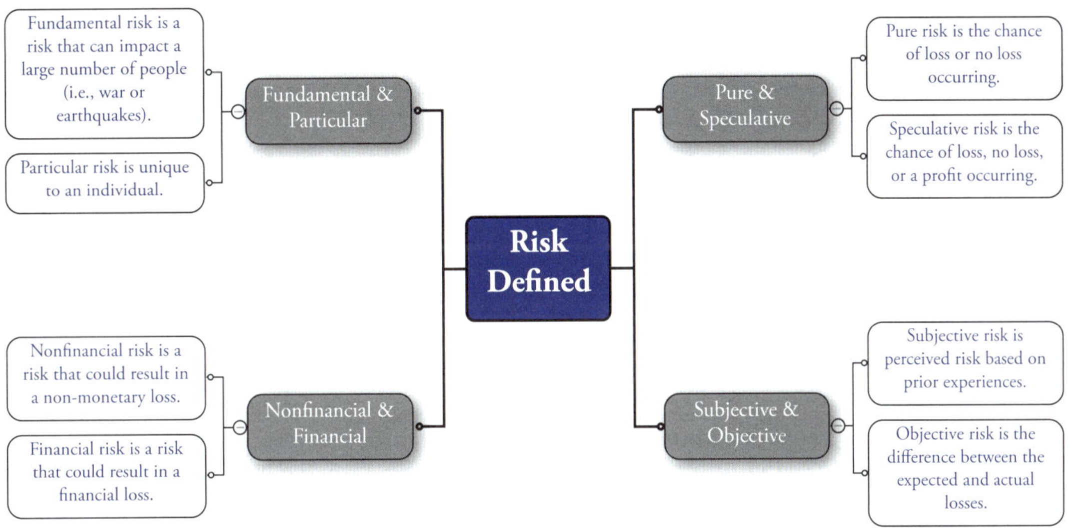

Probability of Loss

The probability of loss is the chance that a loss will occur. For example, suppose historical data establishes that 1 in 10 males (10%) age 50 are going to become disabled in a year. It is possible with a sample size of 10 that all 10 could become disabled or that none of the sample become disabled. As the pool of insureds increases to 100,000, it is more likely that the actual number of disability claims for the pool will be 10 percent as expected. The larger the sample size, the more likely the actual losses will approach the expected losses.

Law of Large Numbers

The **law of large numbers** is a principle that states that actual outcomes will approach the mean probability as the sample size increases. So, if a coin is flipped 10 times, we would expect five heads and five tails. However, with only ten flips, it is more likely that the actual results will be different than a 50/50 distribution between heads and tails. Here is a computer simulation of a coin being flipped 10 times. This exercise was conducted five times, with the following results for each.

Round	Heads vs. Tails	Result
Round 1	2 vs. 8	20/80
Round 2	3 vs. 7	30/70
Round 3	6 vs. 4	60/40
Round 4	4 vs. 6	40/60
Round 5	7 vs. 3	70/30
Total	22 vs. 28	44/56

With a small sample size, the average result was 44 percent heads and 56 percent tails. When the computer simulation determines the outcome of 100 coin flips, the percentage of heads versus tails is 48.5 percent heads and 51.5 percent tails; however at 1,000 flips the percentage is 49.4 percent heads and 50.6 percent tails. As sample size increases, the actual results of the coin flips approach the expected probability of 50/50. The law of large numbers is useful for insurance companies because the larger the insured pool, the more likely actual losses will approach the expected losses, thereby reducing forecasting error and objective risk. This results in insurance premiums that are more efficient and thus are less costly to the insured.

QUICK QUIZ 2.1

1. Pure risks include many of the same risks all individuals are exposed to and the types of risk a planner must evaluate and plan for each client.
   a. True
   b. False

2. Subjective risk is the variation of actual amount of losses that occur over a period of time compared to the expected amount of losses.
   a. True
   b. False

3. The law of large numbers is useful for insurance companies because the larger the insured pool, the more likely actual losses will approach the probability of losses.
   a. True
   b. False

True, False, True.

RISK MANAGEMENT PROCESS

Part of the "analyze and evaluate" step in the financial planning process requires that a planner perform the risk management process. The risk management process includes the financial planner reviewing all of the client's risk exposures and determining the appropriate risk management technique for each risk. The risk management process includes:

- Determining the objectives of the risk management program
- Identifying the risks to which the individual is exposed
- Evaluating the identified risks for the probability and severity of the loss
- Determining the alternatives for managing the risks
- Selecting the most appropriate alternative for each risk
- Implementing the risk management plan selected
- Periodically evaluating and reviewing the risk management program

DETERMINING THE OBJECTIVES OF THE RISK MANAGEMENT PROGRAM

The first step in the risk management process is to determine the objectives of the risk management program. Risk management objectives can range from obtaining the most cost-effective protection against risk to protection of continuing income after a loss. An example of a client's stated objective may be to insure only those risks that have the potential for causing catastrophic financial loss and to do so at the minimum premium.

Identifying the Risks to Which the Individual is Exposed

The next step is to identify all possible pure risk exposures of the client. *Identifying the potential risk* is primarily a function of the client's lifecycle position. The risk exposures for an individual may be subdivided into the following categories.

1. Personal risks that may cause the loss of income (untimely death, disability, health issues), or cause an increase in the cost of living (disability, health issues).
2. Property risks that may cause the loss of property (automobile, home, or other asset).
3. Liability risks that may cause financial loss (injury to another or to property for which the client is determined to be financially responsible).

Key Concepts

1. Explain the risk management process.
2. Describe the four responses to pure risks.
3. Identify the most appropriate risks to insure based on loss severity and loss frequency.

The client's lifecycle position will help to determine if the client needs to protect against premature death, disability, and long-term care. The charts in the following examples identify the likely potential risks for a specific client based on the client's lifecycle position.

Example 2.3

Frank (age 33) and Stephanie (age 31) are married with one child, Frankie (age 10). Frank and Stephanie both work, each earning $60,000 per year. They have a 30 year mortgage, with 25 years remaining, and two car loans. They want to retire at age 62 and they plan to pay for Frankie's college education.

Potential Risks	Relevant	Reason
Life (Premature Death)	✓	They will need a lump-sum amount to retire their debt, and fund their retirement and education goals.
Health	✓	They need health insurance to cover major medical expenses.
Disability	✓	During their working years, disability coverage provides protection if one of them is unable to work because of sickness or accident.
Property	✓	The residence and personal autos should be insured because any loss could have catastrophic financial consequences.
Long-Term Care		They are too young to need long-term care which is more relevant in their 50's.
Personal Liability	✓	The risk of a lawsuit due to their negligence should be insured.

EXAMPLE 2.4

Matt (age 66) and Elma (age 65) are married with four adult children and ten grandchildren. Matt and Elma are both retired, on Social Security, and have significant retirement savings. They own their primary residence and their two autos are debt free. They do not believe they will be subject to estate taxes. Their risks are identified below:

Potential Risks	Relevant	Reason
Life (Premature Death)		They have already reached retirement, have zero debt, and do not need insurance to pay estate taxes.
Health	✓	Health insurance is important, although they qualify for Medicare at age 65. They may consider supplemental insurance to pay for gaps in Medicare (discussed later in the Social Security chapter).
Disability		They are already collecting retirement benefits, so they are not concerned about not being able to work for income.
Property	✓	The residence and personal autos should be insured because any loss could have catastrophic financial consequences.
Long-Term Care	✓	The risk of needing long-term care based on their age is relevant.
Personal Liability	✓	The risk of a lawsuit due to their negligence should be insured.

Evaluating the Identified Risks for the Probability and the Severity of the Loss

Once the potential risks are identified, the planner must analyze each of the risks based on expected loss frequency and loss severity. When evaluating risks based on their expected loss frequency, the objective is to determine how often the event is likely to occur. Loss severity measures the dollar magnitude or the absolute dollar amount of the expected financial loss were it to occur. Based on the relationship between expected loss frequency and loss severity, an appropriate risk management response to the risk can be identified and implemented. Only those risks that have severe financial consequences but occur infrequently are appropriate to transfer or insure. Examples include the inability to work because of sickness or accident, premature death, an auto accident, or a house fire.

Determining and Selecting the Best Risk Management Alternative

Selecting the appropriate risk management technique is the most critical component of the risk management process. A risk that is not properly managed may have severe financial consequences for the client. Determining the appropriate response to a pure risk requires an understanding of the techniques for risk management, which include:

- Risk Reduction
- Risk Transfer
- Risk Avoidance
- Risk Retention

A planner may use a matrix to analyze each risk, such as:

Severity / Frequency	Low Frequency of Occurrence	High Frequency of Occurrence
High Severity (catastrophic financial loss) (e.g., long-term disability)	Transfer and/or Share Risk Using Insurance	Avoid Risk
Low Severity (non-catastrophic financial loss) (e.g., car gets dented in parking lot)	Retain Risk	Retain/Reduce Risk

Risk Reduction

Risk reduction is the process of reducing the likelihood of a pure risk that is high in frequency and low in severity. Examples of risks that are high in frequency and low in severity are: car door dings, the common cold, and damage to inexpensive personal property. Risks that are high in frequency and low in severity are risks that should be reduced by taking steps to reduce the likelihood of a loss occurring.

Risk	Risk Reduction Implementation
Car Door Dings	Do not park a car next to other cars.
The Common Cold	Exercise, take vitamins, eat healthy foods, and wash hands frequently.
Damage to Household Property	Do not let children play with a ball in the house.

EXAMPLE 2.5

Joe and Holly are married with two children, ages 8 and 4. They have a two-car garage where Holly parks her SUV next to Joe's car. Every time Holly parks her SUV next to Joe's car in the garage, the 4 year old opens the door of the SUV and a new ding is put in the side of Joe's car. After six months, there are multiple door dings in the side of Joe's car. The frequency of the door dings is high, but the severity of having the door dings fixed is relatively low. The cost of repair is only a couple hundred dollars.

The appropriate steps for Joe and Holly to reduce their risk would be to help the 4-year old open the door of the SUV or for Joe to park his car in the driveway.

Risk Transfer

Risk transfer involves transferring a low frequency and high severity risk to a third party, such as an insurance company. Examples of risks that are low in frequency but high in severity include disability (or the inability to work), premature death, or damage to a personal residence. These risks do not occur very often, but when they do, there are severe financial consequences that should be transferred and insured.

EXAMPLE 2.6

Erica (age 33) and Daniel (age 35) are married with two children, ages 2 and 4. Erica works as a vice-president of marketing earning $125,000 per year and Daniel works in the home, taking care of the children. Erica and Daniel own a house with an outstanding mortgage of $400,000. They have saved $75,000 for retirement and anticipate needing $1.25 million. They have not started saving for their children's college education but they anticipate needing $80,000. Erica and Daniel are concerned about Erica becoming disabled or dying prematurely. If this were to occur, the family would not have the financial resources to payoff the mortgage or fund their retirement and education goals. Disability and premature death are risks that are low in frequency but high in financial severity. Both disability and premature death are risks that should be transferred using insurance.

Risk Retention or Accepting the Risk

Risk retention is accepting some or all of the potential loss exposure for risks that are low in frequency and low in severity. Examples of risks that are low in frequency and severity include minor property damage to a personal residence or personal auto. Deductibles and co-payments are forms of risk retention where the insured is sharing in the first dollar of a financial loss. Risk retention is an appropriate risk management strategy for risks that are low in frequency and low in severity.

EXAMPLE 2.7

Liz just purchased a 1977 VW Bug for her 16-year old daughter, Ashley, for $500. Liz decided not to purchase collision insurance on the car, since the severity of a loss would be $500. Liz is retaining the risk of the car being totaled and suffering a financial loss of 100% or $500. However, Liz does need liability insurance in the event Ashley was in an accident and sued. A judgment against Ashley (and Liz) could potentially have severe financial consequences and the liability portion of the risk should be transferred/insured.

Risk Avoidance

Risk avoidance is a risk management technique used for any risks that are high in frequency and high in severity. Activities that will very frequently result in severe financial consequences should be avoided.

EXAMPLE 2.8

Dave smokes about 3 packs of cigarettes per day. As a matter of fact, just before he falls asleep at night, he smokes one last cigarette in bed.

EXAMPLE 2.9

Brandon likes to drink heavily while tailgating before a football game. During the football game, Brandon drinks heavily and, after the football game, has a few more drinks before driving home.

Both examples, smoking in bed and drunk driving, are risks that will frequently lead to a loss (house fire or DUI accident) and result in high severity or a large financial loss. High frequency and high severity risks should be avoided. Avoidance can be applied to many pure risks, such as:

- The risk of being injured on a construction site – avoid the construction site.
- The risk of dying in a private plane crash – avoid flying in private planes.
- The risk of getting a DUI – avoid drunk driving.
- The risk of getting into an accident while talking or texting on a cell phone – avoid cell phone use while driving.

Implementing the Risk Management Plan Selected

The planner should work closely with the client to insure implementation of appropriate risk management techniques. Simply identifying and selecting the risk management technique are insufficient without implementation. The risk management plan should reflect the chosen response to a risk scenario. If risk reduction is the appropriate response to a given risk, the proper risk reduction program must be designed and implemented. If a decision is made to retain a risk, the individual must determine whether an emergency fund will be used (e.g., pet needs medical care). If the response to a given risk is to transfer the risk through insurance, an assessment and selection of an insurer usually follows.

Quick Quiz 2.2

1. Selecting the appropriate risk management technique is the most critical component of the risk management process.
   a. True
   b. False

2. Risk reduction is the process of avoiding pure risk that is high in frequency and low in severity.
   a. True
   b. False

3. Risk transfer involves transferring a high frequency and high severity risk to a third party, such as an insurance company.
   a. True
   b. False

True, False, False.

Periodically Evaluating and Reviewing the Risk Management Program

The purpose for periodic evaluation and review is twofold. First, the risk management process does not take place independently from external influences. Circumstances change over time, and risk exposures can change as well. The risk management response that was suitable last year may not be the most appropriate this year, and adjustments may need to be made.

Example 2.10

The first time Kathy met with her financial planner was three years ago. At that time, Kathy was single, age 30, earning $80,000 per year and renting a home. Today, Kathy is married, age 33, and has two young children, John age 1.5 years old and Bob 3 months old. Kathy's salary is now $125,000 per year and her husband works from home and takes care of the children. Three years ago, her financial planner would have recommended disability insurance, renter's insurance, and possibly a small life insurance policy. Now that Kathy is married, with children and a home, the planner would continue to recommend disability insurance, but also homeowner's insurance and significant life insurance. Without periodic monitoring of a client's risks, it is possible to have new risks that are not covered or inappropriately managed. Kathy needed a small amount of life insurance while single; but after getting married, having children, and purchasing a home, she needs significantly more life insurance.

Second, errors in judgment regarding the selected alternatives may occur, and periodic reviews allow the planner and client to discover such errors and revise the risk management plan as appropriate.

CAUSES OF FINANCIAL LOSS

PERILS

Perils are the immediate cause and reason for a loss occurring. Perils can be the result of an accident or sickness. Common perils include:

- Accidental death
- Disability caused by sickness or accident
- Property losses caused by fire, windstorm, tornado, earthquake, burglary, and, collision of an automobile

Perils can be specifically insured (named) in an insurance policy on a "named peril" basis where only the specific perils listed in the policy are covered. Alternatively, a policy can cover perils on an "open perils" basis, which covers all perils unless specifically identified and excluded.

EXHIBIT 2.2

TYPICAL COVERED PERILS FOR AUTO AND HOME

Personal Auto Policy (PAP)	Homeowners Insurance Policy (HO)
Fire	Fire
Storm	Lightning
Theft	Windstorm
Collision	Hail
Hail	Riot
Flood	Falling Objects
Contact with a Bird or Animal	Weight of Ice, Snow, and Sleet
Falling Objects	Smoke
Earthquake	Explosion
Windstorm	Theft

The above list is not complete, but is an example of some of the perils covered by each policy.

HAZARDS

Hazards are specific conditions that increases the likelihood of a loss occurring. A hazard does not cause the actual loss, but simply increases the probability of a loss. There are three types of hazards:

- Moral
- Morale
- Physical

The underwriter of the insurer must be aware of and be able to identify and manage these hazards.

KEY CONCEPTS

1. Identify typical perils covered under a personal auto policy.
2. Identify typical perils covered under a homeowner's insurance policy.
3. Differentiate between moral, morale, and physical hazards.

Moral Hazard

Moral hazard is the potential for loss caused by the moral character of the insured such as the filing of a false claim with the insurance company. Burning down your own house or claiming a theft occurred when it did not are types of moral hazard. Insurance companies cannot afford to insure false claims because insurance is only meant to provide coverage in the event of an actual financial loss, ones that are not intentionally caused or fraudulently claimed by the insured.

EXAMPLE 2.11

Maurice, a famous college football player for State University, filed a false police report that he had $10,000 worth of clothing, cash, and jewelry stolen from a borrowed car. There actually was no theft. The football player was hoping to collect a $10,000 check from the insurance company for the alleged stolen items. However, he found himself in jail charged with filing a false police report.

The filing of a false insurance claim is an example of a moral hazard and cannot be insured. If false claims were paid by insurers, it would result in increased premiums and people that actually need insurance would be unable to afford the insurance products.

Morale Hazard

Morale hazard is defined as indifference to risk due to the fact that the insured has insurance. Consider the person that drives to a convenience store to purchase a gallon of milk. They pull into the parking spot, leaving the car running and doors unlocked while they enter the convenience store. This person is not concerned about their car being stolen perhaps because they have auto insurance.

Insurers want to incentivize an insured to prevent morale hazard. The way an insurer accomplishes this is through the use of deductibles. With a deductible, the insured pays the first dollars of loss until the deductible is satisfied. Thus, when an insured is considering leaving the keys in the ignition and the car running while they are in a convenience store, the insured may stop and think "do I want to risk paying a $500 or $1,000 deductible if my car is stolen?" Deductibles help to align the best interest of the insurer and the insured to reduce the risk of morale hazard.

QUICK QUIZ 2.3

1. Perils can be specifically covered in an insurance policy on a "named peril" basis where only specific perils listed in the policy are covered.
   a. True
   b. False

2. Physical hazard is indifference to a loss created because the insured has insurance.
   a. True
   b. False

True, False.

Physical Hazard

Physical hazard is a physical condition that increases the likelihood of a loss occurring. Examples of physical hazards include wet floors, icy roads or roads with poor lighting. A physical hazard does not actually cause the accident or the loss, it is simply just a condition that increases the probability of a loss occurring.

EXAMPLE 2.12

Peter is walking down the sidewalk to the local hardware store. While looking across the street he doesn't notice the banana peel on the sidewalk, steps on it, slips and falls breaking his arm. The banana peel was a physical hazard that increased the likelihood of someone falling.

REQUISITES FOR AN INSURABLE RISK

Not all risks are created equal, and not all risks are insurable. A risk that is ideally situated to be an insured risk meets the following requirements:

1. It has a large number of homogeneous exposures.
2. The insured losses must be accidental, from the insured's point of view.
3. The insured losses must be measurable and determinable.
4. The loss must not be financially catastrophic to the insurer.
5. The loss probability must be determinable.
6. The premium for risk coverage must be reasonable and affordable.

Items 1 – 5 are required from the insurer's perspective for the insurer to be willing to provide insurance for a particular risk. Item 6 is a requirement of consumers and represents the likely willingness to purchase an insurance product to cover a pure risk.

Large Number of Homogeneous Exposures

There are two important requirements for a risk to be insurable. The first requirement is that there are a large number of exposures. The second requirement is that the large number of exposures is homogeneous. Both of these requirements are important for a risk to be insurable meaning an insurance company can accurately predict future losses and charge affordable premiums based on forecasted claims.

Key Concepts

1. Identify the requisites for an insurable risk.
2. Identify why the law of large numbers is important to insurance companies.

Law of Large Numbers

The law of large numbers tells us that the more similar the events or exposures, the more likely the actual losses will equal the expected losses. This is important for an insurance company so that the actual claims they pay are very close to the probability of total losses. If the pool of insureds is small, the actual losses could vary significantly from the expected losses, which could lead to financial insolvency of the insurer.

EXAMPLE 2.13

Assume the probability of males, ages 55-64, dying this year is 1 out of 1,000, and each insured owns a $1 million death benefit policy. For every pool of 1,000 males, the insurance company is going to charge premiums based upon paying 1 death benefit (or $1 million) claim this year. If the insurance company experienced two, three or four deaths this year from this pool, their actual death benefit claims would be $2, $3 or $4 million, which is significantly greater than the expected total losses of $1 million per 1,000 male pool. The premiums charged for a probability of 1 out of 1,000 may not offset two or more deaths if such variance continued for many years.

EXAMPLE 2.14

Now, assume the probability of males dying this year, between the ages of 55 - 64 is 890 out of 100,000. Now the insurance company is able to base premiums on 890 claims out of 100,000 insureds. If 900 - 910 of the age 55 - 64 group insureds die this year, the deviation from the expected results is much smaller, since the population of insureds is 100,000 rather than 1,000.

Large Number of Homogeneous Exposure Units

An insurance company needs the pool of loss exposures to be homogeneous (alike). This allows the insurance company to more accurately predict the loss probability and charge an appropriate premium. For example, when determining the premium for an auto policy, the type of car driven is a risk factor. The insurance company pools all male drivers of sports cars with turbo V-8 engines into one group of homogeneous risks and charges a risk premium. Other drivers who drive a four-door, four-cylinder Honda Accord are classified into a different homogenous risk pool and charged a lower premium because the risk exposure is greater for a sports car than for a four-door sedan. Also, consider an Alaska King Crab fisherman working on the Bering Sea with 60-foot waves in the freezing cold versus a stand up comedian. The probability of the insurance company paying a disability or life insurance claim on an Alaska crab fisherman is much greater than paying a disability or life insurance claim on a stand-up comedian that gets hit by a tomato for a bad joke.

Insured Losses Must be Accidental

Actual losses must be accidental from the insurer's perspective because premiums are based on the probability of a loss occurring based on historical information and claims. A tree falling on a house during a bad storm is an accidental loss and covered because the insurer can estimate the probability of losses based on historical information and claims of trees falling on a house. However, intentionally burning down a house that you own and insure to collect the insurance proceeds is an intentional act and is not a covered loss. If insurance companies covered intentional acts of insureds, premiums would increase and may become unaffordable for most individuals.

Loss Must be Measurable and Determinable

Since most losses covered by an insurance contract result in a financial payment to the insured, the actual timing of the loss and amount of the loss must be known. A typical insurance contract is going to offer the promise to pay in the event of a loss, but that promise to pay is only good for a period of time. Consider insurance on a primary residence. The premium is paid for the year, so the insurance company agrees to pay in the event of a loss, if the loss occurs during that one-year period. Once that time expires, the insured must pay a new premium to receive the promise from the insurer to pay for a loss over the next one year.

Losses must also be measurable in terms of the amount of loss. If the probability of a loss is too uncertain, the risk will be considered uninsurable. Back in the mid 1950s, it was determined that the loss caused by a nuclear power plant melt down was too uncertain and potentially so severe that the insurance industry excluded the cost of nuclear power plant failures from insurance policies.

When considering insurance on a primary residence, it is fairly easy to determine the amount to rebuild the house in the event it burns to the ground. However, it is more difficult to determine the amount of cash or jewelry kept in the house, in the event of theft or fire. For hard to value items and those that have moral hazard associated, the insurer may place specific limits on such items.

Typical limits placed on items in a homeowner's policy include:

- Money / Cash = $200
- Jewelry, Furs, and Watches = $1,000
- Firearms = $2,000
- Silverware and Goldware = $2,500

If an insured owns items that exceed these limits, it will be necessary to provide the insurance company with documentation regarding the value and then increase the underlying limits of the policy. Riders and endorsements enable an insured to increase these underlying limits for an increased premium and are discussed later in this text.

Loss Must Not be Financially Catastrophic to the Insurer

Some loss exposures are so financially devastating because the loss would impact too big an area or segment of the population, that an insurance company cannot afford to pay all the claims if the event occurs. The amount that an insurance company receives for any loss is relatively small in comparison to the total possible. For example, a war or nuclear hazard could affect such a large area, such as multiple cities and states, and the financial loss would be so severe, that an insurance company could not afford to pay all of the claims. A loss exposure that would be financially catastrophic to the insurer is an uninsurable risk, which is why an insurer excludes perils such as flood, earthquake, nuclear hazard and acts of war.

EXAMPLE 2.15

Hurricane Katrina hit Louisiana and Mississippi in September of 2005 causing over $81 billion in property damage. Much of the damage shown on the news was the result of massive flooding when the levees surrounding New Orleans and the local parishes were breached. Approximately ½ of all residents affected by the flooding did not have flood insurance. Flood is excluded from homeowners' insurance policies; it must be purchased from the National Flood Insurance Program administered by the Federal Emergency Management Agency.[1] One of the issues raised in the aftermath of Hurricane Katrina was whether the property damage and losses were the result of windstorm or flood. Homeowners who did not have flood insurance argued that the damage from a hurricane is due to windstorm, which is a covered peril under a homeowner's policy. However, the insurance industry argued that the damage was caused by flooding when the levees were breached.

The terrorist acts on September 11th, 2001 which, in addition to the loss of over 3,000 lives, caused almost $10 billion in losses for the insurance industry. The insurance companies did not call the events of 9/11 an "Act of War," which is an exclusion on property insurance policies. However, shortly after 9/11, insurance companies began to exclude "Acts of Terrorism" from insurance policies. As a result, The Terrorism Reform Act of 2002 was passed to provide a federal government "backstop" for losses arising out of acts of terrorism. Private insurers are now able to offer coverage for acts of terrorism, with the federal government paying 90 percent of losses above a threshold.[2]

1. FEMA http://www.fema.gov
2. http://www.thefreelibrary.com/Understanding+the+benefits+of+the+Terrorism+Risk+Insurance+Act.+...-a096554237

Quick Quiz 2.4

1. The law of large numbers tells us that the more similar events or exposures, the more likely the actual results will equal the expected results.
   a. True
   b. False

2. Actual losses must be accidental from the insurer's perspective because premiums are based on the probability of a loss occurring based on historical information and claims.
   a. True
   b. False

3. A loss exposure that would be financially catastrophic to the insured is an uninsurable risk.
   a. True
   b. False

True, True, False.

Premium Must be Reasonable

Premiums must be reasonable and affordable for the insured. Before an individual transfers a risk to an insurer, the individual will conduct a cost benefit analysis of the premium relative to the risk and severity being covered.

EXAMPLE 2.16

Sydney, age 17, drives a 15-year-old Honda Accord with 175,000 miles on the car. The fair market value of the car is $800. To insure the car in the event of a collision, the premium is $900. The benefit Sydney would receive if she totals her car would be $800, less any deductible. Sydney would be better off self-insuring against the risk of property damage to her car.

EXAMPLE 2.17

William, age 33, drives a new Mercedes Benz, with a fair market value of $50,000. To insure the car for collision, the premium is $900 per year. The benefit William would receive if he totals his new Mercedes would be $50,000 less his deductible. William is better off transferring the risk of property damage to his $50,000 Mercedes, for the $900 premium, rather than self-insuring.

The insurance company must also conduct their own cost-benefit analysis. The costs of filing and settling small claims, such as minor fender benders, causes auto policy premiums to increase. As a result, insurers use deductibles that require the insured to cover the first dollar in losses. These deductibles are typically $250 to $500, but may be $1,000 to a few thousand dollars, and effectively dissuade small claims. Deductibles prevent the filing of small severity claims, which helps to keep the premiums of auto policies down. Deductibles also reduce morale hazard.

LAW OF INSURANCE CONTRACTS

A contract is a legal agreement that binds two parties to each other to perform certain obligations. The following elements must be present for a contract to be valid:

- Mutual Consent
- Offer and Acceptance
- Performance or Delivery
- Lawful Purpose
- Legal Competency of all Parties

Key Concepts

1. Identify the elements of a valid contract.
2. Define conditional acceptance.
3. Identify the two categories of legal competence.
4. Define the parol evidence rule.

Mutual Consent

Mutual consent implies that both parties to the contract have a mutual understanding regarding the scope of the contract and they are in agreement as to the terms of the contract. Typically contracts may be terminated by mutual consent of both parties.

Offer and Acceptance

Offer and acceptance consists of one party making an offer to purchase a good or service and the acceptance is when consideration is received. Consideration can be in the form of a cash payment or providing a service.

EXAMPLE 2.18

Mike is selling his Mercedes and is asking $50,000. Joe offers Mike $45,000 for the car. Mike agrees to accept $45,000 and Joe hands Mike a check for $45,000. The original offer was $50,000, Joe made a counter-offer of $45,000 and the acceptance was when Mike agreed to the price of $45,000.

EXAMPLE 2.19

Joe went to his insurance agent to apply for auto insurance for his new Mercedes. Joe completes the auto insurance application, however, completing the application is not an offer. The insurance company presenting Joe with a policy and requiring a premium of $1,000 is the offer. Joe writing a check for $1,000 would be acceptance of the offer.

With insurance there is also "conditional acceptance." Conditional acceptance is if Joe had completed the auto insurance application and attached a check for the premium of $1,000. The insurance agent conditionally accepted the policy, upon final review by the underwriter. If Joe leaves the insurance agent's office and gets hit by a bus in his new Mercedes, and the insurance company would typically have accepted his application, Joe would be covered. As long as Joe met the typical underwriting standards of the insurance company, he will have coverage. Coverage would not exist if the premium was returned and Joe was notified that the policy was not accepted.

Performance or Delivery

In order for a contract to be enforceable, the party to a contract must perform a duty under the contract. Using the previous example, if Joe is buying a car from Mike and gives Mike a check for $45,000, Joe has performed under the contract. He would expect Mike to hand him the keys and title to the car. If Joe asked Mike to deliver the car to his front door before Joe pays, then Mike cannot enforce payment from Joe until the car is delivered to Joe's front door.

Lawful Purpose

Another element of a valid contract is that the subject of the contract cannot be contrary to public policy or be in violation of any laws. If the subject matter of the contract is illegal, then the contract is not enforceable. If Joe enters into a contract to pay Mike $10,000, to steal Mike's neighbor's Mercedes, neither Joe nor Mike will be able to enforce the contract, as the contract is not valid. To steal the neighbor's Mercedes is a violation of the law.

Legal Competence of All Parties

When entering into a contract, both parties must be legally competent. Otherwise, the contract is unenforceable. Legal competence includes the following situations:

- **Minors** - In most states, a minor is under the age of 18. If a minor enters into a contract, the minor can void the contract at any time. If one party can void a contract at any time, there really is not an enforceable contract.
- **Lacking Sound Mind** - A person lacking a sound mind does not have the capacity to understand the purpose and terms of the contract. Therefore, the contract lacks a meeting of the minds or mutual consent. Examples of persons lacking sound mind include a person who is drunk, mentally handicapped, or under the influence of drugs.

Other important considerations of a contract include the **parol evidence rule,** which provides that "what is written prevails." Any oral agreements prior to writing the contract have been incorporated into the written contract. Oral agreements that are not reflected in the written contract are not valid.

> **Quick Quiz 2.5**
>
> 1. Typically contracts may be terminated with the consent of at least one party.
>   a. True
>   b. False
>
> 2. If the subject matter of the contract is illegal, then the contract is not enforceable.
>   a. True
>   b. False
>
> 3. If a minor enters into a contract, the minor may only void the contract within 30 days of entering the agreement.
>   a. True
>   b. False
>
> False, True, False.

LEGAL PRINCIPLES OF INSURANCE CONTRACTS

Principle of Indemnity

The **principle of indemnity** asserts that an insurer will only compensate the insured to the extent the insured has suffered an actual financial loss. In other words, the insured cannot make a profit from insurance. However, the principle of indemnity does not assert that an insured will recoup 100 percent of any loss, as most policies have deductibles and limits on the amount of losses covered.

A **subrogation clause** in an insurance policy requires that the insured relinquish a claim against a negligent third party if the insurer has already indemnified the insured. A subrogation clause entitles the insurer to seek a claim against a negligent third party for any claims paid to the insured. The principle of indemnity and the subrogation clause are closely aligned to accomplish the goal of preventing an insured from profiting from insurance.

Principle of Insurable Interest

The **principle of insurable interest** asserts that an insured must suffer a financial loss if a covered peril occurs, otherwise no insurance can be offered. The principle of insurable interest is closely aligned with the principle of indemnity, which both limit the insured from experiencing a gain using insurance.

Property and Liability Insurance

An insurable interest for property and liability insurance must exist both at the inception of the policy and at the time of loss. If no insurable interest exists at the inception of the policy, then there is an incentive on the insured's behalf to damage the property. If there is no insurable interest at the time of loss, then the insured who received a monetary settlement would experience a profit from the insurance claim, which would violate the principle of indemnity.

KEY CONCEPTS

1. Distinguish between the principal of indemnity and subrogation.
2. Identify the difference in insurable interest as between property, liability insurance and life insurance.
3. Identify the difference between a representation, warranty, and concealment.

EXAMPLE 2.20

Rodney purchases a property insurance policy on a wine warehouse, in the amount of one million dollars. Rodney does not have any financial interest in the wine warehouse. Mysteriously, the wine warehouse burns to the ground and Rodney collects the face value of the policy. This scenario would be a violation of the principles of insurable interest and indemnity as Rodney would have experienced a profit from this insurance policy when he had no insurable interest.

EXAMPLE 2.21

For the past ten years, Teresa has owned a wine warehouse and has property insurance on the warehouse in the amount of one million dollars. Teresa decided to sell the wine warehouse, but keep the property insurance policy. Shortly after selling the warehouse, it mysteriously burned to the ground. If Teresa collected under the property policy, it would be a violation of the principles of insurable interest and of indemnity.

Life Insurance

An insurable interest for life insurance need only exist at the inception of the policy. A life insurance policy is not an indemnity policy. It instead pays the face value of the policy based on the "value" of the amount of insurance purchased. Some people refer to this as a "modified" indemnity policy or an "agreed to value" policy.

EXAMPLE 2.22

When Karen and Sam were married, Karen purchased a life insurance policy on Sam and named herself as the beneficiary. After being married for two years, they divorced but Karen continued to pay the premiums on the life insurance policy. Ten years after their divorce, Sam died. Karen will be able to collect the death benefit from the life insurance policy because Karen only needed to have an insurable interest at the inception of the life insurance policy.

To purchase life insurance, the owner of the policy must have an insurable interest in that person's life. An insurable interest exists for a person to purchase life insurance on their own life and name either themselves or someone else as the beneficiary. An insurable interest also typically exists for close family relationships and may also exist for business relationships.

EXAMPLE 2.23

Brian and Jimmy started a pilot training school together and they each own 50% of the business. Brian and Jimmy decide to take out life insurance policies on each other's life, so that in the event one business partner dies, the proceeds from the life insurance policy can be used to buy the deceased partner's share of the business from the decedent's heirs. Since Brian and Jimmy are business partners, they each have an insurable interest in the life of the other.

Principle of Utmost Good Faith

The principle of utmost good faith requires that the insurer and insured act in a manner that is forthcoming with all information about the risks being considered during the underwriting process. The insured and the insurer follow three legal doctrines during the application and throughout the life of the policy:

- Representation
- Warranty
- Concealment

Representation

A **representation** is a statement made by the applicant during the insurance application process. A representation can be an oral statement or information disclosed on an insurance application such as age, gender, occupation, marital status, and family medical history. A misrepresentation during the application process can lead to the insurer voiding the insurance contract. In order for the contract to be voidable, the misrepresentations must be material and the insurer must have relied on the misrepresentation to issue the policy. A misrepresentation is considered "material," if during the application process the insured knew the statement was false, and the insurer would not have issued the insurance contract but for the false misrepresentation. Misrepresentations about age and gender for a life insurance policy are not considered material. The insurance company will simply determine the benefit based upon the actual age or gender of the insured and the amount of premium actually paid.

Quick Quiz 2.6

1. The subrogation clause asserts that an insurer will only compensate the insured to the extent the insured has suffered an actual financial loss.
   a. True
   b. False

2. An insurable interest for life insurance must exist both at the inception of the policy and at the time of loss.
   a. True
   b. False

3. A representation is a statement made by the applicant during the insurance application process.
   a. True
   b. False

False, False, True.

EXAMPLE 2.24

Dana, age 40, has always been told that she has looks ten years younger than her actual age. Dana recently completed a life insurance application and stated her age as 30, rather than 40. Based on a female age 30, the premium for a one million dollar policy was $400. A few months later, Dana was hit by a bus and died. Upon reviewing the death certificate, the insurer realized that Dana was 40 and not 30. The insurer calculated a death benefit of $600,000 based on the amount of coverage a $400 premium would have purchased for a 40-year-old female.

Warranty

A **warranty** is a promise made by the insured that is part of the insurance contract. The warranty can be a promise to perform or take a certain action. Alternatively, a warranty can be a promise by the insured to not do something. A breach in warranty may allow the insurer to void the insurance contract and not pay any claims.

EXAMPLE 2.25

Chuck and Cindy own a baseball hitting facility and are constructing a new addition to their building. In an effort to reduce their insurance premiums and as a requirement of the policy, they agree to install a fire sprinkler system throughout the building. They then warrant in the application that they have installed the sprinkler system. During construction, they decide to not have the sprinkler system installed, as it would cost more than they anticipated. If a fire causes a loss, the insurer will likely avoid paying the claim, as Chuck and Cindy breached the warranty.

Concealment

Concealment occurs when the insured is intentionally silent regarding a material fact during the application process. The insurer has the right to void an insurance contract based on material concealments by the insured. In order for the insurer to void a contract or avoid paying a claim because of concealment, the insurer must prove that the insured knew the concealed fact was material.

EXAMPLE 2.26

Rey is completing a life insurance application and answers questions such as:

- What is your age, marital status, height, and weight?
- Are you a smoker?
- Do you pilot small planes?
- Do you scuba dive?
- Do you have any other dangerous hobbies?

Rey answers "no" to all of the questions on the insurance application. Rey does not disclose that he likes to "base jump," which is jumping off tall buildings and bridges with a parachute in his hand and releasing the parachute at the last possible moment. Rey's insurance company could void paying a claim if Rey dies as a result of a base jumping accident.

UNIQUE LEGAL CHARACTERISTICS OF INSURANCE CONTRACTS

ADHESION

Insurance contracts are contracts of **adhesion**, which is a "take it or leave it" contract. The insured has no opportunity to negotiate the terms of the contract. Before an insurance product can be sold in a state, the state insurance commissioner must approve the product. The product is then sold "as is" and the insured must accept the policy as written. Since the insured has no ability to negotiate the terms of the

KEY CONCEPTS

1. Identify the distinguishing characteristics of insurance contracts.
2. Determine if property and life insurance policies are assignable.

insurance policy, the courts will rule in favor of the insured if there are ambiguities found in the contract. The insurer had the opportunity to draft the contract clearly and therefore will be charged for any ambiguities.

Aleatory

Insurance contracts are **aleatory** in nature, which means the dollar amounts exchanged between the insured and the insurer are unequal. The insured may pay a lifetime of premiums for a disability insurance policy and never collect a benefit under the policy. Alternatively, an insured may pay a small premium for a life insurance policy, and his heirs may collect a large face value after only one premium payment if the insured dies while covered by the policy.

Unilateral

Insurance contracts are **unilateral** in that there is only one promise made, and it is made by the insurer to pay the beneficiary in the event of a covered loss. The insured in not legally obligated to make premium payments. As long as the insured makes the required premium payments, the insurer is legally obligated to provide coverage under the terms of the policy.

Conditional

Insurance contracts are **conditional** in that the insured must abide by all the terms and conditions of the contract if the insured intends to collect under the policy. If the insured has violated any of the terms or conditions under the policy, the insurer may not pay a claim. One of the conditions of a policy is that the insured take steps to mitigate and reduce any additional damage to property after a covered loss. Another condition is that the insured timely pay the premiums.

Quick Quiz 2.7

1. Insurance contracts are aleatory in nature, which means the dollar amounts exchanged are even.
   a. True
   b. False

2. The insured is not legally obligated to make a premium payment.
   a. True
   b. False

3. Property insurance policies cannot be assigned to a third party without the consent of the insurer.
   a. True
   b. False

False, True, True.

Example 2.27

During a severe storm, a tree falls on the roof of Jill's home causing a large hole. Jill discovers the hole immediately but does nothing. The storm continues to rain on Jill's house for the next three days and the rain causes additional damage to the interior of Jill's house. Jill did not take any steps to cover the hole in her roof and the rain causes extensive damage to her walls and floors. The insurance company will pay for the damage to Jill's roof but will not pay for the interior rain damage because Jill did not take the appropriate precautions to prevent (mitigate) further damage after the tree fell on Jill's roof.

Personal

Property insurance polices are personal contracts between the insurer and the insured. Therefore, the policy cannot be assigned to a third party without the consent of the insurer. When applying for property insurance, the insurer evaluates the riskiness of the applicant based on their credit score, work history, and other personal factors. When the property is sold, the new buyer needs to apply for their own property insurance to give the insurance company an opportunity to evaluate the riskiness of the new owner.

Life insurance contracts, unlike property insurance contracts, can be assigned without the consent of the insurer because the contract continues to cover the insured regardless of who owns the policy. Assigning ownership rights to someone else even one who has no insurable interest under the life insurance contract does not change the underlying insurer's risk associated with the insurance contract.

LAW OF AGENCY

The law of agency describes the relationship and authority an agent possesses when acting on behalf of a principal. A principal, such as an insurance company, hires an agent (insurance agent) to act on the principal's behalf and enter into agreements on behalf of the principal. The authority that an agent possesses is the result of express, implied, and/or apparent authority. In the case of an insurance agent, the statements or actions of the agent that are in the course and scope of the agency agreement will bind the insurance company to the insured.

KEY CONCEPTS

1. Differentiate between express, implied, and apparent authority.
2. Identify how a waiver may impact the insurer's ability to deny a claim.
3. Identify how estoppel pertains to insurance contracts.

EXPRESS AUTHORITY

Express authority is given to an agent through a formal written document. In the case of an insurer and insurance agent, the express authority is an agency agreement. The agency agreement specifically outlines the duties, responsibilities, and scope of authority that the agent can act upon and thus bind the principal. The agency agreement stipulates the terms, conditions, and length of period the agent is allowed to sell insurance policies and bind the insurer to the insured.

IMPLIED AUTHORITY

Implied authority is the authority an agent relies on to do their job when the expressed authority is insufficiently precise. It is also the authority that a third party relies upon when dealing with an agent, based upon the position held by the agent. When a customer walks into an insurance agent's office, the customer will see the company logo on the front door, signs on the wall of the agent's office with the company's logo, and business cards on the agent's desk. All of these signs would lead the customer to believe that the agent sitting behind the desk has the implied authority to bind the insurance company if the customer purchases an insurance policy.

APPARENT AUTHORITY

Apparent authority is when the third party believes implied or express authority exists, but no authority actually exists. If an insurance company and agent had an agency agreement which expired, it is the responsibility of the insurance company to lock the door to the office, take down any signs, and remove the business cards and company letterhead. The insurance company must take the necessary steps to remove any indications of implied authority. If a customer reasonably relies on apparent authority and is issued an insurance policy by an agent who no longer has either express or implied authority, the insurance company is bound by the policy.

EXAMPLE 2.28

Randy walks into his insurance agent's office to purchase an auto policy for his new convertible sports car. Randy notices the business cards on the desk with both the insurance company's logo and his agent's name. There is company letterhead on the agent's desk along with policy applications. Randy completes the auto policy application and pays the first year premium. Upon leaving his agent's office, he gets into an accident and totals his new sports car. Little does Randy realize that his agent's agency agreement expired last week, and the agent was not really licensed. However, Randy will still have coverage from the insurer due to the principle of apparent authority.

QUICK QUIZ 2.8

1. Express authority is the agency agreement, which specifically outlines the duties, responsibilities, and scope of authority that the agent can act upon.
   a. True
   b. False

2. Apparent authority is when the third party believes implied or express authority exists, but no authority actually exists.
   a. True
   b. False

3. Waiver is where a person is denied a right he might otherwise be entitled to under the law.
   a. True
   b. False

True, True, False.

WAIVER

A **waiver** is relinquishing a known legal right. If an insurer waives a legal right, it may not deny paying a claim based on the insured violating or breaching that right.

EXAMPLE 2.29

David is applying for a health insurance policy. Before the policy can be issued, David must complete an application and take a physical exam. David completes the application but never takes the physical exam. The insurer issues David the health insurance policy. The insurer cannot later deny paying claims on the policy because David did not take a physical exam because by issuing the policy, the insurer waived the physical exam requirement.

ESTOPPEL

Through the legal doctrine of "**estoppel**," the principal will not be able to deny the insured an insurance contract. Estoppel is where a person is denied a right he might otherwise be entitled to under the law. Estoppel applies when one party relies on information from another party and that information causes harm to the party who relied on the information. The party who made the statements can be estopped from denying the statements.

EXAMPLE 2.30

Walter and his wife walk into an insurance agent's office and take out a $10 million life insurance policy on Walter's life, with his wife as the beneficiary. Walter's wife asks the insurance agent if the policy will pay a death benefit if Walter commits suicide and the agent responds "yes." Two days later, Walter is found dead from an apparent suicide. Walter's wife then attempts to collect the $10M death benefit under the policy. However, the policy has a "Suicide Clause" that stipulates that if the insured commits suicide within two years of the policy being issued, then the premiums will be returned and no death benefit will be paid. Although the insurer will attempt to produce the policy and suicide provision, the insurer may be estopped from denying the claim based on information the agent expressed to Walter's wife, presuming she can prove the agent's statements.

CHARACTERISTICS OF INSURANCE COMPANIES

TYPES OF INSURANCE COMPANIES

KEY CONCEPTS

1. Identify the difference between stock insurers and mutual company insurers.
2. Identify the differences between agents and brokers.
3. Determine the underwriting process.
4. Understand the term adverse selection.
5. Explain why insurance companies are reinsured.

Stock Insurers

A stock insurer is an insurance company that issues stock, and is owned by shareholders with the intent of earning a profit. A stock insurer collects premiums, pays operating expenses, and may return dividends to shareholders based on the performance of the company. The Board of Directors for a stock insurer is responsible for making decisions to pay dividends to the shareholders. Also, shareholders elect the Board of Directors.

Mutual Company Insurers

A mutual company is an insurance company that is owned by the policyholders, not shareholders. The policyholders elect the Board of Directors for a mutual company. Profits earned by a mutual company are returned to policyholders in the form of a dividend. The dividend is not treated as taxable income but it is a return of premiums paid.

AGENTS AND BROKERS

Agents

Agents are legal representatives of an insurer and act on behalf of an insurer. Agents are only permitted to sell the policies written by their company. Agents have the authority to bind the insurer to an individual. There is typically a difference between the authority an agent has when selling a property and casualty policy versus a life insurance policy. An agent may immediately issue a temporary binder on an auto policy over the telephone. A temporary binder is temporary insurance coverage until the insurance company issues the permanent policy. However, an insurance agent may not immediately bind an insurer when selling a life insurance policy. The insurer must approve the life insurance application before coverage is issued.

Brokers

Brokers are legal representatives of the insured and act in the best interest of the insured. A broker may sell insurance polices from any one of a number of different insurance companies. Since the broker does not represent the insurer, they may not bind an insurer.

Insurance brokers typically help individuals obtain property and casualty, life, and health insurance. Some brokers assist in surplus lines market, which are markets where there is a need for a particular type of insurance but no insurance product exists in that state. A broker may use an insurer that is licensed in another state to provide the insurance product.

QUICK QUIZ 2.9

1. Agents are legal representatives of an insured and act in the best interest of the insured.
   a. True
   b. False

2. Brokers can bind insurers the same as agents.
   a. True
   b. False

False, False.

REINSURANCE

Reinsurance is a means by which an insurance company transfers some or all of its risks to another insurance company. The company that transfers the risk is the ceding company, while the company accepting the risk transfer is the reinsurer. The primary reason an insurance company may want to transfer risk is to reduce the exposure in their portfolio of insured risks. A company may decide to transfer some of their risks to create additional portfolio capacity so as to underwrite new policies.

EXAMPLE 2.31

Hurricane Katrina made landfall over Louisiana and Mississippi on August 29, 2005. Hurricane Katrina caused $81 billion in property damage, with approximately $40 billion in losses covered by reinsurance companies. Some of the largest reinsurance companies in the world shared in the losses as a result of hurricane Katrina.

Reinsurance Company	Dollar Amount of Loss from Katrina
Berkshire Hathaway	$3 billion
Munich Re	$1.5 billion
Swiss Re	$1 billion

Market Info Briefing October 21, 2005, Guy Carpenter

IMPORTANT PROVISIONS AND FEATURES OF INSURANCE CONTRACTS

POLICY PROVISIONS

Most insurance contracts are generally designed with similar provisions, including:

- Definitions of terms used in the contract
- Declarations
- Description of what is insured
- Perils covered
- Exclusions
- Conditions

KEY CONCEPTS

1. Identify the typical sections of an insurance contract.
2. Identify examples included in each section of an insurance contract.

Definitions

The **definition section** of an insurance policy defines key words or phrases used throughout the insurance contract. The purpose of these definitions is to define the meaning of the words, phrases, or terms as used in the contract.

- Insured: Upon the insured's death a death benefit is payable to the beneficiary.
- You, Your: Refers to the owner of the policy.
- We, Us, Our: Refers to the insurance company (insurer).

Declarations

The **declarations section** describes exactly which property or person is being covered. For property insurance, the declarations page will describe the property, address, owner of the property, name of the insured, amount of coverage, deductible, and premium. For life insurance, the declarations page will contain the insured's name, face value of the policy, term or length of the policy, and the issue date.

- End of Initial Term Period: This identifies the last date the policy is effective.
- Amount of Insurance: This is the amount of the death benefit or policy limit that is payable to the beneficiary of the policy.
- Premiums: Depending on the type of the policy, this section may identify the amount of the current premium and perhaps any renewable premium.

Description of What is Being Insured

The **description section** describes exactly what is being insured. For a life or health insurance policy, the name of the insured is included in this section. For a property and casualty policy, the address of the property is in the description.

- Insured: Name of the insured
- Effective Date: The start date of when the policy is effective
- Age and Sex of the Insured: Used to determine the insured class and premium due for life, health, and disability policies

> **QUICK QUIZ 2.10**
>
> 1. For a life or health insurance policy, the name of the insured is included in the declarations section.
>   a. True
>   b. False
>
> 2. The exclusion section of an insurance policy will exclude certain perils, losses, and property.
>   a. True
>   b. False
>
> True, True.

Perils Covered

The perils covered section may cover perils on a named peril basis where specific perils are listed as covered in the policy. Alternatively, the policy may cover perils on an open peril basis, which covers all risks of loss that are not specifically identified and excluded in the exclusions section of the policy. For term life insurance, the peril covered is death of the insured within the term period.

Exclusions

The **exclusions section** of an insurance policy will exclude certain perils, losses, and property. Perils are excluded because they may be uninsurable, there is a moral hazard, or the coverage is potentially financially catastrophic to the insurer. Examples of excluded perils for a property insurance policy include:

- War or nuclear hazard
- Flood
- Power failure
- Intentional acts
- Neglect
- Movement of ground

Losses excluded from a policy may be due to the insured not taking steps to mitigate after a covered loss has occurred. Also, some property is not covered such as damaged or stolen business property in the home.

Conditions

Conditions are provisions in an insurance policy that require an insured to perform certain duties. If the policy conditions are violated, the insurer may refuse to pay the full amount of the claim. Examples of conditions include:

- Notifying the insured in the event of a loss
- Filing of a police report in the event of a theft
- Cooperating with the insurer after a loss
- Taking appropriate steps to reduce further damage after a loss

Miscellaneous Provisions

Miscellaneous provisions in an insurance policy cover topics not addressed within other areas of the policy. Examples of miscellaneous provisions include:

- **Errors in Age or Sex:** In the event of a misstatement of age or sex, the death benefit payable under a life insurance policy will be based upon the actual age or sex at death.
- **Suicide Exclusion:** A typical exclusion under a life insurance policy is if the insured commits suicide within the first two years of the policy. Premiums will be returned in the event of the insured committing suicide.
- **Payment of Benefits:** This section will outline where and how the death benefit will be payable to the beneficiary.
- **Grace Period:** The grace period identifies the amount of time after the due date of the premium that the policy will stay in force. If the premium is not paid within the grace period, the policy will lapse. The typical grace period is 31-60 days.

RIDERS AND ENDORSEMENTS

An **endorsement** is a modification or change to the existing property insurance policy. A **rider** is a modification or change to a life or health insurance policy. Riders and endorsements are a way for an insured to customize a policy, since insurance policies are contracts of adhesion and the insured has no opportunity to negotiate the terms of the contract. If there are conflicting terms between the policy and a rider or endorsement, then the rider or endorsement language prevails.

KEY CONCEPTS

1. Differentiate between a rider and an endorsement.
2. Identify the purpose of a deductible.
3. Identify the purpose of coinsurance.

A property insurance policy is typically endorsed when the insured owns property in excess of the coverage limits within the policy. If a policy only provides coverage of up to $2,000 in jewelry, an endorsement can be used to increase the jewelry limit to an amount appropriate for the value of the client's jewelry.

A rider can be added to a disability policy that waives the premium if the insured becomes disabled for a short period of time.

UNDERWRITING AND MANAGING ADVERSE SELECTION

Underwriting is the process of classifying applicants into risk pools, selecting insureds, and determining a premium. An underwriter is responsible for evaluating risks and determining whether the risk is insurable or non-insurable. The underwriter is also responsible for managing adverse selection. **Adverse selection** is the tendency of those that most need insurance to seek it while those with the least perceived risk avoid paying the premiums by not buying insurance. In an ideal world the insurer would only insure those persons least likely to have a claim. However, that would not lead the insurer to profitability as those who are least likely to have a claim are also most likely to self insure. An underwriter wants to maintain an appropriate mix of those that need insurance and are likely to file a claim versus those that are unlikely to file a claim. The underwriter follows underwriting principles that are established by the company. These principles outline acceptable risks, borderline risks, and risks that are unacceptable.

An underwriter groups risks into similar classes and assigns a premium or class rate to all members of the class, such that the premium is expected to cover all claims, operating expenses, and produce a profit.

The underwriter attempts to manage adverse selections with the use of deductibles, co-payments, and coinsurance.

DEDUCTIBLES AND CO-PAYMENTS

Deductibles are the first dollars in a loss, which the insured is responsible to pay. Deductibles may be a flat dollar amount such as $250, $500, or $1,000. A deductible may also be a percentage of the covered loss, which is typical for flood insurance or homeowner's insurance in states like Florida. The purpose of such a deductible is to reduce the filing of small claims, reduce premiums, and eliminate moral and morale hazard. Without deductibles, the paperwork, time, and resources needed to process claims of $50 or $100 would make insurance premiums unaffordable. Deductibles also serve as motivation for an insured to take precautions to avoid losses or to prevent the filing of false claims since an insured with a deductible will not receive 100 percent of the value of loss. An example of a deductible is when a person must pay the first $1,000 of medical expenses each year, and then 20 percent of all expenses over that amount. The insurer pays 80 percent of covered medical expenses that exceed the $1,000 deductible.

EXAMPLE 2.32

> Beth has a two-year-old car she purchased for $40,000 which is now worth $30,000. Her car recently caught on fire and was a complete loss. Her insurance company paid her $29,500, which is the actual value of her car, less her $500 deductible.

Co-payments are paid in addition to deductibles or as a substitute for deductibles and are commonly used in health insurance policies. **Co-payments** are loss-sharing arrangements whereby the insured pays a flat dollar amount or percentage of the loss in excess of the deductible. An example of a co-payment is when a person is covered for health insurance by a HMO, PPO, or POS and pays $25 each time he or she goes to the doctor.

COINSURANCE

Coinsurance defines the percentage of financial responsibility the insured and the insurer must uphold in order to achieve equity in rating. Coinsurance exists primarily in property insurance and encourages insureds to cover their property to at least a stated percentage of the property's value, or else suffer a financial penalty. Because the vast majority of property losses are partial, without coinsurance clauses many insureds would attempt to save money on insurance by purchasing less insurance than the full value of their property. While underinsuring is not illegal, it presents a problem for the underwriter and actuary who base expected loss estimates, and thus premiums, on the full value of the properties in the insured pool.

The amount paid for a property insurance claim with a policy with a coinsurance clause is determined by comparing several values. If the insured purchases coverage that meets or exceeds the coinsurance requirement (usually 80 percent of replacement value for homeowners insurance), then payment on a claim for a loss will be the lesser of the face value of the policy, replacement cost, or actual expenditures. However, if the insured purchases coverage that is less than the coinsurance requirement (say, 60 percent of the replacement value), then payment on a claim for such a loss will be the greater of the actual cash value (ACV) or the result of the following formula subject to the limit of the face value of the policy.

The coinsurance formula is:

$$\frac{\text{Amount of Insurance Carried}}{\text{Amount of Insurance Required}} \times \text{Covered Loss} = \text{Amount Insurer Pays}$$

The purpose of coinsurance in a property insurance policy is to encourage the insured to maintain a stated percentage of minimum coverage. Otherwise the insured will become a coinsurer and proportionately share in any loss.

EXAMPLE 2.33

Jerry owns a home with a replacement cost of $500,000. A tree falls on Jerry's house, causing $100,000 in damage. Jerry has a policy with an 80% coinsurance amount and a $500 deductible.

How much will the insurer pay if Jerry carries $300,000 of coverage?

$$\frac{\$300{,}000}{0.80 \text{ x } \$500{,}000} \times \$100{,}000$$

= $75,000 - $500 = $74,500 (paid by insurer)

EXAMPLE 2.34

How much would the insurer pay if Jerry had $400,000 of coverage?

$$\frac{\$400{,}000}{0.80 \text{ x } \$500{,}000} \times \$100{,}000$$

= $100,000 - $500 = $99,500 (paid by insurer)

EXAMPLE 2.35

How much would the insurer pay if Jerry had $600,000 of coverage?

$$\frac{\$600{,}000}{0.80 \text{ x } \$500{,}000} \times \$100{,}000$$

= $150,000* ($99,500 paid by insurer)

* The insurer payment is limited to the loss of $100,000 less the deductible of $500, therefore $99,500. The insured has over insured but is subject to the principle of indemnity.

The maximum amount the insurer will pay is up to the covered loss or the face value of the policy or policy limits, less any deductible, even though the coinsurance formula may result in a percentage greater than 100 percent.

EXAMPLE 2.36

Gina has a medical procedure costing $12,000. Her deductible is $2,000 and she has an 80/20 coinsurance clause with a stop loss of $5,000. How much will Gina pay for her procedure?

Loss	$12,000
- Deductible	$2,000
Covered Loss	$10,000
Insured Loss	$8,000
Coinsurance	$2,000

Gina will pay $4,000 of the total.

Coinsurance is also a term used in medical insurance indemnity policies. In these policies, coinsurance refers to the percentages paid by the insurer and the insured for claims after a deductible has been met and before the stop-loss limit is reached. For example, in a plan with an 80/20 coinsurance formula, a $1,000 deductible, and a $2,000 stop-loss limit, the insured will pay 100 percent of all covered costs until the $1,000 deductible is reached. After the first $1,000 in claims, the insured pays 20 percent of covered costs until claims reach $6,000 ($2,000 stop-loss / 20% + $1,000 deductible) and then 0 percent. The insurance company is responsible for 100 percent of all covered claims in excess of $2,000 during the policy period.

VALUING PROPERTY FOR LOSSES

Insurance policies must not only specify what perils are covered and what is excluded, but must also explain how losses are to be valued. Without valuation provisions in the policy, the insured and the insurer would not have clarity over how much a particular claim is worth.

KEY CONCEPTS

1. Differentiate between actual cash value, replacement cost, and appraised value.

Insurance policies generally value and pay losses based on one of three valuation methods:

- Actual cash value
- Replacement cost
- Appraised or agreed upon value

ACTUAL CASH VALUE

Actual cash value represents the replacement cost less the depreciated value of the property. Actual cash value is used to value the amount of coverage for a personal auto or personal property in a homeowners policy or business property policy.

EXAMPLE 2.37

Three years ago Bailey purchased a new car for $30,000. Yesterday, she was in an accident and her car was totaled. Her car had depreciated by $12,000 over the three years she owned the car. The actual cash value of the car was $18,000 ($30,000 - $12,000), which is how much the insurer will pay Bailey for her loss, less any deductible.

For personal property in a homeowner's policy actual cash value (ACV) means replacement cost less depreciation.

Replacement Cost

Replacement cost represents the amount to repair or replace property, without any deduction for depreciation. Replacement cost is the method used to value damage to a personal residence (dwelling) under a property insurance policy.

EXAMPLE 2.38

A windstorm blows off a portion of the roof on Sylvia's house. The cost to replace the damaged roof is $75,000. Under the replacement cost method of valuing a loss, the insurer will pay the full $75,000 less any deductible to repair the damaged roof.

Personal property can be valued using actual cash value (ACV) or replacement cost (RC). Replacement cost is preferable to the insured because the insured will receive the full dollar amount to replace the damaged property rather than the depreciated value under actual cash value.

EXAMPLE 2.39

A tree falls on Bob's house damaging his room and crushing his refrigerator. The roof damage is valued at $15,000. He purchased the refrigerator 10 years ago for $2,000. The actual cash value of the refrigerator is now $200. If Bob has replacement cost for the roof but actual cash value for the refrigerator, his insurance company will pay $15,000 for the roof and $200 for the refrigerator less any applicable deductible. However, if Bob has replacement cost for both the roof and refrigerator, Bob will receive $15,000 to repair the roof and $2,000 to purchase a new refrigerator, less any deductible.

QUICK QUIZ 2.11

1. Actual cash value is the method used to value damage to a personal residence under a property insurance policy.
   a. True
   b. False

2. Underwriting is the process of classifying applicants into risk pools, selecting insureds, and assigning a premium.
   a. True
   b. False

3. Replacement cost is how a personal auto policy (PAP) values property or personal auto.
   a. True
   b. False

False, True, False.

Appraised or Agreed Upon Value

Appraised or agreed upon value is when items are hard to value or when the insured owns property that exceeds standard limits of a property insurance policy. Typically jewelry, art, furs, and collectibles are covered using appraised or agreed upon value; such that any underlying limits in the property insurance policy are increased.

REGULATING THE INSURANCE INDUSTRY

The insurance industry is regulated primarily at the state level, but federal law also overlaps state insurance regulation. At the federal level, the Gramm-Leach-Bliley Act of 1999 repealed the Glass-Steagal Act, which prevented banks, investment firms, and insurers from competing outside of their core business. As a result of the Gramm-Leach-Bliley Act, banks and investment firms can sell insurance, and insurance companies can provide banking and investment services. Now that firms in financial services provide insurance, banking, and investment services, the regulatory environment has become more complex with firms now subject to regulation by the Federal Reserve for banking, the Securities and Exchange Commission on investments, and state regulation for insurance products.

The insurance industry is highly regulated by three levels of state government, which are:

- legislative
- judicial
- executive or State Insurance Commissioners

KEY CONCEPTS

1. Identify the three levels of state regulation of the insurance industry.
2. Determine if the NAIC has regulatory power.
3. Identify the goals of the NAIC.
4. Differentiate between various methods to regulate insurance rates.

LEGISLATIVE

The legislative branch of state government passes laws and regulations that regulate how insurance companies conduct business in their state. The legislature defines how insurance products are sold, controls how insurance agents are licensed, and protects consumer rights by passing consumer protection laws.

JUDICIAL

The judicial branch of state government rules on the constitutionality of laws passed by the legislative branch. The judicial branch also rules on decisions and actions taken by the executive branch. The judicial branch provides oversight of the legislative and executive branch, along with the insurance industry.

EXECUTIVE OR STATE INSURANCE COMMISSIONER

All states have a state insurance commissioner, which is an elected or appointed position. The state insurance commissioner is responsible for enforcing the legislature's laws and regulations, licensing of insurance agents, reviewing rate increases, and auditing insurance companies.

NATIONAL ASSOCIATION OF INSURANCE COMMISSIONERS (NAIC)

The National Association of Insurance Commissioners (NAIC) is a voluntary organization of insurance regulators from the 50 states, the District of Columbia and the five U.S. territories (Guam, Puerto Rico, Virgin Islands, American Samoa, and Commonwealth of the Northern Mariana Islands).[1] The mission of the NAIC is to "assist state insurance regulators" in serving the public. The goals of the NAIC are to:

- Protect the public
- Promote competition
- Promote fair treatment of insurance consumers
- Promote the solvency of insurance companies
- Support and improve state regulation of insurance

1. http://www.naic.org/index_about.htm

The NAIC does not have regulatory power, but it does issue model legislation to address problems within the insurance industry. States may or may not adopt the model legislation.

The NAIC also provides a watch list of insurance companies based upon financial ratio analysis. The ratio analysis measures the financial health of an insurance company. To promote solvency and avoid insurers from being unable to pay claims, life and health insurance companies are subject to a Risk-Based Capital test (RBC) that was developed by the NAIC. Risk-based capital measures how much capital is invested and the riskiness of the investments. The more risky the investments, the more capital the insurer is required to maintain. If the insurer does not maintain adequate capital, then regulatory action may be required. Regulatory action may include the state seizing, rehabilitating, or liquidating the company.

Insurance Rate Regulation

The rates that insurance companies use when determining premiums are regulated at the state level. The regulation varies by state and rate laws may also differ based upon the insurance product. Some of the insurance rate regulation laws include:

- Prior Approval Law
- File and Use Law
- Use and File Law
- Open Competition

Quick Quiz 2.12

1. The insurance industry is regulated primarily at the state level.
   a. True
   b. False

2. The NAIC does not have regulatory power, but it does issue model legislation to address problems within the insurance industry.
   a. True
   b. False

3. States that allow a "use and file" law permit an insurance company to file the rate increase with the state insurance commissioner's office and immediately implement the rate increase.
   a. True
   b. False

True, True, True.

Prior Approval Law

Under prior approval law, an insurance company must file the rate increase request with the State's Insurance Commissioner's office. The rate increase will either be approved, disapproved, or modified. During 2009 and 2010, many states denied health insurance rate increases due to the increasing unemployment rate and potential political fallout arising from 10 to 20 percent health insurance rate increases.

File and Use Law

States that allow a "file and use" law permit an insurance company to file the rate increase with the State Insurance Commissioner's office and immediately implement the rate increase. The state insurance commissioner may later deny the rate increase in which case the insurance company must rebate the premiums paid under the denied rate.

Use and File Law

A "use and file" state permits an insurer to increase rates, but they must file the rate increase within a specific time period, as determined by state law. Both the "file and use" and "use and file" laws avoid any delays associated with the rate increases being approved, as they allow the insurer to implement rate increases quickly.

Open Competition

Open competition laws allow insurers to set their own rates, and the State presumes that supply and demand will determine the appropriate rates for various insurance products. The open competition approach assumes that fair competition among insurers will result in efficient premium prices.

SELECTING AN INSURANCE COMPANY

The financial stability of an insurance company is a primary determinant for selecting an insurer. Rating agencies analyze and evaluate the financial health and ability of an insurer to pay claims. The better the insurer's rating, the more likely they are to sell policies, as consumers will have confidence in the insurer's ability to pay claims, should the insurer experience a loss.

Rating Agency	Highest Ratings		Lowest Ratings	
A.M. Best	A++	A/A-	C/C -	D
Fitch	AAA	AA	B	CCC
Moody's	Aaa	Aa2	B1	Caa
Standard and Poor's	AAA	AA-	B+	CCC
Weiss	A+	B -	D	E

A consumer should compare insurer ratings across several rating agencies. An insurer with consistently high ratings across multiple rating agencies is a low risk and acceptable provider. However, an insurer with consistently low ratings from multiple rating agencies is a high risk and should be avoided.

KEY TERMS

ACTUAL CASH VALUE - Represents the depreciated value of the property.

ADHESION - A take it or leave it contract.

ADVERSE SELECTION - The tendency of those that most need insurance to seek it out.

AGENTS - Legal representatives of an insurer and act on behalf of an insurer.

ALEATORY - A type of insurance contract in which the dollar amounts exchanged are uneven.

APPARENT AUTHORITY - When the third party believes implied or express authority exists, but no authority actually exists.

APPRAISED OR AGREED UPON VALUE - Used for hard to value items and where the insured may own property that exceeds standard limits of property insurance policy.

BROKERS - Legal representatives of an insured and act in the best interest of the insured.

COINSURANCE - The percentage of financial responsibility that the insured and the insurer must uphold in order to achieve equity in rating.

CONCEALMENT - When the insured is intentionally silent regarding a material fact during the application process.

CONDITIONAL - The insured must abide by all the terms and conditions of the contract, if the insured intends to collect under the policy.

CO-PAYMENT - A loss-sharing arrangement whereby the insured pays a percentage of the loss in excess of the deductible.

DECLARATIONS SECTION - The section of an insurance policy that describes exactly what property is being covered.

DEDUCTIBLE - A specified amount of money the insured is required to pay on a loss before the insurer will make any payments under the policy.

DEFINITION SECTION - The section of an insurance policy that defines key words, phrases, or terms used throughout the insurance contract.

DESCRIPTION SECTION - The section of an insurance policy that describes exactly what is being insured.

KEY TERMS

ENDORSEMENT - A modification or change to the existing property insurance policy.

ESTOPPEL - The legal process of denying a right you might otherwise be entitled to under the law.

EXCLUSION SECTION - The section of an insurance policy that will exclude certain perils, losses and property.

EXPRESS AUTHORITY - Authority given to an agent through a formal written document.

FINANCIAL RISK - A loss of financial value, such as the premature death of a family's primary wage earner.

FUNDAMENTAL RISK - A risk that can impact a large number of individuals at one time (earthquake or flood).

HAZARDS - A specific condition that increases the potential or likelihood of a loss occurring.

IMPLIED AUTHORITY - The authority that a third party relies upon when dealing with an agent based upon the position held by the agent.

LACKING SOUND MIND - The state of not having the capacity to understand the purpose and terms of the contract, therefore the contract lacks a meeting of the minds or mutual consent.

LAW OF LARGE NUMBERS - A principle that states the more similar events or exposures, the more likely the actual results will equal the probability expected.

MINORS - In most states, a minor is under the age of 18. If a minor enters into a contract, the minor can void the contract at any time.

MORAL HAZARD - The potential loss occurring because of the moral character of the insured, and the filing of a false claim with their insurance company.

MORALE HAZARD - The indifference to a loss created because the insured has insurance.

MUTUAL CONSENT - Common understanding and agreement between parties to a contract regarding what the contract covers and the terms of the contract.

NONFINANCIAL RISK - A risk that would result in a loss, other than a monetary loss.

KEY TERMS

Objective Risk - The variation of actual amount of losses that occur over a period of time compared to the expected amount of losses.

Offer and Acceptance - Consists of one party making an offer to purchase a good or service, and the acceptance is when consideration is received.

Parol Evidence Rule - States that "what is written prevails." Oral agreements that are not reflected in the written contract are not valid.

Particular Risk - A risk that can impact a particular individual, such as death or the inability to work because of a sickness or accident.

Perils - The immediate cause and reason for a loss occurring.

Physical Hazard - A physical condition that increases the likelihood of a loss occurring.

Principle of Indemnity - Asserts that an insurer will only compensate the insured to the extent the insured has suffered an actual financial loss.

Principle of Insurable Interest - Asserts that an insured must suffer a financial loss if a covered peril occurs, otherwise no insurance can be offered.

Pure Risk - The chance of loss or no loss occurring.

Reinsurance - A means by which an insurance company transfers some or all of its risk to another insurance company.

Replacement Cost - Represents the amount to repair or replace property, without any deduction for depreciation.

Representation - A statement made by the applicant during the insurance application process.

Rider - A modification or change to a life or health insurance policy.

Risk - The chance of loss, uncertainty associated with loss, or the possibility of a loss.

Risk Avoidance - A risk management technique used for any risks that are high in frequency and high in severity.

KEY TERMS

Risk Reduction - The process of reducing the likelihood of a pure risk that is high in frequency and low in severity.

Risk Retention - Accepting some or all of the potential loss exposure for risk that are low in frequency and low in severity.

Risk Transfer - The process of transferring a low frequency and high severity risk to a third party, such as an insurance company.

Speculative Risk - The chance of loss, no loss, or a profit.

Subjective Risk - The risk an individual perceives based on their prior experiences and the severity of those experiences.

Subrogation Clause - A clause in an insurance policy that requires that the insured relinquish a claim against a negligent third party, if the insurer has already indemnified the insured.

Underwriting - The process of classifying applicants into a risk pools, selecting insureds, and assigning a premium.

Unilateral - There is only one promise made; and in the case of an insurance contract, it's made by the insurer to pay in the event of a loss.

Waiver - The relinquishment a known legal right.

Warranty - A promise made by the insured that is part of the insurance contract.

DISCUSSION QUESTIONS

1. Describe the personal risk management process.
2. List the four responses to managing risk.
3. Define a peril.
4. Define the three main types of hazard.
5. List some unique characteristics of an insurance contract.
6. Explain the differences between pure risk and speculative risk.
7. Explain the four differences between subjective and objective risks.
8. Describe the law of large numbers and why it is useful for insurance companies.
9. List typical perils covered under a personal auto policy.
10. List typical perils covered under a homeowner's insurance policy.
11. What are the requisites for an insurable risk?
12. Describe the elements of a valid contract.
13. Define conditional acceptance.
14. Define the parol evidence rule.
15. Explain the differences between the principal of indemnity and a subrogation clause.
16. When must an insurable interest exist for property, liability, and life insurance?
17. Define representation, warranty, and concealment.
18. List unique characteristics of insurance contracts.
19. Describe the differences between express, implied, and apparent authority.
20. Identify the differences between agents and brokers.
21. List the responsibilities of an underwriter.
22. Identify why insurance companies are reinsured.

23. List and define typical sections of an insurance contract.

24. Differentiate between a rider and an endorsement.

25. Describe the purpose of a deductible.

26. Describe the purpose of coinsurance.

27. Describe the differences between actual cash value, replacement cost, and appraised value.

28. Identify the three levels of state regulation of the insurance industry.

29. Identify the goals of the NAIC.

30. Describe the differences between various methods to regulate insurance rates.

MULTIPLE-CHOICE PROBLEMS

1. The risk that individuals of higher than average risk will seek out or purchase insurance policies is called?

    a. Peril.
    b. Hazard.
    c. Law of Large Numbers.
    d. Adverse Selection.

2. What type of hazard results from the indifference that a person has to the potential loss because he or she has insurance?

    a. Peril.
    b. Physical Hazard.
    c. Moral Hazard.
    d. Morale Hazard.

3. Which of the following is correct regarding a peril and hazard?

    a. A hazard is the proximate or actual cause of a loss.
    b. A peril is the proximate or actual cause of a loss.
    c. A peril is the condition that creates or increases the likelihood of a loss occurring.
    d. None of the above.

4. Which of the following is not a requisite for an insurable risk?

    a. A large number of homogeneous exposure units must exist.
    b. Insured losses must be accidental from the insured's standpoint.
    c. Insured losses must be measurable and determinable.
    d. The loss must not pose a catastrophic risk for the insured.

5. The principle of indemnity requires that:

    a. A person is entitled to compensation only to the extent that financial loss has been suffered.
    b. Insured cannot indemnify himself from both the insurance company and a negligent third party for the same claim.
    c. The insured must be subject to emotional or financial hardship resulting from the loss.
    d. The insured and insurer must both be forthcoming with all relevant facts about the insured risk and coverage provided for that risk.

6. A subrogation clause means that:

   a. A person is entitled to compensation only to the extent that financial loss has been suffered.
   b. Insured cannot indemnify himself from both the insurance company and a negligent third party for the same claim.
   c. The insured must be subject to emotional or financial hardship resulting from the loss.
   d. The insured and insurer must both be forthcoming with all relevant facts about the insured risk and coverage provided for that risk.

7. When must an insurable interest exist for a property insurance claim?

   a. At the policy inception and time of loss.
   b. At the policy inception only.
   c. At the time of the loss.
   d. Either at the policy inception or at the time of the loss.

8. When must an insurable interest exist for a life insurance claim?

   a. At the policy inception and time of loss.
   b. At the policy inception only.
   c. At the time of the loss.
   d. Either at the policy inception or at the time of the loss.

9. When the insured is silent to a fact that is material to the risk being insured, what has occurred?

   a. Breach of Warranty.
   b. Misrepresentation.
   c. Concealment.
   d. Breach of Indemnity.

10. Jennifer is applying for life insurance, with her two children as the beneficiary. Jennifer has always been told she looks young for her age and although she is 58, she stated that she is 28 on her life insurance application. What would the insurer be most likely to do if Jennifer's beneficiaries attempt to collect on the life insurance policy?

    a. Void the policy.
    b. Require payment on premiums for a 58 year old insured.
    c. Recalculate the face value of the policy based on actual premiums paid.
    d. Bring a lawsuit against the estate.

11. Which of the following statements regarding the characteristics of an insurance contract is false?

    a. They are a contract of adhesion, which means the insured must accept it or leave it.
    b. They are aleatory contracts, which means amounts exchanged may be unequal.
    c. They are unilateral, meaning there is only one promise, which is a promise by the insured to pay the premium.
    d. The contracts are conditional, which means the terms are under the condition that premiums are paid.

12. Joe walks into his insurance agent's office and notices his agent's name on a business card and the insurer's name on letterhead. If an agency agreement exists, what type of authority does Joe believe his agent has to enter into an insurance contract?

    a. Express Authority.
    b. Implied Authority.
    c. Apparent Authority.
    d. None of the Above.

13. Donna owns a house with a replacement cost of $500,000. She purchases $300,000 of insurance with a coinsurance requirement of 80% and a $500 deductible. If Donna's house is hit by a hurricane and she suffers a $150,000 loss, what will the insurer pay?

    a. $74,500.
    b. $112,000.
    c. $119,500.
    d. $149,500.

14. Insurance regulation is primarily conducted by?

    a. The Securities and Exchange Commission.
    b. The State Insurance Commissioner.
    c. The Federal Insurance Commission.
    d. The FDIC.

15. Which of the following statements regarding loss frequency is true?

    1. Loss frequency is the expected number of losses that will occur within a given period.
    2. Loss frequency is the potential size or damage of a loss.

    a. 1 only.
    b. 2 only.
    c. Both 1 and 2.
    d. Neither 1 nor 2.

16. Which of the following statements regarding loss severity is true?

    1. Loss severity is the expected number of losses that will occur within a given period.
    2. Loss severity is the potential size or damage of a loss.

       a. 1 only.
       b. 2 only.
       c. Both 1 and 2.
       d. Neither 1 nor 2.

17. Cate is an inquisitive person and wants an explanation of the legal characteristics of an insurance contract. All of the following statements are correct, EXCEPT:

    a. An insurance contract is a contract of adhesion where the insured accepts the contract as written.
    b. An insurance contract is aleatory in the sense that equal monetary values are exchanged.
    c. An insurance contract is unilateral, where only one party agrees to a legally enforceable promise.
    d. An insurance contract is conditional in terms of claim payment if certain conditions are met by the insured.

QUICK QUIZ EXPLANATIONS

Quick Quiz 2.1

1. True.
2. False. Objective risk is the variation of actual amount of losses that occur over a period of time compared to the expected amount of losses.
3. True.

Quick Quiz 2.2

1. True.
2. False. Risk reduction is the process of reducing the likelihood of a pure risk that is high in frequency and low in severity.
3. False. Risk transfer involves transferring a low frequency and high severity risk to a third party, such as an insurance company.

Quick Quiz 2.3

1. True.
2. False. Morale hazard is indifference to a loss created because the insured has insurance. A physical hazard is a physical condition that increases the likelihood of a loss occurring.

Quick Quiz 2.4

1. True.
2. True.
3. False. A loss exposure that would be financially catastrophic to the insurer is an uninsurable risk.

Quick Quiz 2.5

1. False. Typically contracts may be terminated by mutual consent of both parties.
2. True.
3. False. If a minor enters into a contract, the minor can void the contract at any time.

Quick Quiz 2.6

1. False. The principle of indemnity asserts that an insurer will only compensate the insured to the extent the insured has suffered an actual financial loss. A subrogation clause in an insurance policy requires that the insured relinquish a claim against a negligent third party, if the insurer has already indemnified the insured.
2. False. An insurable interest for property and liability insurance must exist both at the inception of the policy and at the time of loss.
3. True.

QUICK QUIZ EXPLANATIONS

Quick Quiz 2.7

1. False. Insurance contracts are aleatory in nature, which means the dollar amounts exchanged are uneven.
2. True.
3. True.

Quick Quiz 2.8

1. True.
2. True.
3. False. A waiver is relinquishing a known legal right. Estoppel is where through a legal process, you are denied a right you might otherwise be entitled to under the law.

Quick Quiz 2.9

1. False. Agents are legal representatives of an insurer and act on behalf of an insurer. Brokers are legal representatives of an insured and act in the best interest of the insured.
2. False. Brokers do not represent the insurer so they may not bind an insurer.

Quick Quiz 2.10

1. True.
2. True.

Quick Quiz 2.11

1. False. Replacement cost is the method used to value damage to a personal residence under a property insurance policy. Actual cash value is used to value the amount of coverage for a personal auto or personal property.
2. True.
3. False. A PAP uses actual cash value when providing coverage for a personal auto.

Quick Quiz 2.12

1. True.
2. True.
3. True.

CHAPTER

3

HEALTH INSURANCE

LEARNING OBJECTIVES

After reading this chapter, you should be able to:

1. Understand the need for health insurance.
2. Describe the fundamental changes imposed by the Affordable Care Act.
3. Discuss group health insurance and its features and types.
4. Discuss the need for individual health insurance and the different types of policies.
5. Describe the common provisions in a health insurance policy.
6. Differentiate the types of group and individual health insurance plans.
7. Describe the taxation of health insurance policies.
8. Compare and contrast group and individual health insurance alternatives, including fee for service and managed care health plans.*
9. Describe the Consolidated Omnibus Budget Reconciliation Act of 1985 (COBRA).
10. Explain alternatives for acquiring health coverage including COBRA and Medicaid.*
11. Describe health savings accounts and flexible spending accounts.
12. List the activities of daily living (ADLs).

* CFP Board Resource Document - Student-Centered Learning Objectives based upon CFP Board Principal Topics.

INTRODUCTION

Effective financial plans help individuals make appropriate financial choices that improve their financial health. However, without physical health, an individual will not have a good quality of life. Unlike the risks associated with death and disability, most people tend to understand health risks and know that having adequate protection against those risks, in the form of health insurance, is a desirable financial goal. When an individual chooses to self-insure against health risks and a major health problem emerges, all of the individual's assets are at risk. Health care treatments can be expensive, and may deplete a person's accumulated savings (for retirement, children's education, and major purchases), leaving the individual financially insecure. Transferring the risk of incurring major health care costs to an insurer is prudent, especially when there is a possibility that other financial goals will be jeopardized if proper risk management plans are not in place.

KEY CONCEPTS

1. Highlight the two reasons that explain why group health insurance is the most popular type of health insurance.
2. Highlight the two reasons that explain why group health insurance can be provided so cost effectively.
3. Define the two primary types of group health insurance.
4. Describe how a co-pay, a deductible, and a maximum out-of-pocket amount work in conjunction with each other.

When a person who is fully insured under the Social Security system reaches age 65, that person can obtain government-provided health insurance from the Medicare system. Medicare Part A, which is paid for by payroll tax deductions during the participant's working career, covers hospital costs. Medicare Part B, which is paid for by payroll tax deductions plus a monthly premium amount deducted from the participant's Social Security benefits, covers medical costs (doctors bills, lab tests, and the like). Persons receiving Medicare benefits often obtain a Medigap insurance policy to pay for items not provided for by Medicare. The details of Medicare health insurance are covered Chapter 10. This chapter focuses primarily on private individual health insurance.

THE AFFORDABLE CARE ACT

The Patient Protection and Affordable Care Act of 2010 and the Health Care and Education Reconciliation Act of 2010 are collectively referred to as The Affordable Care Act.

The Affordable Care Act (ACA) mandates that individuals obtain health insurance that meets the law's definition of minimum essential coverage. The ACA requires large employers (an employer that, at any time during the year, employs at least 50 people) to provide a minimum level of health insurance coverage to employees or face significant tax penalties. Small employers (those employing fewer than 50 workers at all times during the year) are encouraged by means of tax credits to provide health insurance to their employees. Individuals who do not receive employer-sponsored coverage, and who do not purchase a qualified health insurance contract from a government-sponsored health insurance marketplace or from the private insurance market, are also subject to a tax penalty.

The mandate to obtain a health insurance policy with minimum essential coverage began in 2014. Some individuals are, however, exempt from the mandate.[1] Exempt individuals include:

1. Those who are conscientiously opposed to purchasing insurance based on religious grounds
2. Individuals who are members of a health-care sharing ministry (a tax-exempt organization whose members share both religious beliefs and medical expenses that are incurred in accordance with those beliefs)
3. Individuals who are not citizens or nationals of the United States who are either non-resident aliens or are unlawfully present in the United States
4. Incarcerated individuals
5. Individuals with no affordable coverage
6. Members of Indian tribes
7. Household income below filing threshold
8. Individuals with hardship exemption certification

Individuals who are not covered by an employer plan may obtain a qualified health plan (QHP) offered by a health insurer in the individual market, or may purchase a policy from a government-sponsored health insurance marketplace. The ACA refers to policies acquired in either of these two ways as insurance offered in the individual market.

Health insurance policies obtained in the individual market must provide "essential benefits," including ambulatory services, emergency services, hospitalization, maternity and newborn care, pediatric services, rehabilitation and mental health services, prescription drugs, and laboratory and preventative wellness services. To be classified as a QHP under the Affordable Care Act, the plan must provide an essential benefits package in one of four categories:

1. Bronze Plan - a plan that pays the actuarial equivalent of 60% of the estimated costs of health services.
2. Silver Plan - a plan that pays the actuarial equivalent of 70% of the estimated costs of health services.

1. Treas. Reg. §1.5000A-3.

3. Gold Plan - a plan that pays the actuarial equivalent of 80% of the estimated costs of health services.
4. Platinum Plan - a plan that pays the actuarial equivalent of 90% of the estimated costs of health services.

As plans move from Bronze to Platinum, the premiums increase due to the incremental risks that are transferred to the insurance company offering the package. Low-income taxpayers may qualify for a reduction in the cost of obtaining required health insurance through a premium assistance tax credit, and, if they purchase a Silver plan, they may qualify for reduced cost-sharing expenses.

Catastrophic plans may also be offered to individuals under the age of 30 and individuals who are exempt from the individual mandate. This includes individuals qualifying for hardship exemptions, including those whose plans have been cancelled and who are unable to find another plan that is affordable. A catastrophic plan must be designed so that it provides the essential health benefits listed above, but provides no benefits for any plan year until the individual's share of the cost has matched the out-of-pocket limits for HSAs (excluding coverage for preventive health services). In addition, coverage must be provided for at least three primary care visits.

Individuals who do not maintain QHP coverage for each month of the year after 2013 are subject to an income tax penalty for each month that coverage is not in force equal to the lesser of a flat dollar amount or an amount based on a percentage of the taxpayer's household income, as specified in the following table:

Year	Age 18 and Older	Under Age 18	Percent of Income
2014	$95	$47.50	1.0%
2015	$325	$162.50	2.0%
2016	$695	$347.50	2.5%

The dollar amounts of the monthly penalties are adjusted for inflation after 2016. Beginning in 2014, taxpayers must report on their tax return whether they had coverage each month during the year, and the penalty will be added to the income tax liability calculated on the tax return. Failure to pay the penalty does subject the taxpayer to interest charges on the unpaid balance. However, the IRS is prohibited by the ACA from using deficiency procedures to collect the penalty due from a taxpayer, and may not take criminal action against the taxpayer or impose a levy on the taxpayer's property if the taxpayer does not pay the penalty. The only recourse the IRS has to collect the penalty due is to offset any overpayment of tax due to the taxpayer in current or future tax years.

EXAMPLE 3.1

Grayson, who is an unmarried taxpayer, does not have minimum essential coverage for any month in 2016. Grayson's household income is $120,000. Assume Grayson's applicable filing threshold is $12,000 and the annual national average bronze plan premium for Grayson is $5,000.

For each month in 2016, Grayson's applicable dollar amount is $695. Grayson's flat dollar amount is $695 (the lesser of $695 and $2,085 ($695 × 3)). Grayson's excess income amount is $2,700 (($120,000 - $12,000) × 0.025). Therefore, the monthly penalty amount is $225 (the greater of $58 ($695/12) or $225 ($2,700/12)).

The sum of the monthly penalty amounts is $2,700 ($225 × 12). The sum of the monthly national average bronze plan premiums is $5,000 ($5,000/12 × 12). Therefore, the shared responsibility payment imposed on Grayson for 2016 is $2,700 (the lesser of $2,700 or $5,000).

EXAMPLE 3.2

The facts are the same as in the previous example except Grayson has minimum essential coverage for January through June. The sum of the monthly penalty amounts is $1,350 ($225 × 6). The sum of the monthly national average bronze plan premiums is $2,500 ($5,000/12 × 6). Therefore, the shared responsibility payment imposed on Grayson for 2016 is $1,350 (the lesser of $1,350 or $2,500).

EXAMPLE 3.3

In 2016, Harvey and Julie are married and file a joint return. Harvey and Julie have three children: Ken, age 21, Lisa, age 15, and Morgan, age 10. No member of the family has minimum essential coverage for any month in 2016. Harvey and Julie's household income is $250,000. Harvey and Julie's applicable filing threshold is $24,000. The annual national average bronze plan premium for a family of 5 (3 adults, 2 children) is $15,000.

For each month in 2016, the applicable dollar amount is $2,780 (($695 × 3 adults) + (($695/2) × 2 children)). The flat dollar amount is $2,085 (the lesser of $2,780 and $2,085 ($695 × 3)). The excess income amount is $5,650 (($250,000 - $24,000) × 0.025). Therefore, the monthly penalty amount is $470.83 (the greater of $173.75 ($2,085/12) or $470.83 ($5,650/12)).

The sum of the monthly penalty amounts is $5,650 ($470.83 × 12). The sum of the monthly national average bronze plan premiums is $15,000 ($15,000/12 × 12). Therefore, the shared responsibility payment imposed on Harvey and Julie for 2016 is $5,650 (the lesser of $5,650 or $15,000).

There are exceptions to the penalties. These include:

- Two or more members of a family whose combined cost of employer-sponsored coverage is considered unaffordable.
- Gross income below the applicable return filing threshold.
- Individuals who obtained minimum essential coverage during the open enrollment period on government sponsored health insurance exchanges.
- Certain individuals who applied for CHIP (Children's Health Insurance Program) coverage during the open enrollment.

- Individuals eligible for services through an Indian Health Care Provider.
- Certain individuals residing in a state that did not expand Medicaid eligibility under Section 2001(a) of the Affordable Care Act.

Those claiming a hardship that do not meet one or more of the exceptions listed above must obtain a hardship exemption certification issued by the marketplace.

GROUP HEALTH INSURANCE

Group health insurance is the most common method of obtaining health insurance today for working adults. Most working individuals obtain their health insurance coverage by participating in their employer's group health insurance plans. Self-employed individuals with employees may offer a group health insurance plan as well to attract and retain qualified employees.

The most attractive features of group health insurance are the ability to obtain coverage at a reasonable **premium** and without a physical and proof of insurability. Underwriting a large group of individuals permits the insurer to spread the claims risk among the pool of participants. Having a large group of participants also spreads the administrative costs of the plan across many people. Both of these factors contribute to lower premiums for group insurance when compared to individual health insurance policies.

ELIGIBILITY

To be eligible to purchase group health insurance, an individual has to be affiliated with a group that is covered by a group health insurance policy. Typically, all individuals who are employed on a full-time basis (or are members of a qualifying group) at a company that provides group health coverage are eligible to participate in the group plan. Sometimes non-employer groups provide coverage for their members as well. Common examples are local Chambers of Commerce (which may offer a group plan that can cover the employees of all member companies), labor unions, and professional associations (such as the American Bar Association or the American Institute of Certified Public Accountants). Individuals who obtain health insurance through the government insurance marketplace are also purchasing a form of group insurance, although insurance sold through the health insurance marketplaces is referred to as insurance offered in the individual market.

FEATURES OF GROUP HEALTH INSURANCE

Unlike individual health insurance, which is underwritten by assessing the specific health risks of the individual requesting coverage, group policies are underwritten based on the characteristics of the group to be covered. Individual underwriting and proof of insurability are not required for group health insurance contracts. Instead, the characteristics of the group as a whole are considered, including items such as the average age of the group, and the type of work performed at the company. Most group contracts cover most full-time employees. This coverage helps prevent adverse selection risk for the insurer, which is the risk that healthy members of the group will opt out of coverage, leaving only those with greater expected health care needs covered in the plan. Unlike the situation with employer group insurance plans, which can minimize adverse selection by requiring all employees to be eligible for the plan, the government marketplace health plans, which allow individuals to "opt in," may pose greater adverse selection risk.

The employer typically enrolls all eligible employees in the plan, and pays some of the premiums for coverage. When health care costs were less expensive, employers sometimes paid the entire cost of coverage. However, that is infrequent today. When the employee must pay part of the health insurance costs, those costs are typically paid through payroll deduction. Since the employer shoulders a large part of the administrative burden by enrolling employees and paying premiums, part of the administrative cost savings realized by the insurer can be passed on to the employer in the form of lower group-health insurance premiums.

Quick Quiz 3.1

1. Reasonable premiums and no required proof of insurability (i.e., a physical) are two of the most attractive attributes of group health insurance.
   a. True
   b. False

2. Underwriting a large amount of people spreads the actuarial risk among the pool for group health insurance, but participants drive up the administrative costs.
   a. True
   b. False

3. A group comprehensive major medical insurance plan is a combination plan that covers both basic and major health risks.
   a. True
   b. False

4. Once the insured reaches his out-of-pocket limit, the insurer pays the cost of care in excess of the insured's co-pay.
   a. True
   b. False

True, False, True, False.

Types of Group Health Insurance

There are two primary types of group health insurance:

- Group basic medical insurance
- Group major medical insurance

When the features of these plans are combined into one policy, the policy is a group comprehensive major medical insurance plan.

Group Basic Medical Insurance

Group basic medical insurance covers hospital, physician, and surgical bills, but typically has low policy limits. Due to the low policy limits, group basic medical coverage is often used in conjunction with group major medical insurance. However, today, the Affordable Care Act prohibits health plans from putting annual or lifetime dollar limits on most benefits so group basic medical insurance on a stand alone basis will not meet the requirements of minimum essential coverage under The Affordable Care Act.

Group Major Medical Insurance

Group major medical insurance coverage supplements basic medical coverage by paying for a wider array of services and increasing policy maximums. Sometimes these policies are referred to as group supplemental insurance plans.

Group Comprehensive Major Medical Insurance

Group comprehensive major medical insurance plans combine the benefits of basic medical coverage and major medical coverage. Typically, plan deductibles are low, and the employee may be required to make a co-payment when receiving services. After the plan deductible has been met for the year, the insurance company usually pays 80 percent of the cost of health care and the participant pays the remaining 20 percent until a maximum annual out-of-pocket limit is reached. Once the annual out-of-pocket limit is reached, the insurance company pays 100 percent of the costs of care for the remainder of that year.

EXAMPLE 3.4

Dylan is a participant in his employer's group comprehensive major medical insurance plan. The plan has a $200 deductible and a $1,500 out-of-pocket maximum. If Dylan is injured in an accident and his medical costs total $2,000, Dylan will have to pay the first $200 to cover the deductible and will pay $360 (20% of the remaining $1,800 in medical costs) for a total of $560. The plan will pay the remaining portion of the cost or a total of $1,440. The next time Dylan needs medical attention within the same year, he will not have to pay another deductible since the deductible has to be satisfied only once per year, but he will pay 20% of the costs until his total out-of-pocket costs for the year (including the deductible) are $1,500. In other words, Dylan will have to pay a maximum of $940 more for the year before the insurer pays 100% of future costs for the year.

Traditionally, comprehensive major medical plans were not favored by employees, since they resulted in the employee paying up to the out-of-pocket maximum each year. Many employees and unions favored first-dollar-pay type plans, in which the employee would make a small co-payment (of, perhaps $5 or $10) each time they visited a physician, and the insurance company would pay for the balance of the bill. First-dollar-pay type plans have higher premiums than comprehensive plans due to the increase in benefit payments made by the insurance company, and the increased administrative costs incurred. More recently, however, with the creation of Health Savings Accounts (HSAs) and the new federal requirements concerning health insurance coverage for employees, high deductible plans have enjoyed a renaissance as a means to provide adequate healthcare coverage while cutting premium costs for employers.

INDIVIDUAL HEALTH INSURANCE

NEED FOR COVERAGE

When a client does not have health insurance coverage under a government-sponsored program, such as Medicare or the government health insurance marketplace, and does not have access to employer-provided or other group health insurance, the client should consider purchasing an individual health insurance policy.

KEY CONCEPTS

1. Highlight how the Patient Protection and Affordable Care Act of 2010 is designed to spread the cost of mandatory health insurance.
2. Describe the inverse relationship between deductibles and premiums.
3. Define stop loss limit.
4. Describe what medical expense insurance covers, and name the subcategories of it.

Premiums on individual health insurance are typically higher than premiums on group health insurance, which may encourage some individuals to self-insure instead of purchasing coverage. Everyone should have, at a minimum, coverage for catastrophic medical expense needs, such as unforeseen major surgery or hospitalization, even if they choose to self-insure for routine medical expenses, such as annual physical exams, tests, and office visits.

EXAMPLE 3.5

Dermot is a healthy, unemployed individual who does not qualify for participation in any group health insurance plans. The cost of a health insurance plan that pays everything except a small co-payment per office visit is prohibitive. Therefore, Dermot decides to self-insure for small recurring costs, and purchase insurance to cover only major, unexpected medical expenses. By choosing a policy that has a high deductible, Dermot can minimize the premium cost of obtaining the insurance protection, while also protecting his other assets should he get sick and need major medical treatment.

Subsequent to the passage of the Patient Protection and Affordable Care Act of 2010 and the Health Care and Education Reconciliation Act of 2010, all U.S. citizens and residents are required to obtain health insurance, or face tax penalties for failing to comply. Under current law, obtaining health insurance that meets the minimal essential requirements specified by law is no longer a choice; it is a civic obligation. As mentioned earlier in this chapter, catastrophic plans may also be offered to individuals under the age of 30 and individuals who are exempt from the individual mandate.

Cost of Individual Policies

Unlike group coverage, which is often subsidized by the employer, a person purchasing an individual health insurance policy will typically be responsible for paying the full premium. He or she will not receive the benefits of the risk spreading and administrative efficiencies that reduce premium costs within a group. The individual health insurance plan is underwritten by taking the peculiar risks facing the applicant into consideration, so those who have existing conditions that require regular medical treatment or oversight will likely pay greater premiums.

The Patient Protection and Affordable Care Act of 2010 attempts to lower the cost of individual health insurance for individuals whose income is no greater than 400 percent of the federal poverty level state or federally administered programs to provide low-cost insurance protection to qualified persons. The federal government will provide a tax credit, referred to as the premium assistance credit, or will pay part of the cost of obtaining the insurance directly from the insurance carrier. In addition, individuals who meet specified income requirements and purchase a Silver Plan through an insurance marketplace may be eligible for additional cost sharing assistance from the government.

Eligibility

As with other forms of insurance, in the past individual health insurance can only be obtained if the person seeking coverage is relatively healthy at the time the policy is issued. Those with existing conditions requiring extensive medical treatment traditionally had to pay large premiums to offset the risk that the insurer is undertaking, or the existing condition may have been excluded from the policy. The 2010 health care legislation prohibits exclusions for preexisting conditions on any health insurance policies issued after 2013.

Types of Individual Policies

Major Medical Insurance

Similar to group major medical insurance plans, **individual major medical plans** provide coverage for hospital, physician, and surgeon fees, medications, and durable medical equipment (such as wheelchairs and hospital beds). Routine eye and dental exams are usually not covered under a major medical insurance policy, and the policy often has exclusions for self-inflicted injuries and medical procedures that are purely cosmetic in nature. The coverage provided by major medical policies often differs from carrier to carrier, so it is important to pay attention to the policy terms, coverages, and exclusions when making policy comparisons and selecting coverage. Many carriers, for example, impose maximum charges for various medical procedures or hospital stays, and may also impose additional limits on treatments such as mental health visits.

Traditionally, the lifetime policy limits per covered person on major medical insurance were often high, such as $1 million. The Affordable Care Act has removed the lifetime cap for all policies issued after September 2010.

The annual **deductible** for a major medical policy can vary from a few hundred dollars to several thousand dollars. If the major medical insurance policy covers a family, the deductible typically applies per person, per year. There is an inverse relationship between the amount of the deductible and the size of the premium: as the deductible grows, the premium gets lower since many of the first health care expenses encountered during the year will be paid for by the insured, reducing claims-flow and administrative burdens for the insurer.

For comprehensive individual medical and major medical coverage policies, after the deductible amount has been met, the insurance company pays a percentage of the medical costs (limited to the amount classified as usual and customary expenses), and the insured pays the remainder as a **coinsurance** amount. Typical structures for such a policy are 80%/20% or 60%/40%, up to an annual stop-loss limit. Once the insured's out-of-pocket expenses, including the deductible and coinsurance amounts, equals the annual stop-loss limit, the insurance company pays 100 percent of any additional health care costs for that year.

EXAMPLE 3.6

Randy and Kelly are married and have three children. They are covered by a comprehensive medical and major medical insurance policy with a $250 deductible per person, 80% / 20% coinsurance provision, and an annual stop-loss limit of $2,500. In a softball game this year, Randy slid into second base and dislocated his knee to the point that he needed knee replacement surgery. The surgery cost $25,000. Each of his children had various colds and minor issues, which cost $250 each. Aside from these expenses, there were no other health care costs incurred by the family this year.

Randy's knee replacement surgery will result in him paying a $250 deductible, as will the doctor visits for each of the children, for a total of $1,000. In addition, Randy must pay 20% of the cost of the major medical knee surgery in excess of the deductible amount, up to his stop-loss limit of $2,500. Twenty percent of $24,750 equals $4,950, but Randy will only have to pay $1,500 in addition to the $1,000 deductible, which is the amount that is necessary to bring his out-of-pocket expenses up to the annual stop-loss limit of $2,500. Note that if the policy were not comprehensive, but rather a stand-alone, major medical policy, any deductible would be in addition to the stop-loss limit.

Medical Expense Insurance

Medical expense insurance is similar to group basic medical expense coverage. Unlike major medical insurance policies, medical expense insurance policies only cover specified types of medical expenses and as such, do not meet the requirements for minimal essential coverage under the Affordable Care Act. Medical expense insurance may pay for actual expenses incurred when receiving health care, or may pay a lump sum upon the occurrence of some event affecting one's health. In either case, the policy limits are likely to be very low compared with major medical policies. While obtaining medical expense insurance is better than having no health insurance at all, planners should recognize that the policy limits may not be sufficient to cover the expenses incurred.

The most common types of medical expense insurance include hospital expense insurance, physicians expense insurance, and surgical expense insurance.

Hospital expense coverage, as the name implies, pays for costs of medical care while the insured (or family members, if a family policy) is in the hospital. Amounts billed directly by the hospital are covered, subject to policy limitations, but separately billed items, such as doctor, surgeon, and x-ray fees for services performed outside of a hospital are not covered by a hospital expense policy. Many policies limit coverage to a specified number of days, such as 60, 90, or 180 days.

Physicians expense insurance provides coverage for fees charged by physicians for office visits and tests that are not performed in the hospital (such as blood work, x-rays, and non-surgical procedures).

Surgical expense insurance pays for surgeon's fees when a surgical procedure is not conducted in a hospital. If the surgical procedure was conducted in the hospital, these expenses would be covered by the hospital expense coverage policy.

Health Insurance Policy Provisions

Preexisting Conditions

A preexisting conditions exclusion clause helps control adverse selection. A preexisting condition is defined as a condition for which the insured person was treated during the six-month or one-year period prior to the policy's inception date. Preexisting conditions are not covered under individual health insurance policies, although this exclusion usually lasts for only one or two years, after which treatment for the preexisting condition will be covered, as it would be for any other medical condition. The Affordable Care Act prohibits exclusions based on preexisting conditions for newly issued health insurance policies after 2013, although some grandfathered health insurance plans may still contain preexisting condition exclusions.

Grace Period

A grace period of 31 days is granted to the insured in the event that he or she is late making a premium payment. During the grace period, a policy may not be canceled by the insurer. However, if payment of the overdue premium is not received by the last day of the grace period, the coverage automatically lapses.

Reinstatement

Included in every health insurance policy is a procedure for policy reinstatement should coverage lapse due to nonpayment of premium. Certain policies specify a time limit within which the insured may reinstate the policy without proof of insurability. Other policies require the insured to again submit to the underwriting process before coverage is reinstated. Reinstated policies usually exclude coverage for illnesses incurred during the first ten days after reinstatement (again to control adverse selection problems).

Time Limit Clause

The time limit clause is attached to the policy so that an insurer may void a policy on the grounds of misrepresentation made by the insured on the application for coverage. The insurer must usually discover and contest the misstatement during the first two years the contract is in force. After that time, the policy is incontestable and misstatements may not be used against the insured to void a policy or deny a claim. This is similar to the incontestability clause in a life insurance contract.

Renewal Clauses

Renewal clauses in the individual health insurance policy specify the length of time that an insurance policy can remain in force. This can have a serious effect on the duration of coverage. In the case of group insurance policies, as long as the insured is employed by the group, then he or she may retain coverage.

Guaranteed Renewable

Under a guaranteed renewable clause, the company promises to renew the policy to a stated age, usually 65. The insurance company cannot cancel the insured at any time during the benefit period, regardless of bad health or the number of claims filed by the insured. The renewal of the policy is at the sole discretion of the insured. The insurance company, however, reserves the right to increase premiums as deemed necessary, as long as such premium increases are for the entire group covered.

Noncancelable

A health insurance policy with a noncancelable renewal clause provides the greatest amount of security for the insured. The insurer guarantees the renewal of the policy until age 65, and the premiums may not be increased. Noncancelable premiums are about 25 percent higher than they are for a similar guaranteed renewable policy because the insured is afforded much more protection.

Renewable at Insurer's Option

With this renewal clause, the insurer may not cancel the policy during its term (usually one year), but it may refuse to renew the policy for a subsequent term. Clearly, this provision is not safe for the insured. One should carefully consider the purchase of a policy with this provision.

Conditionally Renewable

A conditionally renewable contract cannot be canceled by the insurer during the policy term (again, usually one year), but it may refuse to renew the contract for another term if certain conditions exist. For example, if full-time employment ceases, the insurer reserves the right to cancel the policy at the end of the last month of employment. Also, renewal may be denied on the basis of unpaid premiums or the insured reaching age 65 and becoming eligible for Medicare coverage. This renewal clause gives the insured more protection than the one discussed previously, but it still is not as safe as the guaranteed renewable and noncancelable options.

Quick Quiz 3.2

1. Once an insured meets the stop-loss limit, not taking into account the deductibles paid, the insurer pays the full amount, up to a specified ceiling.
   a. True
   b. False

2. The high cost of individual health insurance is partly due to the inability of the insurer to spread the risk among the group's participants.
   a. True
   b. False

3. The Patient Protection and Affordable Care Act is designed to administer a program to provide low-cost health insurance to qualified persons.
   a. True
   b. False

4. The most common types of medical expense insurance are: hospital expense insurance, pharmacy expense insurance, and surgical expense insurance.
   a. True
   b. False

False, True, True, False.

EXHIBIT 3.1

SAMPLE INDIVIDUAL HEALTH INSURANCE MONTHLY PREMIUMS

ZIP CODE: 70068 (97 PLANS)	27-Year-Old Female	27-Year-Old Male	47-Year-Old Female	47-Year-Old Male
Premiums	$46.93 - $321.33	$33.28 - $224.58	$78.39 - $536.80	$66.50 - $472.27
Deductibles	$0 - $10,000	$0 - $10,000	$0 - $10,000	$0 - $10,000
Types of Plans	PPO, POS, Network*	PPO, POS, Network*	PPO, POS, Network*	PPO, POS, Network*
Office Visits	Not Covered to $50/Visit	Not Covered to $50/Visit	Not Covered to $50/Visit	Not Covered to $50/Visit
Co-Insurance	0 - 30%	0 - 30%	0 - 30%	0 - 30%

ZIP CODE: 30303 (115 PLANS)	27-Year-Old Female	27-Year-Old Male	47-Year-Old Female	47-Year-Old Male
Premiums	$50.25 - $401.46	$39.81 - 259.86	$94.00 - $665.88	$78.00 - $591.46
Deductibles	$500 - $20,000	$500 - $20,000	$500 - $20,000	$500 - $20,000
Types of Plans	HMO, PPO, POS, Network*	HMO, PPO, POS, Network*	HMO, PPO, POS, Network*	HMO, PPO, POS, Network*
Office Visits	Not Covered to $50/Visit	Not Covered to $50/Visit	Not Covered to $50/Visit	Not Covered to $50/Visit
Co-Insurance	0 - 30%	0 - 30%	0 - 30%	0 - 30%

**Network plan is a variation of a PPO plan.*
www.ehealthinsurance.com

TYPES OF GROUP AND INDIVIDUAL PLANS

Both group and individual health insurance plans can be written on an indemnity basis (reimbursement) or on a managed care basis.

KEY CONCEPTS

1. Describe the differences and similarities between an HMO and a PPO.
2. Explain the reasoning behind the criticism of managed care insurance plans.

INDEMNITY HEALTH INSURANCE

Indemnity health insurance is also referred to as a traditional health insurance plan. Indemnity health insurance plans allow participants the benefit of having a wide range of health care practitioners at their disposal. Indemnity plan participants are not limited to a service network system for medical care. Indemnity health insurance is the most flexible type of insurance policy, but participants also pay some of the highest premiums in order to have the flexibility of choosing their own health care providers. Typically, indemnity plans have deductibles, no copays, and coinsurance for major medical.

Managed Care Insurance

Managed care insurance emerged from a desire to reduce the costs of health care while increasing competition among service providers. When compared to major medical plans, managed care approaches to health care restrict participant choice of health care providers and often require participants to obtain pre-approval from insurance company representatives (who are not always medically trained) as a condition of obtaining covered treatment that is not considered emergency care. Companies offering managed care have also been criticized for prohibiting physicians from discussing alternative options of care with the patients, creating an ethical dilemma for the health care provider who is determined to act in the best interest of the patient. Despite their shortcomings, managed care approaches to health insurance have assisted in somewhat containing the cost of medical services over time.

There are three main types of managed care approaches to health insurance coverage:

- Health Maintenance Organization (HMO)
- Preferred Provider Organization (PPO)
- Point-of-Service Plans (POS)

Health Maintenance Organizations (HMOs)

Health Maintenance Organizations (HMOs) were authorized by the HMO Act of 1973. HMOs consist of a group of physicians who provide comprehensive care for their patients and are organized in an effort to control the rising cost of healthcare. Physicians are employed by the HMO directly or may be physicians in private practice who have chosen to participate in the HMO network. The independent physicians are paid a fixed amount for each HMO member that uses them as a **primary care physician**. Some HMOs require that medical services be performed by the pre-approved physicians who are either employees or independent contractors of the HMO. These HMOs will not pay for health care services obtained outside of their physician network. Other HMOs permit their members to obtain service outside of the insurance company's provider network, but payments for services performed by an out-of-network provider will typically be smaller than claims allowed for similar services provided within the network, which effectively increases the cost to the participant.

One major disadvantage of HMOs is that patient choice is limited to an established network of approved health care providers. Americans, as a group, do not like having their options limited, which may explain why HMOs never became popular vehicles for providing health care services.

Advantages and Disadvantages of HMOs

EXHIBIT 3.2

Advantages

- Fixed fee for health care
- Low co-payments
- Total health care costs are generally lower and more predictable than with PPO or POS

Disadvantages

- Gatekeeper for specialists services so it is often difficult and complicated to get specialized care
- Longer waits for non-emergency doctor appointments
- Any health care costs from out-of-network providers, except in emergencies, are not well covered if at all

Preferred Provider Organizations (PPOs)

A **Preferred Provider Organization** is an arrangement between insurance companies and health care providers that permits members of the PPO to obtain discounted health care services from the preferred providers within the network. Unlike an HMO, which limits choice of physicians and other health care providers, a PPO typically has a larger provider pool for participants to choose from. Participants are not required to receive services from preferred providers, but higher deductibles and coinsurance payments may apply when services are obtained from providers outside of the network. Health care providers are not employed by the PPO, but do receive a fee for serving as primary health care provider for a member of the PPO.

QUICK QUIZ 3.3

1. PPOs typically have a wider network of health care providers from which to choose than HMOs.
   a. True
   b. False

2. The emergence of managed care plans was born from a desire to decrease competition among health care providers.
   a. True
   b. False

True, False.

EXHIBIT 3.3

ADVANTAGES AND DISADVANTAGES OF PPOs

ADVANTAGES

- Health care costs are low when using in-network providers
- No gatekeeper required for specialist consultations, including out-of-network providers
- Primary care physician is not required
- Yearly out-of-pocket costs are limited

DISADVANTAGES

- Out-of-network treatment is more expensive
- Co-payments are generally larger than with HMOs
- May need to satisfy a deductible, especially with out-of-network providers
- Co-insurance may apply when out of network

Point of Service Plans (POS)

A **point of service plan (POS)** is considered a managed care/indemnity plan hybrid, as it mixes aspects of in-network and fee-for-service, for greater patient choice. Members choose which option they will use each time they seek health care.

Like an HMO and a PPO, a POS plan has a contracted provider network. POS plans encourage members to choose a primary care physician from within the health care network. This physician becomes the patient's "point of service." If the patient prefers an out-of-network provider, the in-network primary care physician may make referrals outside of the network, but higher deductibles and coinsurance payments may apply if the insured is receiving services on the indemnity side.

POS plans are becoming more popular because they offer more flexibility, lower costs, and freedom of choice than standard HMOs, PPOs, or indemnity plans.

EXHIBIT 3.4

ADVANTAGES AND DISADVANTAGES OF POS PLANS

ADVANTAGES

- Freedom of choice for managed care
- Not limited to only HMO network providers
- Costs are minimal for in-network care
- Annual out-of-pocket costs are limited
- No referral is needed for choosing an out-of-network doctor

DISADVANTAGES

- Copays for out-of-network providers are high
- There are deductibles for out-of-network providers
- Sometimes difficult and complicated to get specialized care with in-network providers

POLICY PROVISIONS

Health insurance policy provisions for groups are very similar to the provisions typically found in individual policies and in disability insurance policies. A summary of some of the more important policy provisions that are relevant for financial planners is provided below.

KEY CONCEPTS

1. Describe some health insurance policy provisions that are particularly relevant to financial planners.
2. Briefly describe the taxation of an individual's health care benefits.
3. Explain the different coverage periods for different individuals, under the COBRA plan.
4. Describe how HSAs work.

PREEXISTING CONDITIONS

Insurance works by spreading unknown risks (such as the risk of contracting health conditions that require medical treatment) across a pool of individuals. If it were possible for consumers to purchase insurance when they had a known condition or disease requiring medical treatment for a fraction of the cost of the treatment itself, a rational consumer would wait until he or she had a need for insurance (a pending medical expense) to obtain it. Under these circumstances, it would be impossible for the insurance company to spread those risks across the pool of insureds and generate a profit for performing that service.

The purpose of the preexisting condition clause is to prevent adverse selection against the insurance company, and to permit the risk-spreading function to work. If healthy individuals who will not require medical services for the current year are not part of the premium paying pool, there is no way to spread the risk across the pool, and the purchase of a policy by a sick person would be little more than a disguised attempt to transfer a known cost to the insurance company. Despite the potential for adverse selection, the Affordable Care Act does not permit exclusions for preexisting conditions after 2013. As a consequence, applicants cannot be denied insurance due to a preexisting condition. Some health insurance plans with grandfathered status under The Affordable Care Act, however, may contain pre-existing condition clauses and provisions.

INCONTESTABILITY CLAUSE

When a health insurance policy is issued on a noncancelable or guaranteed renewable basis, the policy often includes an **incontestability clause**. The incontestability clause protects the insured by preventing the insurer from challenging the validity of the health insurance contract after it has been in force for a specified period of time unless the insured initially obtained coverage fraudulently.

Grace Period

As is the case with all insurance policies, an insurance company will only undertake the risk the insured is trying to transfer when the insured compensates the company for undertaking the risk. If policy premiums are not paid by the due date, the health insurance policy will lapse. However, when the policy includes a **grace period**, the policy will remain in force and will not lapse as long as the premium is paid within a specified number of days after the due date. A one-month grace period (which usually translates to a period of 31 days), is very common in health insurance policies.

Renewability

Health insurance that is underwritten on an annual basis may prevent insureds from obtaining access to needed health care if they get sick. If, for example, the health insurance company does not reissue the policy when the renewal date is reached simply because the insured had contracted some form of disease or health condition in the prior policy period, access to treatment may be jeopardized. This is the opposite of adverse selection risk. In this instance, once a person becomes sick, the insurance company could decide to drop that person from coverage so that it does not have to pay health care providers for the care given to the participant.

To prevent this from happening, and to give policy holders some protection against policy cancellation, different renewability rights are provided in health insurance contracts, including:

- Noncancelable
- Guaranteed renewable
- Conditionally renewable
- Optionally renewable

Noncancelable

Noncancelable policies prevent the insurance company from cancelling the policy for any reason provided that the policy premium is paid. Usually, the policy will specify that it is noncancelable for a specific period of time, or until the insured reaches a stated age. Some policies also specify that, during the noncancelable period, no changes to the policy may be made, including changes to the premium. Noncancelable policies provide the greatest degree of protection to the insured, since the insured can force the insurance company to provide continued coverage simply by paying the premium on the policy.

Guaranteed Renewable

Guaranteed renewable health insurance policies require the insurance company to renew the policy for a specified period of time or until the insured attains a certain age (such as age 65, when eligibility for Medicare is established). Provided the insured pays the premium, the insurance company must renew the policy during the stated period. Unlike the case with noncancelable policies, which do not permit increases in premiums, the premium on a guaranteed renewable policy may be increased on a class basis (i.e., increased across the board for all similarly situated insureds). The premium may not be increased for one participant simply because he or she has contracted a disease or health condition requiring treatment.

Conditionally Renewable

When a policy is conditionally renewable, the insurance company may not cancel it during the policy term (which is typically one year). However, the insurance company reserves the right to cancel the policy when it is up for renewal. The conditions that will cause the policy to be cancelled on the renewal date are often specified in the contract itself. Planners should be attentive to these provisions when placing conditionally renewable insurance with clients.

Optionally Renewable

An optionally renewable policy permits the insurance company to cancel the policy at any time, except during the term of the existing contract. Unlike a conditionally renewable policy, which specifies the conditions that will result in loss of coverage, under an optionally renewable policy the insurance company can cancel coverage for any reason. Optionally renewable health insurance contracts give the client little peace of mind, and should be carefully considered prior to purchase.

TAXATION AND HEALTH INSURANCE

When an individual receives benefits under a health insurance policy, and those benefit payments are used to pay for health care, no taxable event occurs. In this instance, the benefits are received tax-free. Some health insurance policies, such as dread-disease policies (for example, a policy that pays a specified amount if the insured is diagnosed with cancer), pay a lump sum to the insured regardless of the actual expenses incurred in treating the condition or disease. When lump-sum payments such as these are received, there are no federal income tax consequences as long as the proceeds are used to pay for medical care. Amounts received in excess of the actual cost of care are subject to income tax.

When group health insurance benefits are provided by and paid for by an employer, there is no taxable event for the employee. Furthermore, when the policy pays the actual cost of medical care (as specified above), the insured will not have to report the benefits received as income. Normally, when an employee receives property (such as a health insurance policy) from an employer in return for his or her labor, the fair market value of that policy is subject to income tax the year it is received, under a tax rule known as the economic benefit doctrine. Congress has enacted a specific exception to this rule that allows employees to receive health benefits on an income-tax-free basis in an attempt to encourage employers to provide health insurance coverage to their employees. The employer can deduct the cost of providing group health insurance to its employees as an ordinary and necessary business expense.

QUICK QUIZ 3.4

1. Adverse selection occurs when health insurance plans refuse to renew health insurance for people if they become ill.
   a. True
   b. False

2. Employers may deduct the costs of providing health insurance only if the employee includes the monetary benefit derived from that insurance as income.
   a. True
   b. False

False, False.

CONSOLIDATED OMNIBUS BUDGET RECONCILIATION ACT OF 1985 (COBRA)

In 1985, Congress passed the Consolidated Omnibus Budget Reconciliation Act, which permits individuals who were covered under a group health insurance plan to continue to purchase health insurance coverage at group rates for a certain period of time after they separate from the group. Premiums for group health insurance coverage are typically much lower than the premiums for similar individual health insurance policies. By extending group coverage to individuals who were formerly members of a covered group, Congress made health insurance a bit more affordable for affected individuals.

Employers who offer group health insurance to their employees and have at least 20 employees are required to provide COBRA continuation coverage to their covered employees.

The most common situation in which COBRA applies is when a worker is either laid off or separates from service with an employer that sponsors a group health insurance plan. The former employee can purchase group insurance at the same rate that applies to members of the group plan. In addition, the employer can charge an additional two percent of the premium amount to defray administrative costs.

EXAMPLE 3.7

Topo worked at Digs LLC for the last seven years. He resigned to take another job. Since Digs has more than 20 employees, he is entitled to COBRA. Digs can charge Topo up to 102% of the premium for his health insurance to cover additional administrative expenses.

To be eligible for COBRA continuation coverage, the employee must not have been discharged for gross misconduct. Circumstances that create eligibility for COBRA continuation coverage include:

1. The voluntary or involuntary termination of an employee.
2. A reduction in employment status from full-time to part-time (part-time employees are not usually covered under an employers benefit programs).
3. The death of a covered employee (the employee's dependents may be eligible to purchase group coverage under COBRA).
4. The divorce or legal separation of the covered employee from his or her spouse.
5. The employee becomes eligible for Medicare (which usually occurs at age 65).
6. A dependent child of the employee no longer qualifies for coverage under the employer plan.

In order to balance the interest of employees, who may wish to continue to receive health insurance coverage at reasonable rates, and employers, who are typically not interested in providing services for individuals who are no longer providing services to the company, COBRA continuation coverage is not perpetual. Individuals eligible for COBRA continuation coverage can obtain coverage for the following periods and reasons:

18 Months	• Termination of employment • Moving from full-time to part-time status
29 Months	• The employee meets the Social Security definition of disability
36 Months	• Death of a covered employee • Divorce or legal separation of a covered employee • Loss of dependent status • Eligibility for Medicare

Note that COBRA continuation is typically available for 18 months for the covered worker, and 36 months for survivors or dependents of the covered worker.

EXAMPLE 3.8

Roger, the Senior Vice President of The Amazing Company, died last week. His widow, Rosemary, does not work and is 56 years old. Rosemary can obtain group health insurance coverage under Roger's plan for 36 months after his death.

EXAMPLE 3.9

Charlie, an employee of Electrical Engineering Contractors, Inc., was recently divorced from his wife, Jane. Jane is unemployed, but may obtain group health insurance coverage under Charlie's plan for 36 months after the divorce.

EXAMPLE 3.10

Danielle has recently finished medical school at the age of 27 and is no longer eligible to receive health insurance coverage as a dependent under her parent's group health insurance plan. During her residency, Danielle will not have access to employer-provided group health insurance, so she may receive COBRA continuation benefits under her parent's group plan for 36 months.

EXAMPLE 3.11

Rennie recently retired at the age of 65 and is currently covered by Medicare. His wife, Pat, is 63 and does not yet qualify for Medicare coverage. Pat can obtain health insurance under Rennie's group plan for up to 36 months under COBRA.

HEALTH SAVINGS ACCOUNTS

Health Savings Accounts (HSA) may be set up by individuals or employers. They allow eligible individuals to save for health care costs on a tax-advantaged basis. Contributions made to the HSA by the plan participant are tax-deductible as an adjustment to gross income (above the line), and distributions from the HSA to pay for qualified medical expenses are excluded from income. If an employer makes contributions to an HSA on behalf of an employee, and the contribution limits are not exceeded, the employer contribution is not included in the taxable income of the employee.

KEY CONCEPTS

1. Understand how HSAs are designed to facilitate tax-deferred savings for health care needs.
2. Explain how FSAs can assist employees with health care costs.
3. Contrast HDHPs with HSAs and FSAs.

Some employers offers a **Flexible Spending Account (FSA)**, which permits employees to defer income to the FSA to pay for health care premiums and out-of-pocket health care costs with pre-tax dollars. FSAs require the employee to either use the contributed amounts for medical expenses by 2½ months after the end of the year, or forfeit the unused amounts to the company. The House approved legislation on July 6, 2012 that would amend the "use it or lose it" provision in FSAs. This legislation has not been signed into law, but FSAs after December 31, 2012 are limited to $2,500 (indexed in future years). Unlike FSAs, HSAs permit employees to carry over unused amounts to future years and to invest those amounts so that, over time, the value inside of the HSA can grow.

EXHIBIT 3.5

ADVANTAGES AND DISADVANTAGES OF HSAS AND FSAS

	Advantages	Disadvantages
HSA	• Pre-tax contributions • Funds carry over from year to year • Funds can be invested • Permits reimbursement of over-the-counter medication purchases, if with a prescription • No prescription necessary for insulin	• Must have a high deductible health plan to qualify • Some HSAs have high annual fees
FSA	• Pre-tax contributions • Participants have total control over how to spend the money within the related health care or dependent care options • Can be used for "optional" medical procedures (LASIK eye surgery, braces, etc.) • Can be used for child care or dependent care • Permits reimbursement of over-the-counter medication purchases, if with a prescription • No prescription necessary for insulin	• Money must be used by 2½ months after end of plan year or lose it • Cannot receive distribution amounts that are covered under another health plan • Limited to $2,550 (2015)

From a financial planning standpoint, HSAs are effectively emergency funds for medical care costs. Younger individuals, who are less likely to incur large medical expenses, may choose to use a high deductible health insurance plan and establish an HSA to begin to accumulate a pool of money that can be used for future medical expenses. As the individual ages, and more medical services are needed, he or she can safely continue to use a high deductible health insurance plan (which will have a substantially lower premium compared to plans that pay the first dollar of medical-care costs) because of the presence of the health care emergency fund - the HSA. An individual can minimize insurance (risk-transfer) costs by accumulating HSA funds starting in early years and using high-deductible health insurance plans throughout their work life expectancy.

Eligibility

To be eligible to make HSA contributions, an individual must be covered by a high deductible health insurance plan. Individuals who are covered by Medicare, another health insurance policy, or individuals who are dependents of another person for income tax purposes are not eligible to make contributions to HSAs. One major exception to the dependent eligibility rule is that spouses who independently meet the requirements to establish an HSA may open up their own HSA even though they are listed with the spouse on a jointly filed income tax return.

High Deductible Health Insurance Plans

High deductible health insurance plans (HDHP) include plans with a deductible of at least $1,300 for individual coverage and $2,600 for family coverage in 2015, with a maximum out-of-pocket stop-loss amount of $6,450 for single coverage and $12,900 for family coverage in 2015.

HDHP Deductibles and Out-of-Pocket Expenses (2015 and 2016)

EXHIBIT 3.6

	Individual Coverage	Family Coverage
Minimum annual deductible	$1,300	$2,600
Maximum annual deductible and other out-of-pocket expenses for 2015*	$6,450	$12,900
Maximum annual deductible and other out-of-pocket expenses for 2016*	$6,550	$13,100

* This limit does not apply to deductibles and expenses for out-of-network services if the plan uses a network of providers. Instead, only deductibles and out-of-pocket expenses for services within the network should be used to figure whether the limit applies.

There are some family plans that have deductibles for both the family as a whole and for individual family members. Under these plans, if you meet the individual deductible for one family member, you do not have to meet the higher annual deductible amount for the family. If either the deductible for the family as a whole or the deductible for an individual family member is below the minimum annual deductible for family coverage, the plan does not qualify as an HDHP.

EXAMPLE 3.12

> Bob's annual deductible for the family plan is $3,500. This plan also has an individual deductible of $1,500 per family member. The plan does not qualify as an HDHP because the deductible for an individual family member is below the minimum annual deductible ($2,600) for family coverage.

Contribution Limitations

The maximum amount that can be contributed to an HSA for the calendar year is $3,350 for individual coverage, and $6,750 for family coverage in 2015. Amounts contributed by both the employee and the employer count in this total. In addition, individuals can make a one-time transfer of funds from an IRA to an HSA without tax consequences.

EXHIBIT 3.7

CONTRIBUTION LIMITS (2015 AND 2016)

Year	Individual Contribution Limit	Family Contribution Limit	Additional Catch-Up Contribution (55 or older / Single and Family)
2015	$3,350	$6,650	$1,000
2016	$3,350	$6,750	$1,000

DISTRIBUTIONS

Distributions from an HSA that are used to cover medical expenses are exempt from income tax. All other distributions before age 65 are subject to both income tax and a 20 percent penalty tax. Once the account owner reaches age 65, and is therefore eligible for Medicare health insurance coverage, distributions from the HSA that are not used to pay for medical expenses will be subject to income tax, but no penalty tax will apply.

HSA owners are permitted to roll the funds from one HSA into another HSA once per year without triggering adverse income tax consequences (i.e., the imposition of an income tax on the amount distributed plus, if applicable, the 20 percent penalty). If the rollover is not completed as a trustee to trustee transfer, the participant has 60 days from the date of distribution to roll over the distribution to a new HSA to avoid the imposition of income tax on distributed amounts that were not used to pay for medical costs.

QUICK QUIZ 3.5

1. Upon voluntary termination of employment, one may stay on with the former employer's group insurance plan for 36 months.
   a. True
   b. False

2. If one dies prior to spending all of his or her HSA's funds, the balance can be paid to someone other than the owner's spouse; but that balance is subject to income tax in the hands of the non-spouse beneficiary.
   a. True
   b. False

False, True.

When the owner of an HSA dies prior to distributing all of the assets in the account, the remaining balance can be transferred to another person. If the beneficiary is the spouse, the spouse is treated as owner of the HSA and the normal HSA distribution rules apply. If the account is left to anyone other than the spouse, the death of the participant terminates the HSA, and the remaining balance will be subject to income tax (but not penalty) in the hands of the beneficiary.

CONCLUSION

Health insurance permits clients to purchase a hedge against the risk of incurring large medical care expenses. All U.S. citizens are required, under current law, to maintain adequate health insurance. Planners and clients should carefully consider the most appropriate forms of insurance to purchase so that the appropriate amount of client risk exposure is transferred to insurance companies while protecting the client's asset base to achieve the client's other financial goals.

KEY TERMS

Coinsurance - The amount a patient must pay for major medical care after meeting the deductible.

Deductible - The amount a patient must pay each year before the health insurance plan begins paying.

Flexible Spending Account (FSA) - Employer-sponsored plan that permits employees to defer pre-tax income into an account to pay for health care expenses. FSAs require the employee to either use the contributed amounts for medical expenses by the end of the year, or forfeit the unused amounts to the company.

Grace Period - A provision in most insurance policies which allows payment to be received for a certain period of time after the actual due date without a default or cancellation of the policy.

Group Health Insurance - Health plans offered to a group of individuals by an employer, association, union, or other entity.

Health Maintenance Organizations (HMOs) - A form of managed care in which participants receive all of their care from participating providers. Physicians are employed by the HMO directly, or may be physicians in private practice who have chosen to participate in the HMO network. The independent physicians are paid a fixed amount for each HMO member that uses them as a primary care physician.

Health Savings Accounts (HSA) - A plan that permits employees or individuals to save for health care costs on a tax-advantaged basis. Contributions made to the HSA by the plan participant are tax-deductible as an adjustment to gross income (above the line), and distributions from the HSA to pay for medical expenses are excluded from income.

High Deductible Health Insurance Plans (HDHP) - Plans with a deductible of at least $1,300 for individual coverage and $2,600 for family coverage in 2015, with a maximum out-of-pocket stop loss amount of $6,450 for single coverage and $12,900 for family coverage in 2015.

Incontestability Clause - Clause in a health insurance policy that prevents the insurer from challenging the validity of the health insurance contract after it has been in force for a specified period of time unless the insured fraudulently obtained coverage in the beginning of the policy.

Indemnity Health Insurance - Traditional, fee-for-service health insurance that does not limit where a covered individual can get care.

Individual Major Medical Plans - Major medical insurance coverage purchased independently from an insurance company (not as part of a group).

KEY TERMS

Managed Care Insurance - Health-care delivery systems that integrate the financing and delivery of health care. Managed care plans feature a network of physicians, hospitals, and other providers who participate in the plan. Managed care includes HMOs, PPOs, and POS plans.

Point of Service Plan (POS) - A form of managed care that is considered a managed care/indemnity plan hybrid, as it mixes aspects of HMOs, PPOs, and indemnity plans for greater patient choice. A primary care physician coordinates patient care, but there is more flexibility in choosing doctors and hospitals than in an HMO.

Preferred Provider Organization - A form of managed care in which participants have more flexibility in choosing physicians and other providers than in an HMO. The arrangement between insurance companies and health care providers permits participants to obtain discounted health care services from the preferred providers within the network.

Premium - The amount participants pay to belong to a health plan.

Primary Care Physician - A physician that is designated as a participant's first point of contact with the health care system, particularly in managed care plans.

DISCUSSION QUESTIONS

1. Describe the benefits associated with group health insurance plans.
2. What is the difference between basic and major health insurance?
3. What is the difference between an indemnity type of plan and a managed care plan?
4. Describe the different types of renewal provisions.
5. Explain what a preexisting condition clause does.
6. Which employers are required to provide COBRA continuation coverage to their employees?
7. Who, besides the employee, qualifies for COBRA coverage?
8. Explain the tax benefits of HSAs.
9. Describe the greatest disadvantage associated with FSAs.
10. Describe how a stop loss limit works.
11. What are the major types of individual health and disability coverages?
12. What is the tax treatment of health coverages?
13. How do indemnity plans and managed care plans differ?
14. How can group health coverage be continued or transferred when employment terminates?

MULTIPLE-CHOICE PROBLEMS

1. Noncancelable health insurance contracts are different from guaranteed renewable contracts because:

    a. Noncancelable policies are not guaranteed renewable.
    b. Noncancelable policies cannot be canceled in mid-term.
    c. Noncancelable policies cannot have a premium change.
    d. Noncancelable policies have more liberal disability benefits.

2. Medical insurance is commonly known as health insurance and can be purchased from private insurance companies. Which of the following best describes the classes of medical insurance?

    a. Coverage for hospital expense, surgical expense, physician expense, and major medical expense.
    b. Coverage for hospital expense, nonmajor medical expense, surgical expense, and physician expense.
    c. Coverage for hospital expense, comprehensive major medical expense, nonmajor medical expense, and physician expense.
    d. Coverage for comprehensive major medical expense, nonmajor medical expense, surgical expense, and physician expense.

3. Mr. Johns has a major medical insurance policy with a $1,000 deductible and an 80% coinsurance clause. He becomes ill and is admitted to the hospital for several days. When he is discharged, his hospital bill is $5,000, and his doctor bills are $2,500. What is the amount that his insurance co-pay will pay?

    a. $5,200.
    b. $6,000.
    c. $6,500.
    d. $7,500.

4. In which of the following events would COBRA rules apply for the benefit of the covered employee, employee's spouse, or dependent child?

    1. The death of the covered employee.
    2. The covered employee is fired for incompetence.
    3. The employee changes status from full-time to part-time and, as a result, loses coverage.
    4. The covered employee gets a divorce.

    a. 1 only.
    b. 1 and 4.
    c. 2, 3, and 4.
    d. 1, 2, 3, and 4.

5. Due to a recession, Pat has voluntarily changed her status from full-time to part-time with her employer. Prior to the change, she and her husband were covered under the company health plan. Which statement regarding COBRA is correct?

   a. Because her change is voluntary, COBRA rules do not apply.
   b. COBRA rules allow continuation of health coverage in this situation for up to 36 months.
   c. COBRA rules allow continuation of health coverage in this situation for up to 18 months.
   d. COBRA rules allow continuation of health coverage in this situation for 29 months.

6. COBRA coverage is available for which of the following persons?

   1. A retiring employee.
   2. An employee who is terminated.
   3. Spouses and dependents of a deceased employee.
   4. An employee no longer able to work due to disability.

   a. 3 only.
   b. 3 and 4.
   c. 1, 2, and 3.
   d. 1, 2, 3, and 4.

7. Black Smith is an employee of ABC Corporation. He has just divorced Phyllis who was on all of his group health plan coverages. Phyllis wants to know to what COBRA coverage she is entitled. The following is a list of Black's group health plan benefits, all of which are integral parts of the plan. Which of Black's benefits is/are subject to COBRA rules?

   1. Medical expense plan.
   2. Dental plan.
   3. Vision care plan.
   4. Prescription care plan.

   a. 1 only.
   b. 1 and 4.
   c. 2, 3, and 4.
   d. 1, 2, 3, and 4.

8. The Watson family has a family medical policy that provides the following coverage:

- $250/person deductible (3 person maximum).
- $1,000 out-of-pocket limit.
- 80/20 coinsurance provision.

On a family trip, the Watson's were involved in a car accident. Four family members were hurt. Each person incurred medical expenses of $7,500. How much will the insurance company pay?

a. $23,400.
b. $28,250.
c. $29,000.
d. $29,250.

9. Which of the following is a characteristic of guaranteed renewability?

1. The insurer guarantees to renew the policy to a stated age.
2. The policy is noncancelable and the premium may not be increased.
3. Renewal is solely at insurer's discretion.
4. The insurer has the right to increase the premium rates for the underlying class in which the insured is placed. Note: not for a single individual.

a. 1 only.
b. 1 and 4.
c. 1, 2, and 4.
d. 1, 2, 3, and 4.

QUICK QUIZ EXPLANATIONS

Quick Quiz 3.1

1. True.
2. False. When underwriting a large number of people, the risk, as well as the administrative costs, are spread amongst all participants.
3. True.
4. False. Once the insured reaches his out-of-pocket limit, the insurer pays 100 percent of the cost of care. After the plan deductible is met and until the insured reaches his out-of-pocket limit, the insurer pays the cost of care in excess of the co-pay.

Quick Quiz 3.2

1. False. The stop limit takes into account deductibles paid, as well as co-pay amounts.
2. True.
3. True.
4. False. The most common types of medical expense insurance are: hospital, physician, and surgical expense insurances.

Quick Quiz 3.3

1. True.
2. False. Managed care plans emerged from a desire to decrease health care costs and increase comple-tion amongst health care providers.

Quick Quiz 3.4

1. False. This is actually the opposite of adverse selection, which refers to ill people - or those who would derive the most benefit from insurance - being the only ones who seek insurance, thereby denying the company the ability to spread risk amongst both sick and healthy participants.
2. False. The monetary benefit derived from an employer funded health insurance plan is specifically excluded as income.

Quick Quiz 3.5

1. False. Upon voluntary termination, one may stay on the employer's policy for no longer than 18 months.
2. True.

CHAPTER

4

LIFE INSURANCE

LEARNING OBJECTIVES

After reading this chapter, you should be able to:

1. Describe the purpose of life insurance.
2. Explain the factors commonly used in the life insurance underwriting process.*
3. Identify the parties to a life insurance policy.
4. Identify the various life-cycle stages and their impact on mortality rate.
5. Differentiate between term, whole life, variable, universal, and VUL policies and select the most appropriate type of coverage to match a client's specific circumstances.*
6. Recommend whether a policy should be replaced based upon quantitative and qualitative factors.*
7. Recommend life insurance purchase and benefits distribution options based upon needs, financial resources, and cost.*
8. Calculate a client's insurance needs using alternative approaches, including the needs approach, human life value approach, and capitalized earnings approach.*
9. Identify the types and uses of life insurance in financial planning.
10. Describe a modified endowment contract.
11. List settlement options for life insurance policies.
12. Understand the taxation of life insurance policies.
13. Describe the common contractual provisions in a life insurance policy.
14. Understand tax-free policy exchanges under Section 1035.
15. Discuss viatical settlements and accelerated benefits provisions and their tax consequences.
16. Recognize the complications for a closely held business upon the death of an owner and the need for buy-sell agreements.*
17. Understand the use of life insurance and buy-sell agreements.
18. Distinguish between the three most common types of buy-sell agreements: cross-purchase agreements, entity agreements, and wait and see agreements.*

* CFP Board Resource Document - Student-Centered Learning Objectives based upon CFP Board Principal Topics.

INTRODUCTION

When managing the personal risk exposures of individuals, life insurance, disability insurance, health insurance, and long-term care insurance are frequently purchased to ensure that a person can meet his or her financial goals. This chapter covers life insurance and the planning associated with it. Chapter 3 covers health risks and the use of health insurance. Long-term care is covered in Chapter 6.

It is often said that two things in life are certain: death and taxes. Many individuals tend to ignore these eventualities, particularly those who do their own financial planning without the benefit of a professional advisor. The prospect of paying taxes and contemplating one's own death are not thoughts that people prefer to harbor. The inevitability of death, however, is a very real issue when addressing financial goals. Younger people tend to ignore this risk as something too remote. While they will eventually have to face the inevitability of death, young people tend to believe that they won't have to worry about that for a long time. From a financial planning perspective, however, the younger the person, the more important the management of mortality risk (the risk of dying within the year).

PARTIES TO A LIFE INSURANCE CONTRACT

KEY CONCEPTS

1. Identify the parties to a contract.
2. Understand the "Unholy Trinity."

Three parties have an interest in any life insurance contract issued – the owner, the insured, and the beneficiary. Sometimes, the same person holds all three interests in the policy (if the proceeds are payable to his or her estate). In other cases, different individuals, groups, or legal structures may be the owners and/or beneficiaries of a life insurance policy.

The **insured** is the individual whose life is covered by the life insurance policy. When the insured dies, the life insurance company will pay the death benefit to the named beneficiary.

The **owner** of the policy is the person who can exercise the economic rights of the policy and typically, but not necessarily, pays the premiums. For example, if permanent life insurance is purchased, the owner can borrow from the cash value, pledge the cash value as collateral for a loan, and receive policy dividends (all of these situations will be discussed later). When a client wishes to access the savings element of permanent life insurance policies, he or she must be the owner of those policies. The owner and insured are often the same person. In some cases it makes sense to have the life insurance policy owned by someone other than the insured (such as the insured's spouse, a beneficiary, or a trust created to hold the policy). Typically, when a person other than the insured is the owner of the policy, the insured is attempting to reduce estate taxes, or is attempting to achieve greater asset protection of policy values than might otherwise occur. Often times, irrevocable life insurance trusts (know as ILITs) are used to purchase life insurance so that the proceeds are not included in the gross estate of the insured. ILITs and other life insurance arrangements are beyond the scope of this textbook, but are covered in the Income Tax and Estate Planning courses.

If the owner and insured are different parties, the owner will have to have an insurable interest in the life of the insured at inception to obtain life insurance coverage, or the insured must consent to the owner purchasing coverage on his or her life. An insurable interest is an interest based upon a reasonable expectation of pecuniary advantage through the continued life, health, or bodily safety of another person and consequent loss by reason of that person's death or disability or a substantial interest engendered by love and affection in the case of individuals closely related by blood or law.[1] In other words, an insurable interest exists when there is a financial or other benefit to the continued life of another person. A person always has an insurable interest in himself and his spouse. A person will likely have an insurable interest in other family members and in his business partners. The insurable interest requirement serves the goal of preventing speculation on human life. Without such a requirement, it creates the possibility of betting on the deaths of others.

If the insured was the original owner and transfers the policy to a third party, the insured is deemed to have given consent to that third party to hold insurance on the insured's life. Insurable interest rules are designed to limit exposure to moral hazards (i.e., creating an incentive for the insured to die early as a means of collecting the death benefit).

1. CA Insurance Code Section 10110.

The **beneficiary** is the person entitled to receive the death benefit. With life insurance, as well as other financial accounts that transfer ownership at the death of the owner, there is generally a primary beneficiary and a contingent beneficiary. A primary beneficiary is the person who will receive the proceeds from the life insurance policy upon the death of the insured. The contingent beneficiary is the person or persons who will receive the proceeds in the event of the insured death and in the event that the primary beneficiary is already deceased or chooses to disclaim the proceeds.[1] The owner of the policy can name anyone including himself as the beneficiary. If there is no named beneficiary, the policy death benefit is typically paid to the owner, or if the owner is also the insured, to the owner/insured's estate.

EXAMPLE 4.1

Randy purchased a $1 million life insurance policy on his life to protect his family in the event of his early death. Randy decided to retain ownership of the policy so that he could access the cash value of the policy. Randy did not name a beneficiary, therefore if he dies, the life insurance death benefit will be paid to his estate. The situation would be the same as if Randy had named his estate as the beneficiary of the policy.

As the example above illustrates, the insured, owner, and beneficiary may be the same person. Typically, when the insured is different from the owner, the owner is also named as the beneficiary on the policy.

EXAMPLE 4.2

John is the insured on a $1 million life insurance policy. His wife, Ally, is the owner of the policy. She has named herself as the primary beneficiary, and her son, Ryan, as the secondary or contingent beneficiary. If John dies, the policy will pay the death benefit to Ally (who is also the owner), or if Ally predeceases John, the proceeds will be paid to Ryan.

EXAMPLE 4.3

Bertie is independently wealthy and expects to pay estate taxes at his death. Bertie created a trust and made cash gifts to the trust over time. The trustee used the funds to purchase a life insurance policy on Bertie's life. The trust owns the policy, pays the premiums, and is listed as the beneficiary of the policy. When Bertie dies, the trustee will use the death benefit in accordance with the instructions set forth in the trust document.

It is also possible for the owner, insured, and beneficiary to all be different parties. This is commonly referred to as the "unholy trinity." The unholy trinity is also referred to as the Goodman Triangle since it is a result of the outcome of the court case, Goodman v. Commissioner, 156 F.2d 218 (2nd Cir. 1946). When this occurs, the owner of the policy is deemed to have made a taxable transfer or gift to the beneficiary. Planners need to be very careful about potential gift and estate tax consequences of this type of arrangement (these issues are discussed more fully in the Estate Planning course).

1. Disclaiming life insurance proceeds means that the beneficiary chooses to not accept the funds. A disclaimer may be used as a postmortem estate planning technique. This topic is discussed more in Money Education's Estate Planning textbook.

UNHOLY TRINITY

EXHIBIT 4.1

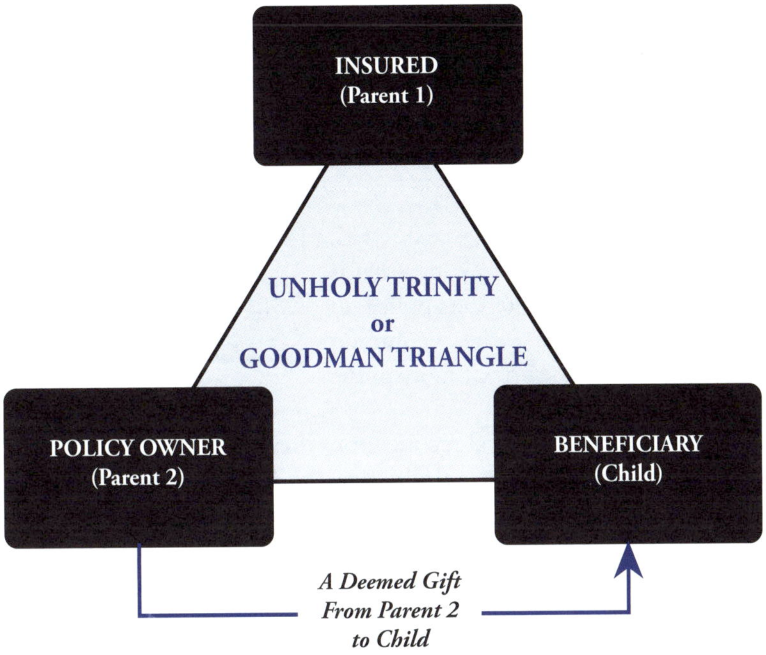

EXAMPLE 4.4

Wally is the insured on a life insurance policy owned by his wife, Hilda. Hilda does not need the money, so she named Wally, Jr., their son, as the beneficiary of the policy. Wally is the insured, Hilda is the owner, and Wally Jr. is the beneficiary. During Wally's life, Hilda can access the cash value of the policy and receive policy dividends. When Wally dies, the death benefit is paid to Wally, Jr., and is considered a taxable gift from Hilda to Wally, Jr., which may cause a gift tax liability.

When clients purchase life insurance, planners should know the identity of the insured, the owner, and the beneficiary. Without this knowledge, the planner will not be able to make appropriate recommendations for managing the client's risk and tax-planning needs.

LIFE INSURANCE UNDERWRITING

Underwriting is the process by which insurance companies decide whether to provide insurance to a customer and under what terms. Underwriters evaluate insurance applications and determine coverage amounts and premiums. They must evaluate the risk exposure and determine the premium that must be charged to insure that risk. When a company "underwrites" a policy, it accepts the risk inherent in the contract. In the case of life insurance, it accepts the risk of the insured dying prematurely and thus, having to pay the face value of the policy sooner than expected based on normal life expectancy. Many factors impact the probability of someone dying within a specific period of time. The underwriter attempts to quantify the impact of these factors on the likelihood of death and then determine an appropriate premium for that level of risk.

There are many factors that affect whether a company will issue an insurance policy on the life of a specific person. These factors will generally include the person's age, height and weight, gender, general state of health, lifestyle, medical history, profession (frequently called avocation by underwriters), financial status, hobbies, driving record, and whether they use tobacco products.

Key Concepts

1. Understand the process of life insurance underwriting.
2. Identify the three stages in the life-cycle model.
3. Highlight/identify the reasons for life insurance.
4. Identify the three methods used to determine life insurance needs.

Depending on the amount of coverage requested, underwriters may request information beyond what is included in the application to evaluate the applicant's medical condition. Some of the common underwriting requirements include one or more of the following:

1. Copies of the applicant's medical records from their doctor(s)
2. An oral swab to check for tobacco or drug use, or the presence of HIV
3. A "mini" medical exam – called a paramedical exam
4. An IBP – an insurance blood profile
5. A HOS, or home office urine specimen
6. An EKG or electrocardiogram to check basic heart health
7. A full medical examination by a physician

A person's health and lifestyle impact the mortality risk. Those with better health will generally have lower premiums. Individuals working in professions with less inherent risk will generally have lower premiums. For example it is more dangerous to work as a deep-sea fisherman or as a logger than as an insurance underwriter. Hobbies can certainly have an impact on the risk evaluation. Hobbies, such as skydiving, rock climbing, and scuba diving subject the person to more risk than other hobbies, such as collecting baseball cards. The exhibit below provides some detail in terms of the impact a specific factor may have on the underwriting process and the resulting policy premium.

Factor	Risk Level & Premium Effect
Height & Weight	Those with a higher BMI (body mass index) are more risky, resulting in a higher premium.
Gender	Women tend to outlive men.
Health	Chronic conditions, diseases, and high cholesterol levels are all higher risk and will result in higher premiums.
Family Medical History	Having a family history of poor health, diabetes, heart attacks or strokes, cancer, or early deaths will result in higher premiums.
Hobbies	People who engage in high risk activities (rock climbing, car racing, scuba diving, non-commercial aviation) will have higher premiums.
Driving	A history of speeding tickets or DWI/DUI arrests will likely result in higher premiums or, possibly, declination.
Financial Stability Status	Those who are more financially stable and well-off tend to be less risky and have lower premiums.

It should be noted that an underwriter will take into consideration the totality of all of the factors in determining whether or not to issue a policy and the amount of the premium. If the underwriter approves an application, the policy may be offered at "standard" rates, or at "preferred" rates if the applicant is deemed to be in better than average physical condition. For applicants who have a higher risk but who are still acceptable at higher premium rates, the underwriter may offer a "rated" policy. Life Insurance Companies frequently have numerous "Table" rating categories, such as Table A - 25% surcharge, Table B - 50% surcharge, Table C – 100% surcharge, etc. Table rates may go up to several multiples of the standard premium rate.

LIFE INSURANCE AND MORTALITY RISK

RISK EXPOSURES FROM DYING EARLY

To understand the risk exposure of early death, it is important to have a general understanding of the life-cycle model of financial planning. Individuals typically progress through three stages from the beginning of their careers to their deaths. These stages include:

1. Asset accumulation phase
2. Conservation/risk management phase
3. Distribution/gifting phase

LIFE-CYCLE STAGES

EXHIBIT 4.2

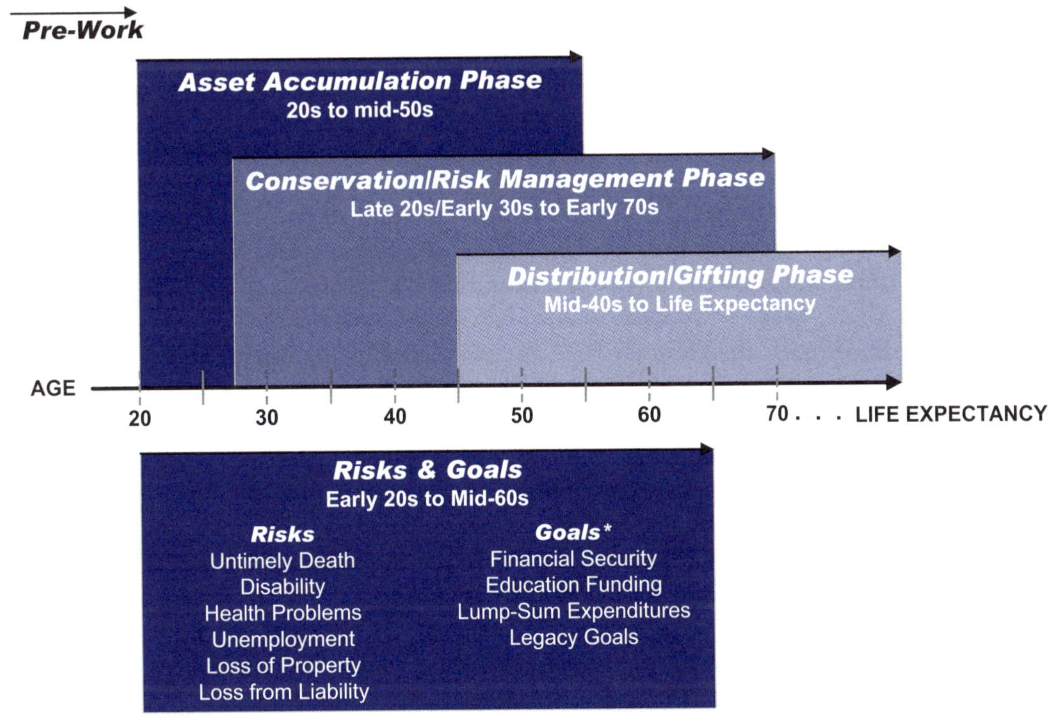

*Financial security means retirement with adequate income to maintain lifestyle.

The **asset accumulation phase** of the life cycle begins after a person completes his or her schooling and enters the workforce and typically lasts until ages 45-55. The early period of this phase is characterized by relatively high debt and low savings. In the early years of the accumulation phase, individuals often marry, have children, purchase houses and cars, and make further investments in their human capital by pursuing professional or graduate education. In the later years of the accumulation phase, debt is declining, savings and investments are increasing, and earnings from work or self-employment are increasing.

During the **conservation/risk management phase** of the life-cycle model, which typically lasts from ages 45-50 until retirement (around age 65), earnings from employment have reached their peak, children enter and exit college, the outstanding balance on the client's mortgage shrinks substantially, and savings increase to support retirement. It is common for individuals in this phase of the life cycle to take a more conservative approach to investing, since retirement is on the horizon. During the early part of this phase, clients become acutely aware of their insurance needs.

The **distribution/gifting phase** of the life cycle begins near retirement and ends at death. During this phase, a person generally begins to spend down his or her accumulated assets and may begin to transfer excess assets to family members and loved ones as gifts. After the person dies, any remaining assets will be transferred to intended beneficiaries by bequest, either through a validly executed will, the probate process, or a non-probate transfer vehicle.

As individuals age, their **mortality risk** (the risk that they will die within the year) increases. While it is unlikely that a healthy 25-year-old person will die this year, some 25-year-olds will pass away. Actuaries measure the likelihood of death at each age by observing the actual incidence of death by age for the population as a whole and then publish these probabilities in mortality tables. Not surprisingly, the risk of dying (mortality risk) increases as a person ages.

If a person dies prior to accumulating sufficient financial assets to meet his or her financial planning goals, the person's family (not the deceased individual) will feel the financial impact. Life insurance can be used as a hedge against the risk of early death so that if the person dies before accumulating the wealth necessary to satisfy his financial objectives, the life insurance death benefit received by the family will cover the cost of unfunded financial goals.

As a person moves through the life cycle from the asset accumulation phase to the distribution/gifting phase, his needs for life insurance as a hedge against early death change. In the accumulation phase of the life cycle, life insurance is often used to:

- Provide an income stream for the family if the breadwinner dies.
- Pay off existing debts (such as outstanding mortgages, car loans, personal loans, and consumer credit accounts).
- Fund financial objectives (such as education for the children).
- Provide a retirement income for the surviving spouse.

Moving from the asset accumulation phase of the life cycle to the conservation/risk management phase, the need for life insurance to fund financial goals and income streams declines, but very slowly (a reverse exponential curve). Everything being equal, if a person dies at an older age compared to a younger age, the need for income replacement declines (assuming that the surviving spouse is roughly the same age). Many financial objectives will already have been partially met, such as paying down the mortgage on the principal residence and helping children to obtain a college education. Once the mortgage is paid and the children have finished school, those objectives may be fully satisfied, and life insurance to fund these objectives may no longer be needed. If the surviving spouse needs supplemental income during retirement, however, life insurance may still be needed to fund this objective.

The conservation/risk management phase may result in increased needs for life insurance as well. If the person started a business, additional life insurance may be needed to:

- Fund buy-sell agreements between the owners of the business when one of the owners dies.
- Provide liquidity for the estate of the business owner so that taxes and administration expenses can be paid without reducing the family's inheritance.

High-income individuals, or those who have accumulated significant assets during the accumulation phase, may also be interested in acquiring life insurance as a way of maintaining and enhancing family wealth. The tax benefits of life insurance make it an attractive tool to help to achieve these objectives.

As the person enters the distribution/gifting phase of the life cycle, income needs are generally not an issue and the retirement income needs should be fully funded. Ideally, when a person retires, most-if not all-of his or her financial goals are met:

- No outstanding mortgage on the house
- Children have completed school and are independent
- Other client objectives have been fully funded

The need for life insurance in the distribution phase of the life cycle often focuses on estate liquidity needs and a desire to create and sustain family wealth. Death benefits paid on a life insurance policy can be used to cover medical expenses prior to death (to the extent that those expenses were not covered by health insurance), funeral expenses, probate and estate administration costs, and estate and inheritance taxes, which allows the full value of the decedent's assets to be transferred to the surviving family. Properly constructed planning arrangements combined with life insurance coverage can also create a pool of capital for the family, allowing someone to achieve financial goals that extend beyond his or her death.

Measuring the Life Insurance Need

Once the need life insurance is determined, a person must then decide how much to purchase. Over time, different approaches to calculating life insurance needs have been developed. Most practitioners use one or more of the following three models to determine life insurance needs:

1. The human-life value approach
2. The needs approach
3. The capitalized-earnings approach

EXHIBIT 4.3

Methods to Determine Life Insurance Needs

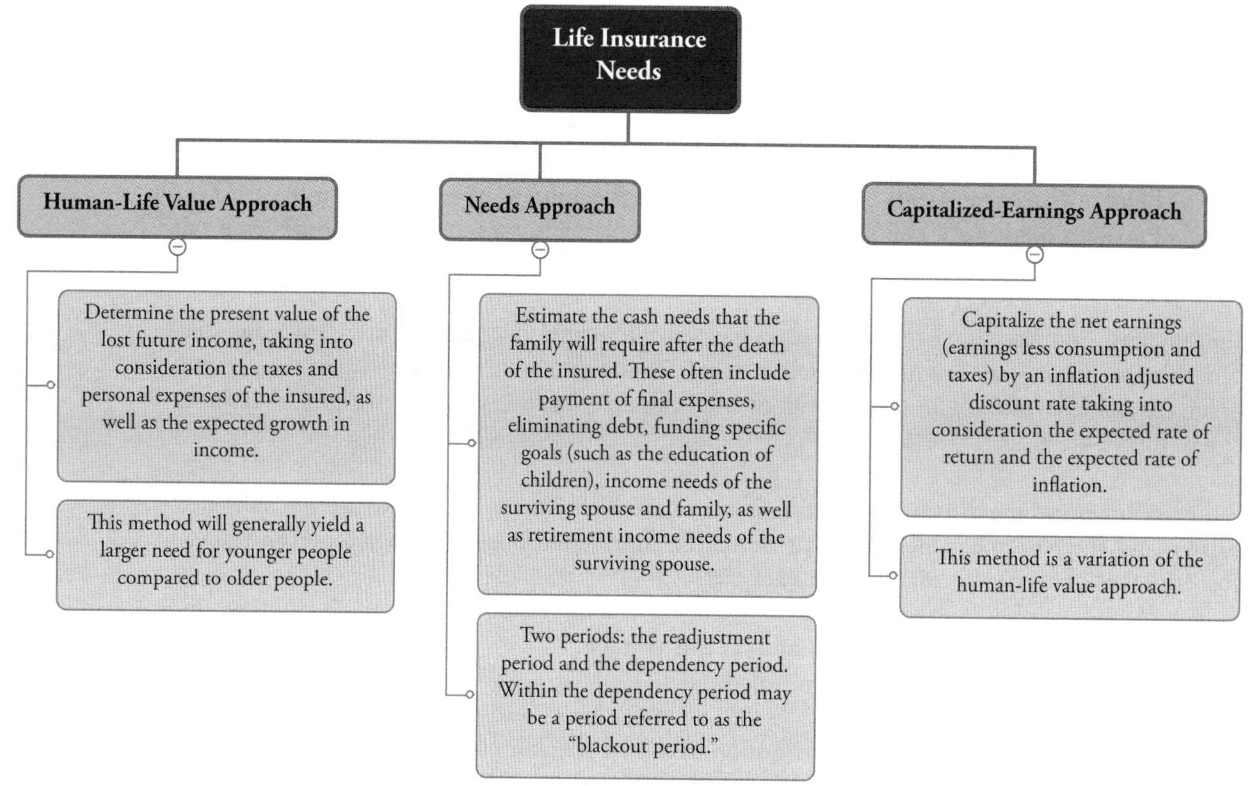

Some advisors routinely use only one of these approaches. However, a better approach is to fit the projection model to the client's circumstances instead of using only one approach. Some advisors use all three models and then consider other issues such as cash flows and bend points to determine how much life insurance to purchase.

Human-Life Value Approach

The **human-life value approach** suggests that the death benefit of a client's life insurance should equal the economic value of his future earnings stream discounted to its present value while considering his tax and consumption patterns. While religious scholars and philosophers teach us that we cannot place a monetary value on human life itself, it is possible to calculate the economic value of a person's expected future earnings. When an individual dies before reaching retirement, the loss of that person's earnings could create a hardship on the family, but with appropriate planning, that income stream can be replaced with the life insurance death benefit. Assuming that a person's income stream will be sufficient to achieve all of his or her financial goals, replacing the lost income stream for the family should permit the family to meet their financial objectives. The human-life value approach was one of the earliest techniques used to estimate life insurance needs. It was espoused by Dr. Solomon Heubner, a professor at The Wharton School of The University of Pennsylvania and founder of the American College of Life Underwriters, who is widely regarded as the "father of insurance education."

The steps in calculating a human-life value include:

1. Determine the person's annual earnings.
2. Subtract personal expenses and taxes that would have incurred (consumption and taxes).
3. Determine work-life expectancy (WLE), or the number of years he or she would have continued to earn income (alternatively stated, the number of years before retirement).
4. Calculate the future value of the lost earnings for the family (sometimes referred to as the family's share of earnings, or FSE), taking into consideration the expected growth rate in earnings.
5. Calculate the present value of the family's share of earnings at the inflation rate to determine the human-life value.

EXAMPLE 4.5

Chelsea is a 30-year-old marketing executive who earns $100,000 per year. She is married to Louis and has two children. She expects her salary to increase at an annual rate of 4% until her retirement at age 65 and anticipates that inflation will average 3%. Chelsea and Louis' income places them in the 25% average tax bracket (including both state and federal taxes), and she uses 15% of her after-tax income for personal consumption. Based on the human-life value approach, how much life insurance should Chelsea purchase?

Using the approach outlined above, we begin by taking Chelsea's income of $100,000 and subtracting the personal expenses that she will incur. The first 25% of her income goes to the payment of taxes, making her after-tax income $75,000. Of this amount, Chelsea uses $11,250 (15% x $75,000) for her own personal consumption and contributes $63,750 (85% x $75,000) of her income toward the achievement of family goals and objectives.

Since Chelsea is 30 years old and will retire at age 65, her work-life expectancy (WLE) is 35 years. The family's share of earnings (FSE) can be calculated by determining the future value of $63,750 per year growing at 4% per year (the expected increase in Chelsea's income) for 35 years (her WLE). Using a financial calculator, the inputs would be:

PMT = -63,750 (Chelsea's annual FSE)

N = 35 (Chelsea's work-life expectancy)

i = 4% (Expected growth rate in Chelsea's salary)

Solve for FV = $4,695,329

If Chelsea died today, her family would lose, in nominal terms, $4,695,329 in future income based on these assumptions. To determine Chelsea's human-life value and the amount of life insurance she should have on her life, we need to calculate the present value of her lifetime FSE (of $4,695,329) at the inflation rate over her work-life expectancy. Using a financial calculator, the inputs would be:

FV = $4,695,329 (Chelsea's lifetime FSE)

N = 35 (Chelsea's WLE)

i = 3% (Anticipated Inflation Rate)

Solve for Present Value = $1,668,642

> Note: This is about 16 times her gross pay!
>
> Using the human-life value approach to calculate life insurance needs, Chelsea should purchase a life insurance policy with a death benefit of approximately $1,700,000. If she had a life insurance policy with this death benefit and she died today, that amount, growing at the assumed annual increase in salary, will provide Chelsea's family with a full replacement of the portion of her income that she contributed toward the attainment of the family's financial goals.

When considering the use of the human-life value approach, a few relationships are worth considering. First, younger individuals have a higher human-life value (all else equal) than older persons because they will earn income for a longer period of time. As a person ages, the human-life value and the need for life insurance protection will decline. Second, as the individual's income rises (all else equal) so will their human-life value. As income increases, a greater amount will have to be replaced in the event that the person dies prior to the planned retirement date. Third, higher inflation expectations will lead to a lower human-life value, since the lifetime FSE is discounted at a higher rate. If a planner would like to make a conservative projection of human-life value, therefore, lower expected inflation rates should be used.

For many people, use of the human-life value approach to determining life insurance needs may be appropriate. If the person will have funded all of his or her financial objectives for the family by retirement, will not have liquidity needs at death, does not have a need to use life insurance for business succession planning purposes, and does not wish to use life insurance to fund family legacies, the human-life value approach to determining life insurance needs will provide an insurance amount that closely approximates the family's actual financial needs.

The Needs Approach

The second approach to estimating life insurance requirements is the **needs approach**. Instead of determining the present value of a future income stream, the planner estimates the cash needs that the family will require at and after the death of the insured. Some of the financial needs that are typically considered when calculating a life insurance amount under the needs approach include:

1. Payment of final expenses, medical care, and adjustment period expenses
2. Eliminating debt
3. Funding specific goals, such as education for children
4. Income needs of the surviving spouse and the family
5. Retirement needs of the surviving spouse

Final expenses typically include funeral costs, administration expenses, taxes (income, estate, inheritance, and generation-skipping taxes), and medical care provided shortly before death. Depending upon the level of service selected, funeral costs can be significant and must typically be paid prior to services being provided. Many people incur most of their lifetime medical expenses within the last few months before their deaths. These expenses usually have to be paid before beneficiaries can receive inheritances. For individuals with tight cash-flow and few liquid assets, including any estimated funeral and medical expenses in the life insurance need calculation is appropriate. Individuals with higher net worth and sufficient liquid assets may not have to include funeral expenses and medical costs when calculating insurance needs since other resources are available to pay these expenses. However, high net-worth individuals are likely to have higher costs of estate administration, and possibly higher transfer taxes that will be due within nine months of death. As an alternative to self-funding or using life insurance to fund these costs, the person can prepay funeral expenses and maintain adequate health insurance during lifetime to ensure that medical expenses are paid.

One way to ease the burden on survivors is to be able to pay off all outstanding debt at death. For example, if a person leaves a mortgaged residence to the surviving spouse, the surviving spouse will have increased cash flow needs to service the mortgage. Paying off the mortgage simplifies matters for the survivor by eliminating the required monthly payments and thereby reducing the survivor's need for cash flow. Individuals may also wish to pay off other forms of debt, such as car loans, personal loans, student loans, and revolving charge accounts. These amounts should be included in the life insurance needs estimate.

Aside from retirement, perhaps the largest funding objective that many families face is the (partial or full) payment of their children's higher education costs. Education is expensive. The cost of tuition and other related costs have consistently increased at a rate greater than inflation. The early death of the family's breadwinner could result in limited funding to cover college education expenses. If education funding is a goal, the planner should calculate the lump sum (present value) needed to pay for the tuition and other related costs at the target college, and include that in the life insurance needs analysis.

An emergency fund should be established to cover unexpected major expenses, and possibly the loss of employment. If a young person dies prior to establishing an adequate emergency fund, however, it may be wise to include a lump sum in the retirement need calculation that can be set aside by the survivors to pay for emergencies so that the other portion of the policy death benefit can be used for its intended purpose.

Finally, when calculating life insurance requirements under the needs approach, the income needs of the surviving spouse and dependents must be considered. Income needs will vary depending upon the family circumstances, the age of the family members, and the availability of public and private benefit payments. These changes to the income needs of the survivors are often broken down into the readjustment period and the dependency period.

The Readjustment Period

After the death of a family's breadwinner, the family will need time to adjust to their new reality – a life without an important member of the family. For a period of six months to two years, the family should have access to the same amount of income that was available when the breadwinner was alive. Often, non-recurring expenses will be incurred as a result of the breadwinner's death. Having the cash flow to cover these expenses without affecting the family's lifestyle may be important.

The Dependency Period

The length of the dependency period is determined by the number of dependents and their ages. Traditionally this period lasts from the end of the readjustment period to the time when all children reach the age of majority. As members of the sandwich generation[1] will suggest, another factor that can extend the dependency period occurs when the decedent's parents are dependents. If parents rely on income to make ends meet, the present value of the anticipated support over the parents' lifetime should also be included in the life insurance needs calculation.

If the surviving spouse has an independent source of income sufficient to meet the needs of him/herself and the family, additional life insurance funding may be unnecessary. In some cases, however, the dependency period may have to be extended to provide supplemental income for the decedent's spouse in the event the spouse cannot work or cannot replace the income lost when the decedent died.

If the surviving spouse is caring for minor children at the time of the decedent's death, both the surviving spouse and the children will qualify for Social Security survivors benefits. When the youngest child reaches the age of 16, survivor benefit payments to the surviving spouse will cease (the blackout period), and the surviving spouse will typically need additional income to act as a substitute for those lost payments. When Social Security payments resume in the form of retirement benefits (as early as age 60 for a surviving spouse), those supplemental income payments can be reduced. The period between the cessation of survivor benefits and the receipt of retirement benefits is sometimes referred to as the "blackout period" by planners. When forecasting the amount of income the surviving spouse will need, be sure to consider the impact of the blackout period on the income needs of the surviving spouse.

> **QUICK QUIZ 4.1**
>
> 1. Generally, people accumulate wealth throughout their lives.
>   a. True
>   b. False
>
> 2. Life insurance can be an effective tool for enhancing a family's wealth.
>   a. True
>   b. False
>
> 3. Death benefits paid from life insurance cannot be used to pay the decedent's hospital bills.
>   a. True
>   b. False
>
> 4. Generally, as clients age, the human-life value and the need for life insurance protection will increase.
>   a. True
>   b. False
>
> False, True, False, False.

After calculating the amount of each of the family's financial needs, these amounts can be added together to determine the appropriate life insurance death benefit for the individual. If the person already has some life insurance coverage, or has existing assets that could be used to fund these needs in the event of an early death, those amounts can be subtracted from the total to determine the net amount of life insurance protection that should be obtained on their life. Example 4.6 provides an analysis of a needs approach to life insurance needs and a graphical presentation of the component parts.

1. The sandwich generation is a term that describes people who must take care of and raise their children as well as provide care and support for their aged parents.

EXAMPLE 4.6

Assume the following information:

Husband	Age 30	$100,000 income
Wife	Age 30	
Child A	Age 4	
Child B	Age 2	

- Social Security Old Age, Survivor, and Disability benefit (OASDI) until Child B becomes age 16, $2,500 per month. The spouse is no longer entitled to benefits after the youngest child turns 16.
- Social Security OASDI benefit until Child B becomes age 18, $1,250 per month. The children stop receiving benefits upon turning 18.
- Social Security OASDI widow's benefit from age 60 to life expectancy age 90, $2,500 per month.
- College education costs $20,000 per year per child in today's dollars, at age 18 for four years.
- Total income needs of spouse for dependency period until Child B is age 22, $5,000 per month in today's dollars.
- Inflation is expected to be 3%.
- Investment rate of return is expected to be 5%.
- Funeral, last medical, and adjustment period expense equal a lump sum of $30,000.
- Mortgage and debt repayment lump sum of $200,000.
- Education inflation rate is 5%.

Present Value Calculations

1			2		
N	=	14 x 12	N	=	2 x 12
i	=	(1.05÷1.03-1)÷12	i	=	(1.05÷1.03-1)÷12
PMT	=	$2,500	PMT	=	$3,750
PV	=	$367,494	$PV_{@44}$	=	$88,205
			$PV_{@30}$	=	$67,385*

3			4		
N	=	14 x 12	N	=	30 x 12
i	=	(1.05÷1.03-1)÷12	i	=	(1.05÷1.03-1)÷12
PMT	=	$5,000	PMT	=	$2,500
$PV_{@46}$	=	$734,987	$PV_{@60}$	=	$681,732
$PV_{@30}$		$540,315*	$PV_{@30}$	=	$382,870*

* Note: The second present value calculation in calculations 2, 3, and 4 use whole years instead of months (e.g., 14 for 2, 16 for 3, and 30 for 4) and use an i of (1.05/1.03 - 1) x 100 and are rounded to whole dollars. The change from months to years for the second calculation was done for simplicity and the keystrokes are not shown.

	Calculation 1	Calculation 2	Calculation 3 Black Out Period*		Calculation 4 Retirement
Redo	$5,000/mo.	$5,000/mo.	$5,000/mo.	$5,000/mo.	$5,000/mo.
OASDI	$2,500/mo.	$1,250/mo.			$2,500/mo.
Net	$2,500/mo.	$3,750/mo.	$5,000/mo.	$5,000/mo.	$2,500/mo.

Age of Spouse	30	44	46	60	90
Age of Child A	4	18	20		
Age of Child B	2	16	18		

PV of Family Costs (30 – 44)	$367,494
PV of Family Costs (44 – 46)	$67,385
PV of College Education	$160,000
PV of Family Costs (46 – 60)	$540,315
PV of Retirement for Spouse (60 – 90)	$382,870
Plus last medical and debt payment	$230,000
Total Insurance Needs	$1,748,064

* Black out period – no Social Security Benefits

The Capitalized-Earnings Approach

The **capitalized-earnings approach** is a modification of the human-life value approach. The differences are that there is no need to determine the work-life expectancy and the investment returns on the life insurance are presumed to be at the long-term investment rate. This is a very efficient method for determining the approximate amount of life insurance needed for one who has dependents and life insurance needs.

This method divides the net earnings (earnings less taxes and consumption) by an inflation adjusted discount rate, which takes into consideration the expected rate of return and the expected rate of inflation.

EXAMPLE 4.7

Assume the following:

Earnings	$100,000
Raise Rate	3%
Inflation Rate	3%
Investment Rate	6%
Consumption by Insured	25%
Federal and State Taxes	25%

The numerator: Earnings - Consumption - Taxes

The denominator: $\frac{1 + \text{Investment Rate}}{1 + \text{Inflation Rate}} - 1$

$$\text{Calculation: } \frac{\$100{,}000 - \$25{,}000 - \$25{,}000}{(1.06 \div 1.03) - 1} = \frac{\$50{,}000}{0.0291262} = \$1{,}716{,}667$$

The amount of life insurance needed using the capitalized-earnings approach in this example is $1,716,667. This amount is comparable to the amount determined using the human life approach. However, the method is significantly easier to use.

Summary of the Three Methods		
Human-Life Value Approach	=	$1,668,642
Needs Approach	=	$1,748,064
Capitalized-Earnings Approach	=	$1,716,667

The three methods coalesce in this case, but in other cases may vary significantly depending on individual circumstances and assumptions used. From numerous applications of the three methods, we have developed a benchmark metric of 12-18 times gross pay as the general guide for life insurance needed. While any rule of thumb, such as this benchmark metric, is a helpful planning tool, it should not be used as a substitute for a complete analysis.

TYPES AND USES OF LIFE INSURANCE IN FINANCIAL PLANNING

Life insurance that transfers the risk of losses associated with early death to an insurance company in return for a fee (the premium on the policy). If the insured party dies, the insurance company pays the specified death benefit to a designated beneficiary. Several types of life insurance policies exist in the market today. The type of policy that is appropriate for one person may not be appropriate for another. Planners need to understand the individual's purpose for buying and holding life insurance and select the policy that most closely matches his or her needs.

The two most common types of life insurance are term and permanent. Permanent life insurance includes universal, whole, variable, and modified endowment contracts, all of which are discussed in this section.

Term Insurance

A **term-insurance** policy, like all other life insurance policies, provides death benefit protection. If the insured dies during the term of the policy, the insurance company will pay the specified death benefit. The term of the policy is typically one year or longer, although many term policies are designed to permit the insured to renew the policy for a longer period of time than the initial term.

When a term-insurance policy is purchased, the owner pays a premium equal to the risk the insurance company is undertaking. Term-insurance policies do not have cash accumulation features and do not provide for continuing insurance after premium payments cease. Quite literally, the owner of a term policy is shifting the financial risk of death for the current year to the insurance company in return for the annual premium. If the owner wishes to shift the financial risk of death to the insurance company in future years, additional premiums must be paid.

As individuals advance in age, the actuarial risk that they will die within the year increases. This means that every year the **mortality cost**, which equals the probability of dying within the year times the face value of the policy, of the term-insurance policy increases to reflect the increased risk of death. The term-insurance premium for a young person tends to be very low due to the decreased risk of death, but term-insurance policies can get very expensive for older individuals. In fact, at age 99, the premium for a term-insurance policy approximates the death benefit of the policy (discounted for a few months of time value) since the risk of death within the year is substantial. For this reason, term-insurance policies tend to be used by younger individuals and for those who need life insurance protection for shorter periods of time to ensure that, in the event of their early death, their financial goals can be met. When the need for life insurance is permanent, some form of cash-value policy will generally be used since the premiums on term insurance at advanced ages become prohibitive.

KEY CONCEPTS

1. Describe the differences between annual renewable term (ART) life insurance, level-term life insurance, decreasing term life insurance, convertible annual renewable term life insurance, and group term insurance.
2. Describe some of the benefits and negatives of universal life insurance.
3. Describe the differences between straight whole life insurance, limited pay whole life insurance, modified whole life insurance, and variable whole life insurance.
4. Describe the income tax benefits that can be arranged with life insurance planning.

EXAMPLE 4.8

Aside from funding her retirement, Maggie's primary financial goal is to pay for the college education costs of her son, Dylan. She is currently 32 years old. Maggie has met with a financial planner and has developed a savings plan that will, over time, meet both her retirement and educational funding needs. If Maggie dies before she can earn the money to fund these objectives, Dylan's education may not be fully funded. To hedge against this risk, Maggie purchases a term-insurance policy with a death benefit of $500,000 so Dylan will be able to attend the college of his choice. If Maggie lives, she will meet the educational funding goal through savings and investments and will no longer need to pay for the insurance. Since Maggie's life insurance need is temporary and she is relatively young, term insurance is a good option.

EXAMPLE 4.9

Bertie (grantor) recently created a Grantor Retained Annuity Trust. He funded the trust with stock of Wooster Enterprises, Ltd. The trust states Bertie will receive an income stream equal to 20% of the value of the stock he transferred to the trust each year for five years (thus the retained annuity). After the five-year period expires, the trust terminates, and whatever is left in the trust will be transferred to his cousin, Claude. If Bertie dies while receiving the income stream from the trust, the value of the trust assets will be taxable in his gross estate.[1] If Bertie purchases a term-insurance policy for the five-year duration of the trust and dies during that term, the policy will provide sufficient money to pay any estate taxes. Since Bertie's need for life insurance is temporary (in this case, five years), term insurance is an appropriate product.

1. IRC Section 2036.

EXAMPLE 4.10

Clarence is the president and CEO of Empress of Blandings Holdings Company, Inc. He owns a 30% interest in the company, and the remaining ownership interest is held by members of his extended family. Since Empress of Blandings is a family-owned company and the owners wish to keep it that way, they have entered into a buy-sell agreement so that if any of the current owners dies, the surviving owners must purchase the deceased owner's interest from his or her estate. The company is a large one, and neither Clarence nor the other owners expect to have sufficient cash on hand to purchase the stock as required by the buy-sell agreement. Instead, they fund the buy-sell agreement using life insurance policies purchased on all of the owners' lives. Since the need for life insurance is permanent in this case, term insurance is not the appropriate type of insurance to purchase.

There are several variations of term insurance in the market today. Perhaps the most common type of term insurance is **Annual Renewable Term (ART)**. An Annual Renewable Term policy permits the policyholder to purchase term insurance in subsequent years without evidence of insurability, but premiums on the policy increase each year to reflect the increasing mortality risk being undertaken by the insurer. Many insurance companies will limit the renewal period to a specified number of years (or to a specific age), at which time the insured would have to then provide further evidence of insurability in order to obtain a new policy. The limitation on renewal protects the insurer against possible adverse selection risk (the risk that only unhealthy insureds will renew their term life insurance coverage).

RENEWABLE TERM PREMIUM AND YEARLY RENEWABLE TERM PREMIUM (ISSUED AT AGE 25)

EXHIBIT 4.4

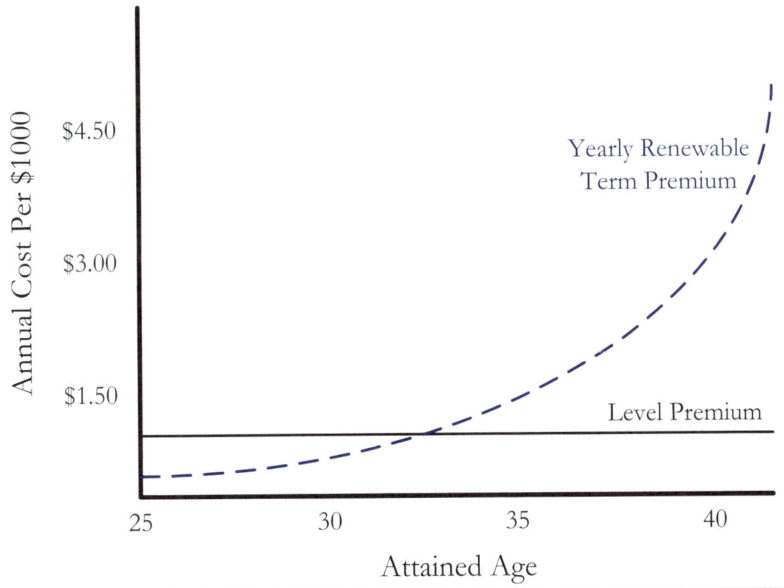

For some individuals, the increasing premium on annual renewable term insurance may be unattractive, and they would prefer to commit to a specific premium amount that will not change over a specific period of time (the term). **Level-premium term insurance** charges a fixed premium each year over a specified period of years (often 5, 10, 15, 20, or 30 years), so the premium does not increase during that period. When a level-term insurance policy is purchased, the premiums paid by the owner will be larger than the premiums on an annual renewable term policy in the earlier years, but will be less than the premiums on an annual renewable term policy in later years. All else being equal, the total premium outlay on an annual renewable term policy will be less than that on a level-term policy since time value of money principles are used to discount the premiums over the leveling period. However, level-premium term may be appropriate for people who prefer simplicity in budgeting, since their insurance costs will be "fixed" over the level premium.

For individuals who do not anticipate having a permanent need for insurance, the life-cycle theory of financial planning suggests that their need for life insurance protection will decrease as they get older. As each year passes and income is earned, that income can be employed to meet their financial goals, thereby allowing them to rely less on life insurance to satisfy those goals in the event of an untimely death. **Decreasing-term insurance** allows the owner to pay the same premium for the insurance protection each year. The death benefit on the policy will, however, decrease each year to offset the increasing mortality cost due to the passage of time.

EXAMPLE 4.11

Randy is married to Kelly, and they have three children. Five years ago, Randy and Kelly purchased a house subject to a 30-year mortgage. Since the children have arrived, Kelly stopped working, and Randy is the sole breadwinner for the family. He has expressed a concern to his financial planner that if he died before the mortgage was paid off, Kelly and the children would not be able to afford to live in the house. Randy purchases a decreasing-term insurance policy that he plans to keep in force for the remaining term of the mortgage. As each year passes, the death benefit will decline, but so will the outstanding balance on the mortgage. The decreasing-term policy allows Randy to budget a fixed dollar amount for insurance protection while ensuring that the balance of the mortgage can be paid off in the event of his untimely death.

A common problem faced by young individuals who have a permanent need for life insurance protection is that they often cannot afford to purchase permanent life insurance. In this situation, term insurance can be used as an interim step to obtaining permanent life insurance protection. Many term-insurance policies permit the insured to convert the term policy into a permanent policy during the renewability period.

EXAMPLE 4.12

Roderick is the 22-year-old heir to Spode Enterprises, Inc. He anticipates receiving large inheritances when his grandparents and parents pass away, and would like to use permanent life insurance policies to pay for estate taxes and administration expenses when he dies. Since he just graduated from college and his salary is relatively modest, he does not currently have the funds to purchase a large amount of permanent life insurance protection. Instead, Roderick can purchase a convertible annual renewable-term life insurance policy. Given his young age, the term-insurance premiums will be manageable now, and he can convert the policy to a permanent policy when his income increases.

Term insurance provides low-cost life insurance protection that can be particularly valuable for younger individuals and for those who have temporary insurance needs. As the person's age increases, so will the premium on the term-insurance policy. Individuals with a permanent need for death benefit protection should consider the use of permanent life insurance policies (such as whole life or universal policies).

The premiums for term-life insurance are very inexpensive and the term of death benefit coverage can be extended well into one's 80s. Below is a table of level premiums for various term policies and for universal insurance, based on the age of the insured.

Life Insurance Premium Costs Comparison for Term and Universal (per $1,000 of coverage)

EXHIBIT 4.5

Age	Term* (10-year)	Term* (25-year)	Term* (30-year)	Universal Life
25	$0.25	$0.52	$0.60	$2.31
30	$0.25	$0.56	$0.64	$2.92
35	$0.26	$0.65	$0.72	$3.77
40	$0.31	$0.96	$1.04	$4.74
45	$0.51	$1.52	$1.68	$5.99
50	$0.83	N/A	N/A	$7.45
55	$1.40	N/A	N/A	$9.05
60	$2.39	N/A	N/A	$11.74
65	$4.08	N/A	N/A	$15.40

Price is per $1,000 of coverage ($ per 000).
For very healthy non-tobacco using male insured.
* Usually available to terminate at or before age 75.

Level-Term Insurance Sample for Male, Age 67

EXHIBIT 4.6

Amount	10-Year Term*	15-Year Term**
$1,000,000	$6,659	$10,454
$2,000,000	$13,249	$20,838

* MetLife Insurance
** Genworth Life Insurance

Universal Life Insurance

Universal life insurance is similar to term life insurance with several additional features or options, including a cash-value accumulation pot. Universal life insurance allows individuals to make premium contributions in excess of the term-insurance premium or not make them at all. If premiums are not paid, ultimately the policy will lapse. Any excess premiums made are deposited into an investment account. The owner of the policy can make contributions to the policy at any time, and each year the insurance company will take enough out of the cash-value accumulation pot to pay the equivalent of the term-life mortality premium. As long as there is sufficient money in the policy to pay the premium, the policy will remain in force. If there is not enough money in the policy to cover the current premium payment, and the owner does not make additional premium contributions to pay for the mortality costs, the policy will lapse.

One of the advantages of universal life insurance is that the owner of the policy can make contributions to the policy when he or she has the cash flow to do so, and the policy will remain in force as long as the term-insurance premium can be paid from the cash value. The cash value is invested by the insurance company, and interest is credited to the accumulation. To the extent that the earnings on the cash accumulation are used to pay for life insurance protection, the growth in investment value is not subject to tax. Over time, this creates the potential for the owner of the policy to pay for the term-insurance protection with pre-tax dollars (from earnings on the cash invested in the policy) as opposed to after-tax dollars (premium payments paid directly by the policy owner).

Universal life policies typically offer two death benefit options, referred to as Option A and Option B. A policy with the Option A death benefit provides a level death benefit. This means that as the cash value accumulation in the policy increases, the amount of death benefit protection decreases. Once the cash accumulation reaches a specified level, however, the death benefit will have to increase to ensure that the policy continues to meet the definition of life insurance. A life insurance policy must have an amount "at risk" (net amount at risk). If the cash value equals the death benefit, there is no longer an actuarial amount at risk.

EXAMPLE 4.13

Edward purchased a universal life insurance policy several years ago and has been making contributions in excess of the term insurance cost. The death benefit for the policy is $100,000, and the death benefit option selected was Option A. The cash value in the policy is $20,000 after the current year's term-insurance premium is paid. If Edward dies this year, his beneficiary will receive a $100,000 death benefit from the insurance company. Since $20,000 of the death benefit is covered by the cash value of the policy, the amount at risk under the policy is only $80,000 ($100,000 - $20,000). Edward's term-insurance premium for the year will be based on an $80,000 death benefit, which will reduce the annual cost he will incur compared to the term-insurance premium on a $100,000 death benefit.

A policy with the Option B death benefit provides an increasing death benefit. If the insured dies, the policy death benefit will equal the specified death benefit in the policy plus the cash value of the policy.

EXAMPLE 4.14

Refer to the facts in the prior example. If Edward chose Option B coverage instead of Option A, and he died this year, his beneficiary would receive a death benefit of $120,000 (equal to the policy death benefit of $100,000 plus the policy cash value of $20,000). The term-insurance premium that Edward will pay is based on $100,000 of insurance protection, which is the amount that the insurance company must pay upon Edward's death. Compared with an Option A death benefit, the annual costs of the Option B policy will be greater because there is a greater amount at risk, and the death benefit received by the beneficiary will be greater as well.

UNIVERSAL LIFE: OPTION A AND OPTION B

EXHIBIT 4.7

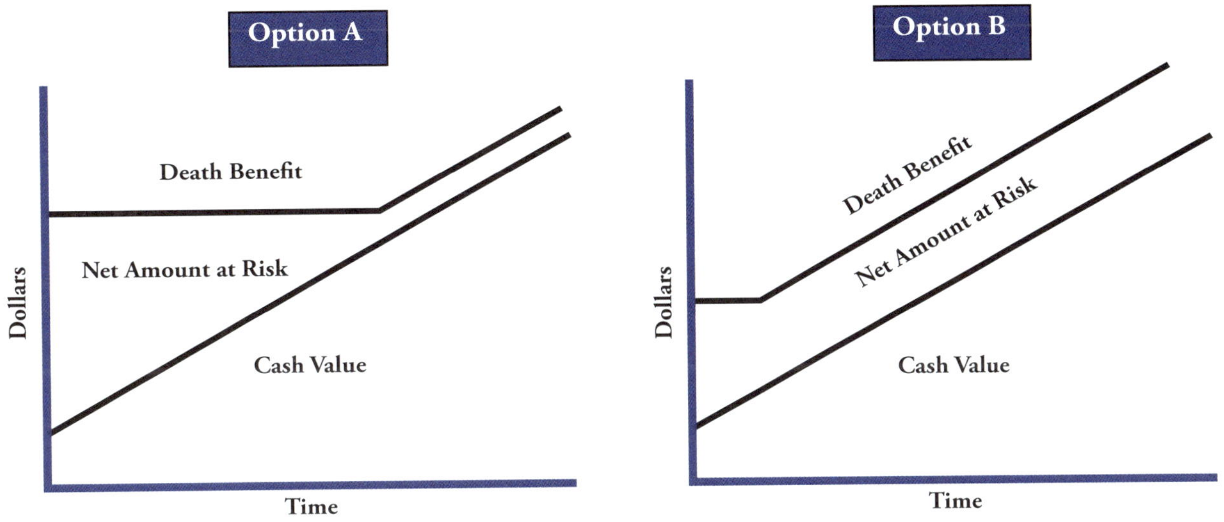

Universal life insurance is attractive for individuals who have temporary needs for life insurance protection and who would like to pre-fund the costs of the term-insurance protection by making contributions to the cash value accumulation pot attached to the policy. Individuals with a permanent need for insurance protection should consider other types of policy alternatives. Because term-insurance costs (mortality costs) increase each year and must be paid to keep the policy in force, a standard universal policy does not guarantee a death benefit unless there is sufficient cash value in the policy to pay the annual mortality cost. However, flexibility in premium payments is one of the attractions of universal life insurance, but that same flexibility may cause the death benefit to be reduced or, in the extreme case, cause the policy to lapse.

WHOLE LIFE INSURANCE

Whole life insurance provides guarantees from the insurer that are not found in term insurance and universal life insurance policies. As long as the premium specified in the insurance contract is paid, whole life insurance will remain in force during the life of the insured even if there is no longer cash in the cash value accumulation pot to pay term-insurance premiums (as is the case with universal life insurance). In arriving at the premium payment amount, the insurer considers the cost of insurance protection over the lifetime of the insured (usually to age 100 or 120), and prices the premium amount accordingly.[1] As a consequence, the premiums on whole life insurance policies are larger than premiums on term life or universal life policies because the insured is pre-funding the cost of insurance protection. The premium payments over the term-insurance cost of protection are invested by the life insurance company, which typically guarantees a minimum investment return. Unlike the situation with a universal life insurance policy, which transfers investment risk to the insured, the insurer retains the investment risk on a whole life policy, and even if the invested excess premium payments are not sufficient to pay the future pure cost of insurance protection (term-insurance cost) each year, the insurer promises to keep the policy in force.

1. Historically, whole life policies have matured at age 100. However, today there are many policies that mature at age 120.

Whole life policies are useful when the person wants to ensure that life insurance protection will be available on a permanent basis. Whole life policies are also useful for middle-aged and older people who need death benefit protection but do not wish to retain investment risk (as would be the case in a universal life insurance policy).

The most common form of whole life policy is often referred to as an **ordinary (or straight) life** policy. It requires the owner to pay a specified level premium every year until death (or age 100 or 120). The premium can be paid on a monthly, quarterly, semi-annual, or annual basis, and the policy will remain in force as long as the premium is paid. Older straight-life policies provided that if the insured lived to age 100, the face amount (the death benefit) on the policy would be paid to the policy owner as a living benefit. If this occurs, the amount received in excess of the owner's basis in the policy would be subject to income tax, so many policies now provide for the insurance policy to remain in force until death, even if the insured lives to or past age 100, to lock in the income-tax-free character of the death benefit.

EXHIBIT 4.8

THE SAVINGS ELEMENT OF A LEVEL-PREMIUM, WHOLE LIFE INSURANCE POLICY

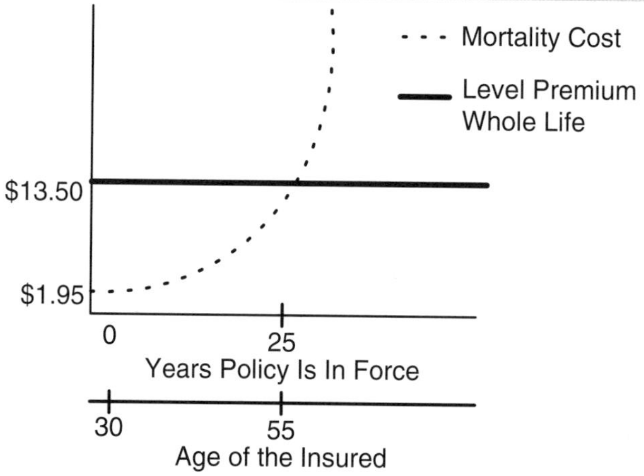

One of the problems with an ordinary (straight) life policy is that premium payments must be made throughout the lifetime of the insured. Many individuals would prefer to make premium payments over a shorter period of time (perhaps their work life expectancy) that will be sufficient to keep the policy in force for their lifetimes. Insurance companies will often provide quotes for whole life policies on a 10 or 20-year payment schedule. At the end of the payment period, the policy is considered to be paid-up, at which time no additional premium payments are due. These policies are referred to as **limited-pay policies.** Of course, the premium on a limited-pay policy will be greater than the premium on an ordinary (straight) life policy since the lifetime premium payments are being front-loaded over the payment period.

While a person may have a need for permanent life insurance protection, the normal premiums on a whole life policy may not be affordable based on the person's current income. However, as income rises in the future, the person may be able to afford the premiums for permanent insurance. For someone in this situation who would like to lock in the insurance protection (to ensure insurability), a **modified whole life policy** should be considered. Modified whole life policies have lower premiums than regular policies for the initial policy period (often three to five years), and increase to a higher premium at the end of the initial period. This type of policy gives a person the opportunity to purchase a whole life policy with initial lower premiums which increase as the insured's income increases. A modified whole life policy is an alternative to convertible term insurance.

Whole life insurance policies can also be purchased on a single-premium basis. A **single-premium policy** requires the owner to pay a lump sum in return for insurance protection that will extend throughout the insured's lifetime. These policies require a substantial initial cash outlay, and are typically used by wealthy individuals for estate and generation-skipping transfer tax purposes. One downside to using a single-premium policy is that if the owner receives lifetime benefits from the life insurance policy by borrowing money from the cash value, income tax must be paid on the cash received to the extent of the growth on policy cash value. A single-premium policy is a form of **Modified Endowment Contract (MEC)**, which has different tax attributes than regular life insurance policies and is discussed in detail later in this chapter.

Some people object to whole life policies on the grounds that the rates credited (earned) to the cash value accumulation within the policy are often low, increasing the premium that must be paid for insurance protection. **Variable whole life policies** provide for a fixed premium payment and permit the cash value of the policy to be professionally managed by the insurance company or an outside investment manager. The policy owner can choose among various investment options to invest the cash value inside the life insurance policy. This type of policy transfers investment risk to the owner, and the amount of the death benefit available on the policy will fluctuate with the performance of the underlying investments. Younger individuals who have long-term investment horizons and those with moderate-to-high risk tolerance may find variable whole life policies appealing since they hope to capture some of the upside benefits of allocating their cash values to equities instead of fixed-income investments. Unlike universal life insurance policies, variable whole life policies have a minimum death benefit that will be paid regardless of the investment performance of the underlying investments. Also, the owner of the policy will be guaranteed the minimum death benefit as long as the scheduled premiums specified in the contract are paid.

Whole life policies can also be tailored to meet specific financial needs. **Second-to-die** policies are often used in estate planning to provide liquidity at the death of the second spouse since this is typically when estate taxes for the couple will be due. A second-to-die policy names two insureds and pays the death benefit only when the second insured dies. Since two lives are covered by the policy, a second-to-die policy is a type of joint life insurance policy. One advantage of a second-to-die policy is that the underwriting is based on the healthier of the two insureds.

Another type of joint life policy is a **first-to-die** policy. Like the second-to-die policy, the first-to-die policy covers two individuals, but the death benefit is paid upon the death of the first individual. First-to-die policies are sometimes used to provide funding to pay off a mortgage at the death of the first spouse, to establish a fund for children's educational costs when one spouse dies early, or to provide a supplemental pool of capital for the surviving spouse to receive additional retirement income.

Policy Dividends

Policy dividends are a non-guaranteed "return of premium" calculated annually based on favorable loss experience, investment performance, and/or expenses.

Whole life insurance policies are permanent policies that are priced using current actuarial mortality assumptions. Over the past century, life expectancies have been increasing, a trend that is expected to continue into the future. Life insurance policies priced using previous mortality tables resulted in higher premiums as compared to premiums calculated using current mortality tables. In addition to favorable mortality experience which occurs when the group of insureds lives longer than they were anticipated to live based on mortality assumptions, the insurance company may realize expense savings, or greater than anticipated returns on investments than it assumed when it originally priced a life insurance policy. Insurance companies return these excess premium payments to policyholders by issuing dividends on participating, or permanent, insurance policies. Unlike a dividend on a stock investment, which is a distribution of corporate earnings and profits and is therefore subject to income tax in the hands of the stockholder, dividends on life insurance policies are treated as a nontaxable return of part of the owner's premium payment.

Policy owners can choose to receive the dividend payments in cash, which could result in taxable income to the extent that dividends exceed the premiums paid, or they may choose one of several other options provided by the insurance company. Insurance companies commonly offer options to use dividends to purchase paid-up additional life insurance protection, purchase one-year term insurance, accumulate interest, or reduce premium payments.

If the policy owner chooses the paid-up additions option, an additional amount of paid up life insurance protection is purchased, which increases the death benefit on the policy. The paid-up additions option is often attractive to individuals who are uninsurable and would like to receive additional death benefit protection.

Instead of purchasing a paid-up addition to the death benefit, the policy owner could also enhance the death benefit by using the dividend to purchase one-year term insurance. This option would provide a greater death benefit if the insured dies during the year when compared to the paid-up additions option, but like all other term-insurance contracts, the coverage will expire at the end of the year unless another dividend distribution is received and is again used to purchase term insurance. Recall that if the dividend stays the same, the amount of one-year term insurance that can be purchased each year will decline due to the increasing mortality risk (and premium cost) as a result of the insured's increasing age.

If the insured does not need additional death benefit protection, the dividends can be left on deposit with the life insurance company, which will pay interest on the dividends. The owner of the policy can access these amounts at any time, and if the dividends and the accumulated interest payments are left with the insurer until the insured's death, they are added to and paid out with the death benefit of the policy. While the policy dividends themselves are not taxable, any interest earned on policy dividends is subject to income tax. Each year that interest is credited to dividends deposited with the insurance company, the insurance company will send the policy owner a Form 1099-INT that will specify the interest payments that are subject to tax.

One use of policy dividends is to use them to offset (decrease) the premium payments due on the policy for the current year. This permits the life insurance premium payments to decline over time if dividends are regularly declared.

Taxation of Whole Life Insurance Policies

Both the growth in the cash value of the policy and the policy death benefit are exempt from Federal income tax as long as the policy is not surrendered.

A policy owner wanting to receive lifetime benefits from a whole life insurance policy without triggering an income tax consequence can achieve this in two ways:

1. By withdrawing the tax basis in the policy.
2. By taking loans against the cash value of the policy. Any outstanding loans against the policy's cash value will be exempt from federal income tax, provided that the policy is in force at the date of the insured's death. However, the death benefit on the policy will be reduced by the amount of the outstanding loan.

IRC Section 101(a) exempts the death benefit on any life insurance policy from income tax provided that the policy has not been exchanged for valuable consideration. A detailed discussion of the Transfer-for-Value Rule is covered later.

Quick Quiz 4.2

1. All else being equal, the total premium outlay on an annual renewable term (ART) policy will be less than a level-term policy.
   a. True
   b. False

2. Universal life insurance is a breed of term life insurance.
   a. True
   b. False

3. Universal life insurance option A provides for increasing death benefits.
   a. True
   b. False

4. Two ways to receive tax-free benefits from a whole life policy during one's life are: taking a loan against the death benefit amount and not withdrawing an amount in excess of the basis.
   a. True
   b. False

True, True, False, True.

Surrender Charges

The insurer incurs several costs when issuing a whole life insurance policy. These costs often exceed the first premium payment. To avoid incurring losses when policy owners purchase and then quickly cancel their insurance contracts, insurance companies typically enforce a **surrender charge** that is designed to compensate them for up-front costs incurred when issuing the policy. The amount of the surrender charge and the length of the surrender-charge period are regulated by state law. Typically, surrender charges decrease over time. After a period of seven to ten years, cancellation of a life insurance policy does not result in the imposition of a surrender charge. In most cases in which careful planning is conducted, surrender charges are not a major concern, since most people who choose permanent life insurance typically want that coverage to stay in force until the death of the insured.

State insurance regulations may provide for a brief "free-look" period during which the policy may be declined for a full refund.

Nonforfeiture Options for Life Insurance

Nonforfeiture options protect the cash values of a policy owner who chooses to discontinue coverage under a whole life policy. This provision states that the insured, by lapsing or surrendering the policy, does not automatically forfeit the cash value accumulation. The nonforfeiture options give the policy owner some choice in how to receive the cash value of the policy.

The most common nonforfeiture options include:

- Cash Surrender Value
- Reduced Paid-Up Insurance
- Extended-Term Insurance

Cash Surrender Value

This option gives the owner immediate access to a certain amount of cash specified in the policy in exchange for terminating the policy. This option should be exercised with care because the same amount of cash may be obtained through one of the other options that provide for a continuing amount of coverage. The need for life insurance declines as people retire, become older, or no longer have dependents. In any other situation in which the need for death protection has ceased or in which alternative death protection has been purchased, cash surrender is a viable option. Consumers who surrender policies may incur an income tax liability on part of the cash value accumulation to the extent that it exceeds premiums paid, so a complete policy surrender should be thoroughly evaluated from a tax perspective. Note that surrender value is usually less than cash value for the first 10 to 15 years of the policy.

Reduced Paid-Up Insurance

This option allows the policy owner to purchase a fully paid-up whole life insurance policy using the cash value of the policy. The face amount of the new policy will be dependent upon the amount of cash value accumulation, less surrender charges. Reduced paid-up insurance is essentially an option to purchase a single-premium whole life insurance policy. It is suitable for someone who wants to maintain some level of permanent death protection but does not want to pay any future premiums.

Extended-Term Insurance

Extended-term insurance uses cash surrender value as a single premium to purchase a paid-up term insurance policy equal to the original face amount for a limited period of time, usually a certain number of years and days. The length of the term protection is dependent upon the insured's age at the time he or she chooses to exercise the option. The length of coverage will also be determined by the company's current premium rates. This option is most suitable for someone who wants to preserve, for only a limited time, death protection equal to the forfeited policy's face value.

Variable Life Insurance

The structure of a **variable life insurance** policy is much like a universal life insurance policy with one major exception – variable insurance policies permit the owner of the life insurance policy to direct the investment of the policy's cash value. In the case of whole life or regular universal life insurance policies, the insurance company invests the cash value and credits a rate of interest to the accumulation. Variable policies typically offer a series of investment options that include investment funds managed by the insurer and outside investment managers. The cash value of a variable life insurance policy is held in a separate account and the policy owner bears all of the investment risk associated with his or her investment choices. If the cash value is invested in funds that increase in value at a rate greater than the crediting rate that the insurance company offers on whole life insurance, the policy owner can benefit from either a decrease in insurance costs (if an Option A level death benefit with a decreasing amount at risk is chosen), or increased death benefits (if an Option B increasing death benefit is chosen), or, in some cases, both.

If the policy owner experiences losses from the investments he or she chooses, this can result in either:

1. increased premium costs for the owner, or
2. a lapse of the policy.

Variable Universal Life Insurance Policies (VULs) are often used by young individuals who have the risk tolerance and time frame necessary to weather equity market downturns. Since VULs have a flexible premium payment option like universal life insurance policies, the policy owner can make large premium payments in early years to fund the cash value accumulation pot, and, if the investments do well over a period of time, have sufficient resources in the cash-value pot to continue to pay the term insurance premium without further premium payments. From a planning perspective, early funding of VULs usually produces the best results, but owners should be aware of the Modified Endowment Contract (MEC) rules. If the policy is funded faster than seven equal payments, lifetime loan benefits that the owner receives from the policy are subject to income tax.

The ability to control the investments in a VUL policy causes the policy to be considered a registered investment security. Life insurance agents and financial planners who sell VULs must be licensed to sell both life insurance and securities.

Feature Comparison of Common Life Insurance Policies

EXHIBIT 4.9

	Term Life	Whole (Ordinary) Life	Universal Life	Variable Life	Variable Universal Life
Premium $	Fixed or Variable	Fixed	Variable, subject to a required minimum	Fixed	Variable, subject to a required minimum
Death Benefit	Fixed	Fixed	May increase above initial face amount, depending on cash value accumulation	Has a guaranteed minimum, but can increase if investment experience on cash value is good	Has a guaranteed minimum, but can increase if investment experience on cash value is good
Policy Owner's Control Over Investments	None	None	None	Complete	Complete
Rate of Return on Investment	None	Fixed rate	May have a minimum guaranteed rate, but can be higher depending on interest rates	No minimum guarantee, but positive investment experience can yield very high returns	No minimum guarantee, but positive investment experience can yield very high returns
Application	Large need, limited resources	Want guarantees	Flexibility without investment responsibility	Flexibility with investment responsibility, fixed premiums	Flexibility with investment responsibility, variable premiums

EXHIBIT 4.10

COMPARISON OF LIFE INSURANCE POLICY COSTS

Subject: 36-year-old female, preferred health, non-smoker
Face Amount: $1,000,000 (death benefit)
Premium paid to age 65 or 66

Policy Type	Universal Life (UL)	Whole Life (WL)	Variable Universal (VUL)	Term (30 Years)
Annual Premium	$4,703	$14,140	$8,403.28	$905*
(Pay to 65)	Yes	Yes	Yes	Yes (66)
Surrender Value	Guaranteed 2%	Guaranteed	Guaranteed	N/A
at 15 years	$70,545	Guaranteed	Guaranteed	0
at 20 years	$94,060	Guaranteed	Guaranteed	0
at 25 years	$117,575	Guaranteed	Guaranteed	0
at 30 years	$136,387	(65) / $480,000	(65)/$210,213	Lapsed
Surrender Value	Non Guaranteed (Projected)	CV not guaranteed	CV not guaranteed	N/A
at 15 years	$70,545	CV not guaranteed	CV not guaranteed	
at 20 years	$94,060	CV not guaranteed	CV not guaranteed	
at 25 years	$117,575	CV not guaranteed	CV not guaranteed	
at 30 years	$136,387	65 / $493,980	65 / $65,377,781	Lapsed
Guaranteed (i)	i = 0.2350	i = 1.2969	i = 2.9626	
Non Guaranteed Return (i) Policy (premium less term premium)	i = 1.2066	i = 1.7429	i = 3.6869	N/A

*** The $905 was the median premium among 15 carriers ($835 - $1,035)**
CV = Cash Value

MODIFIED ENDOWMENT CONTRACTS (MECs)

A modified endowment contract (MEC) is not really another type of life insurance policy, but rather a cash value life insurance policy that has been funded too quickly.

In the 1980s, life insurance was a popular tool for taxpayers who wished to defer income from income tax. Income tax rates in the early 1980s were as high as 50 percent, and it made sense for taxpayers in high brackets to purchase universal, whole life, or variable universal life insurance policies as investments with which to defer the tax on the growth of the policy's cash value until they retired or cashed in the policy. Insureds would then expect to pay income tax on the growth of the cash value at a lower income tax rate. Since life insurance policy cash values grow on a tax-deferred basis (if the policy is cashed-in during the insured's lifetime) or a tax-free basis (if a death benefit is paid when the insured dies), life policies became popular tools to defer investment income. In theory, life insurance is a product designed to hedge against mortality risk faced by the insured, but for high income taxpayers in the 1980s, life insurance became a tool to lower tax rates on investment income. Needless to say, Congress was not amused with this use of life insurance.

In the Tax Reform Act of 1986, Congress enacted the modified endowment contract (MEC) rules.[1] These rules state that if a single-premium life insurance contract is purchased, or if a regular life insurance policy is purchased and is funded too quickly, lifetime benefits received under the policy (in particular, the ability to obtain a loan against the policy's cash value without income tax consequences) would trigger income tax liability.

Congress imposed two tests to determine whether a life insurance contract meets the definition of a MEC:

1. Corridor test
2. 7-pay test

The **corridor test** calls for the policy to be tested using actuarial principles and specifies that the premiums can represent no more than a limited portion of the death benefit. The calculation of the corridor test is beyond the scope of this text.

The **7-pay test** states that if the cumulative premium payments made on the policy are in excess of the net level premium for the policy during the first seven years (or following a material change to the policy), the life insurance contract will be deemed a MEC.

When the insured dies and a MEC pays a death benefit, the death benefit is exempt from income tax. If the insured wishes to access policy values during his or her lifetime, however, distributions in the form of loans or withdrawals are taxed on a last-in first-out (LIFO), or interest-first, basis. The LIFO treatment of a MEC means that, to the extent that the value of the policy exceeds the owner's basis in the policy and the owner takes some form of pre-death benefit, such distributions are subject to income tax. If the owner is under the age of 59½, the distribution may also be subject to a 10 percent IRS penalty tax.

EXAMPLE 4.15

Steady Eddy purchases a whole life policy at age 30 and pays premiums annually. When he turns 50, he borrows some of the cash value from the policy to build a swimming pool. The funds he borrowed do not exceed his taxable basis in the policy and are therefore, not taxable.

EXAMPLE 4.16

Sneaky Pete purchases a single-premium whole life policy ten years ago. Pete decides he needs a pool after seeing his buddy Eddy build one. He also decides to borrow the funds from his whole life policy. However, Pete's policy is an MEC because it is a single-premium policy. As a result, it fails the 7-payment premium test. Because the policy is an MEC, the loans are fully taxable to Pete, to the extent of any gain in the policy.

Group-Term Insurance

As part of their employee benefit packages, many employers offer group term insurance to their employees. **Group-term insurance** covers all eligible employees under a master contract that is obtained by the employer. Employers may offer the group-term insurance as a flat amount (for example, $50,000 or $100,000 of death benefit protection for all employees) or as a percentage of income (one, two, or three times the employee's annual income).

1. IRC Section 7702A.

When offering group term life insurance to its employees, an employer is able to deduct the premium costs that it pays as an ordinary and necessary business expense. An income tax doctrine called the economic benefit doctrine states that when a person receives property in return for services, the value of the property received must be included in his or her income for income tax purposes. The first $50,000 of death benefit protection received by the employees, however, has been excluded from tax by Congress, which means that the employee is not taxed on the value of up to $50,000 of group-term insurance paid for by the employer.[1]

To the extent that the employer pays the entire premium on the group policy and the death benefit protection for an employee exceeds $50,000, the value of the death benefit protection must be included in the employee's income and is subject to income tax. The amount subject to tax equals the amount of death benefit protection in excess of $50,000 multiplied by the applicable premium rate found in Table 1: Uniform Premiums for $1,000 of Group-Term Life Insurance Protection (Table 1).[2] If the employee contributes to the cost of the group term insurance through payroll deduction, that portion of the insurance received is not subject to tax under the economic benefit doctrine.

EXHIBIT 4.11

TABLE 1: UNIFORM PREMIUMS FOR $1,000 GROUP-TERM LIFE INSURANCE

5-Year Age Bracket	Cost per $1,000 of Protection for One Month
Under 25	$0.05
25 to 29	$0.06
30 to 34	$0.08
35 to 39	$0.09
40 to 44	$0.10
45 to 49	$0.15
50 to 54	$0.23
55 to 59	$0.43
60 to 64	$0.66
65 to 69	$1.27
70 and above	$2.06

PROTECTION

Group-term insurance is a very cost effective way of obtaining life insurance protection, even when the employee has to include in his or her income the imputed premium on insurance provided in excess of the $50,000 group term limit. In this case, the employee receives the life insurance protection at a fraction of the cost for which he or she could have purchased the insurance in the private market. In essence, the employee only pays tax on the imputed premium; the employee does not pay the premium itself. Depending on the employee's marginal income tax rate, this results in a significant reduction in the cost of insurance protection.

1. IRC Section 79.
2. This table is found in Treas. Reg. Section 1.79-3(d)(2).

EXAMPLE 4.17

Al, who is 50 years old, works for Pennant Enterprises, Inc. As part of Pennant's employee benefit program, Al receives $150,000 of group-term insurance paid for by the company. Based on the Table 1 Rates and Al's attained age, the imputed premium on the $100,000 of insurance in excess of the tax-free group term limit of $50,000 is 276 ($0.23 x 12 months x 100). At the end of the year, Pennant Enterprises will include an additional $276 in Al's W-2, which will be reported on his annual tax return. Since Al's marginal income tax rate is 25%, the tax he will incur on the inclusion of the imputed premium is $69. For an out of pocket annual cost of $69, Al receives $150,000 of term life insurance protection.

If an employee terminates from service, he or she typically has the option of converting the group term policy into a permanent, cash-value policy at a rate specified in the group contract (and based on the employee's age at the time). This conversion feature may be valuable for individuals who are not insurable since evidence of insurability is not required, and the conversion will preserve the employee's ability to purchase death benefit protection. If a terminating employee is insurable, it may be wise to first consider the cost of commercially available life insurance since the insurance companies underwriting the group plan often assume that those wishing to convert their group-term insurance to permanent insurance upon termination of employment are uninsurable and may therefore charge a higher premium.

Although group term insurance can be very cost effective, the amount of coverage provided rarely covers an employee's needs. Individually owned insurance should be used to make-up the difference between the amount of coverage needed and the amount provided by the group policy.

Other Types of Group Life Insurance

Employers can also provide group whole life insurance, group universal-life insurance, and group variable-universal life insurance to their employees. Often making these types of insurance contracts available on a group basis results in cost savings for the insurer that are passed on to the employees participating in the plan in the form of lower premiums. Sometimes employers pay the premiums on these policies as an employee benefit, while others make the plans available and permit the employees to pay the premiums with after-tax dollars at the lower group rates.

Planners should be aware, however, that the income tax exclusion for the first $50,000 of death benefit protection only applies to group-term insurance plans. Employer-provided group whole life, group universal-life, or group variable-universal life insurance benefits will subject the employee to tax on the economic benefit the employee receives, which is measured by the imputed term cost of the insurance protection received.

COMMON LIFE INSURANCE CONTRACT POLICY PROVISIONS

GRACE PERIOD

Life insurance policy premiums are typically structured to be payable on a monthly, quarterly, or annual basis. To keep the life insurance policy in force, the premium must be paid on time. This requirement is particularly true for term insurance policies, which do not have cash value to keep the policy in force (permanent policies are often structured to borrow from the cash value to pay the premium on the due date unless the insured has already paid the premium). Most life insurance policies provide a **grace period**, typically spanning one month (31 days), after the premium due date for the policy owner to pay an overdue premium. Generally, the insured would not have to provide further evidence of insurability if the premium is paid within the grace period, but once the policy lapses and the grace period expires, the insured may be required to undergo additional underwriting for the policy to be reinstated.

> **KEY CONCEPTS**
>
> 1. Highlight the typical clauses found in life insurance contracts.
> 2. Describe the difference between a survivorship clause and a simultaneous death clause.
> 3. Describe the settlement options: lump-sum, interest only, and the various annuity options.

During the grace period the policy remains in force. If the insured dies during the grace period, the insurance company will pay the death benefit to the named insured and deduct from that death benefit the premium that is due. Some policies may also charge interest on the overdue premium since the insurance company loses the ability to invest the premium proceeds on the due date.

INCONTESTABILITY

In the early days of life insurance, some companies would issue policies to insureds and collect premiums over several years, yet contest the validity of the contract when the death benefit was due based on an alleged misrepresentation, omission of information, or concealment of information by the insured that would have been relevant in making a proper underwriting decision when issuing the policy. The incontestability clause found in life insurance policies today combats this abuse and states that once the policy has been in force for a period of time (typically two years), the insurer may not cancel the policy if it later discovers a material misrepresentation, omission, or concealment. However, the insurer may modify the benefits under the contract.

MISSTATEMENT OF AGE OR GENDER

The cost of life insurance protection is based on the age and gender of the insured. As individuals get older, the likelihood that they will die within the year (as expressed in mortality tables) increases, thereby increasing the risk for the insurer. Furthermore, females tend to live longer and therefore have lower mortality risk when compared to males at the same age. To compensate for this increased risk, the insurance company charges a higher premium for the life insurance protection. If the insured misstates his or her age or gender on a life insurance application, the insurance company can, at any time (even after the death of the insured), adjust the face amount of the policy to the amount that the specified premium would have purchased at the correct age or using the correct gender of the insured. Since the date of the insured's birth will be listed on the insured's death certificate and in the Social Security death index, when processing death claims insurance companies routinely check to make sure that the insured's age, as disclosed in the policy, was correct prior to paying the claim.

EXAMPLE 4.18

> Gloria is trim, fit, and gorgeous at age 48. People think she is close to 30-years old, and she has been lying about her age for years. Gloria purchases a 30-year term policy with a death benefit of $3,000,000 paying the level premium for a 30-year-old, which is $0.60 per $1,000 of coverage. Her total annual premium is $1,800. Unfortunately, three years later she is killed in an automobile accident. The executor of her estate sends the certified death certificate to the insurer who then discovers how old she really was at the inception of the policy. The level premium for a 48-year-old female at the time of issuance was $2.00 per $1,000 of coverage. The insurer will pay the beneficiary $900,000 ($1,800 ÷ $2 x $1,000).

Adverse selection is the risk that an insured facing an almost certain risk of loss will seek to transfer that risk to an insurance company. Adverse selection risk is experienced in all kinds of insurance policies, including life insurance. Individuals more likely to seek to convert their group-term life insurance contracts to permanent insurance when they separate from service are those who need life insurance, are sick, or expect to have a shorter-than-average life expectancy.

SUICIDE

The **suicide clause** in a life insurance policy is designed to hedge against the risk that individuals with suicidal thoughts will purchase life insurance and, shortly thereafter, commit suicide. Since a person who commits suicide has an actual mortality risk of one (or 100%), the normal pricing of a life insurance policy that takes into consideration the actuarial life expectancy of the individual will not result in a premium sufficient to hedge the risk of death for the insurance company. The suicide clause states that, if an insured commits suicide within a specified time (in most states, this time period is two years), the insurance policy will not pay the death benefit to the beneficiary, but will refund the premiums paid (plus possibly interest) on the policy to the named beneficiary. Since it is unlikely that a person would plan to purchase life insurance several years before planning to commit suicide, a two-year exclusion is usually considered sufficient to balance the adverse selection risk of the insurer against the potential loss of the life insurance death benefit for the beneficiaries in the event a suicide does occur.

It should be noted that if a person dies within the two year period, the life insurance company will often scrutinize the claim. The beneficiaries may have to fight to have the proceeds paid.

EXAMPLE 4.19

> Heath Ledger, who is famous for playing the Joker in the movie The Dark Knight, died in early 2008. His death came seven months after he took out a $10 million life insurance policy with his daughter as the beneficiary. The New York Medical Examiner's office ruled that the death was an "accident, resulting from the abuse of prescribed medications." The insurer, ReliaStar Life Insurance Co., investigated the death instead of paying the claim. After a lawsuit was filed, the insurer settled with Ledger's daughter for a sum less than the $10 million.

Reinstatement

If a life insurance policy lapses due to non-payment of premium and expiration of the grace period, the policy may permit reinstatement if the requirements specified in the policy are satisfied. Typically, the policy will specify that reinstatement without evidence of insurability is available for a short time after the expiration of the grace period (usually 31 days). Provided that past premiums plus interest on those premiums are paid to the insurer, and satisfactory evidence of insurability is provided, the insurer may reinstate a life insurance policy up to five years after the policy lapse.

Policy Loan Provisions

One of the benefits of using a permanent life insurance policy is the cash value accumulation that is attached to the insurance. The purpose of the cash value is to accumulate funds to permit the policy owner to spread the cost of the risk of protection over a long period of time, preferably until the death of the insured. The cash value can also be accessed by the policyholder in the form of a policy loan. When a policy loan is issued, there are no income tax consequences for the policy owner provided that the life insurance policy was not classified as a modified endowment contract (MEC), and the interest rate charged on the loan is typically a low rate that is specified in the contract. Policy loans are generally limited to a percentage of the cash value (for example, 90 percent). Any loan outstanding at the death of the insured, plus accrued interest on the loan, is deducted from the death benefit paid to the policy beneficiary.

EXAMPLE 4.20

Tiffany buys a whole life policy and pays premiums for her entire life. The death benefit of the policy is $100,000. During her life, she borrowed a total of $14,000 from the policy. When she dies, her beneficiary receives $86,000, the death benefit less the outstanding loan balance.

In financial planning, the cash value of life insurance policies can be considered part of an emergency fund since the loan provides easy access to cash at a reasonable rate of interest and can be repaid at any time. Sometimes a policy will offer an option that permits the policy owner to use a life insurance policy's cash values to pay the ongoing policy premium. This option may be particularly useful when cash values have accumulated substantially and the policy owner no longer wishes to pay the premium.

Beneficiary Designations

At the insured's death, the policy death benefit is paid to the beneficiaries named by the contract owner, or if no beneficiary has been named, to the estate of the insured individual.

Most beneficiary designations on life insurance policies are revocable, which means that the policy owner can change the beneficiary at any time. In some cases, an irrevocable beneficiary will be named on a policy. For example, a former spouse may be required to maintain life insurance for the benefit of an ex-spouse and/or children, in which case the beneficiary designation is typically irrevocable. In order to change the beneficiary on a policy that has an irrevocable beneficiary designation, the original beneficiary must consent to the change.

The individual or organization that will receive the death benefit upon the death of the insured is referred to as the **primary beneficiary**. More than one primary beneficiary may be named on a life insurance policy, which allows the primary beneficiaries to share the death benefit in the manner specified by either the policy owner or the policy itself.

Contingent beneficiaries will receive the death benefit if the primary beneficiary is not available to receive the policy proceeds. If individuals are named as the primary beneficiaries on a life insurance policy, it is important to consider the possibility that the primary beneficiary may die before the insured, causing the death benefit to be transferred to someone else. If no contingent beneficiary is named, the death benefit is generally paid to the policy owner or to the policy owner's estate (if the policy owner was also the insured). Naming a contingent beneficiary is not as important when the policy death benefit will be paid to either a trust or a corporation, since these entities do not have a natural life and are likely to be in existence when the insured dies.

The naming of beneficiaries on life insurance policies is important and it requires careful consideration to avoid delays in the distribution of benefits. Besides individual or organizational beneficiary designations, group designations can also be used, such as "the children of X." Minors or legally incompetent individuals should not be named as beneficiaries. The use of a trust is a prudent alternative in such situations.

Survivorship Clauses

A **survivorship clause** specifies that the death benefit will only be paid to the beneficiary if the beneficiary survives the insured by a specific number of days (usually 30-60 days). If the beneficiary does not survive by the specified number of days, the death benefit is paid to the contingent beneficiary. If there is no contingent beneficiary, the death benefit is paid to the policy owner or the policy owner's estate. A survivorship clause protects the testamentary intent of the policy owner by ensuring that the appropriate party receives the policy proceeds, and can minimize estate and probate complexities that might be encountered if the policy proceeds are subject to administration in two estates in quick succession.

Simultaneous Death Provisions

A **simultaneous death provision** is similar to a survivorship clause, and is effective whenever the insured and the beneficiary die within a short time of one another and it is impossible to determine who died first. Under the Uniform Simultaneous Death Act, if the insured and the beneficiary die in a common accident and the order of deaths is uncertain, the policy death benefit is distributed as if the beneficiary had predeceased the insured. When the policy owner has named a contingent beneficiary, that beneficiary will receive the death proceeds. If no contingent beneficiary is named, the policy proceeds will be distributed to the policy owner or the policy owner's estate.

Assignment

Assignment is the process of transferring all or part of the policy's ownership rights. A policyholder might wish to assign his or her interest in a life insurance contract to a bank as collateral for a loan, with or without the insurance company's consent. Two main types of assignments exist in today's insurance industry: absolute and collateral. An absolute assignment gives the entity that has received the assignment all policy ownership rights subject to any limitations set forth in the assignment. A collateral assignment is used to serve as security for debt and gives the lender or "assignee" limited ownership rights under the policy. The assignment automatically terminates when the debt is paid, and policy ownership rights are usually exercisable only if the borrower defaults on the loan.

Aviation Exclusion

Though no longer a common exclusion in policies issued today, the aviation exclusion denies coverage for those who die in noncommercial flights, such as private pilots, their passengers, and military pilots. Premiums are usually returned to the beneficiary, but the death benefit is not paid.

War Exclusion

This exclusion allows the insurer to deny the death claim if the insured dies while in the military or as the result of a military action. Premiums are usually returned to the beneficiary with interest and the death benefit is not paid.

SETTLEMENT OPTIONS FOR LIFE INSURANCE

When an insured individual dies and the insurance company is notified of the death, the life insurance benefit becomes payable. The beneficiary can receive the proceeds in a lump-sum payment, but most insurance policies provide several alternative options for the beneficiary to receive the death benefit.

Lump-Sum Payment

Receiving a lump-sum benefit is perhaps the simplest way to complete the life insurance transaction. Sometimes the insurance company will pay the lump sum directly in the form of a check to the beneficiary. More recently, some life insurance companies have been creating an account for the beneficiary at the life insurance company in which the policy proceeds are deposited. The beneficiary receives a check book and can draw any or all of the death benefit out of the account by simply writing a check. Amounts left in the account will earn interest until withdrawn. This approach may be valuable for beneficiaries who would like to receive a lump-sum distribution but who have not yet decided how to invest or otherwise deploy the life insurance death benefit.

Interest Only

The interest-only option allows the beneficiary to keep the death benefit on deposit with the insurance company and receive periodic payments of interest on the policy proceeds. If the owner/insured is concerned about the ability of the beneficiary to manage the insurance proceeds, the interest-only option should be considered. In some cases, the beneficiary is given the opportunity to access some of the principal amount (the death benefit) in addition to receiving payments of income. The primary beneficiary is permitted to name a contingent beneficiary to receive any amounts remaining when the primary beneficiary dies.

Key Concepts

1. Understand the various settlement options available with life insurance policies.
2. Consider the various options available with an annuity settlement option and the impact on the size of the annuity stream.

Annuity Payments from Life Insurance

Life insurance companies provide a variety of **annuity** options for beneficiaries. Annuities are periodic payments to an individual that continue for a fixed period or for the duration of a designated life or lives (joint and survivor annuity). Several of these annuity options are discussed below.

Fixed Amount

When the fixed amount annuity method of distributing the death benefit is chosen, the policy death benefit will be deposited with the insurance company, and the beneficiary will receive fixed payments until the proceeds are depleted. The balance on deposit with the insurance company will be credited with interest each year. As the beneficiary receives payments, the portion of each payment that represents interest earnings will be taxable to the beneficiary. The remaining portion of the payment, which represents part of the death benefit, will not be subject to income tax.

The beneficiary should choose a contingent beneficiary in case the primary beneficiary dies prior to receiving all of the payments from the insurance company. If no contingent beneficiary is named, the remaining amount in the account is typically paid to the estate of the deceased beneficiary.

Life Income

The life income option converts the death benefit into an annuity contract for the life of the beneficiary. When the life income approach is chosen, the amount of the annuity payment will depend on the size of the death benefit paid, and the age and sex of the beneficiary. Each year as payments are received, the beneficiary will pay income tax on a portion of each payment representing the growth in the annuity contract, and the remaining portion will be exempt from income tax. This result relies on the calculation of the exclusion ratio for the policy.[1] The portion of the payments representing the return of the death benefit paid under the life insurance policy will be received by the beneficiary income-tax free. Since the payments will stop when the beneficiary dies, there is no need to name a contingent beneficiary if a life income option is chosen.

Fixed Period

Instead of receiving an annuity payment over the lifetime of the beneficiary, the death benefit proceeds may be used to purchase an annuity certain, which is an annuity that will make payments for a specified number of periods (usually years). When the fixed-period option is chosen, the beneficiary's age and health are not considered in the pricing of the annuity. The only factors that matter are:

- The size of the death benefit
- The crediting rate of interest on the annuity contract

If the beneficiary dies prior to receiving all of the fixed payments, a contingent beneficiary can be named to receive the present value of the remaining payments. If a contingent beneficiary is not named, the payments are made to the primary beneficiary's estate.

1. The exclusion ratio equals the investment in the contract divided by the expected return, which is the total amount of dollar distributions expected under the contract.

A fixed-period annuity with a term less than the life expectancy of the beneficiary will generally result in a higher payment than a life income annuity. In financial planning engagements, using a fixed-period annuity payout may be preferential to the life income method when the beneficiary:

- Needs additional cash flow for a fixed period of time, such as until retirement age (when distributions from retirement accounts will begin).
- Suspects that he or she will have a shorter-than-average life expectancy and would like to preserve some of the death benefit value for a successor beneficiary if the primary beneficiary dies before the term expires.

Life Income with Period Certain

The life income with period certain payout method combines the benefits of the life income method with the benefits of the fixed-period method. This approach transforms the death benefit into a life annuity contract based on the age and health of the beneficiary, yet promises to make a specified number of payments under the contract. If the beneficiary dies early, a contingent beneficiary will receive the remaining payments promised under the contract, or the commuted value in a lump sum.

All else being equal, a life income with period certain payout will provide a lower periodic payment than a straight life payout would, because the insurance company is promising to make payments for a minimum period of time. A guaranteed period payment is appropriate <u>when</u> the beneficiary would like to have the security of annuity payments but suspects that he or she might have shorter-than-average life expectancy.

Quick Quiz 4.1

1. An owner of a life insurance policy is always free to change the beneficiary of the policy.
   a. True
   b. False

2. The suicide clause states that if the insured commits suicide at any time while a life insurance policy is in place, there will be no pay out.
   a. True
   b. False

3. If a client is concerned that his or her surviving spouse will not be able to effectively manage the benefit amount, an interest-only option should be considered.
   a. True
   b. False

4. That portion of the annuity that is attributable to the earnings is subject to taxation to the beneficiary.
   a. True
   b. False

False, False, True, True.

EXAMPLE 4.21

Bryan was named as the beneficiary of his Aunt Josephine's life insurance policy. In his earlier years, Bryan was a free spirit and engaged in several activities that could have shortened his lifespan. Since Bryan has not had a good track record with managing money, he would like to choose a payout method that will give him income for life, but would like to make sure that his son, Garrett, gets something if he dies too soon. Bryan elects to take a life income with a 15-year period certain. If Bryan lives beyond 15 years, he will continue to receive payments for the rest of his life, and the payments will stop at Bryan's death. If Bryan dies 10 years after the payments begin, however, the insurance company will continue to make payments for an additional 5 years to Garrett, whom Bryan named as contingent beneficiary of the proceeds.

Joint and Last Survivor Income

With a Joint and Last Survivor Income settlement option, annuity payments are made over the joint lives of two individuals. When one of the joint annuitants dies, the survivor will receive a reduced payment for the rest of his or her life. Sometimes, a period certain is also incorporated into this option. If the beneficiary of a life insurance policy would like to ensure that another person, such as a spouse, will continue to receive benefits from the policy after the primary beneficiary's death, this type of settlement option should be considered.

TAXATION OF LIFE INSURANCE BENEFITS

Life insurance is generally thought to be tax free. However, the taxation of life insurance is not that simple. There are a variety of tax issues associated with life insurance. Among these are:

- Premium payments
- Death benefits
- Lifetime benefits
- Policy exchanges
- Transfer for value
- Viatical settlements
- Accelerated benefits

KEY CONCEPTS

1. Highlight some of the income tax benefits to be derived from life insurance planning, both to the policy beneficiary(ies) and the owner.
2. Describe FIFO and LIFO treatment.
3. Describe the possible tax consequences for policy exchanges.
4. Describe a viatical settlement.

PREMIUM PAYMENTS

Premium payments on life insurance policies are not tax deductible, with a few rare exceptions. For example, group term insurance premiums on insurance protection of up to $50,000 are deductible by the employer and not included in the income of the employee. Furthermore, certain types of employee benefit plans, such as VEBAs and 415 plans, can be created by an employer and funded with life insurance policies allowing the employer to deduct the premium. Life insurance purchased within a qualified pension plan effectively achieves a tax deduction since the money used to fund the pension plan was tax deductible (many restrictions apply to this, however, and they are covered in detail in a retirement planning course). Finally, life insurance purchased pursuant to a divorce decree may be deductible by the ex-spouse paying the premiums (as alimony), provided that the other ex-spouse is the owner of the policy.

Since the premiums cannot be deducted for income tax purposes, the owner of the policy will have a basis in the policy (representing after-tax investments in the vehicle) equal to the cumulative premiums paid for the policy. The owner's basis may be reduced when the insurance company issues dividends or when the owner makes a withdrawal from the cash value of the policy, both of which are discussed below.

DEATH BENEFIT TAXATION

IRC Section 101(a) states that the death benefit received by a beneficiary of a life insurance policy due to the death of the insured is exempt from federal income tax. The income tax-free character of the death benefit is an important planning consideration. While Congress could subject life insurance death benefits to income tax, it chooses not to as a means of encouraging individuals to purchase life insurance (so that beneficiaries will not have to rely on public assistance).

If an individual owns a life insurance policy on his or her own life, or if the proceeds of the policy are made available to the executor of his or her estate, the death benefit will be included in the owner/insured's gross estate and may be subject to estate tax. Many individuals confuse the income tax and estate tax rules concerning life insurance – they believe that the death benefit is "tax free." If the insured does not own the policy covering his or her life, and the proceeds of that policy are not made payable to the executor of his or her estate, this understanding is correct. Many individuals, however, own the life insurance policies that cover their own lives. When this situation occurs, the death benefit is free from income taxation but is subject to estate taxation if the decedent has a taxable estate.

Taxation of Lifetime Benefits

One of the benefits of owning a permanent life insurance policy during one's lifetime (even on one's own life) is that the owner can obtain several tax-free benefits from the policy prior to the payment of the death benefit.

As discussed earlier, dividends may be issued on life insurance policies when the pool of insured individuals experience better than anticipated life expectancies, the company's expenses are lower than expected, or the company's investment returns are higher than expected. Dividends are treated as a return of premium (a rebate of previously taxed income) and are therefore not subject to income tax. A dividend distribution does, however, reduce the owner's basis in his or her life insurance policy. If dividend distributions exceed the owner's basis, the owner would be subject to tax on those excess dividends, since he or she has already recouped the capital investment in the life insurance policy.

Owners may also withdraw cash value from permanent life insurance policies without being subject to income tax. Withdrawals are treated first as a distribution of basis (which are not subject to income tax) using the first-in, first-out, or FIFO, method of accounting. The exception to this FIFO treatment for loans is an MEC, which follows last-in, first-out (LIFO) rules. For MECs, earnings come out first and are taxable. Once the owner of a non-MEC policy withdraws all of his or her basis, any further withdrawals are subject to income tax because they represent policy earnings, which are not paid out as a result of the death of the insured.

When the owner of a policy has reduced his or her basis in the policy down to zero (through receipt of dividend distributions or withdrawals) and would like to access additional policy values without triggering a taxable event, the owner can borrow from the cash value of the policy (unless it is a MEC). The loan generally carries a favorable rate of interest specified in the life insurance contract and does not have to be paid back, provided that the life insurance policy remains in force during the life of the insured. When the insured dies, the loan plus accumulated interest will be subtracted from the death benefit received by the beneficiary. Provided that the policy remains in force until the death of the insured, the owner of the policy can access cash values on an income tax-free basis (unless it is a MEC).

EXAMPLE 4.22

Tara bought a whole life policy and paid premiums her entire life. The death benefit of the policy is $150,000. During her life, she borrowed from the policy for various reasons. At her death, the outstanding loan, including accumulated interest, equals $32,000. Her beneficiary receives $118,000, the death benefit less the outstanding loan balance.

When a permanent life insurance policy is terminated during the life of the insured (i.e., the policy is surrendered), a taxable event may result. The difference between the amount received by the owner on the surrender of the policy and the basis of the policy in the hands of the owner will be subject to income tax. If the owner of a policy receives less than his or her basis, the payment is considered a return of capital and is not subject to tax or treated as a deductible loss.

EXAMPLE 4.23

Mr. Black purchased a whole life insurance policy, which permitted him to borrow against the policy in an amount not in excess of its cash value. In that regard the policy provided that policy debt consisted of all outstanding loans and accrued interest and that unpaid interest would be added to loan principal. The policy also provided that Mr. Black could surrender the policy and receive as a distribution the cash value of the policy minus any outstanding policy debt. Finally, the policy provided that it would terminate if the policy debt were equal to (or exceed) the cash value.

Over time Mr. Black borrowed $103,548 against the policy. In addition, interest due on each loan accrued at a specified annual percentage rate pursuant to the terms of the policy. Mr. Black did not repay the loans.

Ultimately, the policy was terminated. Upon termination, the outstanding loans were satisfied by policy proceeds and extinguished. At that time the combined balance of the loans, including principal and interest, was $196,230, and Mr. Black's investment in the contract (in the form of aggregate premiums paid) was $86,663.

The insurance company issued to Mr. Black a Form 1099-R (Distributions From Pensions, Annuities, Retirement or Profit-Sharing Plans, IRAs, Insurance Contracts, Etc.) reflecting a gross distribution of $196,230 and a taxable amount of $109,567 ($196,230 - $86,663 = $109,567). The latter amount represented the difference between the combined balance of the loans at the time that the policy was terminated, i.e., $196,230, and Mr. Black's investment in the contract, i.e., $86,663.[1]

When a policy is surrendered, the owner may receive the proceeds in a lump sum, may leave the proceeds with the insurer and receive interest payments on the proceeds, or may choose an installment payment method specified in the life insurance contract. When the installment payment method is chosen, it is possible to spread the taxable gain on surrender of the policy over several tax years using the exclusion ratio approach to calculate the taxable portion of each payment. The installment method may be valuable to a high-bracket income taxpayer who realized a large gain upon surrender of a life insurance policy.

1. See Black v. Commissioner of Internal Revenue, T.C. Memo 2014-27, which is the basis for this example.

SECTION 1035 POLICY EXCHANGES

Many people wish to change life insurance policies or transform them into other types of insurance products as their needs change. Fortunately, the Code specifies that when certain exchanges take place, there is a deferral of gain from one product to the next. Under IRC Section 1035, deferral applies to certain exchanges made between life insurance policies, modified endowment contracts (MECs), and annuity contracts.

As our discussion above highlights, life insurance policies are uniquely tax-favored products due to the income tax exclusion of the death benefit and the ability to access lifetime benefits on a tax-free basis. Modified endowment contracts (MECs) also provide income tax-free death benefits, but if the owner of a MEC attempts to receive lifetime benefits from the policy, those benefits may be subject to income tax (MECs use LIFO, not FIFO treatment, when considering the tax consequences of withdrawals and loans). Annuity contracts provide tax deferral, but ultimately, all gains in the contract will be subject to income tax. Purely from a tax perspective, therefore, life insurance contracts are the best of the three, MECs come in second, and annuities are the least attractive, since they always result in taxable income (except a Roth annuity).

Section 1035 of the Code states that if a policy is exchanged for another similar policy (for example, life insurance for life insurance, MEC for MEC, or annuity for annuity), or for an insurance product that increases the potential for assessment of income tax, the exchange of the policies is a tax-deferred exchange. No income tax will be due at the time of the exchange. If a tax-deferred exchange is desired, therefore, life insurance policies can be exchanged for other life insurance policies, MECs, or annuity contracts. MECs can be exchanged for other MECs or annuity contracts, and annuity contracts can be exchanged only for annuity contracts.

EXHIBIT 4.12

TAX TREATMENT OF EXCHANGE FOR LIFE INSURANCE AND ANNUITIES

	EXCHANGE FROM	
EXCHANGE TO	**Life Insurance**	**Annuity**
Life Insurance	Tax Free	Taxable
Annuity	Tax Free	Tax Free

In the case of a tax-free exchange, the basis of the original contract will carry over to the new contract and will increase if additional premium payments are made to the insurance company.

Nontaxable 1035 Exchanges

EXHIBIT 4.13

L – life insurance

E – modified endowment contract

A – annuity

The acronym LEA can be used to help remember the order for 1035 exchanges. Going from L to E to A is not taxable.

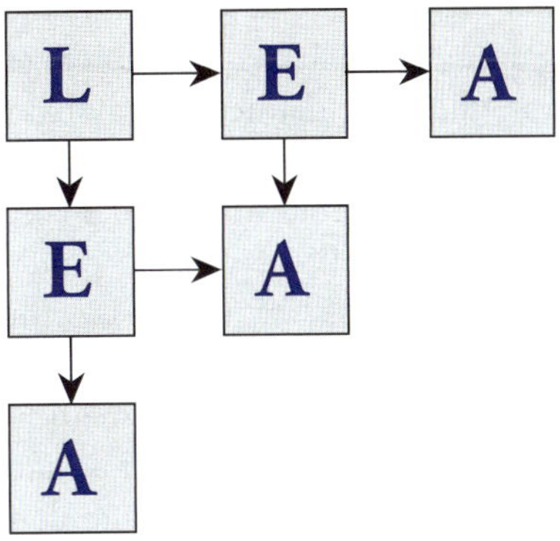

EXAMPLE 4.24

Abe purchased a permanent life insurance policy a number of years ago. His tax basis was $15,000 at the time. He recently executed a 1035 tax-free exchange for a new policy. He has paid $2,000 in premiums since the exchange, which makes his tax basis in the new policy $17,000.

Transfer for Value

If an existing life policy is transferred for valuable consideration (transfer for value), the insurance proceeds are includible in the gross income of the transferee to the extent the proceeds exceed the basis. Thus, the usual income tax exclusion for life insurance proceeds is lost. There are five instances in which the transfer of a policy will not result in inclusion of proceeds in the income of the transferee. They are:

1. A transfer to the insured
2. A transfer to a business partner of the insured
3. A transfer to a partnership of which the insured is a partner
4. A transfer to a corporation of which the insured is an officer or shareholder
5. A transfer that results in the transferee's basis being determined by reference to the transferor's basis, such as a gift

EXAMPLE 4.25

Nick transfers a policy to the NICE partnership of which Nick has a 25 percent interest. The transfer of such a policy will not cause inclusion to Nick.

Viatical Settlements

A **viatical settlement** is the sale of a life insurance policy to a third party. As previously discussed, the surrender of a life insurance policy (which could be thought of as a sale of the policy back to the insurer) results in a taxable event for the owner if the value of the life insurance policy exceeds the owner's basis at the time of surrender. Generally, the same rule applies to viatical settlements – the original owner of the policy will be subject to income tax to the extent that the sale proceeds exceed his or her basis in the policy.

As is the case with most income tax rules, there are exceptions to this treatment. If the owner-insured of a life insurance policy is terminally ill at the time the policy is sold, the gain in the policy is not subject to income tax. Terminal illness is defined as having a life expectancy of less than 24 months, which must be certified by a health care professional. In many cases, when an insured sells a life insurance policy shortly before death, the proceeds are used to pay for his or her medical care. To encourage use of private (as opposed to public) funds to cover these medical expenses, Congress exempts from income tax any gain on the policy realized by the insured. Note that the actual use of the proceeds does not change the result. As long as the insured was terminally ill when the policy was sold, there is no income tax on the gain.

If the owner-insured is chronically ill and the proceeds of the life insurance policy sale are used to pay for long-term care costs for the insured, any gain on the sale of the policy is exempt from income tax. Chronic illness requires that the insured has either a substantial cognitive impairment (suffers from advanced stages of Alzheimer's disease or senile dementia) or is unable to perform two of the six activities of daily living (eating, bathing, dressing, transferring, toileting, and continence) without assistance.

When the purchaser of a policy made by a viatical settlement receives the death benefit, the death benefit is subject to income tax to the extent that the policy death benefit received exceeds the purchaser's basis in the policy. Under the transfer-for-value rule, when a life insurance policy is sold for valuable consideration (as in the case of a viatical settlement), the death benefit is subject to income taxation.

Quick Quiz 4.4

1. If the insured dies while owning the life insurance policy, the value of the policy is not includible in his or her estate for estate tax purposes.
   a. True
   b. False

2. The FIFO method of accounting is preferable to the LIFO method because income tax is deferred until the distributed amount exceeds basis.
   a. True
   b. False

3. If a client exchanges a policy for a similar policy, there is no income tax due at the time of exchange; rather the basis is carried over to the new policy and it is not increased by additional premium payments.
   a. True
   b. False

4. If your terminally ill client sells his life insurance policy and uses the proceeds to pay for a vacation rather than medical expenses, those proceeds, to the extent they exceed the client's basis in the policy, will be subject to income tax.
   a. True
   b. False

False, True, False, False.

Accelerated Benefits Provision or Rider

An **accelerated benefits provision** or rider entitles a qualified insured to receive a pre-death benefit deemed nontaxable. This treatment is similar to a viatical settlement and follows the same rules, except that the only parties involved are the original insurer and the original insured; there are no third parties as in a viatical settlement.

LIFE INSURANCE & BUY-SELL AGREEMENTS

KEY CONCEPTS

1. Highlight the parties to an entity agreement versus a cross-purchase agreement.
2. Distinguish between an entity agreement, a cross-purchase agreement, and wait-and-see buy-sell agreement.
3. Explain why life insurance is a perfect hedge for buy-sell agreements that are triggered on the death of the owner.

In several examples throughout this chapter, we have indicated that life insurance can be used to fund buy-sell agreements for closely held and family-owned business owners. While a complete discussion of buy-sell agreements and their tax consequences is beyond the scope of this chapter, an overview of this common financial planning technique is warranted.

Buy-sell agreements are legal arrangements that require the sale of securities owned by one individual to another individual or entity upon a specified triggering event. Buy-sell agreements are commonly used by business owners to plan for the orderly transfer and control of a business interest, to create a market for stock that is not traded on securities exchanges, and to plan for liquidity in the estate of a deceased business owner.

The most common triggering event that invokes obligations under a buy-sell agreement is the death of the business owner. A properly structured buy-sell agreement requires the estate of the business owner to sell the decedent's business interest to another entity or person, who is often a family member or close business associate of the decedent. Since an obligation to purchase a business interest is triggered at the death of the owner, life insurance is an ideal funding vehicle for buy-sell agreements triggered at death. Typically, either the business itself, or the individual or entity who is obligated to purchase the decedent's business interest will hold a life insurance policy on the decedent's life that has a death benefit sufficient to cover the purchase price of the decedent's business interest.

Other triggering events for buy-sell agreements include disability, divorce, retirement, and withdrawal from the business, but a full discussion of these is beyond the scope of this chapter.

Buy-sell agreements generally are of one of three types:

- entity purchase (sometimes referred to as redemption agreements)
- cross-purchase agreements
- wait-and-see agreements

ENTITY (REDEMPTION) AGREEMENTS

The simplest form of buy-sell agreement is the **entity purchase**, or redemption, agreement. This type of buy-sell agreement obligates the business entity to purchase an owner's interest in the entity upon that owner's death. This type of buy-sell agreement works well for organizations that have a separate legal existence from their owners but would not be appropriate for a sole proprietorship. Sole proprietorships are wholly owned by one person, and when that person dies, so does the proprietorship. The business of a sole proprietor may be transferred to another person or entity at the death of the sole proprietorship through a cross-purchase agreement (discussed below), but the proprietorship cannot purchase itself.

EXAMPLE 4.26

> Cecil is part owner of a luxury resort hotel, Fawlty Towers. Fawlty Towers is organized as a C corporation, and the corporation is wholly owned by members of Cecil's family. To ensure that the ownership of the hotel stays within the family and to make sure that Cecil's estate has sufficient liquidity to cover its expenses at his death, Cecil enters into a buy-sell agreement with Fawlty Towers, Inc. whereby Cecil (through his estate) agrees to sell, and Fawlty Towers agrees to purchase his stock when he dies. The agreement between Cecil and Fawlty Towers is an entity purchase buy-sell agreement.

To fund the purchase obligation under an entity-purchase buy-sell agreement, the business can acquire a life insurance policy on the owner's life with a death benefit sufficient to cover the purchase amount. Life insurance is an ideal vehicle to use for this purpose, since it provides funds at the exact time they are needed (the death of the insured). Furthermore, using the death benefit to meet the purchase obligation under the buy-sell agreement does not affect cash holdings or other assets that the company may need for continued business operations.

What type of life insurance policy should be purchased to fund the buy-sell agreement? The answer, of course, depends on the facts. If the business is family owned, and the owner of the interest is a family member, or if there has been a long-term relationship between the owner and the business with no definitive date when that relationship will end (such as a retirement date), a permanent life insurance policy should be considered. Permanent life insurance costs more up front but provides protection for longer periods of time with guarantees from the insurance company. Using term life, universal life, or variable universal life may be risky, since those policies will only remain in force as long as there is money to pay premiums or in the policy cash value to pay the annual mortality and expense charges. Permanent life insurance guarantees that the money needed to buy the business interest will be there no matter how long the owner lives or continues to be involved in the operation of the business activity.

Sometimes employees of closely-held business interests receive ownership in the business as part of their compensation packages but are not members of the control group or family that want to retain control of the business. Typically, these employee-owners are subject to buy-sell agreements that require them to sell their interest back to the company when they retire, or, if they die before they retire, when they die. Since most people survive until retirement, the most common funding vehicle for this type of buy-sell agreement is a **sinking fund** established and funded by the company so that when the employee retires, the sinking-fund has enough money to purchase the interest. There is mortality risk in these situations, however, that should be addressed. It is possible that an employee-owner will die before retirement and the sinking fund will not have sufficient money to pay for the purchase of the deceased-employee's business interest. As a hedge against this possibility, a life insurance policy could be purchased to cover any shortfall in the sinking fund. Since the life insurance need in this example is not permanent (it expires if the employee lives to retirement), use of term, universal, or variable universal life insurance policies may be appropriate.

Disadvantages

While entity buy-sell agreements have the advantage of simplicity, there is at least one disadvantage to using this structure.

If an entity buy-sell agreement is used, and the surviving owners plan to sell their business interests after the death of the first owner but prior to their own deaths, the entity buy-sell agreement will increase their taxable gain upon sale of their interests. Of course, this would not be an issue for family businesses that are not sold during the lifetimes of the family members. This first disadvantage of entity buy-sell agreements is easily remedied by using a cross-purchase buy-sell agreement.

Cross-Purchase Agreements

A **cross-purchase buy-sell agreement** is an arrangement between individuals who agree to purchase the business interest of a deceased owner. Unlike an entity-type agreement, which involves the business itself, a cross-purchase agreement only involves the owners of the business.

EXAMPLE 4.27

Cecil and his sister, Sybil, are equal owners of a luxury resort hotel, Fawlty Towers. Fawlty Towers is organized as a C corporation, and the corporation has been wholly owned by members of Cecil & Sybil's family since it began. Neither Cecil nor Sybil are married, and neither has any children. To ensure that the ownership of the hotel stays within the family, and to make sure that their estates have sufficient liquidity to cover expenses at death, Cecil and Sybil enter into a buy-sell agreement whereby the first sibling to die agrees to sell (through her estate), and the surviving sibling agrees to purchase the decedent's interest when she dies. The agreement between Cecil and Sybil is a cross-purchase buy-sell agreement.

To fund a cross-purchase buy-sell agreement with life insurance, each party to the agreement purchases a life insurance policy on the life of all of the other parties to the agreement so that the death benefit is sufficient to purchase the interest of any deceased owner. If there are only two parties, this approach is relatively straightforward – each party purchases one policy on the life of the other. When more than two owners are involved, however, things can get complicated, and as the number of owners grows, so does the complexity of the arrangement and the number of life insurance policies that must be purchased.

EXAMPLE 4.28

Bertie, Claude, and Eustice are equal owners of Wooster Enterprises, Ltd. They have entered into a cross-purchase buy-sell agreement triggered upon death. If Bertie dies first, his 1/3 interest would have to be purchased by Claude and Eustis in equal shares. To fund the agreement, both Claude and Eustice should purchase a life insurance policy on Bertie's life that will pay a death benefit equal to 1/6 (1/3 x 1/2) of the value of the company. Bertie and Claude should each purchase a life insurance policy on Eustice's life for the same amount (in case Eustice dies first), and Eustice and Bertie should purchase a life insurance policy on Claude's life in case Claude dies first. As this example illustrates, for a three-owner agreement, six life insurance policies would have to be purchased to fund this buy-sell agreement.

The number of cross purchase policies needed to fully fund the buy-sell agreement can be calculated by using the formula:

$$\text{Number of policies} = N(N-1)$$

Where N = the number of owners subject to the agreement. The greater the number of owners, the greater the number of life insurance policies that should be purchased. For example, four owners would require twelve policies or 4(4-1).

While applying for a large number of life insurance policies does somewhat complicate the administration of a cross-purchase agreement, the real issues emerge in the annual maintenance of the agreement. Each year, each of the owners will pay the premiums on policies they own covering the lives of other owners in order to keep those policies in force. If just one owner fails to pay the premium and another owner dies, the benefits of entering into the buy-sell agreement may be in jeopardy.

An entity agreement is a simple arrangement in which only one policy is purchased on the life of each owner and the premiums are paid by the entity. A cross-purchase agreement is much more complex than an entity agreement.

One of the advantages to a cross-purchase agreement is the ability to increase the surviving owner's basis in his or her shares of the business entity. When life insurance death benefits are received (on a tax-free basis), and are used to purchase the business interest of a deceased owner, each surviving owner's share of the business increases, but so does his or her basis in the business entity. Basis is that portion of the sale proceeds not subject to income tax, so a higher basis results in a higher after-tax benefit to the taxpayer. This benefit is unavailable with entity buy-sell agreements and is often the reason that financial advisors prefer cross-purchase arrangements.

EXAMPLE 4.29

Bertie, Claude, and Eustice are equal owners of Wooster Enterprises, Ltd. The adjusted basis for each 1/3 interest is $100,000. They have entered into a cross-purchase buy-sell agreement triggered upon death. Bertie passed away, and his 1/3 interest in Wooster enterprises was valued at $334,000. The entire business was worth $1 million, leaving $333,000 each for Claude and Eustice. As specified in the buy-sell agreement, Claude and Eustice each purchase half of Bertie's 1/3 interest in Wooster Enterprise, Ltd. for $167,000. After the purchase, Claude's and Eustice's ownership percentages increased from 33% to 50%. Their basis in the ownership interests increased from $100,000 to $267,000 each ($100,000 original adjusted basis + $167,000 paid for acquisition of the interest from Bertie's estate). If Claude and Eustice immediately sold Wooster Enterprises, Ltd. for $1 million, each of them would receive $500,000 (1/2 the proceeds) and would have to pay income tax on a capital gain of $233,000 ($500,000 amount realized - $267,000 adjusted basis).

How would this result differ if the buy-sell agreement was structured as an entity buy-sell, and Claude and Eustice sold the business after Bertie died? As described above, Claude and Eustice would each receive $500,000 (1/2 the proceeds) but would have to pay income tax on a capital gain of $400,000 ($500,000 amount realized - $100,000 adjusted basis). In this instance, the basis of the surviving shareholders is not affected because the corporation, not the individual shareholders, purchased the shares from Bertie's estate.

Cross-purchase agreements are typically preferred from a tax planning standpoint because:

1. they permit the surviving shareholders to increase their basis in the business interest;
2. the death benefit on life insurance owned by individuals is not subject to the possible imposition of the alternative minimum tax; and
3. life insurance owned by business owners outside of a corporation does not trigger any potential accumulated earnings tax.

WAIT-AND-SEE BUY-SELL AGREEMENTS

Wait-and-see buy-sell agreements are a cross between entity and cross purchase buy-sell agreements. Using this approach, the business has the first option to purchase the interest of a deceased owner. If the business entity chooses not to purchase the interest, the surviving owners of the company are given the opportunity to purchase the deceased owner's interest in proportion to his or her ownership interest. If the surviving owners do not exercise their right to purchase the interest, any interest remaining is purchased by the business.

By giving both the company and the owners the right to purchase an interest, the wait-and-see buy-sell maintains flexibility between the simplicity of the entity agreement and the tax advantages of the cross-purchase agreement. Both the company and the surviving owners can assess their respective situations when the death of an owner occurs and act in a way that maximizes their combined benefits.

Wait-and-see buy-sell agreements are very useful for C corporations with large amounts of retained earnings. When retained earnings are distributed to shareholders, they are usually treated as dividend distributions and are subject to income tax. If a corporation redeems shares from the estate of a deceased owner, and the redemption does not exceed the estate and inheritance taxes plus funeral expenses incurred by the deceased owner's estate, the redemption is typically exempt from income tax. This approach results in a reduction in retained earnings at the corporate level (IRC Sec. 303). The reduction in retained earnings reduces the amount of future corporate distributions that are subject to taxes as dividends, which is a significant benefit for C corporations and their surviving shareholders. Under a wait-and-see buy-sell agreement, the corporation will typically exercise its first option to purchase the number of shares necessary to effectuate a Sec. 303 redemption (thereby reducing its retained earnings) and give the surviving shareholders the option to purchase the remaining interest. If the surviving shareholders exercise this option, they will receive an increase in their basis in the business interest, which will reduce their taxable gain in the business entity should they decide to sell their interests before their deaths.

While wait-and-see buy-sell agreements are often used for C corporations, they are not frequently used for S corporations, partnerships, limited liability companies, or limited liability partnerships. Only C corporations issue taxable dividends, so the tax features of the wait-and-see buy-sell agreements are applicable only to C corporations. Wait-and-see buy-sell agreements could still be used with other types of business entities if the primary objective is to maintain flexibility in the repurchase of interests.

Life Insurance is the Perfect Hedge for a Buy-Sell Agreement Triggered at Death

As illustrated in the discussion above, life insurance is a perfect hedge for buy-sell agreements that are triggered on the death of the owner. If life insurance is purchased on the owner's life, the proceeds can be used to purchase the business interest from the decedent owner's estate. This facilitates effective transfer of ownership and control of the business entity and provides liquidity for the deceased owner's estate so that estate and inheritance taxes, funeral expenses, and end-of-life medical care costs can be paid.

CONCLUSION

Life insurance is an effective tool that can be used to hedge against mortality risk that everyone faces. Having a basic understanding of how each policy works, when it is appropriate to use them, and how much coverage should be obtained is important for anyone wishing to provide comprehensive financial planning advice.

Quick Quiz 4.5

1. A cross purchase agreement will increase the income tax basis of survivors/owners.
   a. True
   b. False

2. The number of policies for 5 equal partners in an entity approach to buy/sell is 20.
   a. True
   b. False

3. The number of policies for 5 equal partners in cross-purchase arrangement to buy/sell is 20.
   a. True
   b. False

True, False, True.

KEY TERMS

Accelerated Benefits Provision - Entitles a qualified insured to receive a pre-death benefit deemed nontaxable.

Annual Renewable Term (ART) - Type of term insurance that permits the policyholder to purchase term insurance in subsequent years without evidence of insurability, but premiums on the policy increase each year to reflect the increasing mortality risk being undertaken by the insurer.

Annuity - Periodic payment to an individual that continues for a fixed period or for the duration of a designated life or lives

Asset Accumulation Phase - This phase is usually from the early 20s to late 50s when additional cash flow for investing is low and debt to net worth is high.

Assignment - The process of transferring all or part of the policy's ownership rights.

Beneficiary - A person or institution legally entitled to receive benefits through a legal device, such as a will, trust or life insurance policy.

Buy-Sell Agreements - Arrangements that require the sale and purchase of securities owned by one individual to another following a specified triggering event, such as the death of a business owner.

Capitalized-Earnings Approach - Method to determine life insurance needs that suggests the death benefits of a client's life insurance should equal an income stream sufficient to meet the family's needs without depleting the capital base.

Conservation (Risk Management) Phase - This phase is from late 20s to early 70s, when cash flow assets and net worth have increased and debt has decreased somewhat. In addition, risk management of events like employment, disability due to illness or accident, and untimely death become a priority.

Contingent Beneficiaries - Person(s) or organization named to receive the death benefit if the primary beneficiary is not available to receive the policy proceeds.

Corridor Test - One of two Congress-imposed tests to determine whether a life insurance contract meets the definition of an MEC. This test calls for the policy to be tested using actuarial principles and requires the premiums to represent no more than a specified portion of the death benefit.

Cross-Purchase Buy-Sell Agreement - An arrangement between individuals who agree to purchase the business interest of a deceased owner.

Decreasing-Term Insurance - Type of term insurance that allows the owner to pay the same premium for the insurance protection each year. The death benefit on the policy will, however, decrease each year to offset the increasing mortality cost due to the passage of time.

KEY TERMS

Distribution (Gifting) Phase - This phase is from the late 40s to end of life and occurs when the individual has high additional cash flow, low debt, and high net worth.

Entity Purchase (Redemption) Agreement - Type of buy-sell agreement that obligates the business entity to purchase an owner's interest in the entity upon that owner's death.

First-to-Die - Type of joint life insurance policy that covers two individuals, but the death benefit is paid upon the death of the first individual.

Grace Period - A provision in most insurance policies that allows payment to be received for a certain period of time after the actual due date without a default or cancellation of the policy.

Group Term Insurance - A type of life insurance coverage offered to a group of people (often a component of an employee benefit package) that provides benefits to the beneficiaries if the covered individual dies during the defined covered period.

Human-Life Value Approach - Method to determine life insurance needs that suggests the death benefit of a client's life insurance should equal to the economic value of the client's future earnings stream.

Insured - The person whose life is insured by the policy.

Joint and Survivor Annuity - An annuity based on the lives of two or more annuitants, usually husband and wife. Annuity payments are made until the last annuitant dies.

Level Premium Term Insurance - Type of term insurance that charges a fixed premium each year over a specified period of years, so the premium does not increase over that period.

Limited-Pay Policies - Type of whole life policy with a payment schedule (typically 10 or 20 years). At the end of the payment period, the policy is considered to be paid-up, at which time no additional premium payments are due.

Modified Endowment Contract (MEC) - A cash value life insurance policy that has been funded too quickly. Under an MEC, the death benefit payable to the beneficiary is not subject to income tax, but policy loans or cash value withdrawals are taxable.

Modified Whole Life Policies - Type of whole life policy with lower premiums than a regular policy for an initial policy period (often 3 to 5 years), which increase to a higher-level premium at the end of the initial period.

Mortality Cost - Equals the probability of dying within the year times the face value of the policy.

Mortality Risk - The risk that an individual will die within the year.

KEY TERMS

Needs Approach - Method to determine life insurance needs that suggests the death benefits of a client's life insurance should equal the cash needs that the family will require at death plus income replacement needs.

Ordinary (or Straight) Life - Type of whole life policy that requires the owner to pay a specified level premium every year until death (or age 100).

Owner - Person or institution who owns the policy and can exercise the economic rights in a policy, including assignment, sale, etc. Also the person who is generally obligated for the payment of premiums.

Primary Beneficiary - Person(s) (may be a group designation) or organization to receive the death benefit upon the death of the insured.

Second-to-Die - Type of joint life insurance policy that is often used in estate planning to provide liquidity at the death of the second spouse. A second-to-die policy names two insureds and pays the death benefit only when the second insured dies.

7-Pay Test - One of two Congress-imposed tests to determine whether a life insurance contract meets the definition of an MEC. This test states that if the cumulative premium payments made on the policy are in excess of the net level premium for the policy during the first seven years (or following a material change to the policy), the life insurance contract will be deemed an MEC.

Simultaneous Death Provision - Provision in a life insurance policy for situations in which the insured and the beneficiary die within a short time of one another and it is not possible to determine who died first, Generally the policy death benefit is distributed as if the beneficiary had predeceased the insured.

Single-Premium Policy - Type of whole life policy that requires the owner to pay a lump sum in return for insurance protection that will extend throughout the insured's lifetime. These policies will always be a MECs.

Sinking Fund - A sinking fund is a fund established by a company to pay for future expenses or to retire debt. It is created by setting aside income over a period of time (generally years).

Suicide Clause - Provision in a life insurance policy specifying that the insurance company will not pay the benefit if the insured attempts or commits suicide within a specified period from the beginning of the coverage. The clause is designed to hedge against the risk that individuals with suicidal thoughts will purchase life insurance and commit suicide shortly thereafter.

Surrender Charge - A fee levied on a life insurance policyholder upon cancellation of the policy to cover the up-front costs of issuing the policy.

Survivorship Clause - Provision in a life insurance policy specifying that the death benefit will only be paid to the beneficiary if the beneficiary survives the insured by a specific number of days.

KEY TERMS

Term Insurance - Life insurance policy that states that if the premium has been paid and the insured dies during the term of the policy, the insurance company will pay the specified death benefit.

Underwriting - The process by which insurance companies decide whether to provide insurance to a customer and under what terms.

Universal Life Insurance - Type of term insurance with a cash-value accumulation feature allowing individuals to make premium contributions in excess of the term-insurance premium. The excess premiums are deposited into an account with various investment options.

Variable Life Insurance - Type of life insurance policy that permits the owner of the life insurance policy to direct the investment of the policy's cash value. Variable policies typically offer a series of investment options that often include investment funds managed by the insurer and outside investment managers.

Variable Universal Life Insurance Policies (VULs) - Type of life insurance policy that combines variable and universal life insurance and gives the policyholders the option to invest as well as alter insurance coverage.

Variable Whole Life Policies - Type of life insurance that provides for a fixed premium payment and permits the cash value of the policy to be professionally managed by the insurance company or an outside investment manager.

Viatical Settlement - An arrangement in which a policyholder sells their life insurance policy to a third party.

Whole Life Insurance - Type of life insurance that provides guarantees from the insurer that are not found in term insurance and universal life insurance policies.

DISCUSSION QUESTIONS

1. List and explain the three life-cycle stages.
2. List and explain the three methods used to determine clients' life insurance needs.
3. List the benefits of term life insurance.
4. List the options available with term life insurance.
5. List the benefits of whole life insurance.
6. List the options available with whole life insurance.
7. Describe the income tax consequences associated with whole life insurance plans.
8. Define a modified endowment contract (MEC).
9. Describe the benefits associated with group life insurance plans.
10. List and describe provisions commonly found in life insurance policies.
11. List the settlement options that are available to life insurance beneficiaries.
12. Why are beneficiaries not taxed on life insurance proceeds?
13. Describe why a client might want to take a loan out from a whole life insurance policy and what the consequences of that loan would be.
14. Define a viatical settlement.
15. What are the various needs for insurance on the person in general, and life insurance in particular?
16. What are component needs that make up the needs approach to the amount of life insurance needed?
17. How do term and whole life insurance differ, and what are the advantages/disadvantages of each?
18. What are the various types of term life insurance?
19. What are the various types of whole life insurance?
20. What differentiates variable life insurance from variable universal life insurance?

21. At what threshold is an employee taxed on group term life insurance provided by an employer?

22. What are the various types of annuities that are settlement options from life insurance?

23. What are the tax implications of life insurance?

24. What are the various contractual provisions and options that pertain to life insurance contracts?

25. What is the structure and purpose of an entity purchase, or redemption, buy-sell agreement?

26. What is the structure and purpose of a cross-purchase buy-sell agreement?

27. What are the tax differences between entity and cross-purchase buy-sell agreements?

MULTIPLE-CHOICE PROBLEMS

1. Which of the following life insurance policies provides the highest benefit for the lowest premium and is simply a pure death benefit policy?

    a. Term.
    b. Whole life.
    c. Universal life.
    d. All of the above.

2. Joe, age 33, is married and has a newborn son. Joe is concerned about providing for his family in the event of his premature death. He is concerned about the long-term affordability of life insurance but is able to budget a fixed amount for a period of time. Which of the following policies would you recommend?

    a. Annually renewable term.
    b. Level-premium term.
    c. Whole life insurance.
    d. Single-premium annuity.

3. Ryan and Jody are age 68 and 72, respectively, and are married. They have significant assets that will be subject to estate taxes upon the second spouse's death. Which of the following life insurance policies would you recommend?

    a. Annually renewable term.
    b. Second-to-die whole life policy.
    c. First-to-die whole life policy.
    d. Ordinary whole life.

4. Which of the following life insurance policies contains a cash-value savings component that reaches the face value of the policy at age 100 -120?

    a. Term.
    b. Whole life.
    c. Universal life.
    d. Lifetime annuity.

5. Which of the following life insurance policies has a fixed premium, a cash value and a death benefit that can fluctuate based on investment performance?

    a. Annually renewable term.
    b. Variable renewable term.
    c. Variable whole life.
    d. Variable lifetime annuity.

6. Which one of the following statements concerning whole life insurance is false?

   a. Level-premium whole life insurance accumulates a cash value that eventually reaches the face value of the policy at age 100 - 120.
   b. Whole life insurance offers permanent protection throughout the insured's lifetime.
   c. Whole life insurance can be participating, which means the insured must participate in self-directed investments for the cash value.
   d. Whole life insurance premiums paid throughout the insured's lifetime are ordinary life policies.

7. Which one of the following statements concerning universal life insurance is false?

   a. The insured has the flexibility to adjust premiums, face value and cash value of the policy.
   b. The insured has flexibility without the investment responsibility of the cash value.
   c. The cash value of the policy can be used to pay the premiums.
   d. The death benefit of a universal life insurance policy is fixed.

8. An individual has decided to purchase life insurance and comes to you as his agent. In order to propose a plan of life insurance to meet his individual needs, your first step would be to:

   a. Review his will or have him write a will if he does not have one.
   b. Select an insurance company.
   c. Select the policy type he wants to purchase.
   d. Conduct a needs analysis.

9. When utilizing the needs approach in the determination of the amount of life insurance, which factors should be considered?

   1. The family expenses that will remain after the wage earner dies.
   2. The value of the wage earner's life in the event he or she dies.
   3. The income that can be generated by the surviving spouse.
   4. The number of dependents.

   a. 1 only.
   b. 3 only.
   c. 1, 2, and 3.
   d. 1, 3, and 4.

10. The blackout period is:

    a. The period of time immediately following the death of the wage earner.
    b. The period of time after the death of a wage earner when the family is adjusting to life without the individual.
    c. The period of time when the widow or widower and dependents receive Social Security benefits.
    d. The period of time when the dependents have reached age 18 and the spouse's Social Security retirement benefits have not started.

11. Fred is 30 years old and recently began a job with a salary of $60,000. He is single but has been dating Lisa for 3 years. He expects to marry her within the next 5 years. Fred lives with his parents. What is the amount of life insurance that Fred currently needs?

    a. $0.
    b. $100,000.
    c. $60,000 x 6 = $360,000.
    d. $60,000 x 10 = $600,000.

12. Which of the following is needed to calculate the client's human-life value?

    1. Average annual earnings to the age of retirement.
    2. Estimated annual Social Security benefits after retirement.
    3. Costs of self-maintenance.
    4. Number of years from the client's present age to the contemplated age of retirement.

    a. 3 and 4.
    b. 1, 2, and 4.
    c. 1, 3, and 4.
    d. 1, 2, 3, and 4.

13. Betty owns a $150,000 whole life participating insurance policy that she purchased ten years ago. She has paid premiums of $4,000 each year since she bought the policy and the current cash surrender value is $60,000. Betty has received $10,000 in paid dividends since the policy inception. Which of the following statement(s) is/are correct regarding Betty's policy?

    1. If Betty surrenders the policy now, she will have a taxable gain of $30,000 taxed as ordinary income.
    2. The dividends that were paid on Betty's policy were subject to ordinary income tax treatment.

    a. 1 only.
    b. 2 only.
    c. Both 1 and 2.
    d. Neither 1 nor 2.

14. Marsha, age 35, is a single mother of one daughter, Skyler, age 9. Marsha is a secretary with annual income of $35,000 and a negative net worth. Marsha has two objectives: (1) to protect Skyler in the event of her untimely death and (2) to save for her own retirement. Which of the following life insurance policies should she buy?

    a. A 20-year term insurance policy.
    b. An ordinary whole life insurance policy.
    c. A universal variable policy.
    d. A universal policy.

15. Terry has been advised by his insurance agent to purchase a variable universal life insurance policy. He has sought your advice regarding this purchase. All of the following are characteristics of a variable universal policy, *except*:

    a. The policy features increasing or decreasing death benefits and flexibility of variable premium payments.
    b. The policy owner has exclusive investment control over the cash value of the policy.
    c. The death benefit is guaranteed to be equal to the face value.
    d. The cash value of a variable universal life policy is dependent on premiums and investment returns.

16. Which of the following method(s) is/are appropriate to evaluate a person's life insurance needs?

    1. The human life approach to evaluate life insurance needs takes into consideration the income replacement needs of a person's survivors including income during the readjustment period, income to widow(er), and educational funds for dependents.
    2. The needs approach evaluates the estimated present value of income generated over a person's work-life expectancy that is needed and then adjusts for the expected consumption of the person and for taxes.

    a. 1only.
    b. 2 only.
    c. 1 and 2.
    d. None of the above.

17. Olivia, age 52, purchased a life insurance policy on her own life. All the necessary legal elements of a contract including, (1) offer and acceptance, (2) consideration, (3) competent parties, and (4) legal purpose were met. However, Olivia lied that her age was 42 on the insurance application, and is receiving a premium commensurate with that age. Olivia died two years later in an automobile accident. Her certified death certificate indicated that she was 54 at the time of her death, and that she was 52 when she purchased the policy. Which of the following statement(s) is/are correct regarding this scenario?

    a. The policy could not be voided because her death was two years after the issuance of the insurance of the policy.
    b. The beneficiary can pay in the correct but unpaid premiums and collect the full death benefit.
    c. Her beneficiary will receive a reduced death benefit to reflect her actual age.
    d. All of the statements are correct.

18. Watson, Inc. has four equal partners. All four partners are interested in entering into a buy-sell arrangement. How many life insurance policies would be purchased to properly fund using a cross-purchase agreement?

    a. 4 policies.
    b. 6 policies.
    c. 8 policies.
    d. 12 policies.

19. Which of the following statement(s) is/are correct regarding buy-sell arrangements?

    1. Entity purchase arrangements increase the income tax basis for some survivors upon the death of another owner.
    2. Cross-purchase arrangements increase the income tax basis for all survivors upon the death of another owner.

    a. 1 only.
    b. 2 only.
    c. Both 1 and 2.
    d. None of the above are correct.

QUICK QUIZ EXPLANATIONS

Quick Quiz 4.1

1. False. The asset accumulation phase generally lasts from the time one enters the workforce until retirement.
2. True.
3. False. In the event that the decedent's health insurance policy did not cover all of his or her medical expenses, life insurance proceeds are appropriately used to pay these expenses.
4. False. As clients age, the human-life value and the need for life insurance protection decreases.

Quick Quiz 4.2

1. True.
2. True.
3. False. Option B provides for increasing death benefits - the stated policy amount plus the cash value. Option A provides a level death benefit or the cash value, whichever is greater.
4. True.

Quick Quiz 4.3

1. False. The owner could be under a legal obligation (for example, divorce) to keep a specific beneficiary if the beneficiary designation is an irrevocable election.
2. False. The suicide clause is generally only in effect for a specific amount of time (usually 2 years). During that time, there is no payout, regardless of the reason for death or the cash value.
3. True.
4. True.

Quick Quiz 4.4

1. False. If the insured is the owner, the policy is includible in the decedent/owner/insured's estate.
2. True.
3. False. There is no income tax due, and the basis carries over, but additional premiums increase basis.
4. False. If the seller was terminally ill at the time of the sale, no gain on the sale of the policy is realized, regardless of what the money is actually used for.

Quick Quiz 4.5

1. True.
2. False. An entity approach buys one policy per owner, therefore 5 policies not 20.
3. True.

CHAPTER

5

DISABILITY INSURANCE

LEARNING OBJECTIVES

After reading this chapter, you should be able to:

1. Understand the need for disability insurance.
2. Describe the provisions of an appropriate disability insurance policy including coverage, definition, benefits, taxation, elimination period, residual benefits, and renewability.
3. Describe differences between short-term and long-term disability plans and identify the policy provisions that should be included in privately-purchased disability policies.*
4. Create a plan for meeting individual disability income needs, in consideration of household financial resources, and existing coverage under employer plans, Social Security, and disability income insurance options.*
5. Calculate the tax implications of paying for and receiving disability benefits.*

* CFP Board Resource Document - Student-Centered Learning Objectives based upon CFP Board Principal Topics.

INTRODUCTION

Disabilities are part of life. Approximately 10 percent of the world's population lives with a disability.[1] In America, 56 million, or 1-in-5, live with disabilities. Thirty-eight million disabled Americans, or 1-in-10, live with severe disabilities.[2] As people age, the likelihood of a disability increases significantly.

One of the greatest risks faced by people is the possibility of not being able to work during their earning years – the prospect of becoming disabled. While life insurance acts as a hedge against the possibility of early death, **disability insurance** acts as a hedge against being unable to work. The risk of being unable to work (referred to by actuaries as morbidity risk) at any age is greater than the risk of untimely death (mortality risk). According to statistical data derived from the Society of Actuaries, the National Safety Council, and the Disability Fact Book, the likelihood of disability over death at various ages is:

Age	Likelihood
30	4 to 1
35	3.5 to 1
40	2.7 to 1
45	2.1 to 1
50	1.8 to 1
55	1.5 to 1

While medical science has improved treatments and substantially reduced the risk of death from heart disease and cancer, the risk of disability from these diseases has remained the same or increased. Individuals who rely on employment-related income to meet their current and future financial planning needs should consider hedging their risk of disability with disability insurance policies.

1. United Nations.
2. SSA.gov.

Key Concepts

1. Differentiate between the likelihood of becoming disabled compared to dying prematurely.
2. Describe the moral hazard that is associated with disability insurance.
3. Contrast the importance of short versus long-term disability risk.

There are three primary sources of disability insurance benefits. These sources include the government, employers, and individual or personal policies. Governmental benefits can be provided through the Social Security system or through worker's compensation.

Social Security disability benefits are available to anyone insured under the system who meets the strict definition of disability. However, Social Security disability benefits will not likely provide adequate income replacement, except for those with fairy low incomes, and the Social Security Administration (SSA) has a very strict definition for being classified as disabled. SSA "defines disability as the inability to engage in any substantial gainful activity (SGA) by reason of any medically determinable physical or mental impairment(s) which can be expected to result in death or which has lasted or can be expected to last for a continuous period of not less than 12 months." In addition, there is a five month waiting period before benefits can begin.

Worker's compensation is designed to provide benefits to workers who are injured while working. Worker's compensation laws are designed to eliminate the need for litigation by providing fixed monetary awards to injured workers. It is important to note that this protection applies to injuries sustained while working. Worker's compensation will not provide protection for an employee who cannot work due to an injury outside of work, whereas a private disability policy may provide protection. According to the SSA, 95 percent of all disabling illnesses and accidents happen outside of the workplace.

Employers may provide employees with sick leave, short-term disability benefits, and long-term disability benefits. These benefits are generally provided to all employees in the form of a group benefit. Finally, private disability insurance policies may be acquired directly from an insurance company. This chapter discusses non-governmental disability insurance.[3]

Amount of Coverage

As a rule of thumb, individuals should have a minimum of 60 to 70 percent of their gross income protected with a disability insurance policy. In some cases, the replacement percentage may be greater, particularly for younger individuals with few assets who have families with young children. Due to the moral hazards that can present themselves with this type of coverage, insurance companies will not issue disability insurance policies that will cover more than 100 percent of the insured's income (alone or in combination with other policies) and often will limit coverage to a fraction of the insured's income. The reasoning behind this limitation is that, if the insured has no incentive to work, that may increase disability insurance claims for the insurer, particularly when own-occupation policies (covered below) are issued.

3. Disability benefits under the Social Security system are discussed in the Social Security Chapter.

Group long-term disability insurance offered by employers will generally provide for approximately 60 percent coverage of pre-tax compensation. However, in some cases the amount may be lower or higher. It is important to know that additional coverage can be obtained from other disability insurance companies to increase the coverage to closer to 100 percent. Additional coverage may be important for those who cannot tolerate the risk of a 40 percent reduction in income due to a disability.

EXAMPLE 5.1

Mick worked as a foreman for Acme, Inc., a manufacturing company. Acme provides group benefits for employees, including disability coverage. Mick signed up for the disability protection, which provides for 60 percent coverage in the event of disability due to sickness or accident. Unfortunately, Mick was involved in a motorcycle accident that left him paralyzed. His disability policy will only pay him 60 percent of his pre-tax income. Mick could have purchased an additional policy that would have increased the coverage from an outside insurance company.

Given the facts in the above example, Mick is likely to also qualify for disability benefits under Social Security. As of June 30, 2014, the average Social Security monthly disability benefit was $1,146 for disabled workers.[4] For many, if not most disabled workers, the benefits from Social Security are not sufficient to provide for their required financial needs. Therefore, it is critically important that the right amount of coverage is obtained.

QUICK QUIZ 5.1

1. Americans are far more likely to die prematurely than to suffer a disability?
   a. True
   b. False

2. If a person is covered by a private disability insurance policy, then he or she could also receive benefits from Social Security.
   a. True
   b. False

3. Adequate disability insurance coverage is generally defined as 40 percent to 50 percent of a person's income.
   a. True
   b. False

False, True, False.

TERM OF COVERAGE

Coverage under disability insurance policies is typically split between short-term coverage and long-term coverage. Short-term disability insurance policies often provide benefits for a period of one to two years, while long-term disability insurance policies can provide coverage until normal retirement age or death. When an individual is covered under both short-term and long-term disability insurance policies, the benefit periods should be coordinated so that there is no gap in coverage. For example, if a short-term disability insurance policy covers benefits for two years, the insured's long-term disability policy should provide benefits beginning two years after the disability began (when the short-term disability benefits terminate) to normal retirement age or death. Once the individual reaches normal retirement age, disability coverage is generally no longer needed, since retirement income will commence.

4. SSA.gov: Social Security Program Fact Sheet as of June 30, 2014.

It should be noted that while it is helpful to have short-term disability coverage, it is far more important from a risk perspective to have long-term disability coverage.

CHARACTERISTICS OF DISABILITY INSURANCE POLICIES

Like other insurance, disability insurance is a contract. It is important to understand the various aspects of disability contracts, including the definition of disability, the benefit period, and other policy provisions. These are discussed below.

> **KEY CONCEPTS**
>
> 1. Describe how any occupation disability insurance works in regard to highly skilled professionals.
> 2. Describe what is meant by a split definition of disability.
> 3. Identify conditions under which a disability policy will make payments without a total disability.
> 4. Select the correct elimination period based on other relevant factors.
> 5. Choose other riders that may enhance a disability policy.

DEFINITION OF DISABILITY

Policies specify the conditions under which the insured will be considered "disabled" and therefore entitled to benefits under the contract. Disability policies will generally provide coverage if a person is disabled due to accident or sickness. However, there are policies that may only cover accidents and not sickness. Sickness accounts for approximately two thirds of the disabilities and accidents account for the other third.

In addition to accident and sickness coverage, policies will define a disability in terms of total or partial disability and will define disability in terms of the types of job duties, or occupation, that the insured can no longer perform due to the disability. The three standard definitions in terms of occupation are:

1. own-occupation policies
2. any-occupation policies
3. split (hybrid) definition policies

EXHIBIT 5.1

DEFINITION OF DISABILITY

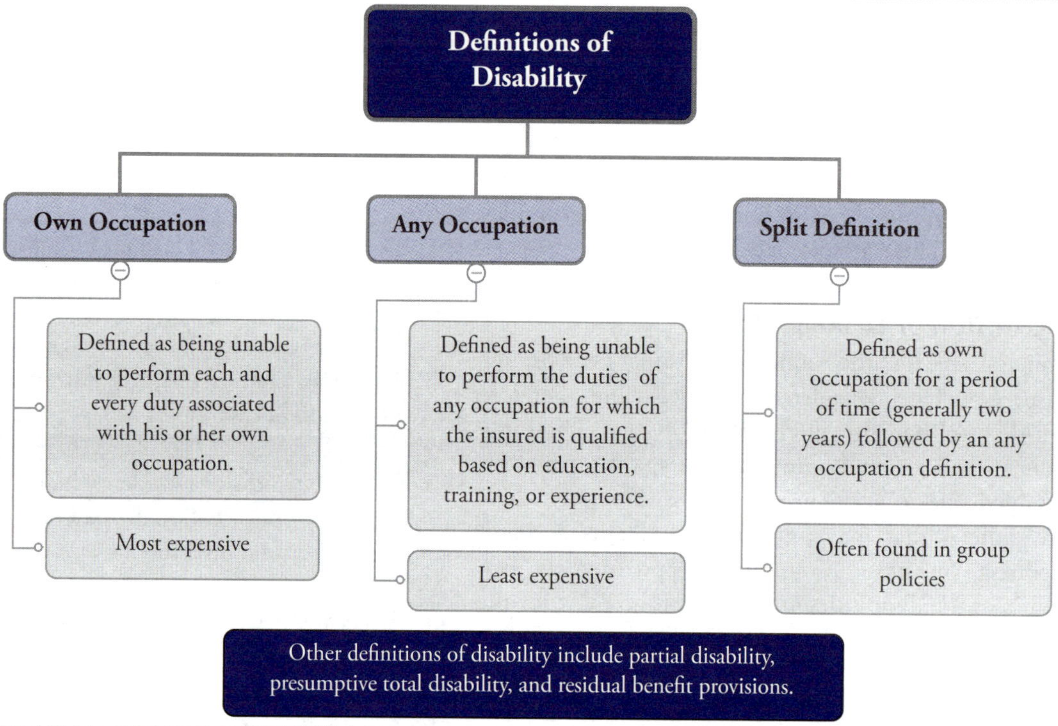

Own-occupation policies state that if the insured is unable to perform each and every duty associated with his or her own occupation, the insured is deemed to be disabled and the policy will provide benefits.

EXAMPLE 5.2

> Rosemary is a concert pianist and has spent her lifetime practicing and performing piano concertos around the world. She recently contracted a disease that affected the dexterity of her hands, which has prevented her from being able to perform at concerts. She purchased an own-occupation disability insurance policy 25 years ago. The insurance policy will pay disability benefits to Rosemary since she can no longer perform the duties of her occupation as a pianist.

Own-occupation policies were popular tools in the late 1980s and early 1990s, particularly with physicians, musicians, and other professionals whose income was dependent on their ability to perform specific tasks. Over time, insurance companies recognized that there was a large adverse selection risk associated with these policies, which are now less available. When an own-occupation policy is issued, the premium is high due to the risks being undertaken by the insurance company.

An **any-occupation** disability insurance policy provides benefits to a policyowner if he or she is unable to perform the duties of any occupation. This type of policy is less attractive to individuals in high-skill professions. A surgeon, for example, would probably not want a policy that will not pay benefits unless he/she could not perform telemarketing services. The courts have limited the interpretation of this definition of disability to mean that the insured can collect benefits if he/she is unable to perform any occupation for which he/she is suited based on training, experience, and educational degrees.[5] Continuing our example, if the surgeon is unable to perform surgery due to an injury to his hands, but could teach medical school to new physicians, he would be expected to earn income in that fashion and would not be considered disabled under the policy contract. The surgeon would not, however, be required to perform telemarketing services as a means of minimizing benefits received under the policy.

Many disability insurance policies, especially group policies, use a **split definition** (hybrid) of disability. Under a split definition policy, an insured will be covered against the risk of not being able to perform his or her own occupation for a period of time and, after that period expires, an any-occupation definition of disability would be used. This type of policy gives the insured a period to adjust to his or her new reality and perhaps get the training necessary to perform other occupations that will allow him/her to replace some or all of the lost income from the old occupation. Some disability policies will provide coverage for retraining.

One of the advantages of an own-occupation definition policy is that if the insured is disabled in terms of their occupation, then they can receive benefits and still pursue another career. However, insurance policies are contracts and thus, the exact language of the contract is critical. It turns out that some insurance carriers market policies as "own occupation" that pay benefits as long as the insured is not engaged in another occupation. The term, "modified own occupation" is often used to describe this type of coverage. In addition, there are other definitions that are used that are variations of the true own occupation definition. For example, there is a specialty own occupation definition that is even more restrictive to the insured. This type of definition would protect a surgeon that had a specific medical specialty, such as a gastroenterologist. With all of the variations in the types of coverage being marketed, it is critical to read the definition in the contract that deals with disability.

EXAMPLE 5.3

Randy went to the LSU School of Dentistry, graduated and has been working as a dentist in Metairie, Louisiana. However, he was diagnosed with a tumor at the top of his spine and is unable to work as a dentist since he cannot bend over. Fortunately, Randy purchased an own occupation policy that now provides him with 60 percent of his prior earnings. In addition, he has been able to obtain an new job as a disability insurance sales person selling disability insurance to dentists. He is the top performing rep in the country and this new occupation does not interfere with his disability benefits.

Presumptive Total Disability Coverage

Many disability policies have a provision, know as **presumptive total disability coverage**, which automatically considers certain conditions to be totally disabling. These conditions generally include loss of sight in both eyes, hearing in both ears, the use of both hands, the use of both feet, and the use of one foot and one hand. If any of these conditions arise, the policy automatically presumes total disability and will begin payments according to the contract. This type of provision expedites income to those who need it without having to go through the normal steps to be considered disabled.

5. See Bacon v. Government of Saskatchewan (1990) 88 Sask. R. 182 (Q.B.)

Partial Disability

Many policies include coverage for **partial disability**, defined as the inability to perform at least one important duty of the insured's normal occupation. The partial disability provision provides payments that are less than those paid for total disability but these benefits usually last for only a short period of time (such as six months). By covering partial disability in this manner, the insurer gives the insured an incentive to return to work sooner than he or she otherwise might.

Residual Benefit Provision

Experiencing a condition that prevents an insured from working for a period of time may lead to a permanent loss of income. This may be particularly true when an insured is covered by an any-occupation disability policy or an own-occupation disability policy that morphs into an any-occupation policy after a specified period of time. While the insured may be able to work, it is possible that the conditions causing the disability will prevent him/her from being able to perform all of the requirements of the prior job, resulting in a loss of income. A **residual benefit provision** will provide continuing benefits for an insured who returns to work but suffers a loss of income due to the disability.

Insurance companies typically use two approaches to determine eligibility for residual benefits: (1) the loss of earnings method or (2) the loss of time or duties method. Under the loss of earnings method, residual benefits are usually payable if the insured's earnings loss exceeds 20 percent. Under the loss of time or duties method, if, as a result of the insured's disability, compensation is adjusted for time away from the job, or the income is adjusted because the insured cannot perform the same duties, a residual benefit may also be available. To qualify for benefits, the insured is required to prove an earnings loss (usually by submitting earnings statements before and after the period of disability). Disability insurance policies often compare income before and after on an average basis, such as the average monthly earnings for the 12-month period immediately preceding disability.

Some residual benefit provisions also index benefits for inflation, usually based on the Consumer Price Index. While this increase may not match future increases in income that would have been attained had no disability been suffered, at least it attempts to preserve the purchasing power of the benefit.

ELIMINATION PERIOD

Most disability policies only provide benefits after an elimination period has been satisfied. The **elimination period** is the period of time, beginning upon injury or sickness, that an insured is disabled but is not yet eligible to collect benefits from the insurer. The elimination period ensures that benefits are not paid unless the insured experiences a disability that could deprive the insured of income for a long period of time, and also helps the insurance company manage the moral hazard associated with fraudulent disability insurance claims.

The elimination period can be as short as one month and can be extended depending on the needs of the insured. If, for example, the insured's employer will continue to pay the employee's salary to the insured for up to three months in the event of a disability, the elimination period on the disability insurance policy can be set to three months. This selection would ensure continuous income for the insured while lowering the cost of the insurance protection. As the elimination period increases up to a point (usually 180 days), the premium for the policy will decrease.

Individuals who do not have short-term disability coverage need to make sure that their emergency fund is sufficient to sustain them throughout the disability elimination period. If the emergency fund and the elimination period are not properly coordinated, then the person may be without income for a period of time until disability benefits begin.

EXAMPLE 5.4

Wade works as a graphic designer and earns $4,000 per month. He has a disability policy that will pay him 60 percent of his benefits, which will cover most of his basic needs. When he bought the policy, he chose an 18-month elimination period to reduce the policy premium. Although he does not have a short-term disability policy, he has a sufficient emergency fund to cover his needs during the 18-month period before any disability benefits would begin.

Benefit Period

Disability insurance distinguishes between short-term and long-term coverage. **Short-term disability** provides coverage for up to two years, and typically has a short elimination period (typically 5-30 days). Many employers offer group short-term disability insurance that provides employees with a percentage of their salary while disabled.

Long-term disability typically has a longer elimination period (30-180 days) and provides coverage until normal retirement age, until death, or for a specified term. The most common benefit period is to age 65, but policies may have benefit periods of 2 years, 5 years, or even lifetime benefits. Some employers offer group long-term disability insurance with premiums generally paid by the employee. Employer-sponsored plans are usually not portable and terminate when the employee leaves the employer unless the reason for leaving employment is directly related to the disability.

Quick Quiz 5.2

1. A 30-year-old has a lower morbidity rate than a 50-year old.
   a. True
   b. False

2. Disabled insureds generally continue to pay premiums while they receive benefits to avoid cancellation of the policy.
   a. True
   b. False

3. The "own-occupation" policy is the most widely sold disability insurance policy.
   a. True
   b. False

False, False, False.

Other Disability Policy Provisions

There are many other provisions that might be included in a disability insurance policy. Waiver of premium, COLA, future increase, automatic increase riders, and Social Security riders are discussed below.

Waiver of Premium Rider

Benefits awarded under a disability income policy are provided because the insured no longer has income, or has reduced income, from employment. Most disability insurance policies waive future premium payments under the policy once the elimination period has been met and the insured is receiving disability benefits under the policy. If the insured regains his or her health and returns to work, the premiums on the policy must be paid in order to keep the policy in force.

This rider is standard in most disability policies and may not increase the cost of the policy.

COLA Rider

Some disability insurance policies also provide a cost of living (COLA) adjustment to the benefit payments. Since the cost of products and services used by the insured increases as inflation increases, a COLA adjustment helps the insured maintain his or her purchasing power during a long period of disability. Typically, COLA adjustments are tied to the consumer price index (CPI). All else being equal, a disability insurance policy with a COLA provision will have a higher premium than one without a COLA provision.

Future Increase Rider and Automatic Increase Rider

In addition to protecting current income, some insureds would like assurance that, as their income increases, they are able to get additional disability income insurance. The following two riders are commonly used to achieve this objective:

- **Future increase option rider** - permits the insured to increase the monthly benefit as the insured gets older. This rider effectively guarantees insurability for a certain period of time (such as to age 55) so that as the insured's income increases, they can acquire additional coverage to maintain the same level or percentage of income replacement.
- **Automatic increase rider** - automatically increases the monthly benefits by a stated percentage every year. The advantage of this rider is that the increase is automatic. It does not require the insured to purchase additional coverage. However, the premiums may increase.

If either of these two options is chosen, the premium on the policy, all else equal, will be greater than a policy that does not provide these protections.

Social Insurance Substitute Benefit, Social Security Rider, or Social Insurance Rider

This type of rider, sometimes referred to as an SIS benefit, effectively integrates the maximum disability benefit with Social Security. It provides for higher benefits during the first year of a disability while the insured is waiting for benefits from Social Security. The rider, which increases the cost of the policy, can be structured as an "all or nothing" benefit or as "an offset" benefit. With an all or nothing rider, the benefit will be paid if Social Security does not pay and will not pay if Social Security does pay. With an offset rider, the benefits are reduced to the extent of benefits received from Social Security.

EXAMPLE 5.5

Jackson buys a disability policy with a base benefit of $8,000 and an SIS offset benefit of $1,500. Jackson becomes disabled and eventually receives $1,000 in Social Security disability benefits. Jackson will initially receive $9,500 in benefits. However, once Social Security begins paying benefits, Jackson will only receive $8,500 from the insurance company.

INCONTESTABILITY CLAUSE

Similar to life insurance policies, most disability policies contain an incontestability clause that prevents the insurer from voiding the contract after the specified period of time (generally two years). This type of clause protects the insured from several potential issues, including preexisting conditions, misstatements or misrepresentations, and unknown conditions. Therefore, after two years, the issuing company cannot claim that the insured misrepresented some aspect of the application. After the two years, the claim must be paid. However, there is one caveat in this type of clause. The clause is not valid if the insured fraudulently or intentionally misrepresented material or substantial information.

EXAMPLE 5.6

Ryan applies for a disability policy with Secure Insurance Company (SIC). During the process of filing out the forms, Ryan put an incorrect birthdate. His birthday is August 1, 1980 or 8/1/80. Instead of filling out his correct birthday, he wrote 1/8/80. Five years later he had an accident with his lawn mower in which he became disabled. Because of the incontestability clause, the company cannot void the contract because of a misstatement or error, as long as it was not intentional.

Renewability

Insured individuals who have disability policies that are renewed each year are potentially subject to a risk of policy cancellation. In fact, it would be in the best interest of the insurance company to cancel policies held by individuals who are likely to become disabled as a means of avoiding benefit payments. To prevent this from happening, and to provide policy holders some protection against policy cancellation, different renewability rights are provided for in disability insurance contracts. These rights include: (1) non-cancelable policies, and (2) guaranteed renewable policies.

Non-cancelable

Non-cancelable policies prevent the insurance company from cancelling the policy for any reason provided the policy premium is paid. Usually, the policy will specify that it is non-cancelable for a specific period of time or until the insured reaches a stated age. Some policies also specify that, during the non-cancelable period, no changes to the policy may be made, including changes to the premium. Non-cancelable policies provide the greatest degree of protection to the insured since the insured can force the insurance company to provide continued coverage simply by paying the premium on the policy.

Quick Quiz 5.3

1. A COLA rider will increase the benefit based on increases in the insured's income.
   a. True
   b. False

2. Generally, an own occupation policy will be slightly less expensive than an any occupation policy?
   a. True
   b. False

3. The premium and the elimination period are generally inversely related.
   a. True
   b. False

4. Incontestability clauses protect the insurance company from misstatements or misrepresentations by the insured.
   a. True
   b. False

False, False, True, False.

Guaranteed Renewable

Guaranteed renewable disability insurance policies require the insurance company to renew the policy for a specified period of time or until the insured attains a certain age. Provided the insured pays the premium, the insurance company must renew the policy during the period stated in the contract. Unlike the case with non-cancelable policies, which do not permit increases in premium, the premium on a guaranteed renewable policy may be increased on a class basis (i.e., increased across the board for all similarly situated insureds), but may not be increased for one participant simply because he or she has been exposed to a disease or health condition that increases the likelihood of suffering a period of disability.

GROUP DISABILITY INSURANCE

Disability insurance is also available on a group basis, and is a benefit that is commonly available to employees of larger companies. Group disability insurance can be provided on a short-term or long-term basis, and in many cases, both short-term and long-term policies are offered or provided. The elimination periods for these policies are typically coordinated so that there is continuous income coverage for the insured. Often, the short-term group coverage will begin after employer coverage for sick time ends, and the long-term group coverage will begin when the short-term coverage terminates. Long-term group disability coverage usually terminates when the insured reaches normal retirement age or dies.

The advantage of group disability coverage is that premiums are typically lower than premiums on individual coverage. Employers may pay the premiums on behalf of the employees or may permit the employees to pay the coverage directly through payroll deduction. While group policies provide coverage to employees at a reasonable cost, they are generally not portable, unlike personal policies. Consequently, employees who anticipate frequent changes in employment may wish to consider the purchase of individual private coverage.

TAXATION OF DISABILITY INSURANCE BENEFITS

KEY CONCEPTS

1. Describe the possible tax consequences of disability benefits.

The taxation of benefits received under a disability insurance policy depends on who paid the policy premiums. If the insured paid the premiums with after-tax dollars (as is the case when individual disability insurance is purchased, or when group insurance is purchased with after-tax dollars), the benefits received under the policy are not subject to income tax. Benefits provided under a policy paid for with pre-tax dollars (such as when the employer provides disability benefits at no cost to the employees as an employee benefit) are subject to income tax.

If given a choice, an employee with access to employer group disability insurance should pay for the coverage with after-tax dollars to ensure that benefit payments are received on a tax-free basis. If the employee receives benefits under the policy, that implies he or she is unable to work, and that would probably not be the best time to have to worry about an additional cash outflow – in the form of income tax. Many employers who offer group disability policies to their employees permit them to pay for the policies with after-tax dollars to achieve this benefit.

Some group disability policies require the employee to pay a portion of the premium, while the employer pays the remainder of the premium. In these type of plans, any income from the policy will be partially taxable and partially tax free. The portion of the income that is subject to tax is equal to the percentage portion of the premium paid by the employer. The portion of the income that is not subject to tax is equal to the percentage portion of the premium paid by the employee with after tax dollars.

QUICK QUIZ 5.4

1. Generally, it is more effective to pay disability insurance premiums with after-tax dollars, to avoid paying income tax on disability benefits.
   a. True
   b. False

True.

Generally, partnerships and S corporations cannot deduct premiums paid for disability policies for partners or owners. In some cases, the company may deduct the premium and report the payment as income to the partner or owner. In either case, the partner or owner is effectively paying for the premium with after-tax dollars. Therefore, any disability benefits received will not be taxable.

EXAMPLE 5.7

Lindy works for Alpha Company, which pays the entire premium for disability insurance for its employees. If Lindy is disabled, her benefits are fully taxable.

EXAMPLE 5.8

Cindy works for Bravo Company, which permits employees to purchase disability insurance as part of a group plan with pre-tax dollars. If Cindy is disabled, her benefits are fully taxable.

EXAMPLE 5.9

Mindy works for Charlie Company, which permits employees to purchase disability insurance as part of a group plan with after-tax dollars. If Mindy is disabled, her benefits are not taxable.

EXAMPLE 5.10

Vindy works for Delta Company, which provides disability insurance for its employees, but only pays 75 percent of the premium. The other 25 percent of the premium is paid by the employee with after-tax dollars. If Vindy is disabled, 75 percent of her benefits are taxable.

It should be noted that the Internal Revenue Code (IRC) provides some relief for those who are disabled. Taxpayers who are blind are permitted to have an additional standard deduction. In addition, IRC §22 provides for a credit for disabled persons that can provide some tax relief.

CONCLUSION

In many ways, disability insurance can be more important than life insurance since the incidence of disability is significantly greater than untimely death. It is important to address and cover the risk of not being able to work. This risk is precisely what disability insurance covers. As with other insurance, there are many choices and many alternatives that one must consider when purchasing disability insurance.

KEY TERMS

Any Occupation - Type of disability insurance policy that provides benefits to a policyowner if he or she is unable to perform the duties of any occupation for which he or she is suited by education, training, or experience.

Automatic Increase Rider - A provision that automatically increases the monthly benefit by a stated percentage each year.

COLA Rider - Provides a cost of living adjustment to benefit payments based on increases in inflation.

Disability Insurance - A type of insurance that provides supplementary income in the event of an illness or accident resulting in a disability that prevents the insured from working at his or her regular employment.

Elimination Period - The period of time, beginning upon injury or sickness, that an insured is disabled but is not collecting benefits from the insurer.

Future Increase Option Rider - A provision that permits the insured to increase benefit coverage as they get older.

Guaranteed Renewable - A provision that requires the insurance company to renew the policy for a specified period of time or until the insured attains a certain age.

Long-Term Disability - Provides coverage for specified term, until specified age, or until death.

Non-Cancelable - A provision that prevents the insurance company from cancelling the policy for any reason provided the policy premium is paid.

Own Occupation - Type of disability insurance policy that provides benefits to a policyholder if he is unable to perform the duties of their occupation. This type of policy is more expensive than an any occupation policy.

Partial Disability - A provision that provides payments that are less than those paid for a total disability.

Presumptive Total Disability Coverage - A provision that automatically considers certain conditions to be totally disabling, such as loss of sight in both eyes, hearing in both ears, the use of both hands, the use of both feet, or the use of one foot and one hand.

Residual Benefits Provision - A provision that will provide continuing benefits for an insured who returns to work but suffers a reduction of income due to a disability.

KEY TERMS

SHORT-TERM DISABILITY - Provides coverage for up to two years, and typically has a 5 to 30 day elimination period (the period an insured must wait before receiving benefits).

SPLIT DEFINITION - Type of disability policy where an insured is covered against the risk of not performing his or her own occupation for a period of time, and after that period expires, an any-occupation definition of disability is used.

DISCUSSION QUESTIONS

1. List and define the three common definitions used in disability insurance policies.
2. List and describe provisions commonly found in disability insurance policies.
3. Explain the relative importance of short versus long-term disability coverage.
4. Explain why it is important to not just accept an own occupation definition as described by a representative or by marketing literature.
5. Describe the impact to disability policy premiums of increasing the elimination period.
6. Compare and contract the future increase option rider and the automatic increase riders.
7. Identify the primary issue in determining whether disability benefits are taxable or tax-free.
8. What is the purpose of disability income insurance, and what are some of the various definitions of disability?

MULTIPLE-CHOICE PROBLEMS

1. Which one of the following statements regarding disability insurance is false?

    a. The longer the elimination period, the less expensive the policy.
    b. An own-occupation policy will provide disability benefits if the insured is unable to perform the duties of his or her own occupation.
    c. An any-occupation policy is less expensive than an own-occupation policy.
    d. A residual benefit clause provides the insured with benefits that extend beyond the disability period.

2. Jack has a disability income policy that pays a monthly benefit of $2,400. Jack has been disabled for 60 days, but he only received $1,200 from his disability insurance. Which of the following is the probable reason that he only received $1,200?

    a. The policy has a deductible of $1,200.
    b. The elimination period is 45 days.
    c. The policy has a 50% coinsurance clause.
    d. Jack is considered to be only 50% disabled.

3. Jared is a university professor who teaches three classes. He developed throat cancer and can no longer lecture. His disability policy is not covering him due to his sickness. What type of policy does he likely have?

    a. Own occupation policy.
    b. Split definition policy.
    c. Modified own occupation policy.
    d. Any occupation policy.

4. Diane, an ER surgeon, buys a disability policy with a base benefit of $6,000 and an SIS offset benefit of $1,200. Diane becomes disabled and eventually receives $1,000 in Social Security disability benefits. How much will she receive from the insurance company initially?

    a. $4,800.
    b. $6,000.
    c. $6,200.
    d. $7,200.

5. Lucy, an ER surgeon, buys a disability policy with a base benefit of $6,000 and an SIS offset benefit of $1,200. Lucy becomes disabled and eventually receives $1,000 in Social Security disability benefits. How much will she receive from the insurance company after Social Security benefits begin?

   a. $4,800.
   b. $6,000.
   c. $6,200.
   d. $7,200.

6. Andrea owns and runs a printing company that is organized as an S corporation. Unfortunately, she has an accident with a printing press and is rendered disabled. She receives $4,000 per month in disability payments. The S corporation had paid the premiums on the policy, but reported the payments on her W-2. How much of the benefit is subject to income tax?

   a. $0.
   b. $2,000.
   c. $3,000.
   d. $4,000.

7. Beth is an associate at GWC Attorneys at Law. The firm has a contributory long-term group disability policy. She is required to pay 60 percent of the premiums. If she becomes disabled, her benefits would equal $4,000 per month. Based on this type of plan, which of the following is correct if she were to become disabled?

   a. She will only receive a benefit of $2,400.
   b. The entire benefit will be taxable.
   c. The entire benefit will not be taxable.
   d. She will receive a benefit of $4,000, but $1,600 will be taxable.

8. Allison is a news reporter with a local station. The news station does not provide disability insurance. She purchases a policy through a local insurance agent that provides a benefit of $3,000 per month. If she is in the 30 percent tax bracket, what will her benefits equal after-tax?

   a. $0.
   b. $900.
   c. $2,100.
   d. $3,000.

9. Which of the following provisions may not increase the cost of the policy?

   a. COLA.
   b. Waiver of premium rider.
   c. Automatic increase rider.
   d. SIS benefit.

10. Which of the following is the most favorable definition of total disability in a disability insurance policy?

    a. Any occupation.
    b. Own occupation.
    c. Modified own occupation.
    d. Split definition.

11. Ralph is an engineer at RTQ Enterprises. The firm does not offer disability policies to employees. Therefore, Ralph is considering purchasing a policy on his own. What percent of his salary will an insurance company typically offer as a benefit?

    a. No more than 1.5 times his salary.
    b. No more than 100 percent of his salary.
    c. Approximately 60 percent of his salary.
    d. No more than 33 1/3 percent since he is covered under Social Security.

12. How long would someone have to wait to receive Social Security disability benefits if they qualify?

    a. 5 months.
    b. 6 months.
    c. 12 months.
    d. Benefits are paid immediately if eligible.

13. Roger has a disability policy with a 12-month elimination period. He was in a bizarre accident involving a crane falling on a building causing part of the building's exterior wall to fall on his van. He lost the use of both of his legs in the accident. If his policy has a presumptive total disability coverage provision, when will he begin receiving benefits?

    a. Immediately.
    b. After six months as the provision accelerates the waiting period.
    c. After a one month statutory administrative time period.
    d. He will have to wait the 12 months.

14. Disability policies have many characteristics and provisions. Which of the following is correct regarding policies that are guaranteed renewable versus non-cancelable?

    a. Non-cancelable prevent the insurance company from cancelling the policy as long as the premiums are paid.
    b. Guaranteed renewable and non-cancelable disability policies often have policy increases.
    c. Guaranteed renewable and non-cancelable disability policies always provide protection for the insured until age 65.
    d. Guaranteed renewable policies can experience premium increases based on the health conditions of the insured.

15. Many disability policies that are provided on a group basis have a spit definition. Which of the following describes such a definition?

    a. Disability will be defined based on the duties of the insured.
    b. Disability will be defined based on any occupation that the insured is qualified for based on experience or training.
    c. Disability will be defined based on the specific duties of the insured.
    d. Disability will be defined based on the duties of the insured for a period of time and then based on any occupation that the insured is qualified for based on experience or training.

QUICK QUIZ EXPLANATIONS

Quick Quiz 5.1

1. False. It is far more likely for people to suffer a disability than to die early.
2. True.
3. False. Generally, people should have between 60 and 70 percent of their income protected by disability coverage.

Quick Quiz 5.2

1. False. Morbidity rates fall with age.
2. False. Generally, once an insured becomes disabled and the elimination period has passed, future premiums are waived.
3. False. Own occupation disability insurance is the least sold type of disability insurance.

Quick Quiz 5.3

1. False. A COLA rider will increase the benefit payments once payments have begun based on increases in inflation. There are other riders that will increase coverage based on increases in income.
2. False. An own occupation policy will be more expensive than an any occupation policy because it is more defined in terms of the duties the insured cannot perform.
3. True.
4. False. Incontestability clauses protect the insured from unintentional misrepresentations or errors, generally after two years.

Quick Quiz 5.4

1. True.

CHAPTER

6

LONG-TERM CARE INSURANCE

LEARNING OBJECTIVES

After reading this chapter, you should be able to:

1. Discuss the aging characteristics of the population of the United States.
2. Explain why there is a need for long-term care services.
3. Identify those persons who need long-term care services.
4. Summarize long-term care services.
5. Compare and contrast long-term care services with traditional medical services.
6. Assess the costs of long-term care services.
7. Discuss alternative ways to pay for long-term care services.
8. Evaluate Medicaid as an alternative to long-term care insurance.*
9. Identify personal risk factors when considering long-term care.
10. Justify the financial considerations and trade-offs relative to purchasing long-term care insurance.
11. Identify the basic factors in establishing premiums for long-term care insurance.
12. Describe common policy features in long-term care insurance policies.
13. Identify services that are excludable in long-term care policies.
14. Discuss the merits of inflation protection in a long-term care policy.
15. Identify and describe the optional benefits in a long-term care policy.
16. Discuss the decision of how long a term of benefits to select for a long-term care policy.
17. Explain the income tax benefits of a long-term care policy.
18. Explain the benefits and limitations of tax-qualified long-term care contracts.
19. Identify activities of daily living that can trigger the need for long-term care.*
20. Develop an appropriate long-term care insurance plan based on needs, financial resources, policy coverage, and cost.*
21. Describe the three methods used by an insurer to pay long-term care benefits.

* CFP Board Resource Document - Student-Centered Learning Objectives based upon CFP Board Principal Topics.

INTRODUCTION

The United States has an aging population. The total population was approximately 309 million as of 2010. Of those, 49,572,181 were age 62 or older (2010) and 40,267,984 were age 65 or older. Today, approximately 10,000 persons turn age 65 each day while only 1,077 children are born each day.[1]

The chart below provides a comparison of the aging population from 2001 to 2010 for the total population as well as by gender. The chart reflects a sizable increase in Americans over the age of 60 for both men and women. However, the increase in men over the age of 60 is significantly higher than for women.

1. The United States Census Bureau "Profile of General Population" 2010. Estimate of boomers turning 65 and new births is based on census data.

U.S. Population Totals by Age Group and Sex in the 2010 and 2000 Censuses

EXHIBIT 6.1

	Total Population		Male Population		Female Population	
	2010 Census	2000 Census	2010 Census	2000 Census	2010 Census	2000 Census
Total US Population	**308,745,538**	**281,421,906**	**151,781,326**	**138,053,563**	**156,964,212**	**143,368,343**
60 to 64 years	16,817,924	10,805,447	8,077,500	5,136,627	8,740,424	5,668,820
65 to 69 years	12,435,263	9,533,545	5,852,547	4,400,362	6,582,716	5,133,183
70 to 74 years	9,278,166	8,857,441	4,243,972	3,902,912	5,034,194	4,954,529
75 to 79 years	7,317,795	7,415,813	3,182,388	3,044,456	4,135,407	4,371,357
80 to 84 years	5,743,327	4,945,367	2,294,374	1,834,897	3,448,953	3,110,470
85 years and over	5,493,433	4,239,587	1,789,679	1,226,998	3,703,754	3,012,589
60 and over	57,085,908	45,797,200	25,440,460	19,546,252	31,645,448	26,250,948
65 and over	40,267,984	34,991,753	17,362,960	14,409,625	22,905,024	20,582,128
70 and over	27,832,721	25,458,208	11,510,413	10,009,263	16,322,308	15,448,945
85 and over	5,493,433	4,239,587	1,789,679	1,226,998	3,703,754	3,012,589

2000 to 2010	Increase	Increase %	Increase	Increase %	Increase	Increase %
60 and over	**11,288,708**	25%	**5,894,208**	30%	**5,394,500**	21%
65 and over	**5,276,231**	15%	**2,953,335**	20%	**2,322,896**	11%
70 and over	**2,374,513**	9%	**1,501,150**	15%	**873,363**	6%
85 and over	**1,253,846**	30%	**562,681**	46%	**691,165**	23%

Source: For 2010 Data: U.S. Census Bureau, 2010 Census.

As medical advances increase average life expectancy, advanced age presents additional medical problems for individuals. Prolonged illness or mental impairments, such as senile dementia and Alzheimer's disease, often require an affected individual to receive assistance for both medical and custodial care. Experts suggest that over 40 percent of people over the age of 65 will require skilled nursing home care at some point during their lives. Sometimes, nursing home care is required for rehabilitation after surgery and is usually for a relatively short duration. Cognitive impairments, however, may prevent a person from engaging in normal **activities of daily living (ADLs)** without assistance, and in these circumstances nursing home stays may last for several years. Activities of daily living include eating, bathing, dressing, transferring, toileting, and continence without assistance.

The cost of receiving nursing home care is expensive. Depending on the area of the country where the services are provided, the costs can range from $60,000 to over $120,000 per year. While medical insurance plans may cover a short stay in a skilled nursing home for rehabilitation purposes after surgery or a hospital stay, medical insurance does not cover the costs of extended nursing home stays. Long-term care insurance can be used to cover the cost of nursing home care that exceeds the coverage provided by medical insurance and Medicare. It is estimated that 70 percent of people over the age of 65 will need some form of long-term care including the 40 percent that required skilled nursing care.

Key Concepts

1. Explain how the aging population in the United States impacts the need for long-term care.
2. Understand how the needs for long-term care increase with age.

EXHIBIT 6.2

The Risk of Adverse Events Impacting Those Age 65 and Older

Adverse Events That Occur	Lifetime Possibility Beyond Age 65	
	Men	Women
Major House Fire Fact: There are 369,500 major house fires annually (2013 statistic)*	2.2%	2.6%
Severe Car Accident Fact: Approx. 2.34 million accidents result in death or injury (2012 statistic)**	15.5%	18.0%
Becoming ADL Disabled or Cognitively Impaired (Based on AARP data)	44.0%	72.0%

Source: The 2014 Sourcebook for Long-Term Care Insurance Information / LTC Facts and Figures / Summarization of data compiled by Dawn Helwig, Miliman.
** National Fire Protection Association*
*** U.S. Department of Transportation*

EXHIBIT 6.3

The Need for Long-Term Care

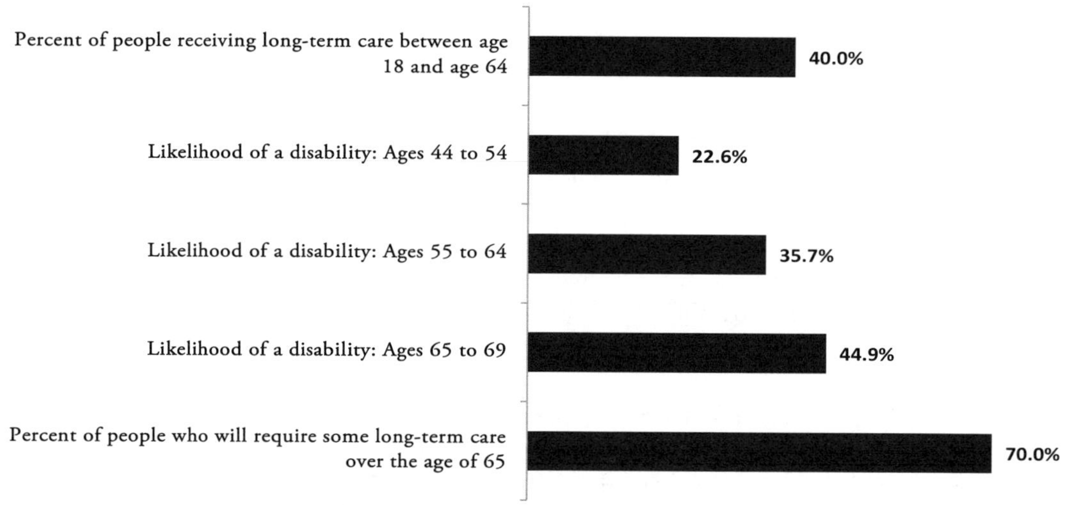

Source: GuidetoLongTermCare.com

This chapter discusses the need for long-term care services, long-term care insurance, the coverages and benefits under these policies, and alternatives to long-term care insurance.

Long-Term Care Services

Key Concepts

1. Describe long-term care services.
2. Explain the costs of long-term care services.
3. Identify the activities of daily living and the instrumental activities of daily living.

Long-term care is a range of personal care and supportive services that a person might need if they were unable to care for themselves because of illness, disability, or cognitive impairment. Long-term care services meet the needs of frail, older people and other adults who lack the capacity for self care.

Long-term care services differ from traditional medical care in that **traditional medical care** attempts to treat or cure illnesses. Long-term care usually does not attempt to improve the medical condition of the recipient but rather helps to maintain lifestyle. Long-term care services help the recipient to manage routine activities of daily living (ADLs) such as eating, bathing, and dressing. Long-term care services can also assist a person who needs supervision, protection, or reminders to take medicine or perform other activities. Thus, long-term care services include ADLs and instrumental activities of daily living (IADLs) such as medication management, housework, and health maintenance tasks.

ADLs vs IADLs

EXHIBIT 6.4

Activities of Daily Living (ADLs)	Instrumental Activities of Daily Living (IADLs)
• Eating	• Medicine Management
• Bathing	• Shopping
• Dressing	• Preparing Meals
• Transferring	• Housekeeping
• Toileting	• Doing Laundry
• Continence	• Using Transportation
	• Handling Finances

Long-term care services are provided in a variety of settings. Long-term care services may be provided in the home, in the community, in a residential setting, or in an institutional setting (nursing home). In the home, the provider is either a home health agency or family or friend. In the community, long-term care services can be provided at an adult day care. In a residential setting, long-term care services are provided by assisted living communities. Nursing homes provide institutional care.

As mentioned above, the average stay for LTC patients may be relatively short or it may extend for years. According to the 2004 National Nursing Home Survey, the average stay in a nursing home is over two years. The next section discusses the cost of long-term care services. However, it is important to keep in mind that many stays in these facilities are relatively short and often long-term care services are provided by family members. Therefore, while the cost of long-term care can be enormous for some patients, it is fairly minimal for many others.

The Cost of Long-Term Care Services

Long-term care services can be expensive. The cost depends on the amount of care and the type of care that one receives. It also depends on where the care is received (both the type of setting and the geographical location) and what type of medical professional provides the service.

EXHIBIT 6.5

Long-Term Care Room Rates (2014)

Type of Facility	Median Daily Rates	Median Annual Rates	Daily Range of Rates Across All States	
			Low	High
Nursing Home - Private	$240	$87,600	$104	$954
Nursing Home - Semi-Private	$212	$77,380	$94	$800
Assisted Living	$115	$42,000	$25	$347

Source: Genworth 2014 Cost of Care Survey

EXHIBIT 6.6

Long-Term Care Assistance Rates (2014)

	Median Rate	Range
Home Health Aides	$20/hr.	$8 - $39/hr.
Homemaker / Companion	$19/hr.	$8 - $39/hr.
Adult Day Services	$65/hr.	$12 - $215/day

Source: Genworth 2014 Cost of Care Survey

Paying for Long-Term Care Services

Given the pervasive need for long-term care for our elderly, the question arises as to how this service is provided. Often, an unpaid caregiver, such as a family member or friend, provides long-term care services. In many other cases, people must pay for the service. There are four common methods for paying for long-term care services. These are:

1. Medicare
2. Medicaid
3. Personal assets and savings
4. Long-term care insurance

Key Concepts

1. Identify the four common methods for paying for long-term care services.
2. Explain why Medicare is not an appropriate option to pay for long-term care services.
3. Describe what options are available to those persons who do not have long-term care insurance and who find themselves in need of long-term care.
4. Understand the limitations of Medicare and Medicaid for long-term care services.

Medicare

Medicare is a federal program that pays for healthcare for persons over age 65 and for people under age 65 with disabilities. Medicare generally does not cover long-term care services. However, Medicare will help pay for a short stay in a skilled nursing facility, for hospice care, or for home health care if the recipient meets the following conditions:

- Has had a recent prior hospital stay of at least three days
- Is admitted to a Medicare-certified nursing facility within 30 days of the prior hospital stay

- Needs skilled care, such as skilled nursing services, physical therapy, or other types of therapy, as a result of some medical condition that caused the hospital stay

If all of these conditions are met, Medicare will pay for some of the costs up to 100 days. However, Medicare payments are limited and, thus, are inadequate to provide for extended care needs as illustrated in the following exhibit.

EXHIBIT 6.7

Skilled Nursing Facility Time Line (2015)

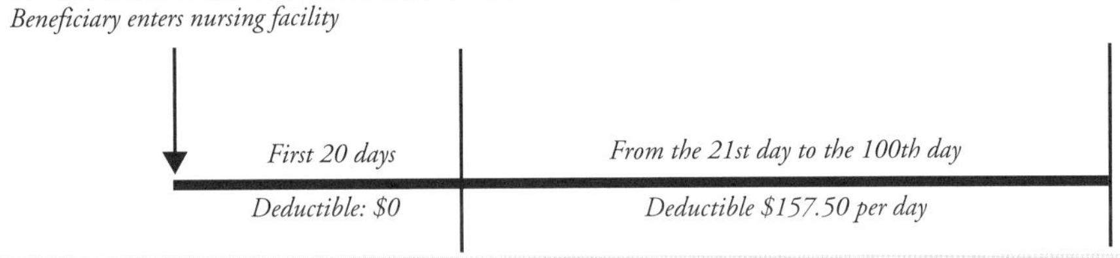

Medicaid

Title XIX of the Social Security Act is a Federal/State entitlement program that pays for medical assistance for certain individuals and families with low incomes and resources. This program, known as **Medicaid**, became law in 1965 as a cooperative venture jointly funded by the Federal and State governments (including the District of Columbia and the Territories) to assist States in furnishing medical assistance to eligible needy persons. Medicaid is the largest source of funding for medical and health-related services for America's poorest people.

Within broad national guidelines established by Federal statutes, regulations, and policies, each State establishes its own eligibility standards; determines the type, amount, duration, and scope of services; sets the rate of payment for services; and administers its own program. Medicaid policies for eligibility, services, and payment are complex and vary considerably, even among states of similar size or geographic proximity. Thus, a person who is eligible for Medicaid in one state may not be eligible in another state, and the services provided by one state may differ considerably in amount, duration, or scope from services provided in a similar or neighboring state. In addition, state legislatures may change Medicaid eligibility, services, and/or reimbursement at any time.

A state's Medicaid program must offer medical assistance for certain basic services to most categorically needy populations. These services generally include the following:

- Inpatient hospital services
- Outpatient hospital services
- Pregnancy-related services, including prenatal care and 60 days postpartum pregnancy-related services
- Vaccines for children
- Physician services
- Nursing facility services for persons aged 21 or older
- Family planning services and supplies
- Nurse-midwife services
- Rural health clinic services
- Home health care for persons eligible for skilled-nursing services
- Laboratory and x-ray services
- Pediatric and family nurse practitioner services
- Federally qualified health-center (FQHC) services, and ambulatory services of an FQHC that would be available in other settings
- Early and periodic screening, diagnostic, and treatment (EPSDT) services for children under age 21

In addition, states may also receive Federal matching funds to provide certain optional services.

While Medicaid will pay for most long-term care expenses for eligible low-income persons, it is often difficult to qualify for the government service. To be eligible, a person must meet both the general requirements as well as meet the financial requirements. In most cases, a person must be one of the following to meet the general requirements:

- Be age 65 or older
- Have a permanent disability as that term is defined by the Social Security Administration
- Be blind
- Be a pregnant woman
- Be a child, or the parent or caretaker of a child

A person must have limited income and limited assets to meet the financial requirements for Medicaid. The amount of income a person can have varies by state, and also varies depending on which eligibility groups each state covers. When the state determines a person's financial eligibility for Medicaid, the state will count certain types of income, but not all of it. A person's income includes these sources:

- Regular benefit payments such as Social Security retirement or disability payments
- Veterans benefits
- Pensions
- Salaries
- Wages
- Interest from bank accounts and certificates of deposit
- Dividends from stocks and bonds

However, Medicaid generally does not count such things as:

- Nutritional assistance (food stamps)
- Housing assistance provided by the federal government
- Home energy assistance

There is another option for those individuals whose income exceeds the state limits, called the special income level group. The special income level group is an optional group for states, meaning that states can choose to cover or not cover this group. Over 40 states have chosen to cover this group though, so it is widely available as a pathway to receiving long-term care services under Medicaid. This group is aimed specifically at people who need long-term care services. The income requirement is significantly higher for this group, but receiving benefits under this category may require the person to "share in the cost" of the service provided. The group has the same general requirements and similar asset requirements.

In the process of a state determining a person's financial eligibility for Medicaid, certain types of assets are counted, while others are excluded. During the Medicaid application process, applicants must provide documentation of the assets they own.

The amount of countable assets a person can have and still qualify for Medicaid varies from state to state. In most states a person can retain about $2,000 in countable assets, and married couples that are still living in the same household can retain about $3,000 in countable assets. This may not sound like much, but it is important to understand that many assets are not counted at all when determining Medicaid eligibility. Assets that are usually counted for eligibility include:

- Checking and savings accounts
- Stocks and bonds
- Certificates of deposit
- Real property other than your primary residence
- Additional motor vehicles if you have more than one

Assets that do not get counted for eligibility include the following:

- Primary residence
- Personal property and household belongings
- One motor vehicle
- Life insurance with a face value under $1,500
- Up to $1,500 in funds set aside for burial
- Certain burial arrangements such as pre-need burial agreements
- Assets held in specific kinds of trusts

A personal residence is often a person's largest and most valuable asset and is not considered for Medicaid edibility purposes. However, there are limits as to the amount of equity that a person can maintain and still qualify for Medicaid. In 2013, the equity limit is in excess of $500,000. Medicaid must deny benefits above this limit.[2]

Middle-income individuals generally cannot qualify for Medicaid, and generally do not have enough resources to adequately self-insure. The Deficit Reduction Act of 2005 (DRA) created the Qualified State Long Term Care Partnership program to encourage more people to purchase long-term care insurance. Residents of some states may be able to find long-term care coverage through

2. States have the option of using a higher limit, which can be as high as $802,000 in 2013. Most states have chosen to use the lower limit, but some states, especially in parts of the country where housing is expensive, use the higher amount. These limits are adjusted each year to account for inflation. (source: http://longtermcare.gov/medicare-medicaid-more/medicaid/medicaid-eligibility/financial-requirements-assets/)

a State Partnership Program that links special Partnership-qualified (PQ) long-term policies provided by private insurance companies with Medicaid. These PQ policies:

- Help people purchase shorter term, more complete long-term care insurance
- Include inflation protection, so the dollar amount of benefits received can be higher than the amount of insurance coverage purchased
- Allow people to apply for Medicaid under modified eligibility rules if there is continued need for long-term care after the policy maximum is reached
- Include a special "asset disregard" feature that allows individuals to keep assets like personal savings above the usual $2,000 Medicaid limit

The following example shows how a Partnership-qualified policy works:

EXAMPLE 6.1

Walter, a single man, purchases a Partnership policy with a value of $100,000. Some years later he receives benefits under that policy up to the policy's lifetime maximum coverage (adjusted for inflation) equaling $150,000.

Walter eventually requires more long-term care services, and applies for Medicaid. If Walter's policy was not a Partnership-qualified policy, in order to qualify for Medicaid, he would be entitled to keep only $2,000 in assets. He would have to spend down any assets over and above this amount.

However, because Walter bought a Partnership-qualified policy, he can keep $152,000 in assets and the state will not recover those funds after his death. Walter would only have to spend down his assets over and above the $152,000 in order to be eligible for Medicaid.

Since Partnership-qualified policies must include inflation protection, the amount of the benefits received can be higher than the amount of insurance protection purchased. For example, if you have a Partnership-qualified long-term care insurance policy and receive $100,000 in benefits from it, you can apply for Medicaid and, if eligible, retain $100,000 worth of assets over and above the state's Medicaid asset threshold. In most states the asset limit is $2,000 for a single person. Asset limits for married couples are often higher.

States must certify that partnership policies meet the specific requirements for their partnership program, including that those who sell partnership policies are trained and understand how these policies relate to public and private coverage options.

Medicaid Planning and the Look Back Period

The Medicaid program provides coverage for long-term care services for individuals who are unable to afford it. Some individuals, with assistance from financial planners and attorneys, have found ways of arranging assets so that the assets are preserved for the individual and/or family members, but are not countable when Medicaid eligibility is determined. The Deficit Reduction Act of 2005 (DRA) addresses key areas related to transfers of assets for less than fair market value and makes it more difficult for individuals with the resources to pay for their own long-term care services to inappropriately transfer assets in order to qualify for Medicaid.

When an individual applies for Medicaid coverage for long-term care, States conduct a review, or "look-back," to determine whether the individual (or his or her spouse) transferred assets (e.g., cash gifts to children, transferring home ownership) to another person or party for less than fair market value (FMV). The DRA lengthened the "look-back period" to 60 months (five years) prior to the date the individual applied for Medicaid.

When individuals transfer assets at less than the FMV they are subject to a penalty that delays the date they can qualify to receive Medicaid long-term care services. Previously the penalty period began with the month the assets were transferred. However, under the DRA, the penalty period, for transfers made on or after February 8, 2006, begins on either the date of the asset transfer, or the date the individual enters a nursing home and is found eligible for coverage of institutional level services that Medicaid would pay for were it not for the imposition of a transfer penalty-whichever is later.

Medicaid planning is often undertaken to preserve assets for children or relatives, or to preserve assets for a spouse. It is also done to preserve assets that could be used to enhance care above what is provided for under Medicaid. There is a valid question as to whether Medicaid planning is ethical and/or moral. There are many advisors and attorneys who assist people in transferring assets to qualify for Medicaid benefits. There are also many advisors and attorneys who believe it is unethical and will not engage in this type of planning. Consider the following two examples:

EXAMPLE 6.2

Barry worked as a plumber since he was 18 years old. He worked hard his entire life and has saved a fair amount of money by not going on vacations, eating at home, and living modestly. He just turned age 65 and has been diagnosed with Alzheimer's disease. He had hoped that he would be able to leave some of his money to his daughter for his grandson's college education. However, he is concerned that he will spend his life's savings on long-term care. He is also concerned that his wife will be without the necessary funds to care for her needs.

EXAMPLE 6.3

Larry worked as a plumber since he was 18 years old. He worked hard his entire life, but also enjoyed his life by buying expensive cars, vacationing every change he had, and always buying the latest in fashion trends. While he has earned a significant amount of money over his career, he has almost nothing saved and lives in an apartment. He just turned age 65 and has been diagnosed with Alzheimer's disease. He is very concerned about the progressiveness of the disease and the prospect of needing long-term care and not being able to afford it.

Despite the fact that Larry has been at least somewhat irresponsible in terms of spending, he is entitled to Medicaid. From an ethical perspective, the case can be made that Medicaid is designed for the poor and therefore Larry should receive it and Barry should not. This outcome may or may not be palatable. Barry, on the other hand, is left with the choice of spending down his assets (using them for long-term care needs) and then applying for Medicaid or engaging in Medicaid planning.

In Helvering v. Gregory, Judge Learned Hand famously wrote about tax planning: "Any one may so arrange his affairs that his taxes shall be as low as possible; he is not bound to choose that pattern which will best pay the Treasury; there is not even a patriotic duty to increase one's taxes." Considering this quote and the idea of preserving assets for a spouse, one might conclude that

Medicaid planning is not unethical. Some might even conclude that Medicaid planning is not only ethical, but also prudent. However, what is certain is that there is an ethical question that must be answered before undertaking this type of planning.

Special Needs Trust

The assets of certain kinds of trusts are not considered for purposes of determining eligibility for Medicaid. These trusts are generally classified as special needs trusts. A **special needs trust** is a specific type of trust that is used to provide benefits to persons or beneficiaries with special needs. Typically, these trusts are established to ensure that benefits available from federal and state agencies are preserved and maintained. The more common special needs trusts are the Third Party Special Needs Trust, the self settled type trust that is established and exempt under 42 U.S.C. Sec. 1396p(d)(4)(A), and what is referred to as a pooled trust, which is exempt under 42 U.S.C. Sec. 1396p(d)(4)(C).

A third party special needs trust is sometimes referred to as a family trust as the trust is a receptacle for funds from a parent, guardian or other family member. The assets of these trusts, if properly structured, are not counted or considered for purposes of available benefits for the beneficiary.

These trusts can be funded by a parent or guardian during life or at death and are sometimes funded through the proceeds from a life insurance policy. The funds are contributed to a trust by the grantor or settlor for the benefit of the person with the special needs (beneficiary). The assets were never the property of the beneficiary and are therefore not counted as assets for purposes of federal benefits.

The trust must be established to not provide food, shelter or any asset that could be converted into food or shelter, such as cash. It may provide for other benefits, such as medical treatment, therapy, education, travel, computer equipment, etc. These types of benefits can improve the lifestyle of the beneficiary and not interfere with governmental benefits.

The assets of the other two trusts are also ignored for Medicaid purposes. However, these two trusts require that assets remaining in the trust be available for state recovery to the extent that state funds were used to care for the beneficiary.

Quick Quiz 6.1

1. Long-term care insurance does not cover hospice care.
   a. True
   b. False

2. Because everyone qualifies for Medicaid, long-term care insurance is only for those who want more choices in long-term care than Medicaid offers.
   a. True
   b. False

3. If Bob had a home worth $300,000, it is possible he could qualify for Medicaid.
   a. True
   b. False

4. Paying for long-term care services out of pocket is not a wise choice for anyone.
   a. True
   b. False

5. Activities of daily living include eating, bathing, dressing, transferring, toileting, continence and exercising.
   a. True
   b. False

False, False, True, False, False.

Personal Assets and Savings

Paying for long-term care out of personal savings can be an option for some. However, it depends on how long the services are needed. In many cases, long-term care services may only be needed for a short period of time. In other cases, individuals may need the service for an extended period of time. In these cases, paying for the service can be financially devastating. However, once a person's assets are depleted, they may become eligible for Medicaid.

It is important to keep in mind that while paying for long-term care services out of savings is devastating to the person who needs the care, it can also be devastating to the person's spouse. Couples accumulate assets together over many years to pay for their needs (and wants) during retirement. If long-term care is needed for one spouse an extended period of time, it can be a financial disaster for the other spouse, who could live for years or decades.

Long-Term Care Insurance

Long-term care insurance is an option that can mitigate the risks of needing and having to pay for long-term care for an extended period of time. Unlike traditional health insurance, long-term care insurance is designed to cover long-term services and supports, including personal and custodial care in a variety of settings. While health insurance may pay the entire bill for a week at a hospital, it will not pay for an indefinite stay at a nursing home. Long-term care insurance pays for home health care, nursing home stays, and hospice care. Long-term care insurance policies have many choices, limitations, and costs that need to be considered.

THE NEED FOR LONG-TERM CARE INSURANCE

Not everyone will need long-term care or long-term care insurance. However, as the average age of the United States population is increasing, and as the life expectancy is increasing, the need for both long-term care and long-term insurance is also increasing.

POPULATION STATISTICS FOR THE UNITED STATES

There are more than 40 million persons over age 65 in the United States. Approximately 70 percent or 28 million will need long-term care services. As of 2010, there were 6.29 million persons receiving Medicaid for the aged. There are 7.8 million people (2009) who have net worth (excluding housing) equal to or greater than \$1 million.

These higher net-worth persons can be presumed to be able to self-insure against the risk of long-term care needs. Another five million could be added to the 7.8 million if the net worth horizon was reduced to \$500,000.[3] The remainder, more than 20 million, people will not qualify for Medicaid and are not sufficiently wealthy to self-insure against the risk of needing long-term care services.

3. Spectrum Group Surveys (2010).

EXAMPLE 6.4

Sal and Darla met while living in a retirement community in Florida. Sal, who is 6'2" and over 200 pounds, was a ship captain on the great lakes. Darla, who is 5'2", was a social worker. They were married 20 years ago when Darla was 75 years old and Sal was 70. Today, they live in a retirement complex in South Florida that offers independent living, assisted living, as well as skilled care and rehab services. Sal, who can see partially but is legally blind, has recently developed dementia and has urinary incontinence. At 95, Darla is incapable of caring for Sal. He needs help getting in and out of bed, getting dressed, and is unaware of his circumstances. However, Sal is perfectly healthy otherwise and is expected to live for another five years or more. Sal needs long-term care but does not have long-term care insurance. They have approximately $400,000 in savings. Based on their assets, he is unlikely to qualify for Medicaid and will have to spend his assets for care. Given the cost of care and his life expectancy, he may outlive their resources. In addition, he is likely to spend the money that would have been used to provide for Darla.

KEY CONCEPTS

1. Understand the U.S. population long-term care statistics.
2. Explain the various factors that influence the need for long-term care.
3. Identify the two primary issues involved in choosing to purchase long-term care insurance.

While many people spend down their assets to meet Medicaid thresholds, many others should consider purchasing long-term care insurance. Their alternative is to self-insure and risk financial disaster. The risk of financial disaster is not only applicable to the spouse who is in need of long-term care, but also the other spouse who may live for years and be in desperate need of financial resources. It is important to consider the needs of both spouses when making the decision to purchase LTC insurance.

In 2012, about 58,500 paid regulated long-term care service providers served about eight million people in the United States. Long-term care services were provided by 4,800 adult day service centers, 12,200 home health agencies, 3,700 hospices, 15,700 nursing homes, and 22,200 assisted living and similar residential care communities. Each day in 2012, there were 273,200 participants enrolled in adult day service centers, 1,383,700 residents in nursing homes, and 713,300 residents in residential care communities. In 2011, approximately 4,742,500 patients received services from home health agencies, and 1,244,500 patients received services from hospices.[4]

Medicaid paid for nearly one-third of the nation's $158 billion of nursing home expenditures in 2012. Federal law discourages individuals from reducing their countable assets, for example by transferring them to family members, to qualify for Medicaid. Although Congress has acted multiple times to address financial eligibility requirements for Medicaid coverage of nursing home care, methods continue to exist through which individuals, sometimes with the help of attorneys, reduce their assets and qualify for Medicaid.[5]

4. Harris-Kojetin L, Sengupta M, Park-Lee E, Valverde R. Long-term care services in the United States: 2013 overview. National health care statistics reports; no 1. Hyattsville, MD: National Center for Health Statistics. 2013.
5. GAO HIghlights, Highlights od GAO-14-473.

Private long-term care insurance (LTCI) paid for less then 12 percent of all long-term care costs in 2012.[6] However, for those who own LTCI, one study reports that the benefits pay for between 60-75 percent of care at any given time.[7] In 2010, between seven and nine million people had LTCI. [8]

Factors that Influence the Need for Long-Term Care Insurance

Long-term care insurance helps protect accumulated assets against the risk of the high cost of extended long-term care. Long-term care insurance makes economic sense if the person has assets to protect. Otherwise, the individual would qualify for Medicaid. Those who have assets that they intend to bequeath to heirs or preserve for a spouse should consider long-term care insurance.

If long-term care insurance is not affordable, a person might be better off simply spending down his or her assets to qualify for Medicaid. To decide whether long-term care insurance is appropriate, one should consider personal risk factors, financial considerations, and other available alternatives, such as living with family.

Personal Risk Factors

Personal risk factors include life expectancy, gender, family situation, and family health history.

Life Expectancy

The longer a person lives, the more likely he is to need long-term care services. An evaluation of the immediate and surrounding family for a tendency for long life expectancy will help to clarify this factor.

If a person is expected to have a long life expectancy (perhaps due to family history or current health status), long-term care insurance should be considered. In fact, the longer the person's life expectancy, the greater the need for long-term care insurance. Recall that 40 percent of adults over the age of 65 will need nursing home care at some point during their lifetimes. The general health of the family should also be considered. If older family members suffer from health ailments that are likely to require nursing home care, such as Alzheimer's disease or senile dementia, the person's risk of developing one of these conditions might be greater than average, suggesting a greater need for long-term care insurance.

Gender

Women are much more likely to need long-term care insurance than are men, because women have longer life expectancies.

Family Situation

If a person has a spouse, adult children, or other family members who can and will care for them at home, he or she may not need a long-term care insurance policy that pays for home health services. Instead, such a person may want to consider a long-term care policy that pays only for facility based services such as assisted living and skilled nursing care.

6. The George Washington University, National Health Policy Forum, "National Spending for Long-Term Services and Supports (LTSS)" (Washington DC: The George Washington University, February 2012).
7. Assistant Secretary for Planning and Evaluation, "Private Long-Term Care Insurance: Following an Admission Cohort over 28 months to Track Claim Experience, Service Use and Transitions: (Washington, DC: Assistant Secretary for Planning and Evaluation, April 2008).
8. AHIP, "Who Buys Long-Term Care Insurance in 2010-2011?" (Washington, DC: AHIP, March 2012).

Family Health History

A person may have a probability of greater need for long-term care if chronic or debilitating health conditions historically run in the family.

Financial Considerations

Long-term care premiums are typically less expensive if a policy is purchased when the insured is younger. The premiums are usually paid until death or until benefits have begun. However, some policies have paid up provisions (e.g., paid up in 20 years). When considering the payment of long-term care insurance premiums, one should consider how current and retirement income will be affected by the payments. It is beneficial to forecast the likely increase in premium costs caused by waiting until a later age to purchase a long-term care insurance policy. Many financial and insurance professionals suggest that the optimal time to purchase a long-term care policy is between the ages of 55 and 65.

The person's financial status is also an important factor when considering long-term care insurance. If long-term care services are needed, and the person does not have sufficient insurance to cover the costs, the person's assets may have to be liquidated

Persons with relatively low net worth and low income may not be able to afford long-term care insurance premiums. Long-term care insurance premiums can be expensive, particularly at older ages, and if the premium represents a significant portion of the person's net worth or income, it may not be an appropriate risk management tool. People with lower amounts of assets have less to lose by self-insuring. Once their assets are depleted, they may be able to qualify for long-term care coverage through Medicaid.

Persons with moderate and above levels of net worth may wish to protect those assets for the benefit of family members (spouse and descendants), and therefore may not want to spend down assets to pay for long-term care needs. Long-term care insurance may be an appropriate solution for these persons, since the risk of paying for long-term care needs is transferred to an insurance company in return for premium payments. Moderate to high net worth clients with significant bequest motives should also consider long-term care insurance as a risk transfer tool.

Some planners believe that wealthy individuals do not need long-term care insurance because they can afford to self-insure and still transfer some of their assets to their heirs. Because long-term care insurance premiums, particularly at older ages, are perceived to be expensive, risk retention is viewed as one alternative choice. However, it may be prudent for high net worth individuals to purchase and maintain long-term care insurance, particularly when bequest motives are strong. In order to self-insure, the person would have to retain sufficient assets to pay for care over an extended period of time, and those assets would have to be retained until death since many long-term care expenses are often incurred shortly before death. By retaining assets to self-insure against long-term care risk, the person cannot transfer those assets to family members as part of a lifetime gifting strategy. This approach could result in higher gift and estate tax consequences for the family upon the person's death.

Paying long-term care premiums so that the insurance company will cover those costs will free-up assets that can be used for transfer tax planning purposes and may result in significant savings of gift and estate taxes. Instead of considering the long-term care premiums solely in dollar terms, it may be practical for higher net worth individuals to consider the premiums as a percentage of their asset portfolio being protected with the long-term care insurance premiums. If the dollar amount of the premium is high, but that dollar amount only represents a small amount of assets when compared to the size of the person's asset base, incurring the premium to protect the entire asset base may be reasonable, and doing so may also create an opportunity for gift and estate planning. In addition, premium payments reduce a person's estate, which may be beneficial from a transfer tax perspective.

Quick Quiz 6.2

1. More than 40 million people in the United States are over the age of 65.
   a. True
   b. False

2. Medicaid pays for approximately 80 percent of the nation's nursing home expenditures.
   a. True
   b. False

3. Men are more likely to need long-term care insurance than women.
   a. True
   b. False

4. Important factors in determining a need for long-term care insurance include the health of the person, the life expectancy of the person and the person's financial situation.
   a. True
   b. False

True, False, False, True.

One final consideration when determining whether or not to purchase long-term care insurance is whether the person wishes to retain the ability to choose care providers. If a person decides not to purchase long-term care insurance and self-insures, he or she can go on public assistance (Medicaid) once his or her assets are spent down. However, the person will receive care at the facility where the first bed becomes available. There is great disparity in the quality of care at various locations, particularly when considering long-term care services. If the person relies on public assistance to pay for these costs, he or she loses the ability to choose the facility where care will be provided. Individuals who purchase long-term care insurance, however, have a choice in the care provider, and can ensure that they will receive a higher quality of care. For some people, having the ability to choose the care provider is a more important consideration than preserving assets for family members or avoiding taxes and should be considered when developing a comprehensive financial plan.

While many nursing homes are adequate, many others have serious deficiencies. The Centers for Medicare & Medicaid Services (CMS) contracts with state survey agencies to conduct inspections, known as standard surveys, and complaint investigations to determine whether nursing homes are complying with federal quality standards. Nursing homes must meet those standards to participate in Medicare and Medicaid. GAO (Government Accountability Office) reports have found that some nursing homes are chronically noncompliant; that is, they have been cited repeatedly by state survey agencies for serious deficiencies such as residents having preventable pressure sores that harmed them or put them at risk of death or serious injury. It is important to research facilities before choosing one for a loved one.

Other Possible Alternatives

It is possible that a person can depend on family or friends to provide long-term care services. In fact, care in the home by a spouse or a child is a very common form of long-term care in the U.S. However, such services and support are generally limited to activities that do not require a skilled background. Often the needs of the person can be challenging to family caregivers because they are not properly equipped or trained. Many family caregivers struggle with their own emotional and physical health when spending countless hours caring for a loved one, and it is often necessary to retain paid help with lifting, walking, bathing, incontinence, toileting, dressing and supervision.

LONG-TERM CARE INSURANCE

As with other financial services products, long-term care insurance has many aspects that must be considered before choosing to purchase a long-term care policy. The various aspects of long-term care insurance policies are discussed below.

LONG-TERM CARE PREMIUM FACTORS

Long-term care premiums are initially based on several factors including the amount and duration of coverage selected, age, gender, the health of the person insured, the area in which he or she lives, and the elimination period.[9] Premium pricing is further affected by inflation and other riders added to the policy.

EXHIBIT 6.8

LONG-TERM CARE PREMIUM VARIABLE

Age and Gender
Benefits (amount and duration)
Health Characteristics
Geographical Location
Elimination Periods
Inflation Protection
Additional Riders

EXHIBIT 6.9

COMMON FEATURES OF LONG-TERM CARE INSURANCE POLICIES

Renewability - Guaranteed renewability
Nonforfeitures Benefits - Return of Premium or Shortened Benefit Period
Waiver of premium while receiving benefits

The policy premium is strictly related to the age and gender of the insured, the benefits provided and inflation protection. As the age of the insured increases, so does the premium. Since 2013, LTC insurance companies are charging higher premiums for women, since more benefits are historically paid to women than to men. As the benefits increase, so does the premium. Inflation protection also increases the premium. The elimination period, however, is inversely related. As the elimination period increases, the premium will decrease.

9. LTC insurance companies began charging higher premiums for women in 2013 due to the higher likelihood of needing the benefits. Genworth Financial, the first company to begin charging women higher premiums, states that women receive approximately 67 percent of LTC benefits.

Long-Term Care Features and Benefits

Long-term care insurance has a variety of features and benefits that are important to understand. Some of these features and benefits are mandatory, while others are optional. Below is a discussion of these characteristics.

Key Concepts

1. Identify the factors that affect premiums for long-term care insurance.
2. Explain the type of benefits provided under long-term care policies.
3. Contrast tax-qualified contracts from those that are not qualified.
4. Recognize required and optional features of long-term care policies.
5. Provide examples of the ways benefit limits may be specified in a long-term care policy.

Renewals and Cancellations

Long-term care policies are **guaranteed renewable**. This means the insurance company must renew the policy each year as long as premiums are paid. Policies can be canceled at any time by notifying the insurance company. Unearned premium payments are returned if the policy is canceled. Premiums are paid on a monthly, quarterly, or annual basis. Unearned premium return does not apply to a single premium policy or to policies that are paid in full in one to four years. Even policies that are paid in full from 5 to 10 years are subject to a return of premium provision.

After a long-term care policy has been in force for a period of two years, the insurer cannot cancel and cannot refuse to pay claims because there was incorrect information provided in the application unless that information is fraudulent. If the policy has been in force for less than two years, the insurer can deny a valid claim or cancel the policy if it can prove fraud or intentional misrepresentation of a material fact.

Types of Care

While long-term care insurance policies are often viewed as policies that cover skilled nursing home costs, the benefits provided under the policy are generally much more extensive, including custodial care, home health care, hospice care, adult day care, assisted living facilities, and other long-term care services.

Skilled Nursing Care

Skilled nursing care refers to a level of care that includes services that can only be performed safely and correctly by a licensed nurse (either a registered nurse or a licensed practical nurse), doctor or therapist. Inpatient care refers to healthcare for those admitted to a hospital or skilled nursing facility.

Custodial Care

Custodial care refers to non-skilled, personal care, such as help with activities of daily living (eating, bathing, transferring, dressing, toileting, and continence). A healthy individual with a cognitive impairment, for example, may not need constant medical attention, but may need assistance so that he or she does not pose a risk to himself, herself, or others.

Home Heath Care

If given the choice, most individuals prefer to live at home rather than move into a nursing home. Most long-term care policies will pay for the cost of care provided at home (referred to as a **home health care benefit**). Home heath care may encompass limited part-time or intermittent skilled nursing care and home health aide services, physical therapy, occupational therapy, speech-language pathology services, medical social services, durable medical equipment (such as wheelchairs, hospital beds, oxygen, and walkers), medical supplies, and other services provided in the patient's home.

Hospice Care

For individuals with incurable illnesses who are in the terminal stages of life, long-term care insurance policies typically pay for the cost of hospice care. **Hospice care** typically utilizes a team-oriented approach to address medical, physical, social, emotional, and spiritual needs of the terminally ill. Hospice also provides support to the patient's family or caregiver. Hospice care is generally short-term, supportive care for individuals who have a life expectancy of six months or less. Hospice care does not provide therapeutic treatment (treatment designed to cure the individual of their condition), but rather provides pain management treatment and psychological and spiritual support services for patients to permit them to die with dignity and comfort. Hospice services, under most policies, can be provided in a dedicated hospice facility, in a hospital, or at the recipient's home.

Adult Day Care Services

A policy may pay for **adult day-care** services. Individuals needing supervision who live with other family members may not need assistance 24 hours a day. Adult day care facilities provide supervision during the day at a community-based center while caretaker family members are at work. Programs address the individual needs of functionally or cognitively impaired adults. These structured, comprehensive programs provide social and support services in a protective setting during any part of a day, but not 24-hour care. Many adult day service programs include health-related services. Given the opportunity, insurance companies prefer to pay for lower-cost alternatives rather than pay for skilled nursing or custodial care.

Assisted Living Facility

A policy may pay for all or part of the costs of an **assisted living facility**. An assisted living facility is a residential living arrangement that provides individualized personal care, assistance with activities of daily living, help with medications, and services such as laundry and housekeeping. Facilities may also provide health and medical care, but care is not as intensive as care offered at a nursing home. Types and sizes of facilities vary, ranging from small homes to large apartment-style complexes. Levels of care and services also vary. Assisted living facilities allow people to remain relatively independent.

Long-Term Care Services

Long-term care services include medical and non-medical care for people with chronic illnesses or disabilities. Most long-term care services assist people with activities of daily living. Long-term care can be provided at home, in the community, or in a facility. For purposes of Medicaid eligibility and payment, long-term care services are those provided to an individual who requires a level of care equivalent to that received in a nursing facility.

Skilled Care and Immediate Care Facilities

A **skilled care facility** provides the highest level of service combining both daily medical and custodial care. An **intermediate-care** nursing facility typically provides custodial care along with intermittent, as opposed to daily, medical care. Services in either a skilled-care or intermediate-care facility are ordered by a physician, and medical treatments are provided under the supervision of a physician.

Coverage

A long-term care policy may pay different dollar amounts for different types of long-term care services. Policies usually pay benefits by the day, week, or month. For example, a policy that pays with the **expense - incurred method** might pay a daily nursing home benefit of up to $200, a weekly benefit of up to $1,400, or a monthly benefit of up to $6,000. The advantage of a monthly benefit period is that the policyholder may receive higher benefits. Consider the following example.

EXAMPLE 6.5

> Mike, who recently had surgery, has a long-term care policy and uses his home health-care benefit to have a licensed aide assist him at home three times each week. Each visit costs $400. If Mike has a daily benefit of $150, he would have to pay $250 out of pocket for each visit. This cost is approximately $3,000 for an entire 30 day month. However, with a monthly benefit of $4,500, his out of pocket cost would only be $300 (12 x $400 = $4,800 - $4,500 = $300). As a result, daily benefit policies are generally cheaper.

If a policy covers home healthcare, the benefit is usually a percentage of the benefit for skilled nursing home care. For example, a policy with a $200 per day benefit for skilled nursing home care may only pay $100 per day for home healthcare. However, many policies pay the same benefit amount for home care as for skilled nursing home care.

An insured can usually choose the benefit amounts. It is important that the insured knows the cost of skilled nursing care, assisted living homes, and home healthcare in the local market before choosing benefit amounts.

Most long-term care policies limit the total amount of benefits that can be paid over the life of the policy. Some policies state the maximum benefit limit in terms of years. Other policies state the maximum benefit limit in terms of dollars. The maximum benefit limit is referred to as the **maximum lifetime benefit** or the **total plan benefit**.

While most skilled nursing home stays are relatively short, there are some illnesses (Alzheimer's) that can last several years or longer. Therefore, selecting the appropriate total amount of coverage or the appropriate term of coverage is important. In general, policies with longer maximum benefit periods provide higher policy limits and are more expensive.

Services Not Covered by Long-Term Care Insurance

Long-term care insurance policies may exclude coverage for some conditions, either completely or for a limited period. Policies typically exclude:

- **Pre-existing conditions.** A pre-existing condition is an illness or disability for which an insured has received previous medical advice or treatment usually within six months prior to the application for long-term care coverage. A long-term care policy may delay coverage on a pre-existing condition for up to six months after the policy's effective date for coverage.
- **Mental and nervous disorders.** Long-term care insurance policies can exclude coverage of some mental and nervous disorders but the policy must cover serious biologically-based mental illnesses and other diseases, such as schizophrenia, major depression disorders, Alzheimer's disease, and other age-related disorders. However, a long-term care insurer may refuse to sell a policy to someone already suffering from these otherwise covered exclusions.
- **Care provided by family members or loved ones.** Many long-term care policies will not pay members of the family of the insured to provide care to the insured. However, some policies will pay to train family members to be caregivers or may provide "respite care" to give the caregiver a "break."

State-Specific Exclusions

Various states permit long-term care insurance policies to exclude coverage for conditions resulting from:

- alcoholism and drug addiction
- suicide, attempted suicide, or self-inflicted injuries
- participation in a riot, felony, or insurrection
- war or an act of war whether declared or undeclared
- service in the Armed Forces
- aviation activities, if the insured was not a fare paying passenger on a commercial airline

Long-term care policies will not pay for care that is covered under a government program. The exceptions are Medicaid and expenses that Medicare pays as a secondary payor.

Optional Features of Long-Term Care Insurance (Required)

Issuers of long-term care policies must offer inflation protection and a nonforfeiture benefit, but probably will charge extra for those features.

Inflation Protection

It could be years before the insured needs long-term care services. During that time, long-term care costs could increase significantly. **Inflation protection** helps the insured to maintain the purchasing power of the original contract benefit. The younger the insured, the more important inflation protection. Long-term care policies must offer inflation protection in at least one of the following ways:

1. benefits automatically increasing by five percent or more each year compounded annually,
2. the policy limits increase three percent compound annually, or
3. the policy limits increase at five percent level per year.

In lieu of automatic inflation protection, some companies offer a **Guaranteed Purchase Option** or a Guaranteed Future Purchase Option which allows the insured to increase the benefits by a stated percentage periodically. The down side to this approach is that the premium increases as the benefit is increased and the right to purchase future increases may be lost if one or more purchase options are not taken.

An insured must be provided with a graphical comparison of benefits for a policy with and without inflation protection for a 20-year period. If the insured does not want inflation protection, it must be rejected in writing. The exhibit below illustrates inflation over the period from 2002 to 2012.

EXHIBIT 6.10

Long-Term Care Inflation Index

Consumer Price Index (CPI) All Urban Consumers (All Items)		Producer Price Index Home Health Care Services		Producer Price Index Skilled & Intermediate Care Facilities (After 2003: Nursing Care Facilities)	
Year	**Annual**	**Year**	**Annual**	**Year**	**Annual**
2002	2.4%	2002	116.6	2002	144.6
2003	1.9%	2003	117.0	2003	149.4
2004	3.3%	2004	119.8	2004	155.6
2005	3.4%	2005	121.1	2005	161.4
2006	2.5%	2006	121.8	2006	166.2
2007	4.1%	2007	124.0	2007	173.5
2008	0.1%	2008	126.0	2008	178.9
2009	2.7%	2009	128.0	2009	185.3
2010	1.5%	2010	129.5	2010	188.6
2011	3.0%	2011	129.7	2011	193.1
2012	1.7%	2012	130.4	2012	196.0
CPI Increase		**Annualized Increase Home Health Care**		**Annualized Increase Nursing Home Care**	
2.41% for years 2002 - 2012		1.67% for years 1996 - 2012 1.12% for years 2002 - 2012		3.81 for years 1994 - 2012 3.09% for years 2002 - 2012	

Source: The 2014 Sourcebook for Long-Term Care Insurance Information / AALTCI's LTC Insurance Inflation & Price Indexes / Data provided by Jason Goetze, a 20+ year veteran of the LTCi industry who runs a consulting practice dedicated to improving the industry.

Non-forfeiture Benefit

The insurer must offer to guarantee that the insured will receive some of the benefits for which the premium was paid, even upon cancellation or lapsed. This guarantee, which can be rejected, is called a **non-forfeiture benefit**. The longer premiums are paid, the larger the non-forfeiture benefit will be. A non-forfeiture benefit will generally be the greater of the total amount of premiums paid or 30 times the daily skilled nursing home benefit at the time the policy lapsed.

Policies with non-forfeiture benefits are more expensive than policies without them. To reject the non-forfeiture benefit the rejection must be made in writing, and the insurer will explain its contingent non-forfeiture benefit. The contingent non-forfeiture benefit comes into being when an insurance company increases premiums to a certain level. At that point, the insured can either choose a reduced benefit amount to prevent premium increases or convert the policy to a paid-up policy. If the insured fails to make an election, the insurance company can change the policy to a paid-up status if that period is longer than 120 days. The paid-up benefit will be the greater of the total sum of premiums paid for the policy or 30 times the daily skilled nursing home benefit at the time the policy lapsed.

Optional Benefits (May or May Not Be Offered)

Several optional benefits may be offered with the purchase of a long-term care insurance policy. Some of these are waiver of premium, refund of premium, restoration of benefits, and bed reservation.

Waiver of Premium

Many policies include a waiver of premium provision. This provision allows the insured to stop paying premiums during the period in which they are receiving policy benefits. However, this provision may only apply to certain benefits, for example, nursing home or home healthcare.

Refund of Premium

The company will refund some or all of the insured's premiums minus any claims paid under the policy if the policy is canceled. The insured's beneficiary will receive such refund if the insured dies.

Restoration of Benefits

Long-term care policies have a maximum benefit amount. Often, policies will restore the maximum benefit amount in the event that the insured receives benefits, but the benefits do not exceed a specific period of time, often 180 days.

EXAMPLE 6.6

Sallie has a policy with a maximum benefit of $100,000. She has already received $30,000 in benefits. Her remaining benefit maximum would be $70,000. If she does not receive additional benefits for a specified period of time, her maximum benefit can be restored to the original $100,000 if she has a restoration of benefits rider.

Bed Reservation

Some policies will pay to reserve a bed in the nursing home when the insured leaves to go into a hospital. This reservation can last a specified number of days or until the insured returns from the hospital.

Shared Benefits

Policies that have this benefit permit a person who has fully exhausted the benefits under his or her own policy to make use of the benefits available under his or her spouse's policy.

The optional benefits above are examples of benefits that may or may not be offered by a specific carrier. There are certainly other optional benefits that may be offered in addition to the ones listed above.

Important Coverages in Long-Term Care Policies

EXHIBIT 6.11

Coverage for Alzheimer's Disease
At least one year of nursing home and/or home health care coverage, not limited primarily to skilled care
Inflation protection
No requirement to first be hospitalized to receive benefits

Long-Term Care Benefit Periods (Benefit Multiplier)

Long-term care insurance policies provide coverage for long-term care costs in one of two ways:

- benefits are provided for a fixed period of time, or
- a fixed dollar amount is available for the payment of long-term care benefits.

Policies that provide coverage for a defined benefit period may specify the maximum number of months or years for which coverage will be provided, or may provide coverage for the life of the insured once the need for long-term care services is established and the elimination period has been met.

Persons who are relatively conservative, or who have family histories indicating that they may be prone to non-life threatening diseases requiring long-term care services (such as Alzheimer's disease and senile dementia), may wish to choose policies that provide lifetime coverage although lifetime benefits are becoming increasingly rare.

Persons who are willing to retain more risk to themselves and whose family histories indicate that they are not prone to long-term debilitating diseases may wish to choose a shorter coverage period, such as three or five years. The average stay in a nursing home is approximately 2.4 years, but there is no guarantee that the persons will fall into the average category.

Long-term care policies that specify a maximum benefit payment amount may also be appropriate, depending on the client circumstances. Once the maximum benefit amount has been distributed, the long-term care policy will not pay for additional care. The dollar limit should be chosen carefully by the planner and client after considering the client's health, family history, and preferences.

Tax-Qualified Long-Term Care Contracts

Most long-term care contracts issued today are tax-qualified contracts. Tax-qualified implies that the long-term care insurance policy is treated as health insurance for federal income tax purposes and is therefore deductible on income tax returns either as self-employed health insurance (an above the line, or adjustment to income deduction), or as a medical expense itemized deduction subject to the adjusted gross income hurdle (below the line deduction). If long-term care insurance premiums are paid for by an employer, the employer may deduct the premium cost as an employee benefit, and the employees will not be required to report the value received in their incomes for the year. Long-term care contracts cannot, however, be provided as a benefit under cafeteria plans.

To meet the definition of a tax-qualified contract, the long-term care insurance policy:[10]

1. must provide benefits that are limited to long-term care services.
2. does not provide a cash surrender value or access to funds that can be paid, assigned, borrowed, or pledged as collateral for a loan.
3. provides that refunds may be used only to reduce future premium payments or increase future policy benefits.
4. must meet consumer protection standards defined in the Health Insurance Portability and Accountability Act of 1997 (HIPPA).
5. must coordinate benefits with Medicare.

Long-term care contracts that do not meet the above requirements are not considered to be tax qualified, and will not permit the policy owner to take a tax deduction for premium payments made on the policy. The maximum deductible long-term care premium (under IRC § 213(d)(10)), which is a deduction for medical expenses, depends on the age of the insured. These limits are reflected for 2015 in the following exhibit.The per diem limitation for tax qualified policies is $330 (2015).

EXHIBIT 6.12

MAXIMUM LONG-TERM CARE PREMIUM TAX DEDUCTION (2015)

Age 40 and younger	$380
Age 41 - 50	$710
Age 51 - 60	$1,430
Age 61 - 70	$3,800
71 and older	$4,750

CONDITIONS THAT TRIGGER LONG-TERM CARE BENEFITS

To receive benefits under a long-term care insurance policy, an insured individual must be classified as either terminally or chronically ill.

KEY CONCEPTS

1. Provide examples of the conditions necessary for benefits to be paid under a long-term care policy.
2. Recall the six activities of daily living.

Terminal illness is defined as having a life expectancy of less than 24 months, and must be certified by a qualified health professional.

Chronic illness is defined as having a physical or cognitive impairment that:

- prevents the insured individual from performing at least two of the six activities of daily living for at least a 90 day period, or
- requiring substantial supervision to prevent the insured from posing a danger to himself, herself, or others.

To be considered chronically ill, the insured individual must be certified as such by a qualified health professional within the previous 12 months.

10. IRC Section 7702B(b).

EXAMPLE 6.7

Roger has been having trouble lately getting dressed and bathing. If, after 90 days, he could be certified as chronically ill, then he would be entitled to benefits under a long-term care policy.

The six activities of daily living are:

1. eating
2. bathing
3. dressing
4. transferring
5. toileting
6. continence

Benefit payments cover expenses actually paid (reimbursement plan) or pay a flat daily or monthly amount, regardless of expenses paid, depending on the contract.

SELECTION OF LONG-TERM CARE POLICY

Long-term care insurance is sold directly to individuals as individual policies. It is also sold through employer group plans or other organizations. With group policies, there may be limited choices in the amount of coverage and options as well as no choice as to provider. With individual policies, there is a wide range of companies and optional coverages.

The most important factor in policy selection is in actually qualifying for coverage. Generally, there is a medical questionnaire frequently followed by a medical interview and sometimes a memory (cognitive) test.

When deciding on a policy, one should consider the following:

- the premium
- the period of coverage or total benefits
- any inflation adjustment
- the elimination (deductible) period
- services covered
- services excluded
- who is the gatekeeper to determine qualification for benefits
- how are benefits paid
- what triggers benefits

QUICK QUIZ 6.3

1. Breathing without a respirator is an ADL.
   a. True
   b. False

2. Transferring from a bed to a chair is an ADL.
   a. True
   b. False.

3. Long-term care insurance is payable only for either a time certain or an amount certain.
   a. True
   b. False

4. One way to qualify as chronically ill is the inability to perform one of the six activities of daily living.
   a. True
   b. False

5. Chronic illness is defined as having a physical or cognitive impairment that prevents the insured individual from performing at least five of the six activities of daily living for at least a 90 day period.
   a. True
   b. False

False, True, True, False, False.

The Period of Coverage (Benefits)

The insured can select terms of coverage of 1, 2, 3, 5, 7, 10 years, or lifetime benefits. Obviously, the longer the term of benefits, the higher the amount of lifetime benefits and the more costly the premiums. The historical average stay in a facility is 18-36 months, but the range is quite wide - one day to over 100 years.

EXHIBIT 6.13

Long-Term Care Insurance Claims - How Long Do They Last?

Length of Claim by Policy Benefit Period (Claim Duration in Months)					Claims Closed Due to Exhaustion of Policy Benefits	
Benefit Period of Policy	**24+**	**36+**	**48+**	**60+**		
2 Years	14.0%	1.4%	0.4%	0.1%	2 Year Benefit Period	9.7%
3 Years	25.0%	10.9%	1.4%	0.3%	3 Year Benefit Period	8.0%
4 Years	23.9%	12.1%	6.0%	1.0%	4 Year Benefit Period	5.1%
5 Years	15.9%	10.2%	6.1%	2.9%	5 Year Benefit Period	1.5%
Lifetime	23.3%	13.9%	7.6%	4.5%		
For the 3-year benefit period, only 8 in 100 claimants exhausted their policies.						

Source: The 2014 Sourcebook for Long-Term Care Insurance Information / A revealing look at the duration of policy claims by individuals with long-term care insurance conducted by Miliman, Inc.

The Inflation Adjustment

The cost of an inflation adjustment is an additional premium from 47 percent to 82 percent (for 66-year-old male, 7-year benefits). The younger a person buys a long-term care policy, the more important inflation protection is as a policy feature. While not all long-term care costs have risen as much, skilled nursing care has been increasing at 6-7 percent per year.[11]

With an automatic inflation adjustment the monthly or daily benefit and the lifetime benefit increases. The inflation adjustment options vary widely with policies but generally include 0, 3 percent compound, 5 percent equal, and 5 percent compound.

11. Long-Term Care Cost Study 2010, Prudential.

ANNUAL COST OF A LONG-TERM CARE INSURANCE POLICY WITH VARIOUS INFLATION ADJUSTMENTS INCLUDING NONE ($3,000/MONTH FOR 60 MONTHS)

EXHIBIT 6.14

YEAR	INFLATION BENEFIT WITH NO ADJUSTMENT		BENEFIT WITH 3% COMPOUND		BENEFIT WITH 5% EQUAL		BENEFIT WITH 5% COMPOUND	
	Per Month	Total	Per Month	Total	Per Month	Total	Per Month	Total
1	$3,000	$180,000	$3,000	$180,000	$3,000	$180,000	$3,000	$180,000
6	$3,000	$180,000	$3,484	$209,040	$3,750	$225,000	$3,850	$231,005
11	$3,000	$180,000	$4,048	$242,880	$4,500	$270,000	$4,941	$296,460
16	$3,000	$180,000	$4,702	$282,120	$5,250	$315,000	$6,341	$380,460
21	$3,000	$180,000	$5,462	$327,736	$6,000	$360,000	$8,138	$488,280
Expected Annual Premium (age 66 male)	$1,755		$2,588		$2,622		$3,195	
% Increase	N/A		+ 47%		+ 49%		+ 82%	

ELIMINATION (DEDUCTIBLE) PERIOD

The period between being eligible medically and when benefits begin is called the elimination period. The elimination period can be considered a deductible or as co-insurance. The elimination period may be 0, 30, 60, 90, or 180 days. The premium will increase as the elimination period is reduced. Elimination period for skilled nursing care may be different from home health care. Some policies count calendar days while others only count days the insured received a covered service. In general, the longer the elimination period, the lower the premium.

SERVICES INCLUDED AND EXCLUDED

Long-term care services may include help with personal care, activities of daily living (ADLs), home health care, respite care, hospice care, and/or adult day care. The care may be provided in the insured's home, at a day care facility, in an assisted living facility, or in a skilled nursing home. Care services can also include the cost of a case manager to determine need and recommend and monitor services. The cost of such a case manager is usually provided as part of the policy and for no additional premium. This cost will not reduce monthly or lifetime benefits.

For home health care, some policies only cover the cost of licensed caregivers or agencies. Some cover non-licensed caregivers, and some may cover related party caregivers who are licensed or not.

Most long-term care insurance policies do not cover:

- mental or nervous disorders other than Alzheimer's or dementia
- alcohol or drug addiction
- illness or injury caused by acts of war
- treatment in a government facility or paid for by the government
- self-inflicted injuries

The Gatekeeper

When selecting a policy, it is important to know who the gatekeeper to benefits is. The policy may require that a case worker for the insurance company evaluate and certify that the insured is eligible for benefits.

How Benefits are Paid

Benefits are generally paid in one of three ways. The first is the expense incurred method (reimbursement). The expense incurred method pays for the actual expense up to the dollar limit whichever is less, which is paid to the providers or the insured. The second way is the indemnity method. The indemnity method is a set dollar amount paid to the insured for each period he or she qualifies. The third method is the disability method in which the insured only needs to meet the eligibility criteria once. Once the eligibility criteria is met, the insured receives the full daily benefit until death or the benefits are exhausted. The most common policy benefit paid method is the expense incurred method (reimbursement).

Another important consideration regarding how benefits are paid is how the insurance company calculates how much it pays. The following two examples highlight the different methods. Both examples assume a $100 per day benefit.

EXAMPLE 6.8 Company A uses a daily limit. On one day, $50 in home health care cost is incurred. The next day, nothing is spent. On the third day, $150 is incurred. In this case, $150 would be paid ($50 + $0 + $100).

EXAMPLE 6.9 Company B uses a monthly limit. $100 x 30 days = $3,000. Assuming the same daily expenses, and assuming the total expenditures for the month do not exceed $3,000, the $200 incurred during the period above would be reimbursed.

Quick Quiz 6.4

1. In order to activate long-term care insurance, an insured generally must not be able to perform 2 of 6 ADLs.
   a. True
   b. False
2. A 5% equal and a 3% compound inflation adjustment are relatively similar.
   a. True
   b. False.
3. Having an inflation adjustment as part of a LTC policy is especially important if the policy is purchased at a young age.
   a. True
   b. False.
4. The most common method of paying benefits is referred to as the indemnity method.
   a. True
   b. False.

True, True, True, False.

There are policies that permit pooled benefits, for example, between spouses.

What Triggers Benefits (Eligibility) of Long-Term Care Insurance

Being unable to perform two or more ADLs will make an insured eligible for benefits from a long-term care insurance policy. Most policies also pay benefits for cognitive impairment, such as dementia or Alzheimer's disease. However, some plans pay a reduced benefit for home health care.

ALTERNATIVES TO LONG-TERM CARE INSURANCE

Key Concepts

1. Compare the costs and benefits of long-term care insurance to the alternatives to long-term care insurance.
2. Understand how long-term care riders can be purchased.
3. Explain how reverse mortgages could be used in lieu of long-term care insurance.
4. Discuss how annuities might be favorable over long-term care insurance.

As discussed earlier in the chapter, certain individuals may be better off not purchasing a long-term care insurance policy. While these policies are appropriate for many individuals, there are risks that need to be considered. Four risks to a standalone long-term care policy include:

- they can be expensive
- they accumulate no cash value
- the premiums may increase
- the underwriting process can be time-consuming

A major problem with long-term care policies arise when they lapse due to the cost. Affordability can be a major issue in purchasing long-term care, especially if premiums increase. As a result, hybrid solutions have been created to meet the needs of long-term care. These include life insurance with accelerated benefits, annuity contracts permitting cash withdrawals without penalty, viatical or life settlement contracts, and reverse mortgages.

Life Insurance with Long-Term Care Rider

Some life insurance policies offer an accelerated benefits rider for long-term care services. These types of policies might be universal life, variable universal life, or whole life policies. Such a policy will pay out a benefit of long-term care if needed and a death benefit to a designated beneficiary if it is not needed.[12] Also, the beneficiary will receive a payment if long-term care expenses do not exhaust the value of the policy. Some people are attracted to this flexibility and like the fact that they will get some money back no matter what happens. However, combination policies typically require a larger up-front payment than traditional standalone long-term care policies. For example, a healthy 60-year-old male non-smoker pays $100,000 in premiums in three annual installments of $33,333. The insured can receive a maximum monthly benefit of $5,787 for a maximum of six years, and if it is not used, his beneficiaries will receive $138,896. There is a third option for a full refund of the $100,000 premiums anytime after five years, as long as scheduled premiums have been paid as agreed. While this example is for a particular hybrid policy, the more common monthly benefit of a life insurance policy with a long-term care rider is two to four percent of the face value depending on the total amount of premiums that have been paid. A comparable standalone long-term care policy would require premiums of $2,100 per year to be paid for life

12. Under accelerated benefit riders, it is not uncommon that only inpatient long-term care is eligible, not home health care.

unless there is a waiver of premium provision. Combination policies generally have large expenses. A combination policy that includes life insurance is only appropriate when the client actually needs life insurance and is adding long-term care insurance as an additional need.

Annuity Contracts with Long-Term Care Provisions

Some annuity contracts allow withdrawals to pay for long-term care services. Such an annuity policy may be either deferred or immediate. With an annuity, the insured can take withdrawals from the accumulated value of the policy to pay for long-term care needs without paying any surrender charge typically imposed on accelerated withdrawals.

Longevity Annuities (Also known as Deferred Income Annuities)

Longevity annuities are contracts between individuals and insurance companies. A contract will often be purchased as a single investment (single premium) in exchange for a guaranteed income stream for life beginning at a later age, such as 80 or 85. The income is based on the premium or investment, the age of the contract owner, his life expectancy and the period over which the income will be paid. The annuity payments can be used to supplement income needs during the later parts of retirement or supplement long-term care needs. The primary advantage of this approach is that the funds can be used for more than just long-term care. This type of alternative can be used to provide protection against outliving assets (superannuation) or for long-term care needs. Longevity annuities are discussed more thoroughly in the Annuities chapter.

Viatical or Life Settlement Contracts

Life settlement plans permit the insured to sell his or her life insurance for its present value to raise cash for any reason. This policy option is usually only available to women age 74 and older and to men age 70 and older. If an insured sells his or her life insurance policy, there may be little or no death benefit left for heirs. Also, the proceeds of the sale may be subject to income tax if the proceeds exceed the premiums that have been paid.

A viatical settlement is a sale of a life insurance policy to a third party. A viatical settlement is like a life settlement but is generally only possible if the insured is terminally ill. During the settlement process, a viatical company pays the insured a percentage of the death benefit on the life insurance policy based on life expectancy. The viatical company then owns the policy and becomes its named beneficiary. The viatical company may also take over the payment of the premiums on the policy. Any payments received by the insured under a viatical settlement are deemed to be tax-free.[13] There are no death benefits paid to the insured's heirs.

13. See IRC Section 101(g).

Reverse Mortgages

A reverse mortgage is a specific type of home equity loan that permits the borrower to receive cash against the value of his or her home without selling the home. In general the money can be received in a lump sum payment, a monthly payment, or as a line of credit. There are no restrictions on the use of the remainder of the money after paying off any initial first and second mortgage. The borrower will continue to live in the home and retain title and ownership of the home and will continue to be responsible for taxes, homeowners insurance, and home repairs. The borrower does not have to repay the loan, instead, the amount that is owed based on the loan payout and interest in expenses on the loan become due when the last borrower (usually the last remaining spouse) dies, sells, or permanently moves out of the home. There are a number of disadvantages to reverse mortgages including the costs and the fact that there may be little or no equity left in the home to go to beneficiaries since the homeowner has a bequest interest.

Quick Quiz 6.5

1. An alternative to long-term care insurance is a viatical settlement contract.
   a. True
   b. False

2. An alternative to long-term care insurance is a reverse mortgage.
   a. True
   b. False

3. Longevity annuities can be used to supplement income needs or to provide for long-term care.
   a. True
   b. False

4. The proceeds from a viatical settlement are taxable to the extent the proceeds exceed the basis.
   a. True
   b. False

True, True, True, False.

A COMPREHENSIVE INDIVIDUAL ILLUSTRATION OF A LONG-TERM CARE POLICY

One of the earlier sections in this chapter discussed numerous long-term care policy features, each of which impacts the cost of the policy depending on what is selected. This section is included to illustrate the impact to the cost of a long-term care policy of various changes in the features of the policy. To illustrate the impact on the price of a policy for various policy changes, a 66-year-old male was chosen to initially price a policy and then to compare the price based on policy feature changes.

This illustration is for a 66-year-old man, in good health, with an initial monthly benefit of $3,500 adjustment for a fiver percent equal inflation for a term of six years (72 months), with 180-day elimination period and an annual premium of $3,059.71 having no return of premium option nor a non-forfeiture option.

It is important to note that policy premiums will be different from what is illustrated in this section depending on the age and health of the insured, as well as other factors. It should also be noted that premium adjustments may occur over time. Below is the policy detail used for these illustrations.

LONG-TERM CARE POLICY DESCRIPTION

LONG-TERM POLICY DESCRIPTION	
Age	66 (male)
Monthly Benefit	$3,500
Period of Coverage	72 Months
Total Initial Benefit	$252,000
Elimination Period	180
Inflation	5% Equal
Restoration of Benefits	Included
Premium Payment	Lifetime
Payment Mode	Annual
Annual Premium	$3,059.71
Non-Forfeiture Option	None
Return of Premium Option	None

The initial policy choices were as follows:

ITEM	RANGE
Monthly Benefit	$2,500 - $4,500
Benefit Multiplies (term)	24 - 120 months
The Elimination Period	0 - 180 days
Benefit Increase Options (inflation)	0 - 5% compounded
Restoration of Benefits	no / yes
Non-Forfeiture Benefit Options	include / exclude
Enhanced Survivorship Option	include / exclude
Return of Premium after 10 Years	include / exclude

Benefit Option Comparison (The Current Policy Features Are in Bold)

Benefit Option	Change Benefit To	New Annual Premium	Amount of Change
Monthly Benefit Maximum	$2,500 per month	$2,185.51	($874.20)
	$3,000 per month	$2,622.61	($437.10)
	$3,500 per month	**$3,059.71**	**0**
	$4,000 per month	$3,496.82	$437.11
	$4,500 per month	$3,933.91	$874.20
Benefit Multiplier	24 months	$1,799.95	($1,259.76)
	36 months	$2,311.24	($748.47)
	48 months	$2,568.50	($491.21)
	60 months	$2,855.81	($203.90)
	72 months	**$3,059.71**	**0**
	96 months	$3,395.69	$335.98
	120 months	$3,635.50	$575.79
Elimination Period	30-Day	$3,558.04	$498.33
	90-Day	$3,227.70	$167.99
	180-Day	**$3,059.71**	**0**
Benefit Increase Option	None	$2,047.92	($1,011.79)
	3% Compound	$3,019.94	$39.77
	5% Equal	**$3,059.71**	**0**
	5% Compound	$3,728.40	$668.69
Restoration of Benefits Option*	None	$2,886.52	($173.19)
Non-Forfeiture Benefit Option**	Include	$3,896.80	$837.09
Enhanced Survivorship 7-Year Option***	Include	$3,204.04	$144.33
Return of Premium Option - After 10 Years****	Include	$4,467.17	$1,407.46

** Restoration of benefits - the benefits in the policy will be restored if the insured gets better. Benefits can be reinstated if there is a six month or longer benefit free period as long as benefits have not been exhausted.*

*** A non-forfeiture option provides some coverage after making premium payments for a specific time period. The option offers protection from cancelation or stopping paying premiums.*

****Enhanced survivorship rider is a spousal survivorship benefit. The surviving spouse no longer has to pay long-term care insurance premiums. The forgiveness of premiums after the death of the first spouse.*

***** Return of premium pays back all premiums paid if policy is cancelled after a selected term.*

Benefit Increase Comparison for Various Inflation Adjustments

	No Increases		5% Equal		3% Compounded		5% Compounded	
Policy Year	Monthly Maximum	Total Personal Benefit Account	Monthly Maximum	Total Personal Benefit Account	Monthly Maximum	Total Personal Benefit Account	Monthly Maximum	Total Personal Benefit Account
1	$3,500	$252,000	$3,500	$252,000	$3,500	$252,000	$3,500	$252,000
5	$3,500	$252,000	$4,200	$302,400	$3,939	$283,628	$4,254	$306,308
10	$3,500	$252,000	$5,075	$365,400	$4,567	$328,803	$5,430	$390,935
15	$3,500	$252,000	$5,950	$428,400	$5,294	$381,173	$6,930	$498,943
20	$3,500	$252,000	$6,825	$491,400	$6,137	$441,884	$8,844	$636,791
25	$3,500	$252,000	$7,700	$554,400	$7,115	$512,264	$11,288	$812,725

Inflation Adjustments

Notice that three percent compounded (the approximate long-term historical increase in the CPI) is very close to five percent equal as are the monthly premiums (See Benefit Option Comparison).

Plan Options Comparison

No Benefit Increases Option						
Elimination Period	Benefit Multiplier					
	36 Months (3 Years)	48 Months (4 Years)	60 Months (5 Years)	72 Months (6 Years)	96 Months (8 Years)	120 Months (10 Years)
30 Days	$1,753.92	$1,899.52	$2,196.32	$2,374.40	$2,611.84	$2,789.92
90 Days	$1,602.72	$1,751.12	$1,988.56	$2,136.96	$2,374.40	$2,552.48
180 Days	$1,512.00	$1,662.08	$1,899.52	$2,047.92	$2,255.68	$2,433.76

5% Equal Benefit Increases Option						
Elimination Period	Benefit Multiplier					
	36 Months (3 Years)	48 Months (4 Years)	60 Months (5 Years)	72 Months (6 Years)	96 Months (8 Years)	120 Months (10 Years)
30 Days	$2,678.36	$2,970.67	$3,323.86	$3,558.04	$3,935.57	$4,205.66
90 Days	$2,440.06	$2,706.52	$3,018.16	$3,227.70	$3,593.95	$3,833.77
180 Days	$2,311.24	$2,568.50	$2,855.81	**$3,059.71**	$3,395.69	$3,635.50

3% Compound Benefit Increases Option						
Elimination Period	Benefit Multiplier					
	36 Months (3 Years)	48 Months (4 Years)	60 Months (5 Years)	72 Months (6 Years)	96 Months (8 Years)	120 Months (10 Years)
30 Days	$2,502.36	$2,790.81	$3,233.94	$3,501.35	$3,880.36	$4,148.08
90 Days	$2,284.33	$2,523.69	$2,942.18	$3,180.22	$3,530.44	$3,773.51
180 Days	$2,175.46	$2,411.80	$2,781.61	$3,019.94	$3,345.53	$3,583.86

5% Compound Benefit Increases Option						
Elimination Period	Benefit Multiplier					
	36 Months (3 Years)	48 Months (4 Years)	60 Months (5 Years)	72 Months (6 Years)	96 Months (8 Years)	120 Months (10 Years)
30 Days	$3,089.32	$3,445.55	$3,992.55	$4,322.59	$4,790.65	$5,120.98
90 Days	$2,820.18	$3,115.51	$3,632.24	$3,926.37	$4,358.51	$4,658.58
180 Days	$2,685.62	$2,977.50	$3,433.98	$3,728.40	$4,130.27	$4,424.70

Cost of Waiting (One and Five Years)

When Purchased	Age	Monthly Benefit Amount	Annualized Premiums (Rounded)	Total Premiums Paid to Age 85 of Proposed Insured	Cost of Waiting
Today	66	$3,500	$3,060	$58,140	$0
In 1 Year*	67	$3,675	$3,524	$63,432	$5,292
In 5 Years*	71	$4,467	$6,172	$86,408	$28,268

** Assuming the insured is still insurable.*

Break Even Analysis in Days of Use

Number of Years Premiums are Paid	Total Premium Paid	Monthly Benefit	Break Even Days
2	$6,119	$3,675	50
5	$15,299	$4,200	109
10	$30,597	$5,075	181
15	$45,896	$5,950	231

PAYMENT OPTIONS COMPARISON

		LIFETIME		10-PAY		PAY-TO-65	
Policy Period	Age	Total Premiums Paid	Policy Paid Up	Total Premiums Paid	Policy Paid Up	Total Premiums Paid	Policy Paid Up
First Year	66	$3,059.71	No	$5,721.71	No	N/A	N/A
After 10 Years	76	$30,597.10	No	$57,217.10	Yes	N/A	N/A
After 20 Years	86	$61,194.20	No	$57,217.10	Yes	N/A	N/A

As illustrated in the exhibits above, there are many variations of long-term care policies. Each of these variations impacts the cost of the policy.

CONCLUSION

Health insurance and long-term care insurance permit clients to purchase a hedge against the risk of incurring large medical and/or nursing home and long-term care expenses. All U.S. citizens are required, under current law, to maintain adequate health insurance. Long-term care insurance should be considered by any client who wishes to retain the ability to choose service providers or who has bequest motives that could be thwarted (or, possibly, be subject to higher gift and/or estate taxes) if long-term care coverage is not purchased. Planners and clients should carefully consider the most appropriate forms of insurance to purchase so that the appropriate amount of client risk exposure is transferred to insurance companies while protecting the client's asset base to achieve the client's other financial goals.

KEY TERMS

ACTIVITIES OF DAILY LIVING (ADL) - Physical functions that an independent person performs each day, including bathing, dressing, eating, transferring, toileting, and maintaining continence.

ADULT DAY CARE - Services provided during the day at a community-based center. Programs address the individual needs of functionally or cognitively impaired adults.

ASSISTED LIVING - Senior housing that provides individual apartments, which may or may not have a kitchenette. Facilities offer 24-hour on site staff, congregate dining, and activity programs. Limited nursing services may be provided for an additional fee.

BED RESERVATION - Some policies will pay to reserve a bed in the nursing home when the insured leaves to go into a hospital. This reservation can last a specified number of days or until the insured returns from the hospital.

CHRONIC ILLNESS - having a physical or cognitive impairment that prevents the insured individual from performing at least two of the six activities of daily living for at least a 90-day period, or requiring substantial supervision to prevent the insured from posing a danger to himself, herself, or others.

CUSTODIAL CARE - Board, room and other personal assistance services (including assistance with activities of daily living, taking medicine and similar personal needs) that may not include a skilled nursing care component.

EXPENSE INCURRED METHOD – this method provides for reimbursement of expense once bills are submitted to the insurance company. The reimbursable amount cannot exceed the benefit amount.

GUARANTEED PURCHASE OPTION - Allows the insured to increase the benefits by a stated percentage periodically.

GUARANTEED RENEWABLE - The company must renew the policy each year as long as premiums are paid.

HOME HEALTH CARE - Limited part-time or intermittent skilled nursing care and home health aide services, physical therapy, occupational therapy, speech-language pathology services, medical social services, durable medical equipment (such as wheelchairs, hospital beds, oxygen, and walkers), medical supplies, and other services provided in the patient's home.

HOSPICE CARE - Offers a special way of caring for people who are terminally ill, typically utilizing a team-oriented approach to address medical, physical, social, emotional, and spiritual needs.

INFLATION PROTECTION - Helps the insured to maintain the purchasing power of the original contract benefit.

KEY TERMS

Intermediate-Care Nursing Facility - A licensed facility with the primary purpose of providing health or rehabilitative services. Typically provides custodial care along with intermittent, as opposed to daily, medical care.

Long-Term Care Insurance - Coverage that pays for all or part of the cost of home health care services or care in a nursing home or assisted living facility.

Long-Term Care Services - Medical and non-medical care for people with chronic illnesses or disabilities that assists people with Activities of Daily Living, such as dressing, bathing, and using the bathroom. Long-term care can be provided at home, in the community, or in a facility.

Maximum Lifetime Benefit - the total amount of money that could be paid under the LTC policy for charges incurred for covered services.

Medicaid - A state and federal assistance program that pays for medical care and most long-term care expenses for eligible persons with low incomes and limited assets.

Medicare - A federal program that pays for healthcare for persons over age 65 and for people under age 65 with disabilities.

Mental and Nervous Disorders - Long-term care insurance policies can exclude coverage of some mental and nervous disorders, but the policy must cover serious biologically-based mental illnesses and other diseases, such as schizophrenia, major depression disorders, Alzheimer's disease, and other age-related disorders. However, a long-term care insurer may refuse to sell a policy to someone already suffering from these otherwise covered exclusions.

Non-Forfeiture Benefit - The insurer must guarantee that the insured will receive some of the benefits paid for even upon cancellation or lapsed coverage.

Pre-Existing Conditions - A pre-existing condition is an illness or disability for which an insured has received previous medical advice or treatment usually within six months prior to the application for long-term care coverage.

Refund of Premium - The company will refund some or all of the insured's premiums minus any claims paid under the policy if the policy is canceled. The insured's beneficiary will receive such refund if the insured dies.

Restoration of Benefits - Some policies restore benefits to the original maximum amounts if the insured no longer needs long-term care services, usually after 180 days.

KEY TERMS

SKILLED CARE FACILITY - Provides the highest level of service combining both daily medical and custodial care.

SKILLED NURSING CARE FACILITY - 24-hour nursing care for chronically-ill or short-term rehabilitative residents of all ages. It provides the highest level of service, and combines daily medical and custodial care.

SPECIAL NEEDS TRUST - A specific type of trust that is used to provide benefits to persons or beneficiaries with special needs. They are designed to protect eligibility for government assistance programs.

TERMINAL ILLNESS - Having a life expectancy of less than 24 months, which must be certified by a qualified health professional.

TOTAL PLAN BENEFIT – The total amount of money that could be paid under the LTC policy for charges incurred for covered services.

TRADITIONAL MEDICAL CARE - Attempts to treat or cure illnesses.

WAIVER OF PREMIUM - Allows the insured to stop paying premiums during the period in which he or she is receiving policy benefits. However, this provision may only apply to certain benefits, for example, nursing home or home healthcare.

DISCUSSION QUESTIONS

1. What is the trend of the average age in the United States?
2. What is an ADL?
3. What are the six ADLs?
4. What is the estimated percent of people over age 65 who will need some form of long-term care?
5. What needs do long-term care services meet?
6. What are IADLs?
7. Where are long-term services provided?
8. What are the common methods for paying for long-term care services?
9. What programs pay for most long-term care services?
10. What factors influence the need for long-term care insurance?
11. What variables influence long-term care insurance premiums?
12. What are some common features of long-term care insurance policies?
13. What are the typical coverages for long-term care insurance policies?
14. What are typical exclusions from long-term care insurance policies?
15. Describe the purpose of long-term care insurance.
16. What are the two primary issues a planner should consider when advising regarding the purchase of long-term care insurance?
17. What conditions will trigger long-term care coverage?
18. What are some of the alternatives to long-term care insurance?

MULTIPLE-CHOICE PROBLEMS

1. Medicare is primarily for those people who meet the following eligibility requirements:
    a. Disabled.
    b. Children.
    c. Low Income.
    d. Elderly.

2. Medicaid is primarily for those people who meet the following eligibility requirements:
    a. Disabled.
    b. Children.
    c. Low Income.
    d. Elderly.

3. What is the primary function of long-term care insurance?
    a. Pay claims for the insured.
    b. Underwrite long-term care policies.
    c. Provide comprehensive coverage.
    d. Protect against catastrophic risks.

4. For Medicare beneficiaries, the maximum stay in a skilled nursing facility during a benefit period cannot exceed how many days?
    a. 20 days.
    b. 60 days.
    c. 90 days.
    d. 100 days.

5. The elderly do not constitute a homogenous group, therefore:
    a. They have more chronic ailments than acute episodes.
    b. Most elderly people can live independently indefinitely.
    c. The long-term care system must be integrated with the rest of the healthcare system.
    d. A variety of services are needed.

6. What is/are the key factors in determining the need for long-term care?
    a. A disabling accident.
    b. An acute episode.
    c. Multiple chronic conditions.
    d. Inability to perform activities of daily living.

7. What is/are the goal(s) of long-term care?

    a. Return the recipient to independent living.
    b. Cure multiple chronic conditions.
    c. Promote function independence.
    d. Make a terminal person comfortable.

8. Custodial or personal care is?

    a. Skilled nursing care provided.
    b. Assistance with daily living tasks.
    c. Making the terminally ill comfortable.
    d. Individualized care.

9. Which of the following is incorrect?

    a. Long-term care insurance is needed for everyone.
    b. Many people do not need long-term care insurance.
    c. Those with millions in net worth do not need long-term care insurance.
    d. Many people who need long-term care insurance do not have it.

10. Tax qualified long-term care insurance policies must offer all of the following features, provisions, or options except:

    a. Guaranteed renewable or noncancelable.
    b. Option to purchase policy that increases with inflation.
    c. A non-forfeiture option.
    d. An option to purchase skilled nursing care coverage only.

11. Long-term care facilities include all of the following except:

    a. Nursing homes.
    b. Adult day care centers.
    c. Ambulatory centers.
    d. Convalescent centers.

12. Approximately, what percent of persons over the age of 65 will require some long-term care services at some point in their lives?

    a. 50%.
    b. 60%.
    c. 70%.
    d. 90%.

13. Which of the following can be excluded in a tax qualified long-term care insurance policy?

   a. Alcoholism.
   b. Schizophrenia.
   c. Alzheimer's.
   d. Major depression disorders.

14. All of the following are activities of daily living (ADLs) as provided under the Health Insurance Portability and Accountability Act (qualified plans), except:

   a. Eating.
   b. Bathing.
   c. Maintaining continence.
   d. Cognitive thinking.

15. Which of the following most accurately describes the criteria required for an insured to qualify for long-term care benefits for a qualified plan under the Health Insurance Portability and Accountability Act?

   a. The insured is unable to perform two of the six ADLs for 90 days.
   b. The insured has substantial cognitive impairment requiring substantial assistance.
   c. The insured must meet both a and b.
   d. The insured may qualify by meeting either a or b.

16. Mr. Butler, who has recently turned 85, has been blind for two years. He has trouble walking and is unable to cook for himself since he lost his sight. His family has told him that he needs to consider entering an assisted living home. Assuming he has a qualified long-term care plan, is he considered chronically ill under the Health Insurance Portability and Accountability Act?

   a. Yes, he has been unable to perform two activities of daily living for over 90 days.
   b. Yes, but he does have to prove to the insurance company he is unable to perform these tasks.
   c. No, sight is not considered an activity of daily living, although cooking is.
   d. No, neither sight nor cooking is considered an activity of daily living.

17. Andrew Smith, who is 76 years old, was diagnosed with Alzheimer's disease last week. He purchased a long-term care policy when he was 50. Would he be covered under the policy if he entered a nursing home?

   a. Yes. If he is unable to perform two or more ADLs.
   b. Yes. He is covered because he has Alzheimer's disease.
   c. Yes. He is over the age of 71.
   d. No. He does not qualify at this point.

18. There is more than one way to obtain benefits for nursing home coverage. All of the following sources provide some benefits, except:

    a. LTC insurance.
    b. Heath insurance.
    c. Medicare.
    d. Medicaid.

19. In terms of qualifying for Medicaid, which of the following is counted as income?

    a. Nutritional assistance.
    b. Veterans benefits.
    c. Federal housing benefits.
    d. Home energy assistance.

20. Which of the following individuals is more likely to have a need for long-term care insurance?

- Tom has always had menial jobs and owns a small home and little else.
- Sarah has worked as a middle manager her entire career and has pension and Social Security income, in addition to a home and a modest amount of savings.

    a. Tom.
    b. Sarah.
    c. Neither.
    d. Both.

21. Which of the following is the highest level of care under the category of long-term care?

    a. Custodial care.
    b. Intensive care.
    c. Skilled nursing care.
    d. Advanced nursing care.

QUICK QUIZ EXPLANATIONS

Quick Quiz 6.1

1. False. Long-term care insurance coverage includes: nursing homes, home health, and hospice.
2. False. One must qualify financially for Medicaid.
3. True.
4. False. For those individuals with significant assets or few assets, it may make sense to pay for the services in lieu of paying for the insurance.
5. False. All are correct except exercising.

Quick Quiz 6.2

1. True.
2. False. Medicaid pays approximately one-third of the cost, not 80 percent.
3. False. Women tend to need it more due to longer life expectancies.
4. True.

Quick Quiz 6.3

1. False.
2. True.
3. True.
4. False. One way to qualify as chronically ill is the inability to perform two of the six activities of daily living.
5. False. It is at least two, not five of the six activities of daily living.

Quick Quiz 6.4

1. True.
2. True.
3. True.
4. False. The most common method is the expense incurred method (reimbursement).

Quick Quiz 6.5

1. True.
2. True.
3. True.
4. False. Proceeds from viatical settlements are not subject to income tax.

CHAPTER

7

ANNUITIES

LEARNING OBJECTIVES

After reading this chapter, you should be able to:

1. Understand how life expectancies have increased and the impact to retirement planning, including superannuation.
2. Discuss the retirement life expectancy concept and the impact inflation has on purchasing power.
3. Recognize the change from employer sponsored defined benefit plans to employer sponsored defined contribution plans.
4. Explain the characteristics of an annuity including contributions and distribution options and differentiating between immediate and deferred annuities.*
5. Identify the use of annuities in retirement planning.
6. List the parties to an annuity.
7. Differentiate between single and joint life annuities.
8. Explain term certain annuities.
9. Identify the characteristics of variable annuities.
10. Discuss equity-indexed annuities.
11. Distinguish between deferred and immediate annuities.
12. List the advantages and disadvantages of annuity contracts.
13. Illustrate the income taxation of annuities.
14. Recognize the estate taxation issues regarding annuities.
15. Define longevity insurance.
16. Describe and discuss the secondary market for annuities.
17. Outline the regulation of annuities.
18. Describe what happens if an annuity issuer fails.

* CFP Board Resource Document - Student-Centered Learning Objectives based upon CFP Board Principal Topics.

INTRODUCTION

One of the common goals for most Americans is to live comfortably in retirement. This objective requires either a substantial accumulation of assets, a reliable source of income during retirement or a combination of the two. Even when individuals have accumulated assets or have reliable income, there can be risks to financial security during retirement. Two important risks to the security of retirement income are superannuation (outliving one's money) and inflation (loss of purchasing power). Superannuation or longevity risk is the risk of running out of money before death due to long life and can be mitigated by using annuities. However, commercial annuities are generally not adjusted for inflation, and therefore do not mitigate the risk of loss of purchasing power. Social Security retirement benefits generally mitigate both of these risks because the benefits last for life and are adjusted for inflation. The increase in benefits due to inflation helps maintain the purchasing power of the benefits. Annuities are not only used to provide income streams for retirees. Annuities are used very frequently as a method of accumulating assets on a tax-deferred basis. This chapter discusses the various features and characteristics of annuities, including types, options, advantages, disadvantages, costs, taxation, as well as the primary uses for annuities.

As medical technology has improved and individuals have led healthier lifestyles over the past century, life expectancy has increased.[1] There is an 80 percent probability that a 65-year-old will live to be age 80 and a 22 percent probability that a 65-year-old will live to age 95 or longer. A longer retirement period increases the chance that an individual will run out of money.

One way to mitigate superannuation is through the use of annuities. Annuities are contracts that can provide income for the life of a person or the lives of a couple. Annuities are more important today due to increased life expectancies and a decline in the number of retirement plans that pay pensions for life.

EXHIBIT 7.1

Life Expectancy for All Individuals and 65-Year-Olds

	2012	1960	1940	1930
Average Life Expectancy	78.8	69.7	62.9	59.7
Males Only	76.4	66.6	60.8	58.1
Females Only	81.1	73.1	65.2	61.6
All 65-Year-Olds	19.3	14.3	13.8	Not Reported
Males Only (Age 65)	17.9	13.2	12.7	Not Reported
Females Only (Age 65)	20.5	17.4	14.7	Not Reported

www.ssa.gov and National Vital Statistics System www.cdc.gov/nchs

Key Concepts

1. Understand inflation and its impact on retirement and purchasing power.
2. Discuss the retirement life expectancy concept.
3. Discuss risk of running out of money for those with longer life expectancies.
4. Understand the risk of defined contribution plans in long-term planning.

The period between retirement and death, sometimes referred to as **retirement life expectancy** is uncertain, but the longer the retirement life expectancy, the greater the risk that a retiree will exhaust his or her retirement assets or capital. Exhaustion of retirement capital can result from an increase in the number of years of retirement, thereby increasing consumption needs during retirement, or from the loss of purchasing power due to inflation.

Inflation is the increase in the general price level and is generally measured by the Consumer Price Index (CPI). When annual inflation is low (in the 1-3% range), it is hardly noticeable, especially for those persons who are employed because wages tend to rise with price increases. However, for a retiree on a fixed income, inflation can have a devastating effect on purchasing power over a long period of time. For example, if a retiree purchases a market basket of goods priced at $1,000 per month, and the annual rate of inflation is 3.5 percent during the retirement period, the cost to purchase the same market basket of goods will increase ratably over the retirement period. The following chart illustrates the cost of that $1,000 basket of goods in future years and the corresponding decline in purchasing power for a person retiring at age 65 (all numbers in the chart are rounded except for age).

1. For a person aged 65 today, there is a life expectancy of about 18 years for males and 20 years for females.

EXHIBIT 7.2

THE EFFECT OF INFLATION ON COST AND PURCHASING POWER

TIME PERIOD	FUTURE VALUE COST	PURCHASING POWER OF $1,000	DECLINE IN PURCHASING POWER OF $1,000
Now (Age 65)	$1,000	100%	0
In 5 Years (Age 70)	$1,188	84%	16%
In 10 Years (Age 75)	$1,411	71%	29%
In 15 Years (Age 80)	$1,675	60%	40%
In 20 Years (Age 85)	**$1,990**	**50%**	**50%**
In 25 Years (Age 90)	$2,363	42%	58%
In 30 Years (Age 95)	$2,807	36%	64%
In 35 Years (Age 100)	**$3,334**	**30%**	**70%**

As the chart above illustrates, a retiree living to average life expectancy (in this case assume age 85) has a decline in purchasing power of 50 percent assuming inflation is 3.5 percent annually. Instead of needing $1,000 to purchase the market basket of goods at age 65, the same market basket of goods would cost approximately $2,000. If the retiree lives to age 100, which is becoming more common today, the decline in purchasing power is 70 percent. The retiree would need $3,334 per month at age 100 to purchase the same goods that cost $1,000 at age 65.

While there has always been inflation, 50 or so years ago life expectancy was much shorter than it is today. Depletion of retirement assets was less likely. Shorter retirement periods meant less consumption needs (fewer years in retirement) and fewer years of purchasing power erosion (caused by inflation).

Historically, individuals received Social Security retirement benefits and a fixed pension during retirement. Pension payments are generally made from retirement plans known as defined benefit plans. These plans would pay fixed pensions to retired workers for life. While Social Security remains, there has been a significant decline in the number of defined benefit plans over the last thirty years. In fact, in 1985, there were about 175,000 defined benefit plans. In 2012, there were fewer than 45,000 defined benefit plans.

When defined benefit plans were prevalent, the risk of superannuation was pooled together. The defined benefit plan was responsible for paying a fixed pension for as long as the retired participants lived. Naturally, some retirees would live longer than others and some would not live very long. Actuaries could mathematically estimate the average life

QUICK QUIZ 7.1

1. The longer retirement life expectancy, the greater the risk that a retiree will exhaust his or her retirement assets.
   a. True
   b. False

2. The average life expectancy for a 65-year-old male is approximately 18 years.
   a. True
   b. False

3. Defined contribution plans pay a fixed annuity for the life of the annuitant.
   a. True
   b. False

True, True, False.

expectancy of the pool of employees and determine the funding necessary to meet those requirements. However, the pooling of risk ceased as defined benefit plans were replaced with defined contribution plans.

No longer is the risk of outliving resources mitigated with shared risk. Now, retirees are responsible for the funds they have accumulated and must determine how to make those funds last throughout their retirements. While self-reliance is generally a great attribute, the reality is that many, if not most, retirees are ill-equipped to manage their portfolios themselves and will need the assistance of financial advisors.

EXHIBIT 7.3

DEFINED CONTRIBUTION VS. DEFINED BENEFIT PLANS

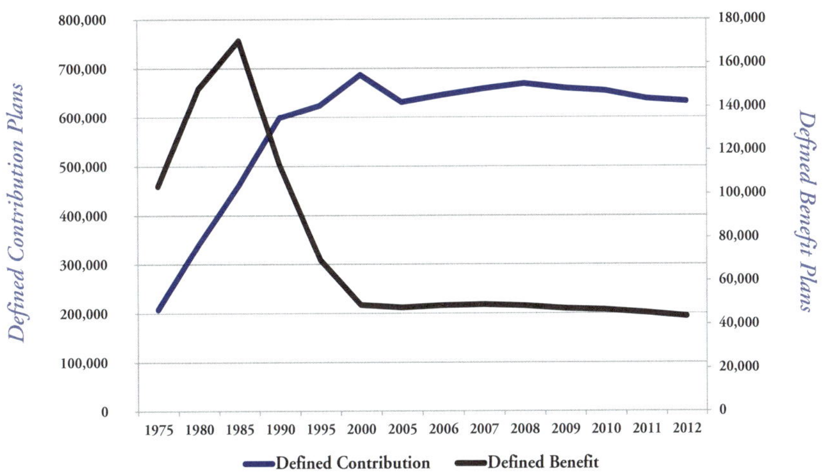

With longer life expectancies and less income from defined benefit plans, it is important for many individuals to mitigate the risk of superannuation. Annuities help individuals mitigate this risk in two ways. First, annuities are often used to accumulate wealth while preserving capital. Secondly, annuities, if annuitized, can provide for lifetime income. Often, annuities are not annuitized and owners simply take withdrawals or surrender the policies. There are numerous features and choices regarding annuities that are discussed throughout the chapter.

CHARACTERISTICS OF ANNUITIES

WHAT IS AN ANNUITY?

An **annuity** is a contract that is designed to provide a specified income that is payable at stated intervals for a specified period of time. Traditionally, individuals received fixed annuities from employer defined benefit plans, from government retirement plans or from insurance companies. However, individuals can purchase commercial annuities from insurance companies and other financial services firms. These annuities are not uniform in any respect. There are many choices a consumer must make when purchasing an annuity. Annuities can be characterized based on several factors, such as the length of payout (fixed or variable), frequency and flexibility of premium (single premium or flexible premium), the timing of when income is payable (immediate or deferred), tax considerations and funding vehicle.

In general, commercial annuities have two phases. The first phase is the **accumulation phase**, which is the period over which funds are accumulated. With deferred annuities, this accumulation takes place over time within the annuity. With immediate annuities, this accumulation of funds comes from some other source, such as life insurance, retirement savings, or an inheritance. The second phase is referred to as **annuitization**, which is when the funds are exchanged for a stream of income guaranteed for a period of time.

Once there is an exchange of funds for the annuity stream, then the owner no longer has access to that sum of funds. It is also important to understand that there are many choices regarding the annuity stream that is chosen. These choices are discussed later in this chapter.

Annuity contracts may protect people from outliving their assets by providing a series of periodic payments to the annuitant, typically lasting as long as the annuitant lives. An annuity is not life insurance, even though it is sold by life insurance companies. Annuities are commonly used to fund retirement benefits.

EXAMPLE 7.1

> Fred retires with $2 million in his 401(k) plan at work. He could attempt to manage the funds himself and budget the money over his retirement years. Alternatively, he could purchase an annuity with all or part of his $2 million that would guarantee a steady stream of income until he dies. The annuity could be paid over his life or could be paid over the joint lives of he and his wife.

Annuity payouts are calculated based on the life expectancy of a group (or pool) of annuity contract owners. Some annuitants live to be age 90 or 100, while others die at much younger ages. Consequently, some annuitants will be paid more money than others and the risk of living "too long" is thus shared among the group. The remaining principal contributed by those who die at younger ages (before their actuarial life expectancy) is used to pay benefits to those who survive (beyond their actuarial life expectancy).

EXHIBIT 7.4

POOLING OF RISK

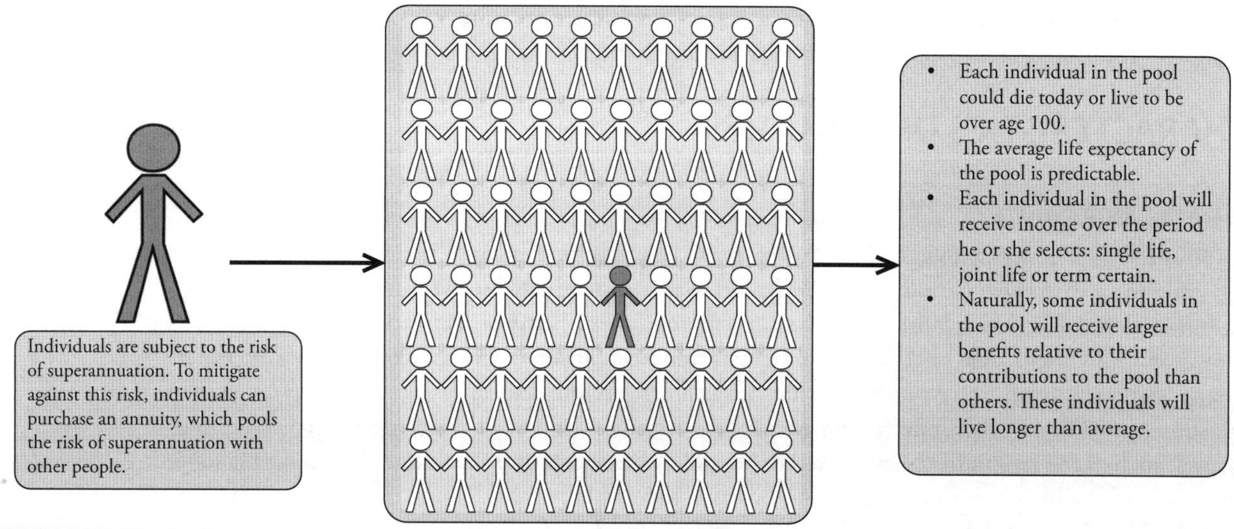

Annuities Summary

Exhibit 7.5

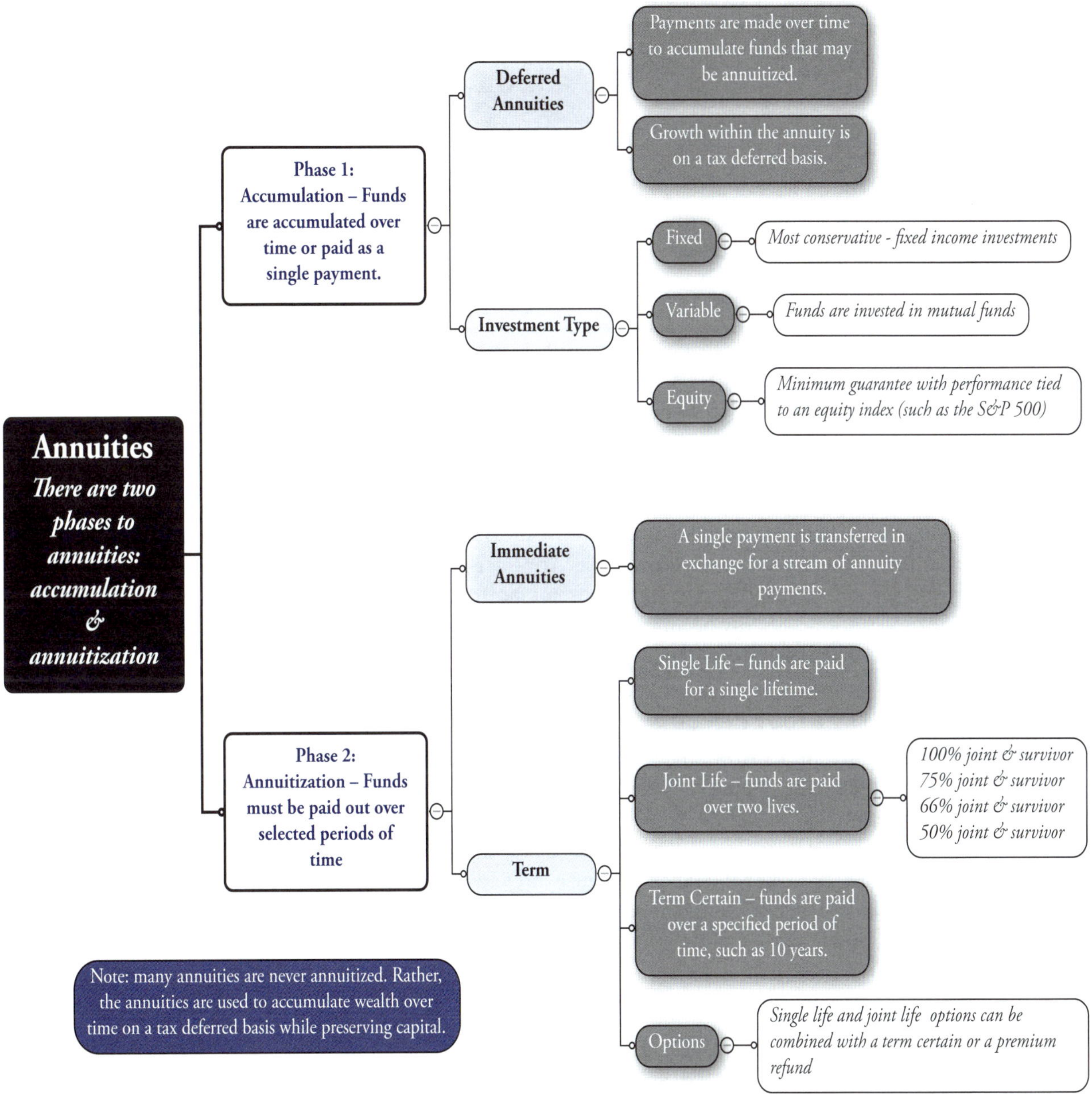

Annuity contracts are not appropriate for all investors. An annuity is designed to provide guaranteed lifetime income and protect against running out of money during retirement. Buyers need to weigh the value of this guarantee against the costs and risks from fees, taxes, and the illiquid nature of annuity contracts. For persons who have bequest motives, it is important to remember that once the premium payments are transferred to the insurance company, they are no longer available to bequeath to the person's heirs and are not directly available for any other expenditures.

EXHIBIT 7.6

ADVANTAGES AND DISADVANTAGES OF ANNUITIES

ADVANTAGES	DISADVANTAGES
• Provides lifetime income • Structure of income can be based on a single life or multiple lives • Eliminates superannuation risk • May provide protection from creditors • Earnings are tax-deferred • Investment options allow for fixed or variable earnings	• Complexity with so many choices is often difficult for investors to understand • Costs and fees reduce returns within the annuity • Once funds are exchanged for the annuity, they are no longer available for bequests or other needs • Taxable benefits consist entirely of ordinary income, as opposed to capital gains and/or qualifying dividends.

PARTIES TO AN ANNUITY CONTRACT

Generally, there are four parties to an annuity contract:

- The **annuitant** is the individual upon whose life the contract is dependent. It is generally the life expectancy of the annuitant that affects the timing and amount of payout under the contract.
- The **beneficiary** is entitled to the death benefit, if such a benefit exists.
- The **owner** owns the annuity contract and names the annuitant and beneficiaries. The owner could also be the annuitant and/or the beneficiary. It is also possible that the owner not necessarily be an individual, but could also be a trust or a company.
- The insurance company issues the contract.

ANNUITY PAYOUT PERIOD

An annuity may provide payments for a fixed term such as 20 years (term certain) or for an indefinite term such as the lifetime of the annuitant (life annuity). Payments may also be based on the life expectancy of two people, such as a husband and wife. The payout periods are discussed further in the following section.

KEY CONCEPTS

1. Define an annuity.
2. Identify the use of annuities in retirement planning.
3. List the parties to an annuity.
4. Define the different payout methods for annuities.

IMMEDIATE VS. DEFERRED

The payout method used by an annuity contract can be either immediate or deferred.

An **immediate annuity** is an instrument created when the contract owner trades a sum of money in return for a stream of income that begins immediately. Immediate annuities are purchased with one, single, lump sum payment. Immediate annuities are commonly used by individuals upon retiring to fund recurring, basic expenses that a retiree faces, such as the costs of shelter, clothing, food, and other necessities of life. Immediate annuities can also be the result of a government obligation, such as Social Security, or a corporate obligation, as in a defined benefit plan.

The benefit of an immediate annuity comes from the certainty it provides. Especially when considering retirement needs, immediate annuities provide a guaranteed income while stocks and the value of other investment securities may fluctuate up or down, resulting in uncertain and potentially risky retirement cash flows. A steady stream of income is particularly important for retirees, at least with respect to their ongoing, basic consumption needs. In theory, many retirees prefer a steady stream of income to cover all of their expenses. In practice, however, many retirees are unwilling to give up ownership of their assets in exchange for a guaranteed steady stream of income. Many retirees take a balanced approach by having a portion of their assets annuitized (including Social Security and other retirement annuities) to cover basic consumption needs while preserving other assets for additional consumption and bequest motives.

Immediate annuities require a sum of money to be exchanged for the annuity payments. However, annuities can be used to accumulate a sum of money over time prior to the funds being paid out (annuitized) in the form of an annuity. These types of annuities are referred to as deferred annuities. A **deferred annuity** is an annuity contract that does not begin distributions immediately, but waits until some future time to start payments. The premium payments used to fund a deferred annuity can be either a single lump sum payment, or a series of payments made over time (generally years). Deferred annuity contracts permit a client to invest the premium payments in various underlying investments inside of the annuity contract for a period of time with the goal of accumulating assets that can then be paid out in the form of a series of periodic payments.

Deferred annuity contracts may be attractive options for both the young and the old. Young individuals with a long work life expectancy may use deferred annuities to accumulate a pool of funds that can be annuitized later. This approach allows them to capture investment growth between the time the premium payments are made and the date of annuitization. It should be noted, however, that there are other investment vehicles that provide the same tax deferral with lower fees and less complexity. Older individuals closer to retirement may use deferred annuities for "longevity insurance," which is a strategy that permits retirees to consume their retirement funds over their normal life expectancy without the fear of living beyond their assets and thus, running out of money. Longevity insurance is discussed later in this chapter.

One of the advantages of annuities is their favorable tax treatment. Income earned within the annuity is not taxable until such time as it is distributed or paid out. This feature allows the annuity to accumulate earnings on a tax-deferred basis. Deferred annuities take advantage of this feature by accumulating assets over a period of years. The taxation of annuities is further discussed later in this chapter.

Flexible Premium vs. Single Premium

As mentioned above, annuities can be purchased with flexible premiums or with a single premium. A **flexible premium annuity** allows the insured the option to vary premium deposits over time. Under a flexible premium plan the insured spreads payments out over a designated period of time by paying periodic premiums. These payments can be made in equal installments or can vary in terms of amount and timing. Earnings on the deposits are tax-deferred until the annuity begins making payments. The size of the annuity payments will be dependant on the premiums that are paid and the earnings accumulated prior to payout.

An annuity purchased with a single lump sum is known as a **single premium annuity**. The funds used for purchasing a single premium annuity can come from various sources, such as life insurance, retirement funds or savings. Proceeds of life insurance policies can be used to purchase single premium annuities at special rates under life income settlement options. Retiring individuals often purchase single premium annuities upon retirement using some or all of their qualified retirement plan money.

EARNINGS

The value of an annuity account will increase due to premiums and will increase due to earnings. Annuities will either be fixed or variable. Fixed annuities invest in less risky investments and will guarantee returns for a period of time. Variable annuities have a wider array of investment choices, including equity investments. These options are more thoroughly discussed later in the chapter.

QUICK QUIZ 7.2

1. The four parties to an annuity contract include the annuitant, the owner, the insurance company issuing the contract, and the beneficiary.
   a. True
   b. False

2. Deferred annuities are always purchased with one, single, lump sum payment.
   a. True
   b. False

3. Annuity benefits are taxed as capital gains.
   a. True
   b. False

True, False, False.

ANNUITY BENEFIT OPTIONS

An annuity is an agreement whereby a person will exchange a sum of money for a series of periodic payments. These payments can be structured in many different ways, which are referred to as benefit options. The standard benefit options are to have the annuity paid over a single life, a specific period of years (term certain), or over the lives of two individuals. There are variations in these standard options, which are discussed below.

EXHIBIT 7.7 ANNUITY BENEFIT OPTIONS

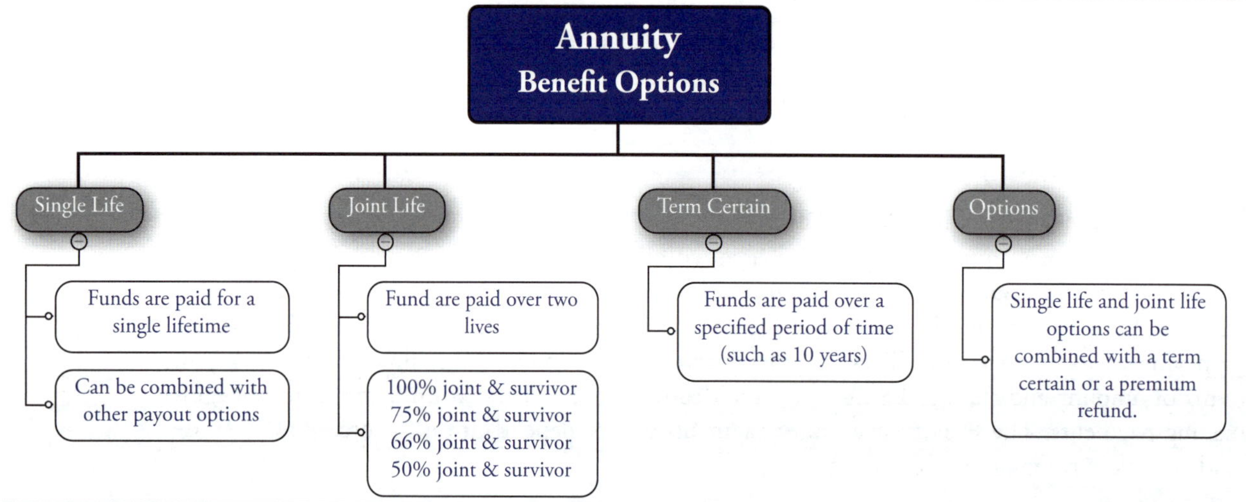

Single Life Annuities

A **single life annuity** is an annuity that only provides payments to one person. The payments from a single life annuity cease when the annuitant dies. A single life annuity has many payout options available. Single life annuities include:

- Straight or pure life annuities
- Installment refund annuities
- Cash refund annuities
- Term certain annuities

Straight or Pure Life Annuities

A **straight or pure life annuity**, provides a stream of income to the annuitant for life. When the annuitant dies, the annuity payments end. Compared to other types of annuity contracts, a pure life annuity provides a greater annuity cash-flow for a given premium payment since only one measuring life is used for determining the annuity payment term.

Key Concepts

1. Differentiate between single life annuities and joint and survivor life annuities.
2. Understand the different payout options with a single life annuity.
3. Understand the different payout options with a joint and survivor annuity.

Many individuals will not purchase single life annuities because the mortality risk is retained by the annuitant. Recall that annuity contracts offer an opportunity for individuals to hedge against the risk of running out of money by transferring that risk to an insurance company. The insurance company pools the risks represented by many annuitants, and uses the premiums paid by those who die early (before actuarial life expectancy) to fund the annuity payments of those who live longer than their actuarial life expectancy. It is possible, therefore, that someone could purchase a life annuity contract and die after receiving only one, or a few, payments. Since there is no guaranteed minimum number of payments on a single life annuity, the annuitant's heirs will receive nothing from the contract once the annuitant has died. For this reason, using all of an individual's retirement savings to purchase a pure single life annuity may be ideal for the person who is very risk averse and seeks to spread income out over his lifetime to smooth his consumption but does not have any bequest motive. If a person has bequest motives, single life annuities may still be valuable in planning for retirement income when used in combination with other strategies. Many individuals will use part of their retirement savings to purchase a single life annuity that covers basic cash flow needs in retirement, such as housing, food, clothing, and medical costs. They retain control of their other retirement assets for use during retirement and for possible distribution to heirs after death. This bifurcated approach allows individuals to transfer part of the risk of running out of money to the insurance company without completely disinheriting heirs.

Installment Refund Annuities

An **installment refund annuity option** provides for the insurer to continue periodic annuity payments after the annuitant has died until the sum of all annuity payments made equals the original purchase price of the annuity. This option reduces the risk that an unexpected early death will result in a large sum of money being exchanged for only a few annuity payments.

Cash Refund Annuities

A **cash refund annuity option** also guarantees that the annuitant or the annuitant's family will receive the premium payments made to purchase the annuity, but instead of continuing to make periodic payments until there is a full recovery of the premium, the remaining balance is paid in cash (lump sum) at the annuitant's death. All else equal, a cash refund annuity will pay a lower monthly income than an installment refund annuity providing the same level of payment since the insurance company's obligation to refund the premium payment may be accelerated at the death of the annuitant.

Both installment and cash refund annuities provide lifetime income for the annuitant. These refunds are only considered if the annuitant dies before the amount of premiums have been paid out. In addition, these options result in a smaller annuity amount as compared to the straight life annuity option because these options have less risk for the annuitant.

Term Certain (Guaranteed Minimum Payment)

A **term certain annuity** (also known as period certain) pays annuity benefits for a specified period of time. This term could be for ten or twenty years. With a term certain annuity, it will pay benefits for only that period of time. Once the final payment is made, the annuity payments are complete. Based on this type of structure, a term certain annuity continues to subject the annuitant to the risk of superannuation.

Two common guarantee options are the ten-year period certain and the twenty-year period certain. If the annuitant dies before the end of the guarantee period, the named beneficiary receives the remaining guaranteed payments. If the annuitant outlives the term certain period, payments continue to the annuitant until the annuitant's death.

While a term certain will only make payments for the specified period of time, a term certain option can be combined with a life annuity. Unlike a straight life annuity, which does not guarantee a minimum number of payments, a life annuity with a term certain provision ensures that the annuitant or his heirs receives a minimum number of payments or, alternatively, if the annuitant lives for a long time, the annuitant will receive a lifetime of income. A term certain annuity acts as a hedge against the mortality risk retained when an individual purchases a single life annuity. In the case that the annuitant dies before his or her life expectancy, it preserves some of the capital for distribution to the annuitant's heirs. This hedge comes at a cost. For a given level of premium payment, the payment received by the annuitant of a single life annuity with a term certain provision will be less than the payment received by the purchaser of a straight life annuity. In the unusual case of a single life annuity with a term certain equal to the life expectancy of the annuitant, the insurance company is retaining both the risk that the insured will die before life expectancy, and the risk that the insured will die after life expectancy. With a straight life annuity, the insurance company retains the risk that the annuitant will die after their actuarial life expectancy.

EXAMPLE 7.2

Scott is retiring and is concerned about the risk of running out of money during retirement. He will receive Social Security benefits, but they are not enough to cover his basic financial needs. He was advised to consider an annuity, which appears to have many advantages. However, he does not want to run the risk of exchanging a large sum of money and then only receiving a few payments if he were to unexpectedly die shortly after purchasing the annuity. Given his fear, he might consider an installment refund annuity, a cash refund annuity or a term certain annuity. Either of these options will "guarantee" a minimum amount of income from the annuity, but they will all have lower payments than a straight or pure life annuity.

Joint and Survivor Life Annuities

A **joint and survivor annuity** promises to make payments over the lives of two or more annuitants, and annuity payments are made until the last annuitant dies. Joint and survivor annuities are commonly used to fund the retirement cash-flow of married couples. Without a joint and survivor option, a surviving spouse could be subject to a significant decrease in income if the annuity payments stopped at the death of the first spouse.

A **100 percent joint and survivor annuity** pays the specified monthly payment to the annuitants while both are alive and continues to make the same payment to the survivor after the first annuitant's death.

Some individuals may determine that, after the first death, the survivor would not need 100 percent of the original annuity payment since the deceased spouse will no longer have consumption expenses. They may choose a joint and survivor annuity that pays the survivor only a portion of the payment that was paid on both lives. For example, a married couple may purchase an annuity that pays $2,000 per month while both spouses are alive, but upon the death of the first spouse, the payment is reduced to $1,500 (75% of the original payment). This form of annuity contract is referred to as a **75 percent joint and survivor annuity**.

When a married person is a participant in a defined-benefit qualified retirement plan, the Retirement Equity Act (REA) requires that the pension benefit be paid in the form of a **50 percent joint and survivor annuity**. Retirement plan participants can elect to increase the payment made to a survivor to a higher percentage, but they cannot reduce the percentage below 50 percent or elect to receive a straight life annuity without the written consent of the nonparticipant spouse. For a given level of annuity benefit, the higher the percentage of the initial payment paid to the survivor of a joint and survivor

Quick Quiz 7.3

1. The term for annuities is always over a single life or a joint life.
   a. True
   b. False

2. A joint and survivor annuity always continues to pay 100% after the death of the first annuitant.
   a. True
   b. False

3. A single life annuity can be combined with a fixed term guarantee.
   a. True
   b. False

4. The amount of a life annuity benefit with a guaranteed term will be less than that without a term guarantee.
   a. True
   b. False

False, False, True, True.

annuity, the lower the amount of periodic income. The premiums for joint and survivor annuities are typically greater than the premiums charged for single life annuities because the insurer promises to make payments over a longer period of time.

EXAMPLE 7.3

Gavin and Clair are 65 years old, have been married for forty years, and are getting ready to retire. They have accumulated $1 million that they would like to convert into an annuity. The annuity company might provide for the following options:

- Single life annuity over Gavin's life of $76,000
- Single life annuity over Clair's life of $65,000
- 100% joint life annuity of $57,000
- 75% joint life annuity of $62,000

They would need to decide if they prefer one of these options over the other. They might also decide to include one of the other options, such as an installment refund annuity option or a cash refund annuity option.

TYPES OF ANNUITY CONTRACTS

Several different forms of annuity contracts are offered for sale to consumers, including fixed annuities, variable annuities, and equity-indexed annuities. Investors will often choose an annuity for potential growth, tax deferred savings and/or principal protection. The annuity may or may not ever be annuitized.

KEY CONCEPTS

1. Define fixed annuity payments.
2. Identify the characteristics of variable annuities.
3. Identify advantages and disadvantages of variable annuities.
4. Describe equity-indexed annuities.
5. Discuss common indexing methods.

- A **fixed annuity** provides payments of a fixed dollar amount that is typically determined when the annuity payments begin. The income is fixed based on the guaranteed returns provided by the insurer in the account.
- **Variable annuities** offer a variable rate of return based on the overall return of the investment options that are chosen. Variable annuities offer potentially higher returns than fixed annuities, but they also carry a greater risk of loss. Variable annuities offer an opportunity to mitigate the risk of inflation by investing in equities. Variable annuities also mitigate against investment risk since they have some minimum guarantees built into the contracts.
- An **equity indexed annuity** has characteristics of both fixed and variable annuities. It offers a minimum guaranteed interest rate combined with an investment return linked to the performance of a specific equity based market index, such as the S&P 500. Equity indexed annuities also mitigate investment risk, longevity risk and inflation risk.

Types of Annuity Contracts by Underlying Investments

EXHIBIT 7.8

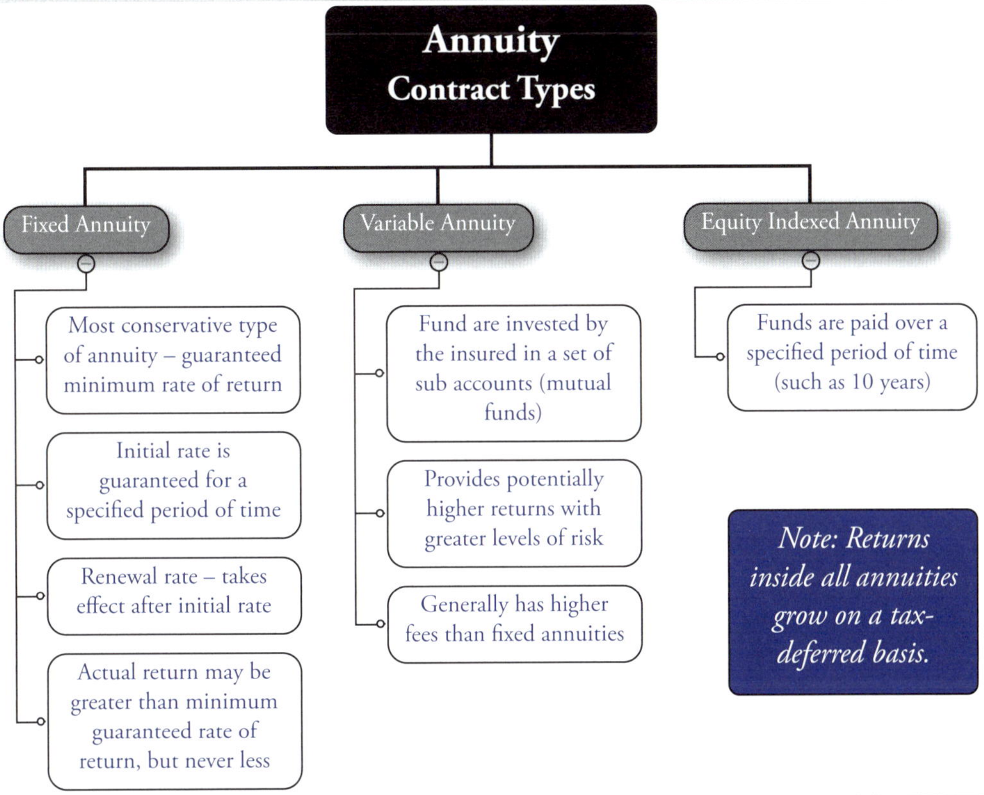

Fixed Annuity

A fixed annuity is the most conservative type. A fixed annuity is a contract that provides full principal protection combined with a guaranteed rate of return that is stated in the annuity contract.

Typically, the premiums paid for the annuity contract will begin earning an interest rate, which is dependent on current fixed income interest rates and known as the **initial rate**. This initial interest rate is guaranteed for a period of time. Once the initial interest-rate-guarantee period expires, a **renewal rate** for the policy will go into effect. This rate will never be less than the minimum interest rate stated in the annuity policy. As a result, the actual rate of return on the contract may be higher than the stated guaranteed rate of return in the contract, depending on prevailing interest rates. However, it will never be less than the guarantee.

Variable Annuity

A variable annuity is a contract between an annuitant and an insurance company whereby the insurance company agrees to make periodic payments to the annuitant in an amount to be determined in the future that is based on the accumulated value of the contract. Variable annuities can be purchased with either a single premium or a series of premiums (flexible premium).

A variable annuity, like all other annuity contracts, has two phases: the accumulation phase and the annuitization, or payout phase. During the accumulation phase the annuitant makes payments into the contract that are invested in various mutual fund investments chosen by the annuitant. The earnings on these investments accumulate on a tax-deferred basis. Variable annuities offer a variable rate of return based on the overall return of the investment options chosen by the contract owner. The payout phase begins when the annuitant elects to annuitize the contract and receive regular payments from the insurance company.

Some older variable annuity contracts require the annuitant to annuitize the contract no later than the attainment of a specified age, such as age 85-90. Once the contract is annuitized, control of the investment account is transferred to the insurance company in exchange for the promise to make annuity payments. Annuitization typically terminates any accumulation-phase benefits, such as living or death benefits, provided for in the contract.

Some people view variable annuities as an investment option that offers features not typically found in other types of non-qualified investments, including: tax-deferred earnings, the ability to avoid income tax when one investment in the annuity contract is sold and replaced with another investment (sometimes referred to as a tax-free transfer among subaccounts), death benefit protection options, living benefit protection options, and lifetime income options.

Since control of the underlying investments in the variable annuity contract rests with the contract holder, variable annuities offer potentially higher returns than fixed annuities but also involve investment risk. The prospectus provided to purchasers of variable annuities contains important information about the annuity contract, including fees and charges, investment options and objectives, risks, death benefits, living benefits, and annuity income options. All of these factors should be carefully considered by purchasers of variable annuities. Variable annuities typically have a trial period of 10 or more days from the receipt of the contract, known as a free-look period. During this time the purchaser can terminate the contract and recover the premium paid without being subject to any surrender charges.

Variable Annuity Fees

Variable annuity products have unique fees and charges designed to cover the cost of contract administration, portfolio management, and insurance benefits (for example, death benefits before annuitization and lifetime income benefits). Fees and charges may be assessed on the original investment, the current account value, or on the benefit's base value (benefit base). Variable annuities may impose a variety of fees and expenses. The most common fees and charges associated with a variable annuity are discussed below:

Mortality and expense risk charges - These charges compensate the insurance company for insurance risks and are deducted from the value of the contract. These expenses are intended to cover the risk of annuitants living too long. The fees for guaranteed death benefits are included in mortality and expense risk charges. The typical mortality and expense risk charge ranges from 1.15% to 1.85% annually.

Administrative and distribution fees - These are the fees that cover the costs associated with servicing and distributing the annuity. These fees typically range from 0% to 0.35% annually.

Annual fee - An annual fee is a flat fee charged for record keeping and administration. The fee typically ranges from $30 to $50 and is charged on the contract anniversary date. This fee is regularly waived for contract values of $50,000 or more.

Sub account fees and expenses - These fees and expenses are charged to the investment subaccounts inside the annuity (mutual funds), and include investment management fees. Additional expenses include the cost of buying and selling securities within the subaccounts. These are asset-based expenses that will vary by subaccount but typically range from 0.7% to 2.5% annually.

Surrender charges - Many variable annuities have sales charges or surrender charges, known as contingent deferred sales charges (CDSC). Most variable annuities do not have an initial sales charge. However, insurance companies often assess surrender charges to annuitants who liquidate their contract during the surrender period.

The surrender charge is typically a percentage of the amount withdrawn and declines gradually over time. The surrender charge is effectively a way for the insurance company to recoup the broker's commission. A typical surrender charge ranges from seven percent to nine percent, decreasing over the surrender period to zero percent. Variable annuities are offered by share class with B shares typically having a six to eight-year period of surrender charges for each contribution, L shares having a three to four-year surrender charge period for each contribution, and C shares having no surrender charge period making them fully liquid. The B shares typically have slightly lower fees.

There is generally a direct link between the CDSC and the commission the broker receives as part of the sale. Often, a seven year CDSC implies a seven percent commission. While this is not always the case, it is important to keep this in mind when selecting annuities.

Not all annuities have sales charges or a CDSC. Annuities that do not have sales charges can be purchased directly from companies such as Fidelity and Vanguard. In addition, fee only advisors also sell annuities that do not charge a sales charge.

EXAMPLE 7.4

> Eddie purchases a variable annuity contract with a $100,000 purchase payment. The contract has a schedule of surrender charges, beginning with a 7% charge in the first year, and declining by 1% each year. In addition, he is allowed to withdraw 10% of the contract value each year free of surrender charges. In the first year, Eddie decides to withdraw $50,000, or one-half of your contract value of $100,000 (assuming the contract value has not increased or decreased because of investment performance). In this case, Eddie could withdraw $10,000 (10% of contract value) free of surrender charges, but he would pay a surrender charge of 7%, or $2,800, on the other $40,000 withdrawn.

During the accumulation phase, a variable annuity offers a wide range of both fixed and variable subaccounts with different investment objectives and strategies. The value of the variable annuity at any point in time will be a function of the performance of the investment options chosen by the contract holder. Variable subaccounts include actively managed portfolios, exchange traded funds, indexed or index-linked portfolios, alternative investments, and other quantitative-driven strategies. The subaccounts invest in various asset classes that include stocks, bonds, real estate, derivatives, commodities, and money market instruments.

Within the variable annuity during the accumulation period, the annuitant can transfer money from one subaccount to another without paying current income taxes on any earnings. The number of transfers per year may be limited by the annuity contract. Variable annuity issuers typically limit the number of transfers to discourage day trading-type activity within the contract.

During the accumulation period the earnings grow on a tax-deferred basis. During the surrender period, variable annuity contracts generally offer the contract holder the right to withdraw up to 10 percent of the contract value annually without incurring a surrender charge. Withdrawal of money from a variable annuity will subject earnings to income tax at ordinary income tax rates, and if a withdrawal is taken prior to the attainment of age 59½, the annuitant may be subject to an additional 10 percent early withdrawal penalty on the amount that is subject to income tax.

Variable annuity contracts, similar to other annuity contracts, allow for the contract value to be paid to a named beneficiary upon the death of the annuitant if the annuitant dies prior to annuitizing the contract. Annuity contracts also frequently provide a standard death benefit that is calculated as the greater of the return of premiums paid on the annuity less withdrawals, or the contract value at the death of the annuitant. Some contracts offer additional enhanced benefits such as the ability to lock in a death benefit equal to the highest value of the contract. Optional death benefits typically cost from 0.25 percent to 1.5 percent annually and may terminate once an income option is elected and the annuitization period or payout period begins.

Guaranteed Living Benefit Riders

The equity markets provide investors with an opportunity to generate investment returns that outperform inflation and taxes and increase wealth significantly over longer compounding periods. The primary concern with equity markets is the significant risk or at least the perceived risk. For example in 1987 (Black Monday), the equity market dropped close to 30 percent in one day. In 2008, the market dropped over 30 percent for the year. Guaranteed living benefit riders are sold and marketed with the notion of combining the upside potential available in the equity markets with a guaranteed rate of return and principal protection.

Many annuities offer living benefits that provide principal and or income guarantees to help protect retirement income from declining markets during the accumulation phase. Living benefit riders provide income protection while allowing for investment growth opportunities. There are three basic types of living benefits:

1. the guaranteed minimum accumulation benefit (GMAB)
2. the guaranteed minimum income benefit (GMIB)
3. the guaranteed minimum withdrawal benefit (GMWB)

The cost of additional optional living benefits typically ranges from 0.3 percent to 2.0 percent annually, and may be either fixed or variable, depending on the contract provisions. Purchasers should be aware that the costs on these riders can greatly decrease the upside growth potential within the annuity.

The general concepts of the GMAB, GMIB and GMWB living benefit riders are discussed below, in addition to the Guaranteed Lifetime Income Benefit (GLIB). However, it is important to understand that the contract from each insurance company may have differences in terms of guarantees, minimums, costs and other variables. Therefore, it is critical to carefully read and understand these types of riders before considering the appropriateness of the annuity or rider.

Guaranteed Minimum Accumulation Benefit

A guaranteed minimum accumulation benefit (GMAB) rider guarantees that for a specified period of time (typically 7-10 years), an investor's contract value will be at least equal to a certain minimum percentage (usually 100%) of the amount invested regardless of investment performance. The rider combines principal protection with potential upside potential. Many GMABs require the funds to be invested in a specified set of sub accounts or in a specified asset allocation.

Guaranteed Minimum Income Benefit

A guaranteed minimum income benefit (GMIB) rider is designed to provide the investor with a minimum amount of lifetime income during retirement, regardless of investment performance. The contract guarantees an income stream based on a minimum benefit base. The benefit base initially equals the initial investment, but will increase over time. Generally, investors must wait for a period of time (often ten years) before annuitizing. The rider guarantees the income even if the benefit base goes to zero.

Guaranteed Minimum Withdrawal Benefit

A guaranteed minimum withdrawal benefit (GMWB) rider guarantees that a certain percentage (usually 5-7%) of the amount invested can be withdrawn annually until the entire amount is completely recovered, regardless of investment performance of the underlying asset base.

If the underlying investments perform well, then there are additional funds in the policy at the end of the withdrawal period. If the underlying investments perform poorly or if the account value drops to zero, the investor can still continue to take withdrawals until the full amount of the original investment is recovered.

There is often a step-up feature that permits the investor to lock in a higher benefit base if the underlying investments perform well.

Guaranteed Lifetime Income Benefit

The Guaranteed Lifetime Income Benefit (GLIB) guarantees that a certain percentage (typically 2-8%, often based on age) of the amount invested can be withdrawn each year for as long as the contract holder lives. The percentage will be lower for younger investors and higher for older investors when withdrawals begin.

These riders have been extremely popular and often misunderstood given the volatility in the equity markets and the low interest rates available on fixed income securities. Most of these riders are available on fixed annuities as well as variable annuities.

Equity-Indexed Annuities

Equity-indexed annuities are fixed annuities, either immediate or deferred, that earn interest or provide benefits that are linked to an external equity reference or an equity index. The value of the index might be tied to an equity index or some other index One of the most commonly used indices for annuity products is the Standard & Poors 500 composite stock price index (S&P 500), which is an equity based index. The value of any index varies from day to day and is not predictable or guaranteed.

An equity indexed annuity differs from other fixed annuities because of the way it credits interest to the contract value. Some fixed annuities only credit interest at a rate set in the contract. Other fixed annuity contracts credit interest at rates that are set from time to time by the insurance company. In contrast, equity-indexed annuities credit interest using a formula based on changes in the index to which the annuity is linked. The formula determines how the additional interest is calculated and credited to the contract. An equity indexed annuity is a compromise between a variable annuity and a straight fixed annuity having little downside risk and modest upside potential.

An equity indexed annuity, like other fixed annuities also promises to pay a minimum (guaranteed but low) interest rate. This minimum rate guarantee is paid regardless of whether the index-linked interest rate is lower than the guaranteed rate. The value of the annuity will also not decline below a guaranteed minimum value because it is guaranteed by the issuer. For example, many single premium annuity contracts guarantee that the minimum value will never be less than 90 percent of the premiums paid plus at least three percent plus annual interest less withdrawals.

Quick Quiz 7.4

1. Mortality and expense charges for a variable annuity may exceed 1%.
   a. True
   b. False

2. Surrender charges are not used for variable annuities.
   a. True
   b. False

3. The annual reset (ratcheting) method is a common indexing method for equity-indexed annuities.
   a. True
   b. False

True, False, True.

The two features of an equity indexed annuity contract that have the greatest effect on the amount of additional interest that may be credited to the contract are:

- The indexing methods specified in the contract
- The participation rate

It is important for contract owners to understand the features of the contract and how those features work together.

The **indexing method** is the approach used to measure the amount of change, if any, in the index. Some common indexing methods include:

- The annual reset (ratcheting) method
- The high watermark method
- The point-to-point method

COMMON INDEXING METHODS

EXHIBIT 7.9

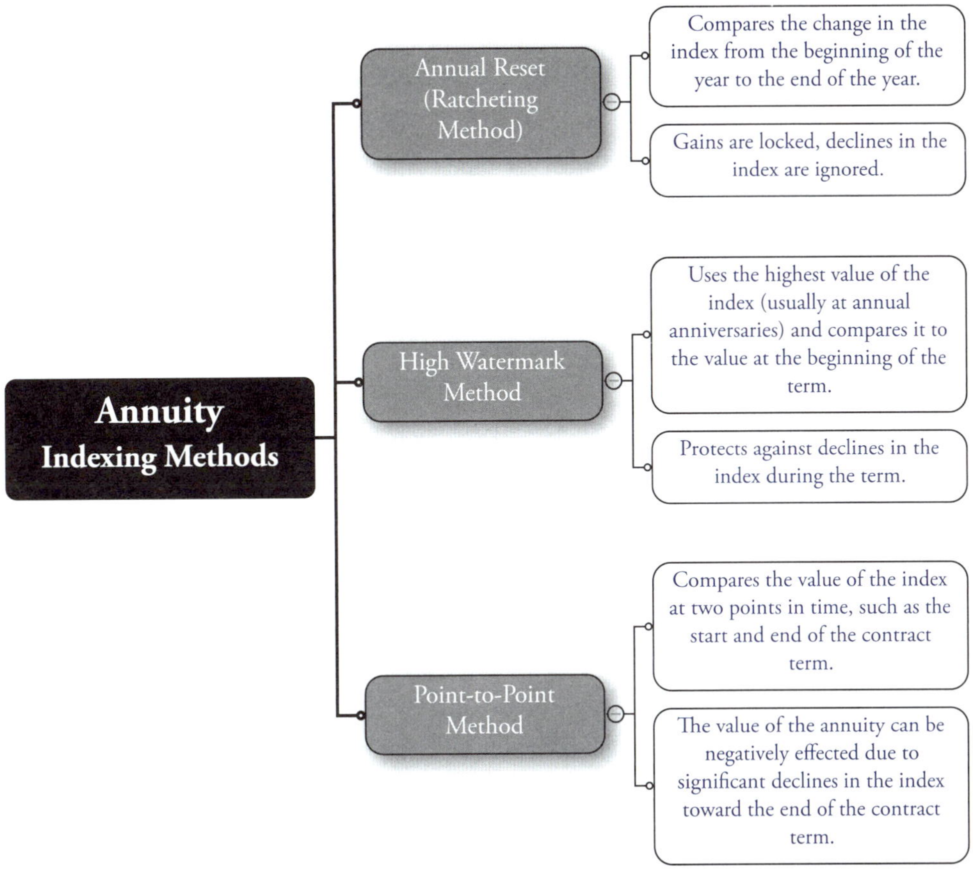

Note: All 3 methods can be combined with various cap rates and / or participation rates.

When the **annual reset method** is used, the index-linked interest crediting rate is determined each year by comparing the index value at the end of the contract year with the index value at the beginning of the contract year. Interest is then added to the annuity each year during the term. The advantage of the annual reset method is that the interest earned is locked in and the index value is reset at the end of each year. Future decreases in the index will not affect the interest already earned and credited to the contract. The trade-off for this indexing method is that the participation rate may change each year and will generally be lower than other indexing methods. Furthermore, an annual reset design may use averaging to limit the total amount of interest earned each year.

The **high watermark approach** to determining index-linked interest is accomplished by comparing the value of the index at various points during the term (usually on anniversary dates). The interest credited is based on the difference between the highest index values and the index value at the start of the term. Interest is added to the annuity at the end of the term. Since interest is calculated using the highest value of the index, this design may credit higher interest to the contract than some other interest crediting designs if the index reaches a high point early or in the middle of the term and then drops off later. The trade-off is that interest is not credited until the end of the term. Equity-indexed annuities taking this approach may cause the loss of interest for the last accumulation period prior to annuitization, since surrendering an annuity before the end of the term will result in forfeiting the indexed-linked interest for that term. Contracts with this design may have a lower participation rate than annuities using other designs, or they may use a cap to limit the total amount of interest that can be earned.

The **point-to-point index-linked crediting method** is based on the difference between an index value at the end of the term compared with the index value at the start of the term. Interest is then added to the annuity at the end of the term. Since interest cannot be calculated before the end of the term this design permits a higher participation rate than annuities using other indexing methods. However, since the term is typically six or seven years, the annuitant may not be able to receive the index-linked interest until the end of the term.

The **index term** is the period over which index-linked interest is calculated. For most equity-indexed annuities, interest is credited at the end of a time period ranging from one to ten years, with six or seven years being the most common. Some indexed annuities offer single terms while others offer multiple, consecutive terms. If an annuity has multiple terms, there will usually be a window at the end of each term (typically 30 days) during which the annuitant may withdraw money without penalty.

The **participation rate** determines how much of the increase in the index will be used to calculate the index-linked interest. For example, if the calculated change in the index is 10 percent, and the participation rate is 70 percent, the index-linked interest will be seven percent. A company may set a different participation rate for newly issued annuities as often as each day. Therefore, the initial participation rate in the annuity will depend on when it was issued. The company usually guarantees the participation rate for a specific period (from one year to the entire term of the contract). When that period is over the company sets a new participation rate for the next period. Some annuities guarantee that the participation rate will never be lower than a specified minimum amount and will never be higher than a specified maximum amount.

Some indexed annuities impose an upper limit on the index-linked interest rate, referred to as the **cap rate**. This rate is the maximum rate of interest that the annuity will earn. For example, if an indexed annuity contract has a 6.5 percent cap rate, only 6.5 percent would be credited to the contract even if the index had a higher return. Not all indexed annuities have cap rates.

The **floor crediting rate** for an indexed annuity is the minimum index-linked interest rate that will be credited to the contract in a given period. The most common floor used in indexed annuities is zero percent. A zero percent floor assures the contract holder that even if the index decreases in value, the index-linked interest credited to the account will be zero (no losses will be allocated to the contract). Purchasers of indexed annuities should be aware, however, that not all annuities have a stated floor on the index-linked interest rates. Those contracts with a floor, however, will retain a minimum guaranteed value.

As an alternative to a cap and floor, some indexed annuities use the average of an index value as the crediting rate rather than the actual value of the index on a specified date. When the averaging approach is employed, the index averaging may occur at the beginning, at the end, or throughout the entire term of the indexed annuity contract.

Some indexed annuities pay simple interest during an index term, while others pay compound interest during the term. In either case, the interest earned in one term is usually compounded in the next term.

In some indexed annuity contracts, the index-linked interest rate is computed by subtracting the margin, or administrative fee. For example, if the calculated change in the index is 10 percent, the annuity might specify that 2.5 percent will be subtracted from the rate to determine the interest rate credited to the contract. In this example, the crediting rate for the contract would be 7.5 percent. The insurance company would only subtract the administrative fee if it would not produce a negative interest crediting rate for the contract.

Equity-indexed annuities provide a variety of death benefits. The most common death benefit is either the guaranteed minimum value of the annuity or the value as determined by the index-linked formula.

QUICK QUIZ 7.5

1. Variable annuities have many fees and costs associated with them.
   a. True
   b. False

2. Variable annuities permit the owner to invest in traditional closed-end mutual funds.
   a. True
   b. False

3. Variable annuities are more complex than fixed annuities.
   a. True
   b. False

True, False, True.

ADVANTAGES AND DISADVANTAGES

ADVANTAGES OF ANNUITY CONTRACTS

Annuities provide several benefits that make them particularly attractive for some individuals.

Individuals concerned with the possibility of outliving their retirement savings may transfer that longevity risk to an insurance company by purchasing an annuity. From a planning perspective, the problem is predicting how long a person will live. With no further advances in medical technology, a male who has attained the age of 66 now has a 50 percent chance to live to age 84 and almost a 20 percent chance to live to age 90. It is prudent, in many situations, to purchase an annuity contract to cover basic consumption needs during retirement so that the annuitant does not have to worry about running out of money at an advanced age.

KEY CONCEPTS

1. Discuss the advantages and disadvantages of annuities.
2. Understand the tax consequences of annuities.

Annuities also provide an opportunity to defer income taxation on the investment earnings in the contract beyond the contribution limitations imposed on ordinary qualified plans and IRAs. Most non-qualified annuities require the account holder to annuitize by a certain age, but many of these contracts impose an age requirement significantly above age 70½, the required beginning date for required minimum distributions (RMDs) from qualified retirement plans and IRAs. Generally, income tax deferral benefits an individual who expects to have a long accumulation period or who expects to be in a lower tax bracket in retirement than when the annuity is funded.

An ancillary benefit to tax deferral is the ability to rebalance the portfolio inside of the annuity contract without incurring any immediate income taxation on asset sales. If investment rebalancing is completed in a non-qualified portfolio outside of an annuity contract, the assets sold in the rebalancing will trigger taxable gain or loss that must be reported on the investor's current income tax return.

Annuities also provide another advantage when unexpected creditor issues arise. Federal law exempts all qualified retirement plans and IRAs from a bankruptcy estate. This exemption means that qualified plan assets and IRA assets are protected from creditors. Annuities are protected from creditors in some states. For example, Louisiana protects most life insurance and annuity contracts.

DISADVANTAGES OF ANNUITY CONTRACTS

While there are many advantages, annuities also have several disadvantages, including complexity, costs, and tax consequences.

Complexity

The complexity associated with annuity contracts is often difficult for investors to understand. The purchase of an annuity contract involves a risk trade-off whereby the risk of living too long is transferred to an insurance company that will pool the funds of many annuitants, using some of the capital paid by those who die before their actuarial life expectancies to pay benefits to those who live beyond their actuarial life expectancies. For many, the possibility of losing capital if they die too young overshadows the benefits of transferring longevity risk to an insurance company. Annuity contracts also have several features such as guaranteed death benefits, guaranteed life income, and guaranteed terms. Each of these features has a cost associated with it, and it is not uncommon for annuity costs to range between 2½ to 3½ percent of invested capital. While these costs are similar to those associated with permanent life insurance, they are expensive when compared with other investment alternatives. One of the reasons for these high costs is that the insurance company cannot predict future medical advances and other items that could dramatically increase life expectancy and therefore significantly increase their costs of providing lifetime income streams for annuitants.

Costs and Fees

One of the major disadvantages of annuity contracts is the costs and fees charged by the insurance company to issue a contract and undertake the longevity risk obligation.

A fixed annuity typically does not impose any direct expense charges on the contract owner other than a surrender charge. Variable annuities, on the other hand, have several types of expenses, including investment management fees for the underlying investment portfolios and annual insurance charges in addition to the surrender charges. These fees and charges were discussed in detail previously in the review of variable annuity contracts.

Surrender charges are commonly used by insurers to recoup the costs of issuing the annuity when the annuitant surrenders the contract within a few years of issuance. These charges typically range from five percent to nine percent of the annuity value and usually decline to zero over a period of time, such as from three to nine years. Each state regulates the maximum term for which a surrender charge may be applied, so the length of the surrender charge period may differ for individuals residing in different jurisdictions.

Insurance charges generally include administrative and distribution charges and mortality and expense risk charges. The administrative and distribution charges pay for all the services involved in the maintenance of variable annuity contracts such as the preparation of the contract statement, mailings, and customer service. Recall that some variable annuity contracts also impose an annual contract fee.

Quick Quiz 7.6

1. Annuities provide an opportunity to defer income taxation on investment earnings.
   a. True
   b. False

2. Fixed annuities generally have significant costs and fees associated with them.
   a. True
   b. False

3. All deferred annuity contracts are subject to the Affordable Care Act surtax of 3.8 percent.
   a. True
   b. False

True, False, False.

Tax Consequences

While one of the benefits of using an annuity contract is the ability to achieve deferral of income taxation on investment gains until amounts are distributed from the contract to the annuitant or a beneficiary, all distributions of income in excess of basis are considered ordinary income, and are subject to tax at the taxpayer's highest ordinary income tax rate. In contrast, investments held outside of annuity contracts do not achieve tax deferral, but they may qualify for favorable capital gains and qualified dividend tax rates that are significantly lower than the tax rates imposed on ordinary income. A more comprehensive discussion of the tax consequences of annuity contracts follows, but it is important to recognize that the purchase of an annuity contract involves a trade-off between the benefits of tax deferral and the benefits of generating investment income taxable at more favorable rates.

Since 2013, distributions from annuity contracts made to high income taxpayers are also subject to the Affordable Care Act surtax of 3.8 percent. A high income taxpayer is an individual with more than $200,000 of adjusted gross income, or a married couple filing jointly with more than $250,000 in adjusted gross income. Currently, the law does not index these thresholds for inflation. Therefore, in addition to all distributions being subject to ordinary income tax (currently, the highest rate is 39.6%), high income individuals may have to pay an additional 3.8 percent tax (raising the income tax rates on annuities to 43.4%). Interestingly, distributions from qualified retirement plans and IRAs are not subject to the 3.8 percent Affordable Care Act surtax, so one way to avoid this additional tax is to purchase an annuity contract inside of a qualified retirement plan or IRA.

TAXATION OF ANNUITIES

INCOME TAXATION

Typically, distributions are not made to the annuitant until the contract is **annuitized**. An annuity contract is annuitized when regular, periodic (such as monthly or annual) payments begin for life or for a specified period of time in excess of one year. In some instances, however, the owner may surrender the contract or decide to take a one-time distribution without annuitizing the contract.

KEY CONCEPTS

1. Explain the income taxation of annuity benefits.
2. Define a non-qualified annuity.
3. Understand the estate tax implications of any remaining value in an annuity at the annuitant's death.

The extent to which distributions from an annuity contract are subject to income tax is determined by reference to the annuitant's basis in the contract. Basis represents after-tax dollars that were invested in the contract. An annuitant who has basis in an annuity contract will receive their basis back income-tax free over their actuarial life expectancy. Distributions from annuity contracts in excess of basis are subject to income tax at ordinary tax rates.

If an annuity owner surrenders the contract, the distribution is taxable to the extent that the distribution exceeds the owner's basis in the contract.

EXAMPLE 7.5

Jasper purchased an annuity contract 10 years ago for $100,000. He feels his retirement funds from other sources are adequate, and needs money now to cover a pressing financial need. Jasper surrendered the annuity contract when the value of the contract was $175,000. Jasper will receive his basis in the contract ($100,000) free of income tax, but will have to pay ordinary income tax on the additional $75,000 he receives when surrendering the contract.

Sometimes, the owner of an annuity does not need to access the full value of the contract, but does need to withdraw some money. When distributions (withdrawals) are taken from an annuity before annuitizing, the entire distribution must be included in the taxpayer's gross income until all of the gain in the contract has been distributed. Once all of the gain in the contract is distributed, further distributions are treated as tax-free returns of invested dollars. Annuity contracts follow a LIFO (last-in, first-out) approach to income reporting in which the gain in the contract (generated from the investment made in the contract) must be fully distributed before a tax-free return of basis may be received. However, annuities issued prior to August 14, 1982 receive FIFO (first-in, first-out) treatment.

EXAMPLE 7.6

Hope purchased an annuity contract 10 years ago for $100,000. The current value of the annuity is $175,000. Hope decides to withdraw $100,000 from the contract to pay for her daughter's graduate education since Hope believes she has enough money saved for retirement. The gain in the contract ($75,000) will be fully subject to income tax when Hope makes the withdrawal, and the additional $25,000 will be treated as a return of Hope's basis. After the withdrawal, Hope will have an annuity contract with a value of $75,000 and a basis of $75,000 ($100,000 original basis less the $25,000 of basis withdrawn from the contract).

Annuities purchased with pre-tax dollars typically do not have any basis (after-tax dollars invested in the contract) for income tax purposes. Examples of annuity contracts that are purchased with pre-tax dollars include annuities purchased with funds in a 401(k) or a deductible traditional IRA plan. In addition, some annuities received as settlements from court cases (to the extent that the payments are not made as compensation for a physical injury) will have a zero basis. Consequently, each payment received by the owner will be fully subject to tax at the owner's ordinary marginal income tax rate.

When an annuitant purchases an annuity contract with after-tax dollars, also known as a **non-qualified annuity**, the after-tax dollars invested in the contract create basis for income tax purposes. Examples of annuity contracts purchased with after-tax dollars include contracts purchased individually by taxpayers outside of retirement plans, annuity contracts received as life insurance settlement options from the death benefits on life insurance policies, and annuities received as settlements from lawsuits to the extent that the damages were for physical injuries sustained by the plaintiffs.

Each annuity payment received from a non-qualified annuity is split into two pieces:

- A tax-free return of basis
- Taxable income

This split is determined by using an inclusion/exclusion ratio similar to that used for the installment method settlement option associated with life insurance death benefits.

The exclusion ratio equals the owner's investment in the annuity contract divided by the expected return on the annuity. The resulting percentage is multiplied by the distribution, or payment, received to calculate the portion of the payment that is not subject to income tax. When performing this calculation, the investment in the contract is the total amount of after-tax dollars invested in the contract, and the expected return is the total amount of dollar distributions expected to be received under the contract. The remaining portion of the payment received by the annuitant is subject to income tax.

EXAMPLE 7.7

Kevin invested $100,000 in an annuity contract. Many years later, he annuitized the contract. The insurance company agreed to pay him $1,388.89 per month for 15 years. His expected return, therefore, is $250,000.02 (15 years x 12 months x $1,388.89 per month). The exclusion ratio is 40%, calculated by taking Kevin's investment in the contract of $100,000 and dividing it by his expected return of $250,000.20. The amount of each payment excluded from tax is $555.56 (calculated by multiplying the exclusion ratio of 40% by the payment of $1,388.89). The difference between the payment of $1,388.89 and the portion excluded from income ($555.56) is $833.34 (60%), which is subject to income tax.

The amount excluded from gross income in a twelve-month period would be $6,666.68 (12 x $1,388.89 x 0.40) and the amount excluded over the entire 15 years would be $100,000 (15 x 12 x $1,388.89 x 0.40). Note that the total amount excluded from income tax in this example equals Kevin's taxable basis in the contract.

The amount included in gross income is the inclusion ratio (60% times each payment received).

Application of the exclusion ratio may be perceived as more difficult if a life annuity payment is chosen instead of a period certain, as illustrated in the preceding example. A simple adjustment, however, is all that is necessary for the exclusion ratio to work. Instead of calculating the return on the contract using the term certain, for tax purposes, it is assumed that the owner will die at actuarial life expectancy. This life expectancy is used as the measuring period for calculating the return on the contract.

EXAMPLE 7.8

Kasey invested $100,000 in an annuity contract. Many years later, he annuitized the contract. The insurance company agreed to pay him $1,388.89 per month for the rest of his life. Using mortality tables provided by the Internal Revenue Service, Kasey's life expectancy was determined to be 15 years. As in the preceding example, the expected return is $250,000.20 (15 x 12 x $1,388.89) and the amounts excluded from and included in gross income are the same.

If an annuitant is receiving a life annuity and dies prior to his or her actuarial life expectancy, the full amount of his or her basis in the contract will not be recovered by the date of death using the exclusion ratio approach to annuity taxation. When this occurs, the annuitant may claim a miscellaneous itemized deduction (not subject to the two percent of adjusted gross income limitation), for the unrecovered basis on his or her final federal income tax return.

If an annuitant is receiving a life annuity and lives beyond his or her actuarial life expectancy, he or she would have recovered the full basis in the contract upon attainment of life expectancy. All payments received by the annuitant after attaining life expectancy, therefore, will be fully subject to tax, and the exclusion ratio will no longer apply.

In addition to the regular income tax that applies to distributions from annuity contracts, two situations will impose additional taxes on the annuitant. If the annuitant takes a distribution of income from an annuity contract before age 59½, a 10 percent penalty tax applies, and if the annuitant is a high income taxpayer and the annuity distribution is not made through an IRA or qualified plan, a 3.8 percent Affordable Care Act surtax will apply.

When taxable income is received from an annuity before the recipient (annuitant) reaches the age of 59½, a 10 percent penalty tax (10 percent of the taxable income) is imposed unless certain exceptions apply, such as distributions made in the form of substantially equal periodic payments to the owner under the provisions of IRC Sections 72(t) or 72(q). This penalty is also waived if the distribution is made due to the disability or death of the annuitant. Prior to annuitization, the last-in, first-out (LIFO) method is used to determine the character of the distribution. This means all of the income of the contract is distributed prior to any distribution of principal. If an annuity owner takes a distribution before reaching age 59½ and the distribution is greater than the income on the contract, the distribution in excess of income is treated as a return of capital and is not subject to income tax or the ten percent penalty.

EXHIBIT 7.10

Taxation Summary Chart

	Qualified Annuity	Non-qualified Annuity
Source of funds	Qualified Plans, IRAs, 403(b) Plans	After-Tax Funds
Tax-deferred earnings	Yes	Yes
Taxation of distributions	Fully Taxable (generally)	Partially Taxable and Partially Return of Basis
10% early withdrawal penalty applies to distributions prior to age 59½	Yes	Yes
Required minimum distributions at age 70½	Yes	No

Furthermore, if the annuitant is a high income individual (defined, for this purpose, as an individual with adjusted gross income over $200,000 or a married couple with adjusted gross income over $250,000), distributions from annuity contracts outside of qualified retirement plans and IRAs will also be subject to the medicare surtax of 3.8 percent imposed by the Affordable Care Act of 2010. Annuity contracts held inside of qualified retirement plans and IRAs are not subject to the 3.8 percent Affordable Care Act surtax.

Annuities Surrendered for a Loss

One of the advantages of variable annuities is that the funds can be invested in assets, such as equities or equity sub accounts, that can provide for sizable growth. However, there are times when the value of an investment in an annuity declines due to changes in the market. In these cases, the owner can surrender the annuity and claim a tax-deductible loss. The annuity must be surrendered and not exchanged. Annuities exchanged for other annuities fall under IRC Section 1035.

The value of the loss on the surrender of an annuity is equal to the investment in the annuity less the value upon surrender. The loss does not include the amount of any surrender charges.

The character of the loss is somewhat unsettled at this point. Annuities are not capital assets. Therefore, the loss is not reported as a capital loss. Annuities produce ordinary income. Thus, there is a case to be made that a loss on a surrendered annuity is an ordinary loss. This approach is more aggressive than the other option, which is to report the loss as a miscellaneous itemized deduction subject to 2 percent of AGI (adjusted gross income).[2]

EXAMPLE 7.9

Jack purchased a variable annuity and invested $150,000. He made a few poor investment decisions, and the market dropped. Like many investors, he decided to sell when the value was low. He decided to surrender the annuity, which cost him a $4,000 surrender fee. He only received $96,000 back. He can take a loss of $50,000. This loss can be taken as an ordinary loss or as an itemized deduction subject to 2 percent of AGI. However, if he takes the loss as an ordinary loss, it could be reversed upon audit.

SECTION 1035 EXCHANGES

As discussed in the Life Insurance Chapter, there are certain tax-free exchanges of life insurance policies and annuities that are permitted under IRC §1035. Section 1035 of the Code states that if a policy is exchanged for another similar policy (for example, life insurance for life insurance, MEC for MEC, or annuity for annuity), or for an insurance product that increases the potential for assessment of income tax, the exchange of the policies is a tax-deferred exchange. No income tax will be due at the time of the exchange. If a tax-deferred exchange is desired, therefore, life insurance policies can be exchanged for other life insurance policies, MECs, or annuity contracts. MECs can be exchanged for other MECs or annuity contracts, and annuity contracts can be exchanged only for annuity contracts.

EXHIBIT 7.11

TAX TREATMENT OF EXCHANGE FOR LIFE INSURANCE AND ANNUITIES

	EXCHANGE FROM	
EXCHANGE TO	Life Insurance	Annuity
Life Insurance	Tax Free	Taxable
Annuity	Tax Free	Tax Free

In the case of a tax-free exchange, the basis of the original contract will carry over to the new contract and will increase if additional premium payments are made to the insurance company.

EXAMPLE 7.10

Brendan purchased an annuity 15 years ago. He has exchanged the annuity for another annuity. This exchange is not a taxable transaction under Section 1035. If Brendan wanted to exchange the annuity for a life insurance policy, then it would be a taxable transaction.

ESTATE TAXATION

The remaining value of an annuity contract held by an individual at death is included in the individual's gross estate for estate tax purposes.

2. See Rev. Rul. 61-201, which provides some support for the more aggressive position of deducting the loss as an ordinary loss. However, losses on IRAs are claimed as miscellaneous itemized deductions subject to the 2 percent limit.

If the owner annuitizes the annuity prior to his death, there is no residual value at the date of the owner's death, and therefore nothing is included in the gross estate for estate tax purposes. Only annuities owned by an individual that had not yet been annuitized, and annuities making term-certain payments extending beyond the date of the original annuitant's death, will be included in the estate of the annuitant at its date of death value.

Annuities are considered **IRD (income in respect of a decedent) assets**. IRD assets represent assets that have a deferred income tax liability that was not paid prior to the date of the owner's death. To preserve the right to subject the deferred income to income tax, the tax law does not permit IRD assets to receive a basis adjustment (equal to the fair market value of the asset at the date of the owner's death) at the death of the owner. Therefore, a beneficiary of an annuity contract will inherit the remaining basis of the original owner, and will pay income taxes on any distributions in excess of basis. To the extent that the inclusion of an IRD asset, such as an annuity contract, in the estate of a decedent increases the decedent's estate tax liability, the increase in estate tax liability becomes an income tax deduction (a miscellaneous itemized deduction not subject to the two percent AGI limit) in the hands of the beneficiary.[3] This income tax deduction offsets some of the income included in the beneficiary's income tax return as a result of receiving the annuity payments.

Quick Quiz 7.7

1. A non-qualified annuity is an annuity purchased with pre-tax dollars.
   a. True
   b. False

2. The exclusion ratio equals the portion of the payment that is subject to income tax.
   a. True
   b. False

3. A single premium deferred annuity purchased with after-tax funds will be subject to the minimum distribution rules.
   a. True
   b. False

4. Annuities are considered IRD assets.
   a. True
   b. False

False, False, False, True.

EXAMPLE 7.11

Pursuant to a retirement plan, ABC Company (ABC) was paying Fred an annuity for life. Fred died at age 92, at which time the annuity payments stopped. No part of the annuity is included in Fred's gross estate.

EXAMPLE 7.12

Meg, who is quirky and unmarried, retired at age 62 and purchased an immediate annuity for $1 million. She was concerned that if she died prematurely she would have wasted her savings. As a result, she decided to purchase a single life annuity with a ten-year term certain option. She named her friend Jeremy as the beneficiary. Unfortunately for Meg, she was hit by a baseball and died four months after purchasing the annuity. Since the annuity will continue to make payments for the remainder of the ten years, that value is included in Meg's gross estate.

3. IRC §691(c).

EXAMPLE 7.13

John, who just died, purchased an annuity contract under the terms of which the issuing company agreed to pay an annuity to the decedent for his life and, upon his death, to pay a specified lump sum to his designated beneficiary. John was drawing his annuity at the time of his death. The amount of the lump sum payment to the beneficiary is includible in the John's gross estate

EXAMPLE 7.14

Pursuant to a retirement plan, ABC Company (ABC) was paying Fred an annuity for life, and was to provide Helen, Fred's wife, upon his death after retirement, with a similar annuity for life. Assume that Fred died at age 67, after the annuity began, when he fell of a treadmill while working out. The value of the wife's annuity is includible in the Fred's gross estate.

EXAMPLE 7.15

Ira has always been a planner and very methodical about his finances. Twenty years ago, he purchased a deferred variable annuity that is now worth $1 million. Unfortunately for Ira, he stepped on a piece of glass and the wound got infected. The infection went untreated, and he died. The value of the annuity, which was not annuitized, is included in his estate.

As the examples above illustrate, if annuity payments continue beyond death, then the value of those payments will generally be included in the owner's gross estate. Depending on the size of the estate, the decedent's estate may or may not be required to pay estate tax. The lifetime exclusion is well over $5 million per person and effectively over $10 million for a married couple. From an income tax perspective, the beneficiary will have to recognize some or all of the payments as income, depending on the basis in the contract.

USES AND APPLICATIONS

Use of Annuity Contracts

There are two primary sources of funding for annuity contracts. Annuity contracts purchased with funds in a qualified retirement plan or IRA are referred to as **qualified annuities**, since the annuity is funded with pre-tax dollars. Annuity contracts purchased with funds outside of qualified retirement plans or IRAs (for example, from investment accounts or private savings) are referred to as non-qualified annuities. Both qualified and non-qualified annuity contracts can be used to supplement an individual's cash-flow during retirement.

Key Concepts

1. Discuss uses of annuities in retirement planning.
2. Define longevity insurance.
3. List the sources of annuities in the secondary market.
4. Identify the risks associated with the purchase of annuities in the secondary market.

Annuities may also be used as structured settlements to fund damages awarded in lawsuits. It is common when the plaintiff in the lawsuit has ongoing needs for cash to pay medical and personal expenses over a long period of time. If there is concern that a lump-sum payment awarded to the plaintiff might be managed, the court may order the defendant to provide a life annuity instead of a single payment.

Lottery winners are frequently given the choice of taking a lump-sum payment for their winnings or receiving a series of payments in the form of an annuity. Usually, the lottery winnings are stated in the amount that a person would receive if the annuity option were selected. The lump-sum payment is always less than the annuity option. With a lottery annuity, the entire payment will be subject to ordinary income tax.

Life insurance policies typically permit beneficiaries of the policy to receive an annuity payout instead of a lump-sum payment. These life insurance settlements consist of the basis from the life insurance proceeds and ordinary income from the earnings.

The tax consequences of receiving annuity payments depends partly on the source of funds used for the purchase of the annuity contract. Income tax consequences are discussed in greater detail later in this chapter.

Use of Annuities in Retirement Planning

Annuity contracts are often used to provide a stable cash-flow stream so that retirees insure that they have enough money during retirement to cover basic consumption needs.

The benefit of an immediate annuity from the perspective of the client is certainty. Immediate annuities are often purchased when an individual retires, since this type of annuity offers a guaranteed income, insulating the owner from the ups and downs of the stock market. In retirement planning, a steady stream of income to cover basic and recurring expenses during retirement is important. In theory, many retirees would prefer a steady stream of income; but, in practice, those same retirees may be unwilling to give up ownership of their assets in exchange for a guaranteed steady stream of income. Retirees may look upon annuities as a gamble on life expectancy with those who live longer winning the bet, and those who die younger losing the bet. Retirees with single life annuities may be concerned that they will die early (losing the annuity life expectancy bet) and, as a consequence, will have squandered their assets.

When an individual approaches retirement, he or she should make a detailed budget for retirement expenses taking into consideration monthly expenses and those expenses that are only paid on an annual basis. In addition, a potential retiree should project the budget forward three or four years to see if these expenditures might change or if major purchases, such as a new vehicle or other durable goods, may be necessary. Once the retirement needs budget has been established, the pre-retiree, or his or her advisor, should determine the sources of retirement income, such as Social Security retirement benefits, government or private pensions, and private savings. Many retirees prefer to have recurring expenses during retirement covered by guaranteed income sources, such as Social Security, defined benefit pension plans, and annuity distributions.

There has been significant academic research published in recent years evaluating sustainable withdrawal rates for retirement portfolios. Traditionally, practitioners have felt comfortable using a four percent withdrawal rate to prevent a retiree from running out of money during retirement. While the four percent withdrawal rate has been criticized by some as being too high, it is still a useful starting place to ascertain how much of a retiree's retirement savings should be annuitized. If

Social Security benefits plus pension benefits plus four percent of the retiree's retirement savings equals or exceeds 100 percent of the retiree's projected retirement needs, there is a reduced need for the purchase of annuities to fund the retirement.

EXAMPLE 7.16

Jay, who is single and age 70, has determined after a detailed budget analysis that his retirement needs are $100,000 per year on a pre-tax basis. His Social Security retirement benefits, which he plans to claim this year, will be $36,000 per year. In addition Jay has $2 million of investment assets. Four percent of $2 million is $80,000, which, when added to the Social Security benefit of $36,000 equals $116,000. In this case, Jay has 36% of his retirement needs in Social Security and the balance is made up of withdrawals from his capital accounts. Upon further analysis, Jay decides that he will prepare a bare-bones budget. This kind of budget takes all discretionary expenditures away from the budget to determine the minimum amount that Jay would need to live on. Jay has determined that his bare-bones budget is $48,000 per year and thus 75% of his bare-bones budget is met by Social Security retirement benefits. After conducting this analysis Jay concludes that he has no need for an individually-owned annuity contract.

EXAMPLE 7.17

John and Mary are both age 62. Both of Mary's parents are still living and are in their 90s. John's mother is also living in her 90s. Both family histories suggest that almost everyone lives into their mid 90s with some family members living beyond 100. John and Mary's Social Security retirement benefits are as follows: John: $20,000 at age 62, $28,571 at age 67, and $35,429 at age 70. Mary has been a stay-at-home mom and has never worked outside of the home. They have estimated that at their retirement age of 66 they will need $100,000 of pretax income to meet their retirement budget, two-thirds of which will need to be inflation adjusted. They have calculated that their combined Social Security benefits will be roughly $40,000 at age 66. In addition to their Social Security benefits they expect to have $1 million in retirement savings at age 66. Using the 4% withdrawal rate plus the $40,000 of Social Security retirement benefits would only give them $80,000 of income. Presuming they have a bare-bones budget of $75,000 per year they may want to use some of their capital to purchase a joint and survivor annuity policy to reduce the risk of running out of money.

Longevity Insurance

Medical science has made significant progress in extending life expectancy over the past century. As life expectancies increase, the possibility of running out of money in retirement increases. One of the most difficult assumptions to make when calculating and funding retirement needs is the number of years an individual will be living in retirement. If retirement funding was based on the assumption of too short a life expectancy, an individual may run out of money during retirement, reducing the enjoyment of later retirement years.

As a hedge against running out of money in retirement, individuals purchase life annuity contracts. **Life annuity contracts** guarantee payments for as long as an individual lives. Using all of one's retirement savings to purchase annuity contracts, however, may not be prudent. Individuals who purchase immediate life annuities at retirement and die before life expectancy will have reduced their potential consumption during retirement years, and have nothing left for transfer to their heirs. On the other hand, those who live beyond actuarial life expectancy benefit from the purchase of an annuity contract, recall that annuity contracts are expensive - there are numerous fees and charges - so placing all of one's retirement funds in an annuity contract may still reduce lifetime consumption due to the transfer to the insurance company in the form of annuity contract expenses.

An intermediate approach to dealing with this problem is **longevity insurance**. Longevity insurance is a sophisticated name for a deferred annuity purchased by an individual at or before retirement that will not begin to make payments until that person reaches an advanced age. The size of the payment on the longevity insurance contract is often designed to cover non-discretionary expenses during retirement after taking into consideration other fixed lifetime income sources available to the retiree, such as Social Security and pension payments. Typically, longevity insurance contracts begin making payments (are annuitized) at age 85. If a longevity insurance contract is purchased, the retiree does not have to worry about running out of money if he or she lives to an advanced age, and his or her remaining retirement funds can be consumed from the date of retirement to age 85, potentially increasing the total amount of consumption that can be enjoyed by the retiree.

The cost of longevity annuity contracts is very reasonable compared to the promised payments on the contract for two reasons. First, the contract is purchased at or before retirement, and payments do not generally begin until age 85. This allows a 20+ year accumulation period for the typical longevity insurance annuity. The longer the accumulation period, the more benefit the owner will receive from compound growth of the investments backing up the annuity contract. Second, since payments on the contract do not begin until age 85, and average life expectancy is about 81 years, more than half of those purchasing longevity annuities will not receive any payments, preserving that capital for those who do live beyond average life expectancy. While those who die before life expectancy do not receive payments on the annuity contract, the overall cost of longevity insurance contracts is reduced due to this actuarial adjustment, and those dying early can preserve the rest of their retirement assets for transfer to heirs without having to worry about running out of money.

EXAMPLE 7.18

Travis, who is 50 years old, has developed a thoughtful retirement plan. He expects that as long as the rate of return on his portfolio yields approximately 300 basis points in excess of inflation, he will be fine. That conclusion assumes he does not live beyond about age 90. However, two of Travis's grandparents lived to age 90 and one is approaching age 100. Given his family longevity and his propensity to be active and health conscious, he is concerned about outliving his retirement assets. He realizes that the return on his assets may or may not exceed his expected return. In addition, he thinks he might very well live beyond age 100. Given these facts, he is considering using 10 percent of his portfolio to purchase a longevity annuity that would begin at age 85, assuming he lives to that age.

On July 1, 2014, the IRS issued final regulations governing the tax treatment of longevity insurance. As our discussion on the taxation of annuity contracts highlighted, high income taxpayers should purchase retirement annuity contracts inside qualified retirement plans and IRAs to avoid the 3.8 percent Affordable Care Act surtax. If a deferred annuity contract is purchased inside a qualified plan or IRA, however, it can pose a problem since its value must be included when determining required minimum distributions, but the money inside of the annuity will not be available for distribution until the retiree attains age 85. The longevity insurance regulations address this problem by specifying that if a qualified longevity insurance contract is purchased inside of a qualified retirement plan or IRA, the value of the contract will not be considered when calculating required minimum distributions. To be considered a qualified longevity insurance contract, the premium for the deferred annuity purchased must not exceed the lesser of 25 percent of the account balance or $125,000, and upon issuance, the contract must be specified to be a longevity annuity contract at issuance. For years beginning after 2014, the $125,000 threshold will be indexed for inflation in $10,000 increments.

Social Security

While many retirees do not view Social Security payments as annuities, Social Security payments have all the characteristics of annuity contracts, and under current law are indexed for inflation. As the examples earlier in the chapter illustrate, since Social Security payments are received on an inflation adjusted basis for the life of the taxpayer, Social Security reduces the need to purchase annuity contracts to cover basic necessities of living during retirement.

Structured Settlements and the Secondary Market

Sometimes, persons are entitled to a pension or are awarded a series of payments over time (an annuity) as the result of a lawsuit or from winning a state lottery (instead of a lump sum payment). After receiving the annuity, some individuals decide they want their cash now and that they do not want to wait to receive the periodic payments. An annuity contract can be sold to someone else in exchange for a lump-sum payment today, discounted for the time value of money. The purchase and resale of these annuities form the secondary market for annuity contracts.

Sometimes these **secondary market annuities** are called pre-owned annuities or in-force annuities. These annuities can be purchased from the original owner at a discount or from a third party, and the stream of income is assigned to the purchaser. Secondary market annuities typically offer a rate of return or yield that is well above the yield available on standard fixed annuities, immediate annuities, or even bonds of a similar credit quality. The increased yield is created when the original owners sell the annuity payments at a discount. It is not the result of the insurer paying a higher rate of return. The insurance company that originally issued the annuity is obligated to make the annuity payments regardless of whether the original owner, or the new owner, is entitled to the payment. When the original payment streams on the annuity were calculated, current market rates were used to determine the payment.

EXAMPLE 7.19

Alice is injured by Barb in an automobile accident. The claim is not settled and ultimately goes to court. Alice wins the case and settlement money is offered to pay Alice either a lump-sum payment or a structured settlement making payments over Alice's lifetime. Alice, who is now unable to work, accepts the structured settlement annuity. The court order specifies that Alice shall receive $2,000 per month for life, with a 20-year guaranteed payment period. Neither Alice nor the court want Barb or Barb's auto insurance company to pay the annuity. Therefore, Barb's insurance company purchases an annuity from a major life insurance carrier to pay the annuity of $2,000 per month with a 20-year guarantee. Barb's auto insurance company is the owner of the policy, the life insurance company is the issuer, and Alice is the payee. If, by chance, the life insurance company goes out of business and the state-guarantee funds that guarantees insurance also go out of business (not likely), then Alice can go back to the original automobile insurance company and demand that they make the required payments as specified in the court settlement.

Five years into the annuity, Alice needs money, and because she does not work, she decides to sell some or all of her annuity payments in return for a lump-sum payment. Alice sells the annuity at an 8.5% discount rate and receives $203,000 from the structured settlement company. The structured settlement company then re-offers the annuity for $253,000 (equating to a yield of approximately 5%) over the term of the annuity. The yield is substantially higher than the yield on CDs or treasuries. A similar 15-year guaranteed annuity of $2,000 per month might cost $300,000 and yield 2.5%.

There are, however, risks when purchasing structured settlement annuities.

The SEC has issued an investor bulletin on pension or settlement income streams to advise annuitants of what they need to know before buying or selling annuities. The person or structured settlement companies purchasing annuities are sometimes called factoring companies. Factoring companies offer a lump sum which is less than the total of the periodic payments that the seller would otherwise receive. They then sell these income streams to retail investors through financial advisors, brokers, or insurance agents. These investments from a purchaser's point of view can be risky and complex.

In a typical transaction, the recipient of the pension or structured settlement will sign over his or her rights to some or all of his or her monthly payments to the factoring company in return for a lump sum amount. Many states require factoring companies that purchase structured settlements to disclose the difference between the lump sum payment that they are offering and the present value of the future income stream discounted at an appropriate interest-rate (for example, the federal AFR for the appropriate time period).

There are several factors to consider before selling rights to a pension or structured settlement annuity. Transactions costs including brokerage commissions, legal and notary fees, and administrative charges may all be deducted from the lump sum proceeds. The SEC suggests asking the following questions:

1. Is the transaction legal? Federal or state law may restrict or prohibit retirees from assigning their pensions to others. The secondary sale of a structured settlement frequently must be approved by a court in keeping with the Uniform Periodic Payment of Judgments Act.
2. Is the transaction worth the cost? This is a simple comparison of the present value of the annuity stream discounted at the federal AFR and compared to the lump sum payment net of all fees and costs charged by the factoring company.
3. What is the reputation of the factoring company?
4. Will the factoring company require life insurance? Should the annuitant die before all payments that were assigned to the factoring company have been received, funds will be paid by the life insurance policy to cover any remaining balance. Purchasing life insurance will add to the annuitant's transaction expenses and reduce the lump sum payout.
5. What are the income tax consequences? The lump sum payments received may be subject to federal and state income tax.
6. Does the sale fit the annuitant's long-term financial goals? There may be better alternatives than selling a structured annuity.

Quick Quiz 7.8

1. Annuity contracts can provide a steady cash flow to retirees but the retiree must give up ownership of the assets used to purchase the annuity in exchange.
   a. True
   b. False

2. Longevity insurance is a fixed annuity.
   a. True
   b. False

3. An annuitant cannot sell or transfer the annuity to someone else.
   a. True
   b. False

True, False, False.

From the buyer's perspective, the recent stock market volatility and low interest rate environment have encouraged investors to look for more attractive returns. Buying the rights to someone else's pension or structured settlement income stream may look like a good alternative to other options because advertised yields from 5.75 percent to 7.75 percent are common. However, these pensions and structured settlement income streams are generally not registered with the SEC. As such, reliable information about these products may be difficult to find, and resolving disputes may be difficult. These products are illiquid, which means they may be difficult to sell later. Purchased rights to an income stream could face legal challenges later, and it could be difficult to legally force the original owner to forward or assign their income to the factoring company or the investor.

It is clear that both sellers and buyers of annuities should conduct substantial due diligence prior to entering into this type of transaction. The following exhibit includes a sample of annuities that might be sold on a secondary market.

EXHIBIT 7.12

SAMPLE OF SECONDARY MARKET ANNUITIES

COMPANY	COST	PAYOUT	RATE	INCOME AMOUNT	FREQUENCY	START DATE	END DATE
Allstate	$70,826	$130,000	4.59%	$130,000	1 lump sum	12-15-28	12-15-28
Allstate	$67,545	$87,448	3.84%	$550	159 monthly	1-20-16	3-20-29
Genworth	$7,571	$10,000	4.04%	$10,000	1 lump sum	7-11-22	7-11-22
Genworth	$119,271	$180,000	4.25%	$1,000	180 monthly	5-9-18	4-9-33
MetLife	$24,961	$31,224	3.50%	$6,000	5 annually	12-5-19	12-5-23
MetLife	$48,402	$131,000	5.28%	$600	60 monthly	4-9-28	3-9-33
NY Lottery	$124,890	$150,000	4.00%	$33,015	3 annually	1-15-19	1-15-21
NY Lottery	$62,445	$75,000	4.00%	$16,508	3 annually	1-15-19	1-15-21
Prudential	$56,865	$69,658	3.00%	$69,658	1 lump sum	4-5-22	4-5-22
Prudential	$53,449	$166,800	5.39%	$695	240 monthly	2-1-28	1-1-48

REGULATION OF ANNUITY CONTRACTS

Most annuity contracts are regulated by the state insurance commissioner in the state in which the contract is sold. The state insurance commissioner approves the annuity contract forms to be issued by insurance companies in that state, and requires that insurance companies keep specified reserves to ensure that they will be able to make promised payments to annuitants. The state insurance commissioner also requires insurers to provide detailed reports on the investments backing up annuity contracts, including an assessment of the investment risk undertaken by the insurance company in investing the money of the annuity pool. The investment risk assessment is sometimes referred to as **risk-based capital**.

Variable annuities provide consumers with an opportunity to tailor the investments backing up the annuity contract to their unique needs, and equity-indexed annuities provide investment returns linked to market-based indexes. Consequently, individuals selling variable annuities are required to obtain state insurance licenses from the State Insurance Commission, as well as securities licenses from FINRA in order to sell these products. These licensing requirements are designed to ensure that individuals offering annuity products for sale to the public have a specified level of knowledge about the product, and about the suitability of the product for consumer needs.[4]

4. FINRA Rule 2111 requires, in part, that a broker-dealer or associated person "have a reasonable basis to believe that a recommended transaction or investment strategy involving a security or securities is suitable for the customer, based on the information obtained through the reasonable diligence of the [firm] or associated person to ascertain the customer's investment profile." In general, a customer's investment profile includes the customer's age, other investments, financial situation and needs, tax status, investment objectives, investment experience, investment time horizon, liquidity needs and risk tolerance. The rule also explicitly covers recommended investment strategies involving securities, including recommendations to "hold" securities. The rule, moreover, identifies the three main suitability obligations: reasonable-basis, customer-specific, and quantitative suitability. Source FINRA.

THE IMPORTANCE OF COMPANY CREDIT RATING

Annuity contracts require the payment of an up-front premium by the contract holder in return for the insurance company's promise to make payments under the contract for years into the future. The financial stability of the company issuing the annuity contract is of major concern to contract holders, and should be a consideration in determining which annuity contract to purchase. The insurance company offering the smallest premium for a given annuity payment may not be the most appropriate choice if its financial stability is in question.

Several rating agencies assess the financial strength of insurance companies issuing annuity contracts. These include A.M. Best (with a rating scale from A++ to S), S&P (with a rating scale of AAA to R), and Moody's (with a rating scale from Aaa to C).

While a full review of the rating scales of these various companies is beyond the scope of this textbook, financial advisors should take into consideration company rating agency scales when making recommendations to clients, and clients should also take this information into account when making their purchasing decisions.

WHAT HAPPENS IF AN INSURANCE COMPANY FAILS?

Insurance company ratings are important, and consumers should attempt to purchase annuities from companies with a strong likelihood of survival. What happens when a company that issues an annuity contract fails? All states have **guarantee funds** run by the state insurance commission that act as the payor of last resort in the case of an insurance company failure. Each year, insurance companies that issue annuities pay a premium to the state guarantee fund. If a company fails with outstanding annuity obligations, the guarantee fund makes the promised annuity payments to contract holders. In the event that the guarantee fund does not have sufficient funds to make those payments, the guarantee fund will assess the surviving annuity contract issuers to obtain the money to make payments, or will arrange to have existing insurance companies take over the payment of the obligations. While a few insurance companies have failed, no annuity contract holder in the United States has been deprived of promised payments to date. In many ways, the state guarantee fund acts as an insurer of insurers to make certain that consumer interests are protected.

KEY TERMS

Accumulation Phase - The period over which annuity funds are accumulated.

Annual Reset Method - The index-linked interest crediting rate is determined each year by comparing the index value at the end of the contract year with the index value at the beginning of the contract year. Interest is then added to the annuity each year during the term.

Annuitant - The individual upon whose life the contract is dependent. It is generally the life expectancy of the annuitant that affects the timing and amount of payout under the contract.

Annuitization - The time when annuity funds are exchanged for a stream of income guaranteed for a period of time.

Annuitized - The time when regular, periodic (such as monthly or annual) payments begin for life or for a specified period of time in excess of one year.

Annuity - A contract between an individual (annuitant) and an insurance company which promises to pay an income on a regular basis for a specified period of time.

Beneficiary - Those persons entitled to the death benefit of the annuity.

Cap Rate - Some indexed annuities impose an upper limit on the index-linked interest rate.

Cash Refund Annuity - Guarantees that the annuitant or the annuitant's family will receive the premium payments made to purchase the annuity, but instead of continuing to make periodic payments until there is a full recovery of the premium, the balance is paid in cash at the annuitant's death.

Deferred Annuity - An annuity contract that does not begin payments immediately, but waits until some future time to start payments.

Equity-Indexed Annuities - Have characteristics of both fixed and variable annuities, either immediate or deferred, that earn interest or provide benefits that are linked to an external equity reference or an equity index.

Fixed Annuity - The most conservative type of annuity that earns a minimum guaranteed rate of return.

Flexible Premium Annuity - Allows the insured the option to vary premium deposits.

Floor Crediting Rate - An indexed annuity is the minimum index-linked interest rate that will be credited to the contract in a given period.

Guarantee Funds - Run by the state insurance commission, they act as the payor of last resort in the case of an insurance company failure.

KEY TERMS

High Watermark Approach - Determining index-linked interest is accomplished by comparing the value of the index at various points during the term (usually on anniversary dates).

Immediate Annuity - An instrument created when the contract owner trades a sum of money in return for a stream of income that begins immediately.

Index Term - The period over which index-linked interest is calculated for equity-indexed annuities.

Indexing Method - The approach used to measure the amount of change, if any, in the index. Some common indexing methods include: (1) the annual reset (ratcheting) approach, (2) the high watermark approach, and (3) the point-to-point approach.

Inflation - The increase in the general price level and is often measured by the Consumer Price Index (CPI).

Initial Rate - The first rate of interest that is earned under a fixed annuities contract and is guaranteed for a specified period of time.

Installment Refund Annuity - A special type of term certain annuity whereby the insurer promises to continue periodic annuity payments after the annuitant has died until the sum of all annuity payments made equals the purchase price of the annuity.

IRD Assets - Assets that have a deferred income tax liability that was not paid prior to the date of the owner's death.

Joint and Survivor Annuity - Promises to make payments over the lives of two or more annuitants. Annuity payments are made until the last annuitant dies. This is commonly used to fund the retirement cash-flow needs of married couples. A 100 percent joint and survivor annuity pays the specified monthly payment to the annuitants while both are alive and continues to make the same payment to the survivor after the first annuitant's death. A 75 percent joint and survivor annuity pays the specified monthly payment to the annuitants while both are alive and continues to make a payment equal to 75 percent of the original payment to the survivor after the first annuitant's death. A 50 percent joint and survivor annuity pays the specified monthly payment to the annuitants while both are alive and continues to make a payment equal to 50 percent of the original payment to the survivor after the first annuitant's death.

Life Annuity Contracts - Protect clients from outliving their assets by providing a series of periodic payments to the annuitant, typically for as long as the annuitant lives.

Longevity Insurance - A sophisticated name for a deferred annuity purchased by an individual at or before retirement that will not begin to make payments until that person reaches an advanced age.

Non-Qualified Annuities - Annuity contracts purchased with funds outside of qualified retirement plans or IRAs (for example, from investment accounts or private savings).

KEY TERMS

OWNER - Person, trust, or company that owns the annuity contract and names the annuitant and beneficiaries. The owner could also be the annuitant and/or the beneficiary.

PARTICIPATION RATE - Determines how much of the increase in the index will be used to calculate the index-linked interest.

PARTIES TO ANNUITY CONTRACT - The annuitant, the beneficiary, the owner, and the insurance company.

POINT-TO-POINT INDEX-LINKED CREDITING METHOD - based on the difference between an index value at the end of the term compared with the index value at the start of the term.

POOLING OF RISK - The spreading of risk among a large number of similar contributors to the pool. Protection is provided to the entire pool of contributors. With annuities, the risk that is being spread is the risk of outliving retirement funds, or superannuation.

QUALIFIED ANNUITIES - Annuity contracts purchased with funds in a qualified retirement plan or IRA.

RETIREMENT LIFE EXPECTANCY - The period between retirement and death.

RISK-BASED CAPITAL - The investment risk assessment undertaken by the insurance company in investing the money backing up the annuity pool.

SECONDARY MARKET ANNUITIES - Called pre-owned annuities or in-force annuities. These annuities can be purchased from the original owner at a discount or from a third party, in which the stream of income is assigned to the purchaser. These typically offer a rate of return or yield that is well above the yield available on standard fixed annuities, immediate annuities, or even bonds of a similar credit quality.

SINGLE LIFE ANNUITY - Also known as a straight life annuity, provides a stream of income to the annuitant for life.

SINGLE PREMIUM ANNUITY - An annuity purchased with a single lump sum.

STRAIGHT OR PURE LIFE ANNUITY - An annuity that provides a stream of income to the annuitant for life.

TERM CERTAIN ANNUITY - Acts as a hedge against the mortality risk retained when an individual purchases a single life annuity by preserving some or all of the capital for distribution to the annuitant's heirs, but this hedge comes at a cost.

VARIABLE ANNUITIES - Provide consumers with an opportunity to individually tailor the types of investments backing up the annuity contract to their unique needs, and equity-indexed annuities provide returns linked to market-based indexes.

DISCUSSION QUESTIONS

1. What major risk to retirement income do annuities mitigate?
2. Discuss the impact of Social Security retirement benefits on superannuation.
3. What is the impact of inflation on retirement income?
4. What role did defined benefit plans play in retirement income when they were prevalent?
5. Discuss the impact of the shift from defined benefit plans to defined contribution plans for retirees.
6. Define an annuity.
7. List the parties to an annuity.
8. What is the annuity payout period?
9. What is the difference between an immediate annuity and a deferred annuity?
10. What is the difference between a flexible premium annuity and a single premium annuity?
11. Identify the different types of annuity benefit options.
12. Define the types of single-life annuity options.
13. What is a benefit of a term certain (or period certain) annuity?
14. Define joint and survivor life annuities.
15. Explain the difference between a fixed annuity, a variable annuity, and an equity indexed annuity.
16. What are the common fees and charges associated with variable annuities?
17. List the advantages of an annuity contract.
18. List three disadvantages of annuities.
19. How are annuities subject to income tax?
20. Define longevity insurance.
21. What are the estate planning issues regarding holding a single-life annuity versus a joint and survivor annuity?

22. What are the risk factors to consider when selling an annuity in the secondary market?

MULTIPLE-CHOICE PROBLEMS

1. Which of the following is true?

    a. A fixed annuity mitigates the risk of superannuation.
    b. A fixed annuity mitigates the risk of superannuation and inflation.
    c. A fixed annuity is always a deferred annuity.
    d. A fixed annuity is always for a single life expectancy.

2. Which of the following risks can an annuity mitigate?

    a. Superannuation.
    b. Mortality.
    c. Superannuation and purchasing power.
    d. Mortality and purchasing power.

3. Bill, age 33, plans to retire at age 67. Bill is a consultant and his income varies widely on a monthly basis. Bill wants to invest in an annuity over his work life expectancy. Which of the following annuities is most suitable for Bill?

    a. Fixed premium, immediate annuity.
    b. Single premium, immediate annuity.
    c. Fixed premium, deferred annuity.
    d. Flexible premium, deferred annuity.

4. Kim, a single 40-year-old, would like to invest in the stock market but wants her principal guaranteed against losses. What type of annuity is most suitable for Kim?

    a. A deferred, fixed annuity.
    b. A single-premium, variable annuity.
    c. A flexible variable annuity.
    d. An equity-indexed annuity.

5. Arline is a 70-year-old widow with no dependents. She wants to invest in an annuity that will produce income now. She has $100,000 to invest and wants to receive the most she can in monthly income. Which of the following is the most suitable annuity for Arline based on her objectives?

    a. A longevity annuity.
    b. A 20-year term certain, fixed annuity.
    c. An immediate, single-premium life annuity.
    d. A deferred, fixed annuity.

6. Patrick is age 67 and receives Social Security retirement income that covers 60 percent of his monthly expenses. He has no dependents. He would like to invest $200,000 in an annuity that will mitigate inflation and provide him with the highest monthly income. Although he has a 20-year table life expectancy, he thinks he has a much longer life expectancy. Which annuity is most suitable for Patrick?

   a. A single-premium annuity.
   b. A deferred, fixed annuity.
   c. A single-premium, variable annuity.
   d. A single-premium, variable annuity with a guaranteed term equal to his table life expectancy.

7. Harold wants to participate in the stock market by purchasing a deferred annuity but wants protection against the loss of his principal. What annuity is best suited for Harold?

   a. An equity-indexed annuity.
   b. A variable annuity.
   c. A fixed annuity.
   d. A single-premium, variable annuity.

8. Neil is 67 years old and about to retire. His table life expectancy is 20 years. He has $25,000 in a retirement plan for which there is no lump-sum withdrawal option. Neil has 2 children and wants to make sure he receives all of the $25,000 and that he can leave his other assets to his children. He wants to participate in equity returns. Which is the most suitable for Neil?

   a. A single-life annuity.
   b. A joint-life annuity with his children.
   c. A single-life, fixed annuity with a term certain of 20 years.
   d. A single-life, variable annuity with a term certain of 20 years.

9. Harry, age 63 purchased an immediate annuity. The annuity will provide monthly payments to Harry for as long as he lives. If he dies before receiving payments for 20 years, the remaining payments will go to his beneficiary. What type of annuity did Harry purchase?

   a. A life annuity with a term-certain guarantee.
   b. An installment refund annuity.
   c. A straight-life annuity.
   d. A joint and survivor annuity.

10. When determining the percentage of an annuity income that is not taxable, the investment in the annuity is divided by the total of the expected payments to be received. What is this quotient is called?

    a. The inclusion ratio.
    b. The exclusion ratio.
    c. The current ratio.
    d. The working capital ratio.

11. Meg has money in a 401(k) plan with her employer. She has no dependents or heirs and wants to maximize her monthly income. She is retiring and wants to move the money into an annuity contract. Which would be the best option for Meg?

    a. Single-premium life annuity.
    b. Flexible-premium annuity.
    c. Deferred annuity.
    d. Installment refund annuity.

12. Which of the following parties to an annuity contract serves as the measuring life?

    1. Owner.
    2. Annuitant.
    3. Beneficiary.

    a. 1 only.
    b. 2 only.
    c. Both 1 and 3.
    d. Both 2 and 3.

13. Clara purchases an annuity with after-tax dollars and wants payments to begin next month. What type of annuity did Clara purchase?

    1. Immediate Annuity.
    2. Deferred Annuity.
    3. Qualified Annuity.
    4. Nonqualified Annuity.

    a. 1 and 3
    b. 2 and 3.
    c. 1 and 4.
    d. 2 and 4.

14. At the age of 40, Kennedy deposited $50,000 in a nonqualified, single-premium deferred annuity. Ten years later, she surrenders the contract for a lump-sum distribution of its $100,000 value. Which of the following statements is correct?

    a. Kennedy will owe taxes on $50,000.
    b. Kennedy will owe taxes on the full $100,000.
    c. Kennedy will owe taxes and a 10% penalty on the full $100,000.
    d. Kennedy will owe taxes and a 10% penalty on $50,000.

15. Which of the following statements about annuities is not correct?

    a. Term certain and joint life terms are not mutually exclusive.
    b. Variable annuities can be invested in subaccounts that invest in fixed income securities.
    c. The annuity benefit payment for a 20-year term certain will be more than the annuity payment for a single life annuity with a 20-year term certain option for an annuitant whose life expectancy is 20 years.
    d. All annuities are subject to minimum distribution rules.

16. Jason owns a life insurance policy. He decided that he no longer has a need for life insurance and wants to exchange it for an annuity. To get the annuity he wants, he will have to exchange the life policy and add additional money. Which of the following is correct?

    a. He can make the exchange, but it will be taxable to the extent of the cash value.
    b. He can make the exchange, but it will be taxable to the extent of the cash value less the additional money he puts into the annuity.
    c. He can make the exchange, which will not be taxable.
    d. He can make the exchange, which will not be taxable, but his basis will not reflect any of the investment into the life insurance policy.

17. Parker, who is now 70 years old, was a diligent saver during his working years and accumulated $100,000 at age 60. He used his savings to purchase a single premium annuity, which pays him $1,000 per month. If his life expectancy was 25 years when he purchased it, how much of each payment is subject to tax?

    a. $333.
    b. $555.
    c. $667.
    d. $1,000.

18. Hugh purchased a single premium annuity for $200,000. The annuity pays him $1,000 per month. If his life expectancy was 20 years when he purchased it, how much of each payment is not subject to tax?

    a. $177.
    b. $475.
    c. $833.
    d. $1,000.

19. Mig purchased a straight life annuity from Confident Results Annuity Provider using funds from his 401(k) plan. Which of the following is correct

    a. His annuity will make payments for his life and that of his beneficiary.
    b. His annuity cannot be a variable annuity.
    c. His annuity will be included in his gross estate at death.
    d. His annuity will have no return of basis.

20. Scott is a drug rep and planning on retiring next month. He is using his accumulated $200,000 to purchase an annuity. Which of the following options will give him the largest monthly annuity payment assuming his life expectancy is 20 years and his wife's life expectancy is 22 years.

    a. 10 year term certain.
    b. Single life annuity over Scott's life.
    c. 100% joint life annuity over Scott and his wife's lives.
    d. 75% joint life annuity over Scott and his wife's lives.

21. There are several types of annuities. Which of the following orders the investment options from least risky to most risky?

    a. Fixed, variable, equity-indexed.
    b. Variable, fixed, equity-indexed.
    c. Equity-indexed, variable, fixed.
    d. Fixed, equity-indexed, variable.

22. Claire is retiring in the next month. She was the bread winner in the family while John was the stay-at-home dad. They have limited assets but will receive Social Security. Which of the following is the best type of annuity for her to select?

    a. A 20-year term certain annuity.
    b. A straight life annuity on her life.
    c. A joint-life annuity on the lives of Claire and John.
    d. A joint-life annuity on the lives of Claire and John with a 10-year term certain.

23. There are many options regarding the type of annuity one can purchase. Which of the following is correct?

    a. A fixed annuity will have the initial rate, which lasts until the end of the first life.
    b. A variable annuity always has funds invested in equity sub accounts.
    c. An equity-indexed annuity generally has less risk than a variable annuity.
    d. Earnings within fixed, variable and equity-indexed annuities are never subject to income tax until annuitization occurs and distributions begin.

24. Perry, who is 50 years old, was building a new home for his family. However, he was running out of money and could not afford the pool they fell in love with. Since his family was upset, he decided to take a withdrawal from his annuity. He had contributed $100,000 to the annuity, and the value of the annuity today is $300,000. He decided to take a withdrawal of $60,000 from the annuity. Which of the following is correct?

    a. $40,000 is taxable as ordinary income.
    b. $40,000 is taxable as ordinary income and subject to the early withdrawal penalty.
    c. $60,000 is taxable as ordinary income.
    d. $60,000 is taxable as ordinary income and subject to the early withdrawal penalty.

25. Harry purchased a life insurance policy with a face value of $100,000. Unfortunately for Harry, and his wife, Barbara, he died racing "import cars." At the time of death, the life insurance policy had a cash value of $40,000. The beneficiary was his wife. Barbara, who has a life expectancy of 40 years, decided to take the single life annuity option with the life insurance proceeds. This option will pay her $500 per month for the rest of her life. How much of the monthly payment is taxable?

    a. $208.
    b. $292.
    c. $500.
    d. None, as life insurance proceeds are almost always tax-free to the beneficiary.

26. Cody decided to purchase a variable annuity and invested $50,000. He made a few poor investment decisions and the market dropped. Like many investors, he decided to sell when the value was low. He surrendered the annuity and received $27,000, after the $3,000 surrender fee. Which of the following is true?

    a. The loss is not deductible.
    b. He can take an itemized deduction of $23,000.
    c. He can take a capital loss of $20,000.
    d. He can take an ordinary loss of $20,000.

27. When Art was 45 years old, he invested $60,000 in an annuity. Ten years later, the value of the annuity was $180,000. He took a withdrawal from the annuity in the amount of $10,000. How is the withdrawal taxed?

   a. The $10,000 is taxable as ordinary income.
   b. The $10,000 is taxable as ordinary income and is subject to the 10 percent early withdrawal penalty.
   c. $6,666 of the $10,000 is taxable as ordinary income.
   d. $6,666 of the $10,000 is taxable as ordinary income and is subject to the 10 percent early withdrawal penalty.

28. Annuities provide many benefits and have many advantages over other alternative investments. Which of the following is not an advantage of a single life annuity?

   a. The annuity mitigates the risk of superannuation.
   b. Earnings within the annuity are tax deferred.
   c. Distributions receive favorable capital gain treatment.
   d. The owner's estate excludes the value of the annuity.

29. With an equity-indexed annuity, there are several indexing methods. Which of the following is not one of them?

   a. Oscillation neutrality method.
   b. Annual reset (ratcheting method).
   c. High watermark method.
   d. Point-to-point method.

30. Ted just retired and has several sources of income. He has Social Security and a pension from his employer, HTD Enterprises. Social Security is adjusted for inflation, but his pension is not. Ted is concerned about outliving his funds. What might he purchase to provide protection against running out of money late in retirement?

   a. Immediate variable annuity.
   b. Deferred fixed annuity.
   c. Longevity annuity.
   d. Life insurance.

QUICK QUIZ EXPLANATIONS

Quick Quiz 7.1

1. True.
2. True.
3. False. Defined benefit plans paid out of a fixed annuity for the life of the annuitant, and in many cases a joint and survivor annuity for the benefit of a surviving spouse. Today, defined contribution plans are used.

Quick Quiz 7.2

1. True.
2. False. Immediate annuities are purchased with one, single, lump sum payment. However, the premium payments used to fund a deferred annuity can be either a single lump sum payment, or a series of payments into the future.
3. False. The income earned from a deferred annuity is treated as ordinary income for federal income tax purposes only upon receipt of distributions.

Quick Quiz 7.3

1. False. The term may be for a specific number of years or over the life of a person or persons.
2. False. A joint and survivor annuity will pay the survivor the contracted percentage.
3. True.
4. True.

Quick Quiz 7.4

1. True.
2. False. Surrender charges are prevalent in variable annuities prior to annuitization.
3. True.

Quick Quiz 7.5

1. True.
2. False. Variable annuities permit the owner to invest in subaccounts of the fund manager.
3. True.

Quick Quiz 7.6

1. True.
2. False. Fixed annuities typically do not impose any direct expense charges on the contract owner other than a surrender charge. Variable annuities have several types of expenses, including investment management fees, annual insurance charges, and surrender charges.
3. False. Since 2013, distributions from annuity contracts made to high income taxpayers (more than $200,000 AGI) are subject to the Affordable Care Act surtax of 3.8 percent.

QUICK QUIZ EXPLANATIONS

Quick Quiz 7.7

1. False. A non-qualified annuity is an annuity contract purchased with after-tax dollars. The after-tax dollars invested in the contract create basis for income tax purposes.
2. False. The exclusion ratio equals the owner's investment in the annuity contract divided by the expected return on the annuity. The resulting percentage is multiplied by the distribution or payment received to calculate the portion of the payment that is not subject to income tax.
3. False. Qualified annuities are subject to the minimum distribution rules, but not non-qualified annuities.
4. True.

Quick Quiz 7.8

1. True.
2. False. Longevity insurance is a deferred annuity purchased by an individual at or before retirement that will not begin to make payments until that person reaches an advanced age.
3. False. An annuity contract can be sold to someone else in exchange for a lump-sum payment today, discounted for the time value of money.

CHAPTER

8

PROPERTY AND LIABILITY INSURANCE

LEARNING OBJECTIVES

After reading this chapter, you should be able to:

1. Identify personal property and liability insurance risks.
2. Differentiate among the basic homeowners insurance (HO) forms and features and explain how to evaluate and compare policies.*
3. List the general exclusions to homeowners policies.
4. List the common provisions in homeowners insurance policies.
5. Describe the automobile insurance legal environment.
6. Identify the primary components of automobile insurance and assess any potential property damage or liability exposures.*
7. Understand personal automobile policy limits.
8. Explain the role of personal and business liability insurance in comprehensive financial planning and how a personal liability umbrella policy (PLUP) and business liability insurance interacts with other property and liability insurance products.*
9. Describe the defenses to liability.
10. Identify the various business and professional property and liability insurance policies and compare them to individual policies.

* CFP Board Resource Document - Student-Centered Learning Objectives based upon CFP Board Principal Topics.

INTRODUCTION

The professional planner should be as knowledgeable about property and liability risks associated with a client's property as with life, health, disability, and long-term care insurance. While property insurance protects the assets the client already owns, liability insurance protects the client against financial loss from legal action. Therefore, both property and liability insurance coverages are essential parts of a client's overall risk management and financial plan.

KEY CONCEPTS

1. Identify the three types of insurance that are most commonly purchased to protect against liability and risks to personal property.
2. Identify and describe the four areas of coverage in Section I of a homeowners insurance contract.
3. Describe coinsurance.
4. Identify and describe the two areas of coverage in Section II of a homeowners insurance contract.

Property insurance includes homeowners insurance, renters insurance, automobile insurance, and insurance on boats and other assets. The home is one of the largest single purchases that individuals make during their lifetimes. Although the frequency of perils causing financial losses to the home is small, the severity of any loss is potentially large. The automobile insurance policy is used to mitigate the risk of loss to the automobile and those involved in an automobile accident. It may be among the most expensive aspects of owning a car for the client. The personal liability umbrella policy (PLUP) provides coverage in excess of the underlying liability coverage provided by the homeowners, automobile, and other property insurance policies.

The commercial package policy, the business owner's policy, professional insurance, and business automobile insurance policies provide protection for business owners and self-employed professionals for property and liability risks.

This chapter introduces each of these types of insurance to help the planner adequately evaluate the client's property and liability needs and recommend appropriate coverage.

PERSONAL PROPERTY AND LIABILITY INSURANCE

This chapter introduces the three insurance policies most commonly used to protect against personal property and liability risks. The three insurance policies are:

- the homeowners insurance policy
- the automobile insurance policy
- the personal umbrella liability insurance policy

Homeowners and automobile insurance are package policies that provide both property and liability coverage in one contract. The personal liability umbrella policy (an excess liability policy) provides a layer of personal liability protection above the liability coverages provided in the underlying homeowners and automobile policies, in the unfortunate event that those policies are insufficient to cover a claim.

Each of the following discussions is based on the standard policy forms issued by the Insurance Services Office (ISO). Since insurance is regulated at the state level, each state may require certain modifications to the standard ISO form. Thus, the ensuing discussions are general in nature. Absolute statements cannot be made about any particular policy without thoroughly reading that particular policy.

HOMEOWNERS (HO) INSURANCE: BASIC COVERAGES

Homeowners insurance is usually provided in a package policy covering both property and liability. There are a variety of alternative contractual forms that a homeowner may select. Each different **homeowners insurance** form includes two sections: Section I provides property insurance coverage, and Section II provides liability coverage. Exhibit 8.1 presents an overview of the different types of perils covered as well as the different forms of homeowners insurance available. The specific HO forms and their general and unique contractual provisions are discussed later in this chapter.

LIST OF COVERED PERILS

EXHIBIT 8.1

BASIC-NAMED PERILS	
1. Fire	2. Vehicles
3. Lightning	4. Smoke
5. Windstorm	6. Vandalism or malicious mischief
7. Hail	8. Explosion
9. Riot or civil commotion	10. Theft
11. Aircraft	12. Volcanic eruption

Broad-Named Perils Includes Coverage for Basic-Named Perils (1-12) plus 13-18
13. Falling objects
14. Weight of ice, snow, sleet
15. Accidental discharge or overflow of water or steam
16. Sudden and accidental tearing apart, cracking, burning, or bulging of a steam, hot water, air conditioning, or automatic fire protective sprinkler system, or from within a household appliance
17. Freezing of a plumbing, heating, air conditioning, or automatic fire sprinkler system, or of a household appliance
18. Sudden and accidental damage from artificially-generated electrical current

Open Perils (Include Coverage for Basic and Broad Perils)
Open perils means the insurance covers any risk that is not excepted in the policy.

Coverage for Different Forms of Homeowners Insurance - Section 1

	HO-2	HO-3	HO-4	HO-5	HO-6	HO-8
Coverage A Dwelling	Broad	Open	N/A	Open	Broad	Basic
Coverage B Other Structures	Broad	Open	N/A	Open	N/A	Basic
Coverage C Personal Property	Broad	Broad	Broad	Open	Broad	Basic
Coverage D Loss of Use	Broad	Broad	Broad	Open	Broad	Basic

Summary of General Exclusions (Perils Excluded)

Each HO form specifies which causes of loss (perils) it covers and which it excludes. Later in this chapter, the different HO forms and the perils covered by each are presented. Listed below are the general exclusions to all homeowners' policies:

- Movement of the ground (earthquake, mudslide, and sink hole)
- Ordinance or law
- Damage from rising water
- War
- Nuclear hazards
- Power failure
- Intentional acts
- Neglect

Movement of the Ground
Property damage arising from earth movement is excluded. This includes damage from an earthquake, volcanic eruption, landslide, and sink hole. Sink hole collapse and earthquake coverage are available by **endorsement**.

Ordinance or Law
A loss due to an ordinance or law that regulates the construction, repair, or demolition of a building or structure is excluded.

Damage from Rising Water
Property damage from the following are specifically excluded from coverage under the homeowners policy:

- Floods, surface water, waves, tidal water, and overflow or spray of a body of water.
- Water below the surface of the ground that exerts pressure on or seeps through a building, sidewalk, driveway, foundation, swimming pool, or other structure.
- Water backing through sewers or drains.

Coverage for naturally occurring floods is available through the National Flood Insurance Program offered by the federal government. Coverage for sewer backup is available in some areas as an endorsement to the HO policy.

War or Nuclear Hazards
Property damage from war or nuclear hazard, including radiation or radioactive contamination is excluded. If a radiation leak from a nuclear power plant near an insured's home contaminates his or her property, there is no coverage for the loss.

Power Failure
Losses due to power failure caused by an uninsured peril, such as a freezer thawing out and its contents spoiling because of local power plant malfunctions, are not covered. If, however, a covered peril such as fire or lightning on the premises causes the power failure, then the resulting damage is covered. Refrigerated property coverage is available by endorsement.

Intentional Acts
If a loss is discovered to be an intentional act on the part of any insured, it is not covered. For example, an insured cannot intentionally burn his or her house down and recover insurance benefits.

Neglect
If an insured fails to use all reasonable and necessary means to save and preserve his or her property during or after the loss, or when the property is endangered by an insured peril, the loss is not covered.

Summary of Section I Coverages

Section I consists of five sections, four specific property coverages (identified as A through D) and additional coverages:

- Section A - Dwelling
- Section B - Other structures
- Section C - Personal property
- Section D - Loss of use
- Additional coverage - Debris removal, damage to trees, credit card loss, etc.

Coverage A: Dwelling

This coverage pays for repair and/or replacement of damage to the house, attached structures, and building materials on the premises. The homeowner typically buys an amount of coverage equal to the replacement cost of the **dwelling**. In some cases, the homeowner will be required to maintain higher coverage if the property is mortgaged. A mortgage lender generally demands an amount of coverage on the dwelling at least equal to the total amount owed on the mortgage.

Covered losses to the dwelling and other structures are paid on the basis of replacement cost with no deduction for depreciation. **Replacement cost** is the amount necessary to purchase, repair, or replace the dwelling with materials of the same or similar quality at current prices. Many contracts require the insured to carry insurance of at least 80 percent of the replacement cost (coinsurance) at the time of the loss or the insured will not be fully covered for a loss that is partial. If the insured carries less than the coinsurance provision requires, the insured will receive a payment for a partial loss, calculated as follows:

$$\frac{\text{Amount of Insurance Carried}}{\text{Coinsurance Requirement}} \times \text{Amount of Loss}$$

EXAMPLE 8.1

Bill owns a home with a replacement cost of $400,000. He purchases $200,000 of property insurance with a coinsurance requirement of 80%. If Bill experiences a $50,000 loss, the insurance company will pay:

$$\frac{\text{Insurance Purchased}}{\text{Coinsurance Requirement}} \times \text{Amount of Loss}$$

$$\frac{\$200{,}000}{80\% \times \$400{,}000} \times \$50{,}000 = \$31{,}250$$

Bill will receive $31,250 less his deductible. Note, he will not receive the loss of $50,000 even though his total coverage is $200,000.

Certain properties attached to the dwelling, or considered an integral part of the dwelling, are covered only on an actual cash value basis. These properties include awnings, household appliances, outdoor antennas, outdoor appliances, and non-building structures. Building glass is replaced with safety-glazing materials, if required by local building codes.

Coverage B: Other Structures (Detached)

In addition to the main house, some homeowners have small, detached structures on their property. These include detached garages, small greenhouses, or storage buildings. Coverage B pays for damage to these structures. The limit of insurance in Coverage B is typically 10 percent of the Coverage A (dwelling) limit. This coverage also pays on a replacement cost basis (just as for the dwelling).

Keep in mind that **other structures** may not be eligible for coverage if they are used for business purposes. If another structure is rented to someone who is not a tenant of the dwelling, no coverage applies (unless the structure is rented for use solely as private garage space).

Coverage C: Personal Property (Tangible Personalty - Moveables)

The value of a homeowner's **personal property** should not be underestimated. Imagine what it would cost to replace the typical family room's furniture, entertainment equipment, music collection, videos, tables, paintings, lamps, and books. All of the HO forms provide coverage for the personal property of the insured (and resident family members), irrespective of where the property is located at the time of loss. The limit of insurance for Coverage C is typically equal to 50 percent of the Coverage A (dwelling) limit.

Note that the standard HO form provides only actual cash value (ACV) coverage for personal property. An optional endorsement is available to add replacement cost coverage to personal property, and this option is strongly recommended for most homeowners. **Actual cash value** is the depreciated value of personal property. Since the contents of a home depreciate rapidly, a homeowner could suffer a serious financial loss if replacement cost coverage were not provided.

EXAMPLE 8.2

> Lisa bought a new 52" television for $2,800. Three years later the television was stolen. The television had depreciated by 60% in the three years. Today, the same television costs $1,500. Lisa will receive $600 ($1,500 - $900 depreciation) in actual cash value. She will receive the full $1,500 if she has replacement cost coverage.

Certain kinds of personal property have dollar limits on the amount that the insurer will pay for any loss. A typical HO policy contains the following personal property limits:

$200	-	money, bullion, coin collections, and bank notes
$1,500	-	securities, bills, evidence of debt, airline tickets, and manuscripts
$1,500	-	theft of jewelry, watches, gems, precious metals, and real furs
$1,500	-	watercraft, including trailers (not boat affiliated) and equipment
$2,500	-	theft of firearms
$2,500	-	theft of silverware, goldware, pewterware, and similar property
$500	-	loss of business use property not on premises
$2,500	-	loss of business use property on premises
$1,500	-	loss of electronic apparatus

If the insured owns personal items that have values beyond the limits stated above, it may be possible to purchase additional amounts of insurance beyond the special limits listed above or purchase a separate policy for such coverage. The additional increments of insurance purchased are listed in what is referred to as a schedule. A **schedule** is a list of dollar limits or amounts of insurance provided for specified personal items attached to the homeowners policy. Note, however, that scheduled assets are no longer covered under the general HO. Scheduled items also have no deductibles and are valued at agreed-upon values.

Certain items of personal property are excluded from coverage because they are either uninsurable or outside the "normal" range of properties owned by the typical homeowner. Homeowners having these unusual types of personal properties and, thus, unusual risk exposures, must request special coverage in addition to that provided by their HO form.

The following personal property items are specifically excluded from coverage in most package homeowners policies:

- Animals, birds, and fish
- Articles separately described and specifically insured
- Motorized land vehicles used off premises
- Property of roomers or boarders not related to the insured
- Aircraft and parts
- Furnishings on property rented out to others
- Property held as samples, held for sale, or sold but not delivered
- Business data, credit cards, and funds transfer cards
- Business property held away from the residence premises

Coverage D: Loss of Use

Loss of use is defined as a combination of additional living expenses for that part of the premises occupied by the insured and for any loss of rental income. Coverage is generally limited to a maximum of 30 percent of the Coverage A (dwelling) limit. However, for HO6 (condo), the limit is 50 percent of Coverage C, and for HO8 (modified), it is 10 percent of Coverage A.

A direct property loss can result in a family having to live in a hotel or apartment for days, weeks, or even months. The incremental difference between the cost of living in these temporary arrangements and normal costs that would have been incurred had there been no loss is known as additional living expense. The increase in housing costs, food, transportation, laundry, and so on are all examples of additional living expenses. Benefits are provided only for the additional (incremental) costs required to maintain the homeowner's normal standard of living.

Under loss of use, a lessor may recover the loss of fair rental value on property held for rental purposes by the insured lessor. Benefits are paid on the basis of rental value less charges and expenses that do not continue during the period in which the property is uninhabitable.

EXAMPLE 8.3

George (lessor) owns a house in which he rents a room to a student (lessee) for $400 per month. If the house is deemed uninhabitable for two months following a fire, George can recover $800 for loss of rent if he is insured.

If a civil authority prevents an insured from using his or her premises due to damage by a covered peril to a neighborhood or neighbor property, loss of use coverage will be provided for up to two weeks. This is a unique feature of the HO form, considering that the insured need not suffer damage to his own property to collect from the policy. The value of this coverage should not be underestimated. Consider the various forest fires in California or hurricanes in Louisiana. If a civil authority orders a homeowner to vacate the premises, the cost of putting a family of four in a hotel room, plus paying for restaurant meals, laundry service, pet boarding, and so on, can amount to several thousand dollars in a very short period of time.

Additional Coverages

In addition to providing Coverages A through D, Section I provides supplementary coverages as follows:

- All-risk coverage is provided for *property while it is being moved from one place to another,* and for an additional thirty days thereafter.
- The cost of *removing debris of covered property* damaged by an insured peril is paid for.
- A *fire department service charge* is covered up to $500 for loss by an insured peril; however, a fire department call for rescuing a cat from a tree or people in a home being threatened by a flood is not covered.
- The additional coverages under the homeowners policy also pay for *reasonable repairs to protect the property from further damage* after a covered loss occurs.
- An additional amount of insurance is provided to *cover damage to trees, shrubs, plants, and lawns* from all covered perils except for wind (limited to five percent of the dwelling coverage, but not more than $1,000 for any one tree or plant).
- Up to $1,000 per loss for *assessments against an insured* by a group of property owners arising from loss or damage to property jointly owned by all of the members collectively (for example, condominium owners or cooperative apartment projects).
- Coverage may exist for damage to property arising from *the collapse of a building* caused by an insured peril in addition to several circumstances per the insurance contract.
- Damage caused by *breakage of glass or safety glazing material* that is part of the building, storm doors, or storm windows is covered.
- Up to $2,500 may be paid for *damage to landlord's furnishings* in an apartment on the insured's dwelling premises.
- Up to $500 of coverage for loss due to *unauthorized use of credit cards*, fund transfer cards, forgery of checks, acceptance of counterfeit money, and any incurred court costs or attorney fees may be available.

Summary of Section II Coverages

Section II coverages are all the same for homeowners' policies, except the policy limits may be different. The coverages are Coverage E for various forms of personal liability and Coverage F for medical payments to others.

Coverage E: Personal Liability

Coverage E protects the named insured and all resident family members against liability for bodily injuries and property damage they or their resident premises cause others to suffer. The minimum limit of coverage is generally $100,000 per occurrence, although some homeowners carry a $200,000 or $300,000 limit. In addition to the liability coverage, the insurer pays all legal defense and settlement costs associated with a claim for damages made by an injured party as long as the insurer is unwilling to pay the limit on the policy.

This coverage provides liability coverage for *personal* (that is, nonbusiness) activities. The insuring agreement is quite broad and simply agrees to protect against claims or suits for bodily injury or property damage. The coverage is then narrowed to exclude most nonpersonal liability situations and other uninsurable exposures. Exhibit 8.2 lists the exclusions that apply to both Coverage E and Coverage F.

EXHIBIT 8.2

LIABILITY EXCLUSIONS APPLICABLE TO COVERAGES E AND F

EXCLUSION	COVERAGE E: PERSONAL LIABILITY	COVERAGE F: MEDICAL PAYMENTS
Intentional Injury	✓	✓
Business & Professional Activities	✓	✓
Rental of Property	✓	✓
Professional Liability	✓	✓
Uninsured Premises	✓	✓
Motor Vehicles	✓	✓
Watercraft	✓	✓
Aircraft	✓	✓
War	✓	✓
Communicable Disease	✓	✓
Sexual Molestation or Abuse	✓	✓
Nuclear Exclusion	✓	✓
Workers Compensation	✓	✓
Controlled Substance	✓	✓
Contractual Liability	✓	–
Property owned by or in the custody of the Insured	✓	–
Residence Employee Away from Premises	–	✓
Persons Residing on Premises	–	✓

Coverage F: Medical Payments to Others

This coverage pays necessary medical expenses to others that result from bodily injury. The bodily injuries must arise out of the insured's activities, premises, or animal(s). Medical expenses must be incurred within three years of the accident, and it is important to note that this coverage will *not* pay for medical expenses incurred by the insured or any regular resident of the household, except a residence employee (such as a maid or butler).

This coverage may seem to duplicate the coverage provided in Coverage E; however, there is an important difference between the two. Coverage F is a "no-fault" coverage that will automatically pay for bodily injuries, while Coverage E pays for both bodily injuries and property damage *for which the insured is legally liable.*

EXAMPLE 8.4

Jordan is celebrating her 6th birthday with a party at her house. One of her guests, Dylan, age 6, falls and hits his head causing a gash on his forehead. Donna, Jordan's mother, rushes Dylan to the emergency room where he receives 6 stitches and returns to the party as a hero. Coverage F of Donna's homeowners policy will pay for the emergency room expenses for Dylan. If Dylan's mother later sues, any judgment for the fault will be paid under Coverage E.

In summary, Coverage F pays regardless of fault, while Coverage E pays only when the insured is legally liable. A typical amount of coverage purchased under this policy is $10,000 per person per occurrence.

EXAMPLE 8.5

If guests at John's dinner party get sick from eating bad oysters, each one of them may receive up to $10,000 to cover necessary medical expenses that result.

The standard homeowners policy contains three different types of exclusions: those that apply to both Coverages E and F, those that apply only to Coverage E, and those that apply only to Coverage F.

Exclusions to Both Coverages E and F

Neither Coverage E nor Coverage F will pay for injuries or damages:

- That are *expected or intended* by the insured.
- Resulting from the *insured's business or professional activities.*
- Resulting from the *rental of premises.* However, coverage will be provided when:
  - Part of an insured location is rented either on an occasional basis, or when part of an insured location is rented out solely as a residence to no more than two roomers or boarders; and
  - Part of an insured location is rented out as an office, school, studio, or private garage.
- Arising out of premises the insured owns, rents, or leases to others that have not been declared an insured location.
- Arising out of the *ownership or use of watercraft, motorized vehicles, and aircraft.* However, certain vehicles and watercraft are covered for liability:
  - Trailers that are not connected to a motorized land conveyance.
  - A vehicle designed primarily for use off of public roads that the insured does not own or that the insured does own but that is on an insured location.
  - Motorized golf carts while being used on a golf course.

QUICK QUIZ 8.1

1. The three types of insurance most commonly purchased to protect against liability and risks to personal property are: homeowners insurance, automobile insurance, and personal umbrella liability insurance.
   a. True
   b. False

2. Section I of a homeowners insurance contract covers: the dwelling, other structures, personal property, and loss of use.
   a. True
   b. False

3. Both Coverage E (Personal Liability) and Coverage F (Medical Payments to Others) pay claims regardless of fault.
   a. True
   b. False

True, True, False.

    - Vehicles not subject to motor vehicle registration that include lawn mowers, motorized wheelchairs, and vehicles in dead storage on the insured location.
    - Nonmotorized watercraft (canoes and rowboats, for example).
    - Low-powered boats the insured owns or rents, or small sailboats (under 26 feet long).
    - Model or hobby aircraft that are not designed to carry people or cargo.
    - Note that the exclusions of watercraft liability are very detailed. Any time the insured plans to purchase, rent, or use a watercraft, the HO policy should be consulted to determine whether or not coverage exists.
- Caused by *war or nuclear weapons* of any kind.
- Caused by the *transmission of a communicable disease.*
- Arising out of *sexual molestation, corporal punishment, or physical or mental abuse.*
- Arising out of the *use, sale, manufacture, delivery, transfer, or possession of a controlled substance* other than legally-obtained prescription drugs.

An exception to all of these exclusions includes liability coverage for injuries to a residence employee (housekeeper, butler, nanny, and so on). This type of liability coverage is provided to protect homeowners against injuries to domestic help when the homeowner is not required to purchase workers compensation coverage for such workers.

Exclusions to Coverage E Only

Certain exclusions pertain only to Coverage E of the policy. They are:

- Damage to *property of any insured* (covered under Section I).
- Damage to *premises the insured is renting* or has control of, unless caused by fire, smoke or explosion.
- *Contractual liability* (however, two types of contractual liability are covered). First, where the insured has entered into a contract that directly relates to the ownership, maintenance, or use of an insured location, coverage is provided. Second, where the liability of others is assumed by the insured in a contract prior to an occurrence, coverage is provided.
- Liability for *loss assessments charged against the insured* as a member of an association or organization of property owners (one example is a condominium association, which may charge individual unit owners for damage to community property).
- Liability for injuries to employees that falls under a *workers compensation or other disability law.*
- Liability for bodily injury or property damage for which the insured is also covered by a *nuclear energy liability policy.*

QUICK QUIZ 8.2

1. In a partial loss scenario, an insured could be paid less than the full loss amount due to coinsurance requirements.
   a. True
   b. False

2. Coverage F of a homeowners policy pays medical expenses relating to a bodily injury suffered by someone who lives in the home.
   a. True
   b. False

True, False.

Exclusions to Coverage F Only

Coverage F will not provide coverage for bodily injuries:

- Sustained by the *insured* or any *family member.*
- Sustained by a *regular resident* of an insured location.
- Sustained by a *residence employee* of the insured that occur outside of the scope of employment.
- Sustained by anyone eligible to receive benefits for their injuries under a *workers compensation or similar disability law.*
- Resulting from *nuclear reaction radiation*, etc., regardless of how caused.

HOMEOWNERS (HO) INSURANCE: BASIC FORMS

The basic homeowners (HO) insurance[1] forms available are:

- HO-2: Broad Form
- HO-3: Special Form
- HO-4: Contents Broad Form (designed for tenants)
- HO-5: Comprehensive Form
- HO-6: Unit Owners Form (for condominium owners)
- HO-8: Modified Form

HO-2: Broad Form

The HO-2 provides coverage for basic perils (1-12) plus coverage for seven additional perils: falling objects, weight of ice, snow, sleet, accidental discharge or overflow of water, bursting of steam appliances or hot water systems, freezing, and accidental damage caused by artificially-generated electrical current. The dwelling is covered for replacement costs but the personal property is only covered for actual cash value (ACV).

HO-3: Special Form

The HO-3 provides all of Coverages A through F, but offers greater protection for the dwelling by providing coverage on an "open-perils" (formerly called "all-risks") basis. Specifically, the HO-3 covers physical damage to the dwelling and other structures on an open-perils basis and personal property on a named-perils broad form basis. The dwelling is covered for replacement costs, but the personal property is only covered for actual cash value (ACV).

"Open-perils" means that unless a peril is specifically excluded in the policy, it will be covered. All of the perils in the HO-2 are covered, and all of the exclusions mentioned previously (war, nuclear, etc.) are included in the policy. The value of the HO-3 is that it will cover certain unusual losses not specifically named as perils in the HO-2. For example, suppose the insured under a HO-2 has his house trampled by a herd of cattle. As none of the named perils addresses this particular situation, the loss would not be covered. With the HO-3, however, there is no such exclusion, so the damage would be covered.

1. HO-1 has been discontinued in most states.

HO-4: Contents Broad Form (Designed for Tenants/Renters)

The Contents form (HO-4) is designed for tenants who do not own their rented dwelling premises. In such cases, what the tenant really needs is personal liability coverage, plus coverage for personal contents and loss of use. Therefore, the HO-4 policy does not provide Coverages A or B. The Contents Broad Form provides coverage for the losses caused by the same perils as HO-2. Once again, the personal property (contents) is only covered for actual cash value (ACV).

> **Key Concepts**
>
> 1. Describe the difference between Replacement Value and Actual Cash Value.
> 2. Describe the difference between Open Perils coverage and Broad coverage or Named Perils Coverage.
> 3. Describe an "endorsement."

The minimum amount of coverage sold under the HO-4 is $6,000 of personal property coverage (Coverage C). The Coverage D (Loss of Use) limit is equal to 30 percent of the Coverage C limit.

HO-5: Comprehensive Form

The HO-5 is similar to HO-3 except for the coverage of personal property. HO-3 covers personal property on a broad perils basis. HO-5, however, covers personal property on an open perils basis. Until recently, this type of coverage was added to HO-3 policies through an HO-15 endorsement. In 2000, ISO created the HO-5 form and eliminated the HO-15 endorsement. Unfortunately, the coverage for personal property under this contract is once again only actual cash value basis unless the insured endorses the valuation to replacement cost.

HO-6: Unit Owners Form (for Condominium Owners)

The condominium association insures most condominium buildings; however, the unit owner may be responsible for insuring certain components of real property, such as additions, improvements and betterments (carpeting, etc.). The HO-6 provides the unique coverage needed for these special exposures. This form covers the same perils as the HO-2 and HO-4, but it does not provide building coverage other than for additions and alterations. The minimum amount of insurance that must be purchased for Coverage C (personal property) under HO-6 is $6,000. Loss of use coverage is limited to 40 percent of Coverage C. Content is covered on an actual cash value basis unless endorsed to replacement value.

HO-8: Modified Form

The HO-8 policy provides repair cost coverage instead of replacement cost coverage for damage to property by a covered peril. The HO-8 form makes homeowners' insurance affordable for persons who live in older homes that can be quite expensive to repair if the insurance is required to use original construction materials and workmanship. Therefore, the functional replacement cost of the home might be much less than the actual replacement cost. The HO-8 provides coverage for basic perils, except that it provides "functional replacement cost" coverage. The insured's damaged dwelling and other structures will be repaired or replaced in the event of a covered loss, but the insurer pays only for currently accepted building materials and workmanship.

HOMEOWNERS (HO) INSURANCE: AVAILABLE ENDORSEMENTS

REPLACEMENT COST FOR PERSONAL PROPERTY

All of the HO forms previously discussed provide only actual cash value (ACV) coverage for personal property. This endorsement adds replacement cost coverage on the personal property of the insured. Since the ACV of household contents is typically only about 25 percent of the replacement cost value, the replacement cost coverage option is strongly recommended. (This may not be available in all states.)

ALL-RISKS COVERAGE FOR PERSONAL PROPERTY (OPEN PERILS)

All-risk coverage, also known as "**open-perils**" coverage, provides for a much broader and more comprehensive protection program than named-perils coverage. Under an all-risk policy, an insurance company must provide evidence that the loss is not covered under the policy before it can deny payment. The burden of proof lies with the insurer. Depending on the policy form purchased, some amount of all-risk coverage may be included on certain types of property. However, if it is not included, its purchase is recommended on both dwelling and personal property.

INFLATION PROTECTION

To avoid a coinsurance penalty, or an "under-insurance" situation, a homeowner should consider adding an inflation-guard endorsement to the homeowners policy. This endorsement increases the face value of insurance on both the dwelling and other coverages by a specified percentage every three months, such as 1, 1½, or 2 percent.

It is rare that insurance coverage amounts will increase at precisely the same rate as inflation in property values. Although an inflation-guard endorsement is a worthwhile purchase, it is not a complete form of protection against inflation and should not be a substitute for regular and careful review of the adequacy of insurance coverage. As expected, the insured's premiums will increase as coverage increases.

EARTHQUAKE AND SINK HOLE COLLAPSE INSURANCE

Earthquake or sink hole collapse endorsements can be added to any homeowners policy to provide coverage for earthquakes, landslides, and earth movement. A minimum deductible of $250 applies to any one loss, and there is a two to five percent deductible of the total amount of applicable insurance that applies to the loss.

REFRIGERATED PROPERTY COVERAGE

Refrigerated property coverage covers damage to property stored in refrigerators or freezers caused by the interruption of electrical service. There is usually a $500 limit and a $100 deductible.

SEWER BACKUP COVERAGE

A sewer backup coverage endorsement provides coverage under Section I for property damage caused by sewer backup problems.

Personal Injury

Section II of the standard HO policy protects the insured only against liability for bodily injury and property damage. An insured may be liable for personal injury or damage to someone's reputation, as well. The HO policies can be endorsed to provide limited personal injury protection to the insured. This endorsement adds coverage for the following *unintentional* offenses (remember that if the loss is intentionally caused, the policy will not provide coverage):

- False arrest, detention or imprisonment, or malicious prosecution.
- Libel, slander, defamation of character, or violation of the right of privacy.
- Invasion of right of private occupation, wrongful eviction, or wrongful entry.

Business Pursuits

A business pursuits endorsement provides the insured with liability for business activities, as long as the insured does not have an ownership or controlling interest in the business. This endorsement is designed to protect the insured as an employee of someone else who may or may not provide liability protection for the insured.

Watercraft

Certain types of watercraft can be added back onto the homeowner's policy for coverage; however, a separate boat owner's policy is generally the wisest choice for any insured who owns a watercraft. The boat owner's policy is quite similar in format and coverages to the Personal Auto Policy, which will be discussed later in this chapter.

Other Endorsements

Many other endorsements for additional premiums are available to meet the specific needs for coverage for various homeowners. The following are a few of the wide variety of endorsements available.

- An "other members of your household" endorsement extends the definition of the insured to include non-relatives over 21. This endorsement is in response to our changing society and the increase in nontraditional households.
- An "assisted living endorsement" extends the definition of the insured to provide coverage for personal property of relatives, not necessarily a household member, in a care facility. The endorsement includes loss of use and liability coverages.
- An "open-perils endorsement" for computers used in the home.
- An "endorsement available for golf carts" can be added to the homeowner's policy and is generally owned to cover property damage. This endorsement is usually subject to a $500 deductible and can also include collision liability coverage.

Quick Quiz 8.3

1. Replacement cost is generally a higher than actual cash value.
   a. True
   b. False

2. In an open perils coverage policy the burden lies with the insured to prove that the damages were caused by an insured-against event.
   a. True
   b. False

3. It is possible to obtain an endorsement for liability insurance against unintentional damage to another's reputation.
   a. True
   b. False

4. While you could insure a small sailboat (under 26 feet long) under a homeowners policy, it is wiser to purchase a separate boat owner's policy.
   a. True
   b. False

True, False, True, True.

HOMEOWNERS INSURANCE CONTRACTUAL CONDITIONS

SECTION I CONDITIONS

Duties of the Insured after a Loss

If there is a loss to an insured's property, the insured is required to fulfill a number of obligations before the loss can be settled. Immediately following the loss, the insured must:

1. Give notice immediately to the insurance company or agent.
2. Protect the property from any further damage.
3. Prepare an inventory of loss to the building and personal property.
4. File written proof of the loss with the insurance company, given the company's time constraints. The insurer must provide a state-promulgated form for the proof of loss.

KEY CONCEPTS

1. Highlight the obligations of the insured.
2. Highlight the obligations of the insurer.
3. Describe how a claim will be paid when the loss is insured by more than one insurer.
4. Highlight the differences between the different standard HO forms 2 – 6.

Loss Settlement

This condition specifies how certain property items will be valued, whether on an ACV basis or a replacement cost basis. The coinsurance provision of the policy is also contained in this clause.

Loss to a Pair or a Set

When there has been a loss to a pair or a set, such as a partial loss of a set of china, or the theft of only one earring, the insurer may either repair or replace the damaged/lost items, or pay the difference between the value of the property as a set before the loss and the value after the loss.

Appraisal

This clause gives the insured the right to dispute the amount of settlement offered by the insurer. If either the insured or the insurer disagrees on the amount of loss, either person may demand an appraisal by a competent appraiser. Then, both the insurer and the insured hire their own appraisers. If the two appraisers cannot reach an agreement on the loss amount, an umpire may be chosen to mediate their differences. Each party pays for its own appraiser, and both the insured and the insurer equally share the expense of hiring the umpire.

Other Insurance

When a loss covered under this policy is also covered by some other policy, the insured cannot collect from each policy in full. To do so would violate the principle of indemnity. The Other Insurance clause states that when another policy also covers a loss, the insurer will only pay a proportion of the loss based on the limits of coverage provided by each policy.

EXAMPLE 8.6

Suppose Phyllis has two HO policies. One provides a limit of $100,000 and one provides a limit of $200,000. Her house is worth $100,000, and after a fire destroys it, she will collect a proportion of the loss from each insurer. Because the first insurer provides 1/3 of all coverage provided ($100,000/$300,000), it will pay 1/3 of the loss, or $33,333. The second insurer will pay 2/3 of the loss, or $66,667.

Suit Against the Insurer

This clause gives the insured the right to sue the insurer *only after* the insured has complied with all of the policy provisions. It also requires that the suit be brought within one year of the date of the loss.

Settlement at Insurer's Option

The insurer retains the right to repair or replace any part of damaged property with similar property, as long as it notifies the insured of this right within 30 days after receiving the insured's sworn proof of loss.

Loss Payment

The insurer has 60 days *after* an agreement is reached regarding the amount of loss to provide payment to the insured. Most insurers will of course pay sooner, but the standard HO policy does give the insurer 60 days to actually make payment.

Abandonment of Property

The insurer does not have to accept property abandoned by an insured. A homeowner who suffers fire damage, for example, might try to force the insurer to take control of the house and be responsible for cleanup and repairs, and even mortgage payments.

Mortgage Clause

Because many homes are mortgaged, the insurer includes this clause to protect the mortgagee's (lender's) interest in the insured home. This clause gives the mortgagee important rights. The mortgagee has the right to receive payment for valid claims on the property, even if the insurer has denied the insured's claim, which would happen in the case of misrepresentation by the insured or an intentionally caused loss. Next, the mortgagee has the right to receive notice of policy cancellation or nonrenewal at least 10 days before the coverage on the property ends.

This clause also imposes certain obligations on the mortgagee. The mortgagee is responsible for notifying the insurer if there is a change in ownership or occupancy of the mortgaged property. The mortgagee must also pay any unpaid homeowner premiums that are due and file proof of loss statements if the insured fails to do so.

No Benefit to Bailee

If the insured has left property with a bailee, such as a moving company or dry cleaner, the insurer will not pay for loss or damaged property on behalf of the bailee. This clause does not say that claims by the insured will not be paid; it merely states that the coverage will not protect or benefit the bailee. If, for example, a fire on the premises of a dry cleaner destroyed the insured's personal property, the insurer would pay the insured's claim; however, it would then subrogate against the dry cleaner.

Recovered Property
When the insured or the insurer recovers property for which the insurer has already paid a claim (as might be the case following a theft), each must notify the other party of the recovery. The insured then has the option either to return the recovered property to the insurer or to keep the recovered property. If the insured keeps the property, the loss payment must be adjusted accordingly.

Volcanic Eruption Period
All volcanic eruptions occurring within a 72-hour period are considered one occurrence. Because volcanoes tend to erupt gradually over a period of days, this clause protects the insured from having to pay a new deductible for each eruption.

SECTION II CONDITIONS

Limit of Liability
The insurer will not pay more than the policy's coverage limit for each occurrence, regardless of the number of suits or claims filed against the insured for any one event.

Duties after a Loss
The insured is expected to give notice of any accident or occurrence to the insurer or its agent. The insured must also promptly forward to the insurer all summons and demand letters. The insured must cooperate and assist the insurer in the investigation and settlement of any claims. Finally, the insured must not voluntarily make payments for anything other than first aid at the time a bodily injury is sustained.

Duties of an Injured Person - Coverage F
An injured person or a representative must give the insurer written proof of a claim as soon as practical after a loss and give the insurer permission to obtain medical records of the injured person. The injured person must also submit to a physical exam by the insurer's doctor if instructed to do so by the insurer.

Payment of Claim - Coverage F
This clause states that paying any claim under Coverage F is in no way an admission of liability by the insurer or the insured.

Bankruptcy of an Insured
The bankruptcy or insolvency of any insured does not terminate coverage or relieve the insurer of its obligations under the policy.

QUICK QUIZ 8.4

1. If a homeowner has two HO policies on the home and suffers a loss, the formula for determining the payout by each insurer is to put the total amount of all insurance as the denominator and each insurer's policy's limits in the numerator.
   a. True
   b. False

2. The insurer may owe a duty to the mortgagee of the home.
   a. True
   b. False

3. Generally, the insurer has one year to pay the insured for a loss suffered.
   a. True
   b. False

4. Generally, the insurer may cancel the policy at any time by notifying the insured.
   a. True
   b. False

True, True, False, False.

Sections I and II Conditions

Concealment or Fraud

Dishonesty either before or after a loss may void the policy. Examples of dishonesty that will void the policy include intentionally concealing or misrepresenting material fact, and intentionally causing losses to occur.

Cancellation and Nonrenewal

Every state imposes its own restrictions on the insurer's right of cancellation and nonrenewal, so it is important to examine the specific policy to understand what is allowed. Generally, however, the insured may cancel the policy at any time by notifying the insurer, while the insurer may cancel the policy only for certain reasons: nonpayment of premium, material misrepresentation of fact, or a substantial change in the risk. In most cases, the insurer must only provide a 10-day notice of cancellation when it is canceling a newly issued policy or when it is canceling for nonpayment of premium. Other cancellations and nonrenewals usually require a 30-day notice. Cancellations generally result in a pro-rata refund of unused premium.

Assignment

The insured may not assign rights under the policy without the insurer's written consent.

Subrogation

The insurer may require the insured to assign rights of recovery for payments made by the insurer. This allows the insurer to take over the insured's subrogation rights against negligent third parties. The insurer does not, however, subrogate for claims made under Coverage F of the policy.

Exhibit 8.3 summarizes the preferred provisions of homeowners insurance.

EXHIBIT 8.3

Homeowners Checklist for Preferred Provisions

Part A - Dwelling	• Replacement cost • Open perils
Part B - Other Structures	• Replacement cost • Open perils
Part C - Personal Property	• Replacement cost • Open perils
Additional Endorsements and Riders	• Extra coverage for valuable personal property • Aircraft • Watercraft • Furnishings on property rented out to others • Business property • Earthquake insurance • Sewer backup coverage

EXHIBIT 8.4

Summary of Homeowners Insurance Policies

	HO-2 (Broad Form)	HO-3 (Special Form)	HO-5 (Comprehensive Form)	HO-8 (For Older Homes)	HO-4 (Renter's Contents Broad Form)	HO-6 (For Condominium Owners)
Perils covered	Perils 1 - 18	All perils except those specifically excluded on buildings; perils 1 - 18 on personal property	All perils except those specifically excluded	Perils 1 – 12	Perils 1 – 18	Perils 1 – 18
Section 1: Property coverages/limits						
House and any other attached buildings	Amount based on replacement cost, minimum $15,000	Amount based on replacement cost, minimum $20,000	Amount based on replacement cost, minimum $20,000	Amount based on actual cash value of the home	10% of personal property insurance on additions and alterations to the apartment	$1,000 on owner's additions and alterations to the unit
Detached buildings	10% of insurance on the home	10% of insurance on the home	10% of insurance on the home	10% of insurance on the home	Not covered	Not covered
Trees, shrubs, plants, etc.	5% of insurance on the home, $1,000 maximum per item	5% of insurance on the home, $1,000 maximum per item	5% of insurance on the home, $1,000 maximum per item	5% of insurance on the home, $1,000 maximum per item	10% of personal property insurance, $1,000 maximum per item	10% of personal property insurance, $1,000 maximum per item
Personal property (contents)	50% of insurance on the home	50% of insurance on the home	50% of insurance on the home	50% of insurance on the home	Chosen by the tenant to reflect the value of the items, minimum $6,000	Chosen by the home-owner to reflect the value of the items, minimum $6,000
Loss of use and/or add'l living expenses	30% of insurance on the home	30% of insurance on the home	30% of insurance on the home	10% of insurance on the home	30% of personal property insurance	50% of personal property insurance
Credit card, forgery, counterfeit money	$500	$500	$500	$500	$500	$500
Section 2: Liability						
Comprehensive personal liability	$100,000	$100,000	$100,000	$100,000	$100,000	$100,000
Damage to property of others	$250 - $500	$250 - $500	$250 - $500	$250 - $500	$250 - $500	$250 - $500
Medical payments	$1,000	$1,000	$1,000	$1,000	$1,000	$1,000
Special limits of liability	Special limits apply on a per-occurrence basis (e.g. per fire or theft): money, coins, bank notes, precious metals (gold, silver, etc.), $200; securities, deeds, stocks, bonds, tickets, stamps, $1,500; watercraft and trailers, including furnishings, equipment, and outboard motors, jewelry, watches, furs, $1,500; silverware, goldware, etc., $2,500; guns, $2,500.					

AUTOMOBILE INSURANCE

Automobile insurance is required in virtually every state, either expressly or implicitly. Mandatory automobile insurance laws exist in many states, and they expressly require the purchase of liability insurance before owning or operating a motor vehicle. Some states further require the purchase of "no-fault" coverages that pay for bodily injuries on a first-party basis, meaning that each insured pays for his and his passengers' injuries without regard to fault. Other states implicitly require automobile insurance by requiring motorists to be "financially responsible" for a minimum amount of bodily injury and property damage. Purchasing automobile insurance generally proves financial responsibility, although some automobile owners opt to post a bond or other proof of financial responsibility.

KEY CONCEPTS

1. Describe the three major risks that should concern an automobile owner/operator.
2. Highlight what could be defined as "your covered auto" in a standard PAP.
3. Highlight the six parts/categories of a standard PAP.
4. Describe several exclusions that are regularly found in standard PAPs.

In addition to these state statutory requirements, many people purchase automobile insurance because their automobile is financed, and the lender requires the borrower to carry coverage for direct physical damage to the automobile. Finally, many people purchase automobile insurance because they recognize that the financial burden associated with an automobile accident could be devastating to their financial well being. One at-fault accident could injure or kill one person or many people, and the insured could be responsible for those damages. In addition, with many new cars costing over $20,000, the damage to the insured's own vehicle could cost thousands of dollars to repair.

THE LEGAL ENVIRONMENT FOR THE AUTOMOBILE

The automobile is one of the most widely-owned and used major assets of consumers in the United States. The automobile presents great risk of economic loss to the owner including both property and liability damage.

The liability of the owner or operator for an automobile is generally governed by the tort laws of negligence. However, some states have modified the negligence law to also include **vicarious liability** responsibility for owners of automobiles for the negligent acts of family members or members of the household who are operating the automobile or for damage caused by a minor while driving the insured automobile. These laws take the form of family purpose doctrine or permissive use statutes. Essentially these laws make both the driver and the owner jointly liable for damages.

All states have financial responsibility and compulsory automobile liability insurance laws with Maine having the highest requirements (expressed as 50/100/25) and Louisiana and Oklahoma having the lowest (10/20/10). In Maine, the bodily injury liability per person minimum limit is $50,000, the bodily injury liability per accident minimum limit is $100,000 and the property damage per accident minimum liability limit is $25,000.

In spite of compulsory liability laws, there are many uninsured motorists. A few states have created special low-cost automobile insurance policies to deal with densely-populated urban areas where the poor may not be able to afford the relatively high automobile liability insurance premiums. The fact that there are many uninsured motorists is an essential reason to consider adding uninsured motorists coverage for both bodily injury and property damage caused by an uninsured or under-insured motorist.

Cost of Automobile Insurance

Automobile insurers determine premiums using three basic sets of factors:

- Age and sex of operators
- Use of the automobile
- Driving record of the operators

In addition, the premiums vary with the location in which the automobile is operated or garaged. For example, less populated areas are generally less expensive. Premiums are increased for increases in coverage and for more valuable automobiles. Some insurers have begun using credit ratings (FICO Scores) to adjust premiums up or down for perceived risk.

Initial premiums are adjusted down for youthful operator discounts (for driver training and good students), safe driving ratings (no tickets or accidents), and the number and types of automobiles.

Summary of Automobile Coverage

To summarize, the owner and operator of an automobile should be concerned about the following risks:

- Liability for injuries and damages to persons outside of the insured vehicle
- Liability for injuries and damages to persons inside the insured vehicle
- The cost to repair or replace a damaged or stolen insured vehicle or other property

In the next section of this chapter, the personal auto policy (PAP) is discussed. This package policy can provide protection against the three major losses listed above.

PERSONAL AUTO POLICY (PAP) COVERAGES

The ISO's **personal automobile policy** is the policy that is sold in almost every state; however, various state laws may result in different policy provisions and coverages. It is always important to read each policy and policy provisions carefully. The following discussion focuses merely on the basic ISO PAP.

Eligible Autos

The PAP may be used to insure four-wheel passenger automobiles, pickup trucks, and vans that are owned by individuals or leased for at least six months. Pickups and vans must have a gross vehicle weight of less than 10,000 pounds and must not be used primarily for business purposes other than farming, ranching, and some sole proprietorships. The policy may be used to insure one vehicle or all the vehicles owned in a household, but is usually subject to a maximum of four vehicles on one policy. It is generally cheaper to insure all the vehicles in one household on the same policy than to insure each individual vehicle with a separate policy.

The PAP may be used to insure vehicles that are used for pleasure and recreation, driving to and from work, farming and ranching, and even for business use by a sole proprietor.

Important Policy Definitions

The PAP contains a section of definitions that are important for reference purposes when reading the policy. Each defined word is put in quotation marks whenever it is used in the policy. While many of the terms are straightforward, the definitions of some are covered below before the various coverages are discussed.

"Your covered auto" is defined as any of the following:

- Any vehicle shown in the policy declarations.
- Any new vehicle *in addition to* those shown in the declarations, but only for 30 days or until the new vehicle is reported to the insurer. The insurer will charge a premium from the date the vehicle was acquired. The new vehicle will have the broadest coverage provided on any declared vehicle for the 30-day period.
- Any new vehicle *that replaces* a vehicle shown in the declarations. The new vehicle will have the same coverage as the vehicle it replaced. The insured must report the new vehicle within 30 days *only if* coverage for damage to your auto is desired.
- Any trailer the insured owns.
- Any auto or trailer that the insured does not own, but that is used as a temporary substitute while a covered vehicle is unavailable due to loss, breakdown, repair, service, or destruction.

The reason this definition is so important is that sometimes coverages are provided for *any* auto, while others are provided only for "your covered auto." Thus, this distinction is important to remember when determining which losses the PAP covers.

Throughout the policy, "you" and "your" refer to the named insured. These terms will not be put in quotation marks. The parts to an automobile insurance policy are A-F.

- Part A - Liability coverage
- Part B - Medical payments
- Part C - Uninsured motorists
- Part D - Damage to your auto
- Part E - Duties after an accident or loss
- Part F - General provisions

Part A: Liability Coverage

Part A agrees to provide liability protection for bodily injuries and property damages caused by an auto accident for which any insured becomes legally liable. The insurer retains the right to defend or settle any claim or suit, and any settlement and defense costs are paid in addition to the policy limits.

Covered Persons and Autos

Who is an insured under Part A? The policy clearly defines an insured as one of four parties:

- You or any family member for the ownership, maintenance, or use of any auto or trailer. This includes the use of borrowed autos, and even rental cars.

- Any person using "your covered auto" with permission.
- Any organization that is responsible for the conduct of someone driving "your covered auto," such as an employer or charitable organization.
- Any organization that is responsible for your conduct or the conduct of a family member while you are driving a nonowned automobile, such as an employer that might be responsible for your actions when you are using a coworker's car for business purposes.

Exclusions

PAP liability coverage is quite broad in nature. It excludes coverage only for the following persons and situations.

- *Vehicle used by auto dealer* - No coverage is provided for any auto dealer or other person in the auto business who is driving your car. The person in the auto business should have their own liability coverage.
- *Bodily injury to an employee* - No coverage is provided for injuries to an employee, because those should be covered by workers compensation benefits. One exception is that the insured will be covered for liability for injuries to a domestic employee.
- *Insured's owned property* - Liability insurance is designed to pay for damages to third parties that are caused by the insured. By definition, liability insurance cannot pay for damages to the insured's owned property. Therefore, in an auto accident, damages to the insured's car and its contents are not paid by the liability coverage. Damage to the car would have to be covered by Part D, and damage to contents of the vehicle would have to be paid by the homeowners coverage.
- *Property in the insured's care, custody, and control* - Along the same lines as the previous exclusion, this one prohibits the insured from recovering under his or her own liability insurance items that are not true liability losses. When property such as a rental car is damaged in an automobile accident, the PAP treats it as if it were the insured's owned auto. The insured may not use the liability coverage to pay for damages to the rental car.
- *Intentional acts* - Any person who intentionally causes an auto accident is not covered for liability by the policy.
- *Public livery* - Coverage is not provided for any person or vehicle while transporting people or property for a fee. A share-the-expense car pool is not considered a for-fee activity and is, thus, covered.
- *Commercial vehicles used in business* - This exclusion eliminates coverage for business use of automobiles, but then gives back coverage for business use of any private passenger auto, or any owned pickup or van, or any temporary or substitute pickup or van. The intent is to limit business coverage on autos to either private passenger autos or owned pickups and vans.
- *Using auto without permission* - No coverage is provided for any person who uses an automobile without having a reasonable belief that he or she has permission to do so.
- *Regular use of nonowned or nondeclared automobile* - When the insured has the regular use of an automobile that is not shown on the declarations page, either because the employer provides a company car or because the insured owns a nondeclared vehicle, coverage is not provided. If the insured has a company vehicle, the employer should provide coverage or the insured should declare the vehicle as a nonowned vehicle and purchase coverage for it. Recall that the named insured is covered while using "any" auto. If this exclusion were not in the policy, the insured could own ten vehicles, buy coverage on only one, but have cov-

erage on all ten. This exclusion makes it clear that the insurer will only cover those owned vehicles that have been declared and for which a premium has been paid.

- *Autos with fewer than four wheels* - Motorcycles and recreational vehicles having fewer than four wheels must be specifically insured under a different policy. No coverage is provided for these types of vehicles, regardless of whether they are owned or borrowed.

Coverage Limits

The limits of coverage for Part A are shown on the declarations page, and in most cases there are actually three separate liability coverage limits: two for bodily injury and one for property damage. All limits are on a per occurrence basis. The first bodily injury limit is the per person limit. A per person limit of $100,000 indicates that any one injured person may not receive more than $100,000 for bodily injuries. The second bodily injury limit is the per occurrence limit for all bodily injuries. If this limit were $200,000, the insurer would pay up to $200,000 for all the bodily injuries sustained in one accident, regardless of the number of persons injured. The property damage limit is also a per occurrence limit and specifies the most the insurer will pay for all property damages caused by one accident.

These "**split limits**" are often written as follows: 100/300/50. The first number is the per person bodily injury limit, the second number is the per occurrence bodily injury limit, and the third number is the property damage liability per occurrence limit. These numbers represent thousands of dollars. In other words, $100,000/$300,000/$50,000 of coverage.

EXAMPLE 8.7

Assume that the insured carried 100/300/50 limits and had a major accident that is deemed to be his fault. Imagine the following claims filed by injured parties in the other vehicle: X sustains $110,000 in bodily injuries, Y sustains $120,000 in bodily injuries, and Z sustains $170,000 in bodily injuries. X, the other driver, also incurs $35,000 in automobile repair and rental car costs. W, a nearby homeowner, sustained $21,000 in property damage. Assume that all claims are settled in the order they are mentioned above.

First, address the bodily injury claims. X is allowed to collect $100,000, because that is the per person liability limit. Note that X likely will sue for the $10,000 deficiency. Y will collect $100,000. Z will collect only $100,000 because at that point, the $300,000 per occurrence limit has been reached. Claims are paid in the order in which they are settled, not on a pro rata basis, so it is important that claimants begin the settlement process as soon as possible. Z will likely sue the insured for the $70,000.

Next, consider the property damage claims. The policy provides a total of $50,000 of coverage, yet there is a total of $56,000 in property damage claims. Thus, the insurer will pay all of X's damages, and W will receive only $15,000 and may sue for the additional $6,000.

Increased Limits While Driving in Another State

As mentioned previously, all states require some minimum level of financial responsibility or automobile liability insurance. When the insured, a resident in one state, drives within another state and has an accident, the insured must generally have sufficient limits to meet the minimum requirements of the state in which the accident occurred.

A driver from Louisiana, who has only the minimum required liability limits of 10/25/10 drives through Texas, where the minimum liability limits are 20/40/15, and would be expected to have those coverage limits if an accident occurred in Texas. The PAP automatically provides the increased limits required by the state law in which the driver has the accident. Therefore, the Louisiana driver's insurance policy would pay up to 20/40/15 if an accident occurred while the insured was driving in Texas.

EXAMPLE 8.8

It is important to note that this policy provision never reduces the limits of liability the insured has purchased. If a Texas driver has 20/40/15 coverage limits and drives to Louisiana, his policy will pay up to those purchased liability limits for any accident.

Liability Loss Sharing with Other Coverage

When more than one auto policy covers a liability loss, the general rule is that the insurance on the automobile is primary, while the insurance on the driver is secondary and excess. The same is true for damage to the insured's auto.

If Brian borrows Beth's car and has an accident while driving it, Beth's PAP coverage will pay first. When Beth's limits of coverage have been exhausted, then Brian's policy will pay on an excess basis. If more than one policy is primary (for example, if an automobile is declared and covered by two separate policies), then the primary policies share losses on a proportionate basis (as discussed under homeowners insurance).

EXAMPLE 8.9

PART B: MEDICAL PAYMENTS

Medical payments are optional no-fault, first-party coverage designed to pay for bodily injuries sustained in an auto accident. Expenses must be incurred within three years of the auto accident. Limits of insurance are provided on a per person, per occurrence basis. A typical limit of coverage is $5,000/person/occurrence. This means that if four covered persons are injured in an auto accident, each may collect up to $5,000 for reasonable and necessary medical and funeral expenses.

Who is Covered?

An insured in this coverage is defined as any of the following:

- You or any family member while occupying a motor vehicle
- You or any family member as a pedestrian when struck by a motor vehicle
- Any other person while occupying "your covered auto"

Exclusions

Medical payment coverages exclude the following:

- *Public livery* - Again, no coverage is provided while the vehicle is used to carry persons or property for a fee.
- *Auto used as a residence* - Although trailers are included as covered autos, this exclusion prevents someone from having medical payments coverage on a house trailer. This type of nonstandard risk must be specifically insured.
- *Injury while working* - Any benefits that are payable under workers compensation or other disability benefit laws preclude coverage under this policy.
- *Using auto without permission* - No coverage is provided for any person who uses an automobile without having a reasonable belief that he or she has permission to do so.

- *Regular use of nonowned or nondeclared auto* - Once again, when the insured has the regular use of an automobile that is not shown on the declarations page, either because the employer provides a company car or because the insured owns a nondeclared vehicle, coverage is not provided.
- *Autos with fewer than four wheels* - Motorcycles and recreational vehicles having fewer than four wheels must be specifically insured under a different policy. No coverage is provided for these types of vehicles, regardless of whether they are owned or borrowed.
- *Auto used in insured's business* - The same exclusion that was discussed in Part A applies here. Coverage is again provided for private passenger autos used in business and for owned pickups and vans used in business.
- *War and nuclear hazard injuries* - Consistent with other policies, this coverage does not apply to any injuries sustained because of acts of war or because of nuclear contamination or radioactive hazards.
- *Racing* - No coverage is provided when the vehicle is located inside a racing facility or when the vehicle is practicing for, preparing for, or competing in any type of racing or speed contest.

PART C: UNINSURED MOTORISTS

Purpose

Because so many drivers do not obey financial responsibility and compulsory automobile insurance laws, the PAP offers insureds the option of purchasing uninsured motorist coverage that acts as the liability insurance for an uninsured or underinsured motorist.

What is Covered?

Part C will pay for bodily injuries and, in many states, property damages that are sustained by an insured because of an uninsured or underinsured motorist. In simpler terms, this coverage will pay what the uninsured, at-fault motorist's liability insurance *should* have paid, had it existed.

Who is Covered?

An insured for this coverage is defined as follows:

- You or any family member
- Any other person occupying "your covered auto"
- Any person who might also be entitled to damages (such as a spouse or child) for the injuries sustained by a person described above

Definitions of an Uninsured / Underinsured Auto

An **uninsured or underinsured motorist** is defined as one who has no liability coverage, one who has limits of liability coverage less than those required by the insured's home state law, one who is an unidentified hit-and-run driver, or one who has liability insurance, but whose insurer cannot or will not pay the claim. Once again, it is important to emphasize that for the insured to collect from this coverage, the uninsured or underinsured driver *must be at fault* in the accident.

Exclusions and Limitations

Many of the exclusions contained in Part B are repeated in this coverage:

- Public livery
- Regular use of nonowned auto

- Injury while working
- Regular use of nondeclared auto
- Using auto without permission
- Auto used in insured's business

In addition, the insurer will not pay for any bodily injuries when the insured or their legal representatives settle a bodily injury claim without the insurer's consent. Furthermore, this coverage will not pay for punitive or exemplary damages.

Part D: Coverage for Damage to Your Auto

Coverage D provides direct damage coverage on "your covered auto," plus any "nonowned auto." "Your covered auto" was defined previously, so it is only necessary to define "nonowned auto." A "nonowned" auto is any private passenger, auto, pickup, van or trailer not owned by or furnished for the use of a family member that is in your (or a family member's) custody. This would include a borrowed car, a rental car, and a temporary substitute auto.

Two Coverages Available

Part D provides the insured with two different direct damage coverages: collision and comprehensive. The insured may purchase one or both of these coverages, though automobile lenders will generally require the insured to carry both.

Collision coverage protects the insured against upset and collision damages, such as those sustained in an accident involving other vehicles, or those sustained when an auto runs off the road and into a lake. These types of accidents are generally viewed as the insured's fault because if there were another party to blame for the accident, the insured could ask that party's liability insurance to pay for the damages.

Comprehensive (sometimes referred to as "other than collision") coverage protects the insured against the following perils: missiles or falling objects, fire, theft, explosion, earthquake, windstorm, hail, water or flood, malicious mischief or vandalism, riot or civil commotion, contact with bird or animal, and breakage of glass. These perils are typically viewed as accidental and out of the insured's control. Thus, the premium for this coverage is lower than that for collision coverage.

Dispute Resolution (Appraisal Clause)

If the insured and the insurer do not agree on the amount of a loss, the insured may demand an appraisal process similar to that provided for in the homeowners policy.

Loss Payment

The insurer retains the sole option either to pay for repairs or to declare the vehicle a "total loss" and pay the actual cash value of the vehicle, less any deductible. The collision coverage deductible is typically twice as high as the "other than collision" deductible. In most cases, insureds should carry a minimum $250 "other than collision" deductible and $500 collision deductible. Higher and lower deductibles are available. However, higher deductibles generally reduce premiums.

Loss Sharing with Other Policies - Collision

As with a liability loss, when more than one auto policy covers a loss by collision, insurance on the automobile is primary, while insurance on the driver is excess. Therefore, if Joe borrows Fred's car and has an accident while driving it, Fred's collision damage coverage will pay first. Joe's policy will pay on an excess basis, but will not pay more than the loss, and will still require Joe to pay his own deductible.

If more than one policy is primary (for example, if an automobile is declared and covered by two separate policies), then the primary policies share losses on a proportionate basis (as discussed under homeowners insurance).

Exclusions

Many of the exclusions described in other coverages apply here:

- Public livery
- Custom furnishings on a pickup or van
- Using auto without permission
- Radar detectors
- Racing
- Most electronic equipment, except permanently-installed sound reproducing equipment
- War
- Nuclear damages

As with most direct property coverages, the PAP excludes coverage for normal wear and tear and ordinary maintenance losses such as road damage to tires. Loss caused by destruction or confiscation by governmental authorities is also excluded, as could occur if the insured vehicle were involved in a crime. Losses to nonowned autos are not covered when the auto is used or maintained by anyone in the automobile business.

Finally, no coverage is provided for a rental vehicle if the insured has purchased a loss damage waiver from the rental car company. Loss damage waivers relieve the insured of liability for damage to the rented vehicle, so the insurer will not provide coverage.

Part E: Duties after an Accident or Loss

Most of the duties required of the insured are common sense: notify the insurer, file proof of loss, and cooperate with the insurer in the investigation and settlement of any claim. In addition, the insured must file a police report to have theft coverage for a stolen vehicle or to have uninsured motorist coverage for a hit-and-run incident.

Quick Quiz 8.5

1. An automobile owner/operator should only insure against risks to persons inside the vehicle.
   a. True
   b. False

2. In a standard PAP, "your covered vehicle" includes a new automobile for no more than the first thirty days of ownership or until the insurer is notified.
   a. True
   b. False

3. There may be three separate liability coverage limits.
   a. True
   b. False

4. If you drive "your covered vehicle" into Mexico, your PAP coverage is effective.
   a. True
   b. False

False, True, True, False.

Part F: General Provisions

There are several general provisions and conditions of the auto policy that are similar to those contained in HO policies. One, however, deserves special attention: the PAP coverage territory.

The PAP provides coverage *only in* the United States, its territories and possessions, Puerto Rico, and Canada. When the insured travels to Mexico (where auto accidents are automatically criminal offenses) or to any other country outside the coverage territory, it is important to realize that the PAP is NOT effective. If the insured intends to drive in such a locale, the appropriate local coverages must be arranged.

LEGAL LIABILITY

The categories of liability to which clients are exposed are: torts (civil wrongs), breach of contract, and crimes (public wrongs). Liability insurance will cover certain classes of torts but not breach of contract or criminal offenses. If a court decides that an individual is liable for a civil wrong that causes injury to another, the individual will be required to make restitution, usually in the form of monetary compensation.

Key Concepts

1. Identify the three types of standards of care.
2. Differentiate between contributory negligence, comparative negligence, and the last clear chance rule.

There are three general types of torts related to liability: intentional interference, strict and absolute liability, and negligence. **Intentional interference** is, as it sounds, an intentional act committed against another that causes injury. Many of the actions that fall under intentional interference are also criminal acts and would not be covered under liability insurance. Slander and libel, however, are usually covered under personal liability insurance policies. **Slander** is defamation or harm caused by a verbal statement, and **libel** is defamation caused by a written statement.

Strict and absolute liability occurs as a result of law. One party is held legally liable regardless of who is responsible for the injury. Workers' compensation laws are examples of strict liability. Under workers' compensation laws, the employer is liable for any injury to an employee while he or she is engaged in business activities. Even if the employee causes injury to himself, the employer will be liable unless the employer can prove the injury was due to intoxication or failure to follow orders. If workers' compensation laws provided for absolute liability, the employer would be liable even if the employee was intoxicated. Under strict liability, responsible parties have few options for defense, but under absolute liability, the responsible party has no options for defense.

If an individual causes harm to another by failing to act with appropriate care, he or she will be subject to liability due to **negligence**. In determining whether an individual has acted with appropriate care, the courts use the "prudent man" standard. The standard is met if a reasonable person confronted with the same circumstances would have performed the same acts. Direct negligence refers to acts or omissions directly attributable to an individual. An individual may also be liable for vicarious acts, which are negligent acts performed by someone else but for which the individual is held at least partially responsible. For example, in many states bartenders are vicariously liable for the negligent acts of intoxicated patrons. Liability insurance generally covers both types of negligence.

Standards of Care

Negligence is defined as the failure to act in a way that a reasonably prudent person would have acted under the circumstances. In short, negligence is imprudent to behavior. Types of liability created from negligent behavior include:

- **Strict (Absolute) Liability** - The two terms are used interchangeably. It is a liability without regard to negligence or fault. It applies to damage resulting from some extraordinarily dangerous activity or other statutorily defined activity (e.g., product liability, hazardous materials, blasting operations). Negligence does not have to be proven; however, defenses may be allowed to refute or lessen liability. Workers are indemnified for employment-connected injuries regardless of who was at fault (e.g., workers compensation). Negligence does not have to be proven on the part of the employer nor are defenses permitted by the employer to refute or lessen liability.
- **Negligence per se** - The act itself constitutes negligence, thereby relieving the burden to prove negligence (e.g., drunk driving). Burden of proof is initially borne by the injured party. Standard of proof in most civil cases is the preponderance of the evidence (more than 50%). Other concepts to consider include *res ispa loquitur* ("the act speaks for itself"). **Res ispa loquitur** is a doctrine of the law of negligence that is concerned with the circumstances and the types of accidents that permits the use of reasonable evidence when a specific explanation of negligence is not available. For example, if a plane crashes, there is negligence. It does not have to be proven. There mere fact that a plane crashes implies negligence. Planes do not just fall out of the sky.

Damages

A tort can result in two forms of injury - bodily injury and property damage. Bodily injury may lead to medical expenses, loss of income, pain and suffering, mental anguish, and loss of consortium. The damages for bodily injury can be:

- Special damages to compensate for measurable losses.
- General damages to compensate for intangible losses (pain and suffering).
- Punitive damages - amounts assessed against the negligent party as punishment.

Property damage is usually measured by the actual monetary loss.

The **collateral source rule** holds that damages assessed against a negligent party should not be reduced simply because the injured party has other sources of recovery available such as insurance or employee benefits (health or disability insurance).

Vicarious Liability

One person may become legally liable for the torts of another (e.g., parent / child, employer where the employee is acting in the scope of employment).

Defense to Negligence

There are various defenses available to alleged negligent parties that can relieve them of legal liability in spite of negligent behavior.

Assumption of the risk - The injured party fully understood and recognized the dangers that were involved in an activity and voluntarily chose to proceed. This defense is not available in all states.

Negligence on the part of the injured party - This can be either **contributory negligence**, where there is evidence that the injured party did not look out for his own safety, or **comparative negligence**, where the amount of damage is adjusted to reflect the injured party's proportion of contribution to the cause of the injury (same with multiple defendants). Contributory negligence theories often result in the entire action failing. Many states allow recovery for that portion of damages not caused by the injured party (comparative negligence). The "**last clear chance**" **rule** may apply. This rule states that a claimant who is endangered by his own negligence may recover if the defendant has a "last clear chance" to avoid the accident and failed to do so.

PERSONAL LIABILITY UMBRELLA POLICY (PLUP)

PURPOSE

The **personal liability umbrella policy (PLUP)** is designed to provide a catastrophic layer of liability coverage on top of the individual's homeowners and automobile insurance liability coverages. A standard amount of coverage is $1 million, although higher limits may be purchased. The need for the PLUP is largely dictated by the insured's personal wealth. The more the insured has at risk, the more likely it is that a PLUP is a suitable purchase.

KEY CONCEPTS

1. Describe the categories of liability to which one may be exposed.
2. Describe the purpose of PLUP.
3. Describe some insurance needs faced by businesses.

CHARACTERISTICS

Most PLUP insurers will require the insured to maintain certain underlying limits of coverage through an HO and a PAP. If the insured also has other liability exposures to insure, such as watercraft liability, minimum limits of coverage will be required for those policies as well.

The PLUP provides the insured with a large amount of coverage at an affordable price. A $1 million PLUP limit might cost as little as $300 per year. The coverage provided is generally quite broad, and may even provide coverages in addition to those provided by the underlying policies. For example, the PLUP might provide personal injury coverage (for defamation of character, false arrest, etc.) even though the underlying HO policy does not. Where these additional coverages are provided, the insured is usually required to pay a **self-insured retention** (SIR) for each loss. This SIR is similar to a deductible.

PLUP coverage provides for legal defense of claims in addition to the claim itself. The cost of legal defense is not charged against the policy. Recall, however, if the insured is willing to pay the face of the policy, there is no requirement to provide legal defense.

When both the umbrella and an underlying policy cover a loss, the umbrella does not pay any claims until the underlying coverage has exhausted its limits. From there, the umbrella picks up with no SIR imposed on the insured.

EXAMPLE 8.10

If Joe has an HO policy with a Coverage E limit of $300,000, and a $1 million PLUP, and is held liable for bodily injuries to another totaling $900,000, his HO policy will pay the first $300,000 of the claims, then the PLUP will pay the remaining $600,000.

EXCLUSIONS

PLUP forms are nonstandard, so it is difficult to generalize about what exclusions are included in each policy. Certain exclusions almost universally found in PLUPs include: damage to the insured's property, injuries sustained by the insured or a family member, injuries that were intentionally inflicted or caused by the insured, injuries to another party that should be paid under a workers compensation law, and business and professional liability incidents.

BUSINESS AND PROFESSIONAL PROPERTY AND LIABILITY INSURANCE

Similar to individuals, businesses also have insurance needs. Some of the policies used by businesses to cover property and liability include the commercial package policy, inland marine policies, the business owners policy, business liability insurance, workers compensation, business automobile, business liability umbrella policies, professional insurance, and errors and omissions.

The Insurance Services Office (ISO) has developed a commercial insurance program including a package policy with two or more coverages.

THE COMMERCIAL PACKAGE POLICY (CPP)

The commercial package policy (CPP) is both a property and a liability coverage combined into a single policy. The advantages of such a policy include lower premiums and fewer gaps in overall coverage. Workers compensation coverage and surety coverages are not part of a CPP. A CPP policy format includes:

- a declarations page
- a policy conditions page
- two or more coverage parts or forms (property, general liability, crime, boiler and machinery, inland marine, commercial auto, or farm)

Each part or form of the CPP will specify:

- covered property
- additional coverages
- extension of coverages
- other provisions
- deductible
- coinsurance
- valuation provisions
- optional coverages
- a cause-of-loss form

Coverages for causes of loss are basic, broad, special, or earthquake form. These forms are similar to the parallel homeowners forms. Business interruption insurance may be added. Also, a builders-risk-coverage form can be added to the CPP for buildings under construction.

Inland Marine Policies

Inland marine policies cover domestic goods in transit, property held by bailees, mobile equipment and property, property of certain dealers and means of transportation and communication. They may also be used to increase coverage limits on movables, such as furs and jewelry.

The Business Owner's Policy (BOP)

The business owner's policy is specifically designed for the needs of small-to-medium-size businesses and covers buildings and business personal property. It comes in two forms: basic and special. The basic form covers listed perils, as distinguished from special, which covers all perils not excluded. The policy has a standard $250 deductible and covers business liability for bodily injury and property damage.

Business Liability Insurance

General liability is the legal liability arising out of business activities excepting autos, motorized vehicles, aircraft, and employee (workers' compensation) injuries. Liability issues, not including exceptions mentioned, are covered by commercial general liability policies (CGL). CGL can be written either as a stand-alone policy or as a part of a commercial package policy (CPP). The usual coverage, Coverage A, is for bodily injury, property damage and legal defense, but it has significant exclusions. Coverage B is for personal and advertising injury liability. Part C covers medical payments.

Workers' Compensation Insurance

Most businesses are required to carry workers' compensation insurance. The usual workers' compensation policy is a package that provides for the following coverages: workers' compensation insurance, employer liability insurance, and other state insurance. The workers' compensation insurance covers benefits provided by the insurer (state). Part two covers lawsuits by employees injured in the course of employment, but not covered by state workers' compensation law. Part three provides coverage for other listed states (business trips, etc.).

Business Auto Policy (BAP)

Businesses also use commercial automobile insurance policies covering both physical damage to property and liability insurance. The business auto package policy is referred to as BAP.

Commercial Liability Umbrella Policy

Businesses may make use of commercial liability umbrella policies for coverage on liability beyond the firm's basic liability policy.

Malpractice Insurance

Most people understand malpractice insurance as liability insurance for health service providers, especially physicians and surgeons. Malpractice insurance, however, is available for all professional service providers and generally covers intentional acts as well as unintentional negligent acts committed by the insured. A typical policy will have a maximum per incident limit and an aggregate limit. The insurer is usually allowed to settle claims out of court without obtaining consent from the insured.

Errors and Omissions Insurance

Errors and omissions coverage provides protection against loss from negligent acts, errors, and omissions by the insured. Many professionals (real estate agents, insurance agents, accountants, stockbrokers, attorneys, engineers) need errors and omissions coverage for negligent acts, omissions, or failure to act within their own profession that may cause legal liability. Policies usually have large deductibles of $1,000 or more.

A special type of errors and omissions coverage, called Directors and Officers Errors and Omissions insurance, is available for business executives. Directors and Officers insurance provides protection against liability due to mismanagement. Policies usually have high deductibles and require that the insured be financially responsible for a percentage of any claims.

Products Liability Insurance

Businesses that manufacture products are subject to liability with respect to those products. Acts that can expose a company to product liability include:

- Manufacturing a harmful product
- Selling a defective product
- Packaging the product inappropriately
- Providing insufficient directions or warnings for use

Quick Quiz 8.6

1. Courts generally use the "prudent man" standard to determine whether one acted with the appropriate amount of care in a given situation.
   a. True
   b. False

2. PLUP forms are considered standard forms, and thus, it is easy to generalize about PLUP coverage.
   a. True
   b. False

3. Only doctors need malpractice insurance.
   a. True
   b. False

4. The commercial package policy (CPP) is business property and business liability coverage combined in one policy.
   a. True
   b. False

True, False, False, True.

EXHIBIT 8.5

Insurance Concept Summary for Businesses and Professionals

Insurance Needs	Businesses	Professionals
Property Insurance - Buildings	CPP	CPP
Property Insurance - Personalty	CPP	CPP
General Liability Insurance	As needed	As needed
Inland Marine Coverage	If transporting goods	If transporting goods
Business Interruption Coverage	As needed	As needed
Builders Risk Insurance	If construction	If construction
Workers' Compensation	If employees	If employees
Business Automobile Policy	If autos/BAP	If autos/BAP
Commercial Liability Umbrella Policy	Excess liability coverage	Excess liability coverage
Malpractice Insurance	N/A	Yes
Errors and Omissions Insurance	N/A	Yes
Products Liability Insurance	If manufacturer	N/A

KEY TERMS

Actual Cash Value - The depreciated value of personal property.

Assumption of Risk - The injured party fully understood and recognized the dangers that were involved in an activity and voluntarily chose to proceed.

Collateral Source Rule - Holds that damages assessed against a negligent party should not be reduced simply because the injured party has other sources of recovery available such as insurance or employee benefits (health or disability insurance).

Collision - Auto insurance coverage that protects the insured against upset and collision damages, such as those sustained in an accident involving other vehicles, or those sustained when an auto runs off the road and into a lake.

Comparative Negligence - The amount of damage is adjusted to reflect the injured party's proportion of contribution to the cause of the injury.

Comprehensive (or Other than Collision) - Auto insurance coverage that protects the insured's auto against perils out of the insured's control, such as missiles or falling objects, fire, theft, earthquake, hail, flood, and vandalism.

Contributory Negligence - Negligence on the part of the injured party that contributes to the harm and, therefore, the injured has to bear some responsibility for the injury.

Dwelling - Residential structure covered under a homeowners insurance policy.

Endorsement - Attachment or addition to an existing insurance policy that changes the original terms.

Homeowners Insurance - A package insurance policy that provides both property and liability coverage for the insured's dwelling, other structures, personal property, and loss of use.

Intentional Interference - Intentional act committed against another that causes injury.

Last Clear Chance Rule - This rule states that a claimant who is endangered by his own negligence may recover if the defendant has a "last clear chance" to avoid the accident and failed to do so.

Libel - A written statement that causes harm to another.

Loss of Use - Under homeowners insurance coverage, loss of use is a combination of additional living expenses and loss of rental income.

Medical Payments - A no-fault, first-party insurance coverage designed to pay for bodily injuries sustained in an auto accident.

KEY TERMS

Negligence - Harm caused by failure to use reasonable care.

Open Perils - All-risk coverage for personal property that provides for a much broader and more comprehensive protection program than named-perils coverage.

Other Structures - Small detached structures on the insured's property in addition to the main house, such as garages, greenhouses, or storage buildings.

Personal Automobile Policy - Insurance policy that covers liability for injuries and damages to persons inside and outside the vehicle and covers the cost to repair/replace a damaged or stolen vehicle.

Personal Liability Umbrella Policy (PLUP) - Coverage designed to provide a catastrophic layer of liability coverage on top of the individual's homeowners and automobile insurance policies.

Personal Property - Valuable items owned by the insured that are covered under homeowners insurance.

Replacement Cost - The amount necessary to purchase, repair, or replace the dwelling with materials of the same or similar quality at current prices.

Res ispa loquitur - A doctrine of the law of negligence that is concerned with the circumstances and the types of accidents, which affords reasonable evidence if a specific explanation of negligence is not available.

Schedule - Attachment or addition to an existing insurance policy that lists individual items.

Self-Insured Retention - A payment similar to a deductible that an insured is usually required to pay for each loss under a personal umbrella policy.

Slander - Verbal statement that causes harm to another.

Split Limits - Three separate liability coverage limits covering bodily injury (per person and per occurrence) and property damage.

Strict and Absolute Liability - Liability resulting from law. Strict liability allows for defense, absolute liability does not.

Uninsured / Underinsured Motorist - Motorist without liability coverage or whose insurer can/will not pay claim, hit-and-run driver, or motorist with insufficient liability coverage according to state law.

Vicarious Liability - One person may become legally liable for the torts of another (e.g., parent / child, employer where the employee is acting in the scope of employment).

DISCUSSION QUESTIONS

1. Explain the need for property insurance.
2. What are the basic, broad, and open-perils coverages provided by a homeowners policy?
3. Identify the various homeowners forms that are available.
4. What do Sections I and II of a homeowners policy provide?
5. What is a named-perils policy?
6. Identify and explain the various contractual options and provisions in homeowners insurance.
7. Explain why intentional acts are not usually covered by insurance.
8. What legal principle implies that property insurance policies only pay for the policy owner's insurable interest in a loss?
9. What are the ways in which property insurance policies determine how losses are valued?
10. List two major general exclusions in almost all homeowners insurance policies that cover real property.
11. What are the coverages provided by a personal automobile insurance policy (PAP)?
12. Identify and explain the various contractual options and provisions in a PAP.
13. What is the need for a personal umbrella policy, and what are the umbrella's distinguishing characteristics?
14. What are three types of property and liability loss exposures facing families and businesses?

MULTIPLE-CHOICE PROBLEMS

1. Bill rents an apartment for $500 per month and has $50,000 content coverage. If he is unable to occupy his apartment due to a negligent fire caused by a neighbor, for up to how many months could he rent another apartment if the cost of the new apartment is $750 per month?

    a. 60 months.
    b. 6 months.
    c. None because negligent acts are not covered.
    d. None because content coverage does not cover reimbursement for rent.

2. Mary lives in Idaho where she carries the state-mandated minimum liability insurance on her car (15/30/10) through her personal automobile policy (PAP). She is driving through Oklahoma and has a wreck with Gerri. Oklahoma requires minimum liability insurance of 30/50/20. Gerri suffers bodily injury in an amount of $40,000 and Gerri's vehicle is damaged in an amount of $22,000. How much will Gerri collect from Mary's PAP policy?

    a. BI $40,000 and property $22,000.
    b. BI $15,000 and property $10,000.
    c. BI $30,000 and property $20,000.
    d. BI $30,000 and property $22,000.

3. Tom and Tim are brothers who frequently drive each other's cars. Their automobiles are insured as follows:

Insured	Insurance Company	Amount
Tim	ABC Co.	40/50/10
Tom	LMV Auto	100/300/25

Tom is negligently driving Tim's car and has an accident causing bodily injury to the other party involved in the accident in the amount of $50,000. Which insurer will pay, and how much?

    a. ABC will pay $40,000, and LMV will pay $10,000.
    b. LMV will pay $50,000, and ABC will pay nothing.
    c. ABC will pay $40,000, and LMV will pay nothing.
    d. ABC will pay $25,000, and LMV will pay $25,000.

4. Under the HO-3 policy, all open-perils are covered, with some exceptions. All of the following are perils that are excluded from a HO-3 policy, except:

    a. Termite damage.
    b. Flood.
    c. Earthquake.
    d. Tornado.

5. John, who has retired to Miami, decided to purchase a condominium unit on the beach. Which of the following homeowners policies would be most appropriate for John to purchase?

    a. HO-3.
    b. HO-4.
    c. HO-5.
    d. HO-6.

6. Jennifer lives by herself and rents a one-bedroom apartment in Manhattan. Which of the following homeowners policies would be most appropriate for Jennifer to purchase?

    a. HO-3.
    b. HO-4.
    c. HO-5.
    d. HO-6.

7. Section II of a HO-3 policy provides what type of protection for the homeowner?

    a. Dwelling.
    b. Damage to other's property.
    c. Loss of use.
    d. Personal property.

8. Raymond lived in New Orleans during hurricane Katrina. His home was destroyed by wind damage, and he was forced to live in a hotel for three months. Which section of his homeowners policy would reimburse him for the increased living expenses associated with the hotel stay?

    a. Dwelling.
    b. Other structures.
    c. Loss of use.
    d. Personal property.

9. Which of the following offers identical coverage for all forms of a homeowners insurance policy?

    a. Section I.
    b. Section II.
    c. No form is identical.
    d. All forms are identical.

10. Which of the following would not be considered an insured person for the purposes of Part A (Liability Coverage) for a Personal Auto Policy?

    a. You.
    b. Any family member.
    c. Any person using "your covered auto" with permission.
    d. Any person using "your covered auto" without permission.

11. Resident family members are covered for the purposes of Part A (Liability Coverage) for a Personal Auto Policy when operating all of the following except:

    a. Their auto.
    b. A rented auto.
    c. A borrowed auto.
    d. A replacement auto after 31 days.

12. Mike has the following split limits of coverage on his Personal Auto Policy of 100/300/50. Which of the following best describes Mike's coverage?

    a. $100,000 per person for bodily injury, $300,000 per occurrence for bodily injury and $50,000 for property damage.
    b. $100,000 per covered auto, $300,000 per occurrence for covered auto and $50,000 for uninsured motorist.
    c. $100,000 per person for bodily injury, $300,000 per occurrence for property damage and $50,000 for uninsured motorist.
    d. $100,000 for property damage, $300,000 per person for bodily injury and $50,000 for property damage.

13. All of the following statements are correct regarding a Personal Auto Policy Part B (Medical Payments) coverage except:

    a. Provides payment for medical expenses of an insured due to an auto accident.
    b. Provides medical payments if struck as a pedestrian.
    c. Provides payments for medical expenses for household pets if struck by the covered auto.
    d. Provides payment for medical expenses of anyone occupying the insured's covered auto.

14. All of the following statements are correct regarding a Personal Auto Policy Part C (Uninsured Motorists) coverage except:

    a. Payment for property damage.
    b. Payment for lost wages.
    c. Payment for punitive damages.
    d. All of the above.

15. All of the following statements are correct regarding a Personal Auto Policy Part D (Coverage for Damage to Your Auto) coverage except:

    a. Collision applies when your car hits another vehicle.
    b. Comprehensive covers fire, theft, or vandalism.
    c. Collision covers damages to a borrowed or rented vehicle.
    d. Collision coverage includes contact with an animal or bird.

16. All of the following statements are correct regarding a personal liability umbrella policy except:

    a. The PLUP provides protection above and beyond the liability limits of your homeowners and automobile insurance policies.
    b. The PLUP requires the insured to carry certain underlying minimum amounts of liability for homeowners and PAP.
    c. The PLUP insurer provides legal defense to the insured.
    d. The PLUP is only appropriate for individuals with a high net worth.

QUICK QUIZ EXPLANATIONS

Quick Quiz 8.1

1. True.
2. True.
3. False. Liability is only paid when there is legal liability, whereas medical payments to others pays claims if someone is injured, regardless of fault.

Quick Quiz 8.2

1. True.
2. False. Coverage F pays necessary medical expenses suffered by someone other than the insured or any regular resident of the household, except a domestic employee.

Quick Quiz 8.3

1. True.
2. False. In an open-perils policy, the insurance company must prove that a loss is not covered under the policy before it can deny payment.
3. True.
4. True.

Quick Quiz 8.4

1. True.
2. True.
3. False. Generally, the insurer has sixty (60) days after an agreement is reached regarding the amount of loss.
4. False. Generally, the insured may cancel the policy at any time by notifying the insurer.

Quick Quiz 8.5

1. False. The three major risks to insure against are for liability and injury to those inside and outside the vehicle, as well as to the vehicle itself.
2. True.
3. True.
4. False. PAP coverage is only within the U.S. and its territories and possessions.

Quick Quiz 8.6

1. True.
2. False. PLUP forms are nonstandard. It is difficult to generalize about the coverage provided and excluded.
3. False. All professional service providers face liability risks; malpractice insurance is a necessity.
4. True.

CHAPTER

9

CREDIT PROTECTION

LEARNING OBJECTIVES

After reading this chapter, you should be able to:

1. Understand the importance of consumer spending in the economy.
2. Identify the types of loans and credit that make up consumer lending.
3. Contrast secured and unsecured loans.
4. Identify the three major credit reporting agencies.
5. Summarize the most important information in a credit report.
6. Explain how frequently and under what conditions a consumer has free access to his or her credit reports.
7. Discuss the likelihood of errors in credit reports and how to fix those errors.
8. Understand credit scores, especially FICO and Vantage, and the factors that influence the scores.
9. Justify the purpose of credit scores.
10. Describe factors that positively and negatively impact FICO scores.
11. Review a consumer's credit report and identify how different debt management approaches will impact the consumer's credit score and develop a plan to maximize the ccredit score over the short and long run.*
12. Understand how to establish good credit.
13. Know what actions damage an otherwise good credit score.
14. Differentiate among credit cards, debit cards, and charge cards.
15. Recall how identity theft is committed.
16. Understand identity theft, its sources and consequences.
17. Explain what to do if a person is a victim of identity theft.

* CFP Board Resource Document - Student-Centered Learning Objectives based upon CFP Board Principal Topics.

INTRODUCTION

As Ben Franklin said, "glass, china, and reputation are easily cracked, and never well mended." Reputation is an important element of credit because they both involve trust. Granting credit to someone is a decision based on the borrower's reputation. The creditor is seeking certainty of behavior. This certainty includes repayment of debt, on time, and under the terms of the agreement. Any negative deviation from the terms of the agreement, no matter how small, could change the expectations of the creditor from certainty to uncertainty (known as risk). Future creditors decide whether or not to extend credit to a potential debtor based on the reported experiences of previous creditors.

HISTORY OF CONSUMER LENDING

Individuals have entered into debt obligations for thousands of years, but consumer credit is a relatively modern concept. Debt was a part of American colonial life, but failing to repay obligations was met with harsh punishment, including imprisonment.

Beginning in the nineteenth century, installment payment plans were made available by sellers for purchases of furniture, sewing machines, and other durable domestic goods. However, before the 1920s, there was little demand for credit for automobiles, college tuition, home modernization and repairs, and durable goods, that make up the bulk of consumer credit today. Financial institutions in the nineteenth and early twentieth centuries were less willing to extend consumers credit as lenders did not have sufficient information to assess the creditworthiness of individual borrowers.

Today, the credit reporting system is extremely efficient and almost everyone uses debt for some or all of their purchases. Consumers use debt for everything from gas and groceries to mortgages. The chart below depicts the increase in consumer debt over the last six decades compared to the U.S. population.

EXHIBIT 9.1

CONSUMER DEBT & U.S. POPULATION

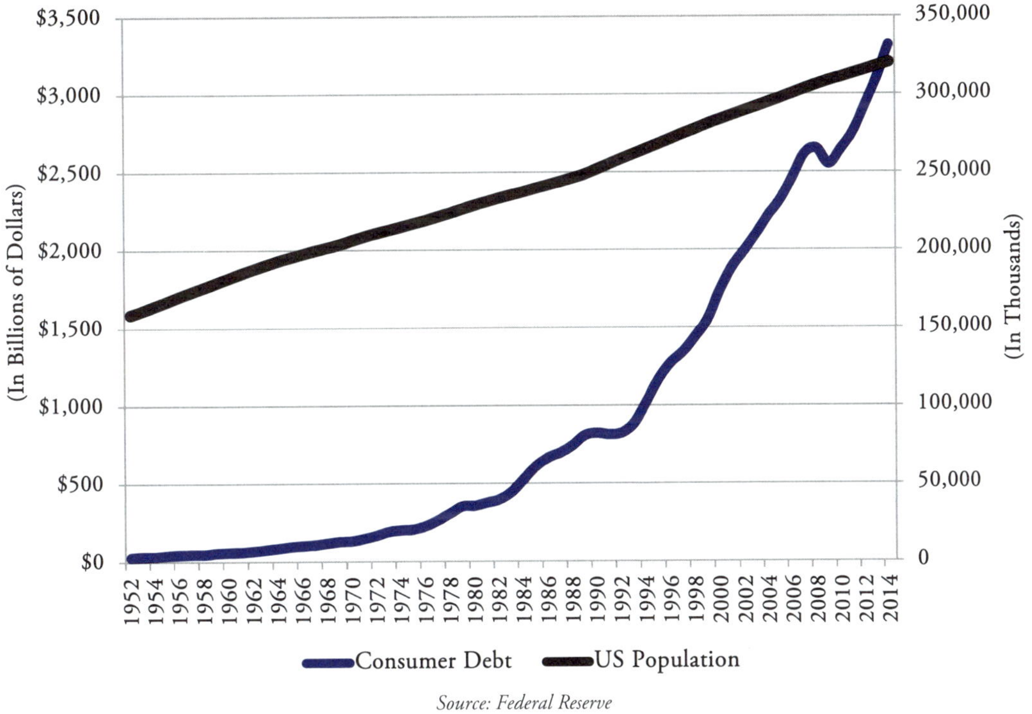

Source: Federal Reserve

CONSUMER LENDING

Consumer lending is a broad field that has a significant economic impact on the country. Sixty to seventy percent of GDP growth in the United States is a result of consumer spending. Credit cards, home equity loans, home equity lines of credit, auto loans, other recreational vehicle loans, and appliance loans are all included in consumer lending.[1]

Consumer confidence plays a significant role in the overall lending industry. When consumer confidence is high, consumers are more willing to borrow money and spend more. Lenders are also more confident of being repaid and are, therefore, more willing to lend more. This positive scenario generally occurs when the economy is expanding and jobs are plentiful. The converse is

1. The Federal Reserve excludes debt secured by real estate from the definition of consumer credit.

also true. When the economy is contracting, it is generally more difficult for businesses and consumers to obtain credit.

SECURED VS. UNSECURED LOANS

Consumer lending may either be secured or unsecured. Secured loans are secured by collateral that may be repossessed if the loan is not repaid as agreed. Examples of secured loans are mortgages and automobile loans, where the house or car is considered collateral towards the debt. If the consumer defaults on the loan, the lender seizes the property. An unsecured loan has no such collateral and is only backed by the borrower's promise to pay. Examples of unsecured loans are personal loans and non-secured credit cards. Secured loans are considered higher quality loans by lenders because of the collateral.

KEY CONCEPTS

1. What percentage of GDP growth in the United States is a result of consumer spending?
2. Recognize how consumers spend and borrow when confidence is high versus low.
3. Identify the three major private credit reporting agencies.
4. Identify the relationship between credit and personal reputation.
5. Identify the information (data) included in a credit report.

There are numerous risks associated with lending money or extending credit. Specifically, not being repaid or not being repaid within the terms of the lending agreement. Banks, mortgage companies, and other creditors accept these risks when they make loans to consumers. The approval of and terms for consumer loans are highly dependent on a borrower's credit rating. If the potential borrower has a poor credit history as determined by the potential lender, the lender has choices. One choice is simply to not extend the credit. Other choices include charging a higher interest rate, or requiring a larger down payment. This is particularly true for unsecured loans or general credit loans. These loans are a bigger risk for lenders and, therefore, generally have higher interest rates than secured loans.

CREDIT REPORTS

Today, credit reports are available on almost everyone. Creditors and lenders report their customers' borrowing activity and history to credit agencies. There are three major credit reporting bureaus or agencies that collect credit information.

- Experian: www.Experian.com
- Equifax: www.Equifax.com
- TransUnion: www.Transunion.com

These **credit agencies** are for-profit companies and not government agencies. They compile and maintain credit information from credit card companies, banks, mortgage companies, and other creditors for the purpose of creating a personal in-depth credit report on individuals. Lending institutions and other creditors electronically send updated consumer credit information to one or more of the three major credit reporting agencies on a monthly basis.[1] This information includes how much an individual consumer owes and whether payments are on time. In addition, whenever

1. According to the Consumer Financial Protection Bureau, banks, credit unions, retail credit card issuers, auto lenders, mortgage lenders, debt collectors and others voluntarily send information to credit reporting companies.

a consumer submits an application for credit, all of that application information is sent to the credit reporting agencies. The credit reporting agencies also review public records for financial information, such as court records of liens, judgments, foreclosures, and bankruptcies. In other words, a consumer's credit report is a record of credit history and serves as a credit reference for creditworthiness.

The information within the credit report is used by the credit reporting agency to calculate a credit score. A credit score estimates a consumer's creditworthiness with one numerical value, while a credit report shows how well the consumer repays debt obligations in a detailed manner.

Credit agencies share this information with their members when there is an inquiry. There are two types of inquiries: hard and soft. **Hard inquiries** are made by creditors or potential creditors when making a lending decision. **Soft inquiries** are made by the consumer or by a prospective or current employer, typically as part of a background check. When a consumer applies for credit, the bank or credit card company contacts one or more of the credit reporting agencies to review the credit report and credit score. Based on the information provided and any other criteria the lender chooses, the lender decides whether to extend a loan and at what interest rate.

EXHIBIT 9.2

HARD VS. SOFT INQUIRIES

Hard Inquires	Soft Inquires
• Occur when a consumer is applying for an auto loan, mortgage, student loan, personal line of credit, or credit card. • May occur when renting an apartment or opening a checking or brokerage account.	• Occur when a consumer is checking his or her own credit score or when a potential employer is conducting a background check. • May occur when renting an apartment or opening a checking or brokerage account.

The three credit reporting agencies are independent companies that each collect information in different ways. Therefore, a credit report from one agency may contain slightly different information than a credit report from another agency. Not every creditor or lending institution reports to all three credit agencies, leading to the potential for differences between and among the different agencies reports.

A credit report generally includes the following information:

- Personal information, such as name, address, Social Security number, date of birth, and employment information. These factors are not included in the calculation of a credit score.
- Credit account information, such as the type of account (credit card, auto loan, mortgage, etc.), the date the account was opened, the credit limit or loan amount, the account balance, and the payment history.
- Any inquiries, such as creditors who accessed the credit information within the last two years.
- Delinquency information and other negative items such as late payments.
- Any information from collection agencies.

- Any public record information from state and other courts, including liens, garnishments, legal suits and judgments, foreclosures, and bankruptcies.

The Fair Credit Reporting Act of 1971 provides that U.S. citizens have free access to their credit reports and credit scores from the three national credit reporting agencies. In the case of a denial of credit based on such a report, citizens also have the right to know exactly why their credit request was denied.

KEY CONCEPTS

1. From the creditor's point of view, why is a credit score superior to a full credit report?
2. Explain why credit scores are used.
3. Explain how a FICO score is determined.
4. Understand what is not included in a credit score.

Consumers should examine their credit report regularly because they frequently contain errors. A study was conducted by the Public Interest Research Group (PIRG) in 2004. Approximately 200 credit reports were reviewed. The researchers discovered that almost 80 percent of the credit reports reviewed contained errors, with many of the errors considered serious. Some of the most common errors were:

- a report containing information on someone else with the same name
- different reports associated with different addresses
- information reported twice (either positive or negative)
- incorrect public information such as court records and bankruptcy reports
- the failure of credit card companies to report credit limits thus distorting the credit utilization ratio of the debtor

PIRG has conducted several follow up studies that have yielded similar results. In addition, The Federal Trade Commission has conducted several studies with similar conclusions. It is obvious that every person should regularly review and monitor each of his or her credit reports for accuracy and completeness. Free credit reports from all three major reporting agencies are available from annualcreditreport.com.[1] Consumers need to be careful when checking their credit score as there are many phishing and imposter sites offering free access to credit reports. These sites are scams and sell consumer information. See further discussion of identity theft later in this chapter.

Repairing a Credit Report

Repairing a credit report requires planning, due diligence, and persistence. Any negative information in the report that is incorrect should be addressed immediately and in writing (limited to 100 words) to the credit reporting agency. It is helpful to include any documentation to support and clarify that the negative information reported is incorrect. The credit reporting agency has 30 days to investigate and reply in writing to the consumer with its findings. If the reporting agency's findings do not support a correction, the consumer can still request that his or her letter be appended to the credit report. Such an addendum helps to notify third parties as to the nature and details of the disagreement.

If the credit report identifies negative, but not incorrect items, it is a good idea for the consumer to negotiate directly with the creditor and attempt to have such things as late payments, charge-offs,

1. This site is maintained by Central Source LLC, which is sponsored by Equifax, Experian and TransUnion.

or collections removed from being reported and then removed from the credit report. The creditor is not obligated to remove negative items, but may do so if there is a compelling reason.

Credit Scores

A **credit score** is a number that summarizes a person's credit risk based on an evaluation of his or her credit report at a particular point in time. Credit scores are calculated using a formula with four or more variables with various weightings. Credit scores are often referred to as FICO scores because most credit agencies' scores are produced from software developed by FICO (formerly named Fair Isaac Corporation). However, there are various credit scoring companies and many different credit scores. The most important credit score for a consumer is the one the lender is using to grant credit.

The two most well-known credit scores are FICO and Vantage. However, even these two provide a large number of different scores for the same person depending on the particular credit granting user. A particular user (creditor) simply changes the weights or the variables in the formula for different uses. All of the scores are based on payment history, debt utilization, age of credit accounts, credit type mix, and credit inquiries. All scores are designed to predict the likelihood of debt repayment.

The credit score actually used by a particular lender is unlikely to be the exact credit score either provided by one of the credit reporting agencies or the particular credit company, and the lender/creditor is unlikely to reveal the actual scoring method it is using.

TransUnion conducted a survey in 2015 to determine how well the public understood what was included in a credit score. Some of the results are reported in Exhibit 9.3.

EXHIBIT 9.3

What is Not in a Credit Score

- **Pay raises:** 48 percent of those surveyed erroneously believed that an increase in income improves their credit scores.
- **Credit inquires:** 40 percent surveyed were unsure of the impact of checking a credit score. 20 percent surveyed erroneously believed checking a credit report causes it to go down.
- **Paying down debts:** 61 percent erroneously believed paying off debts from late payments automatically increases their score.
- **Trended information:** 70 percent of those who have checked their reports in the last year incorrectly assumed that they reflected recent changes or trends in their finances over time.

Source: TransUnion Survey (released March 12, 2015).

FICO Score

The **FICO score** is calculated using a formula that evaluates many types of information in the credit report at that credit reporting agency and ranges from 300 to 850. The FICO score estimates the level of future credit risk. FICO scores can be delivered electronically almost instantaneously, helping lenders speed up the time for loan approvals to minutes rather than hours or weeks.

The FICO scoring system dramatically lowers the cost of borrowing and the cost of capital in the United States. Quick, easy access to credit is a major source of economic strength and stability for consumers and businesses alike. It also differentiates the Untied States from other emerging economies.

Factors such as gender, race, religion, nationality and marital status are not included in FICO scores. Below is a chart with the interpretation of the various ranges in FICO scores.

EXHIBIT 9.4

FICO Score Range

FICO Score	Description of Credit
740 - 850	Excellent
680 - 739	Good
620 - 679	Fair
550 - 619	Poor
300 - 549	Bad

These are generally accepted among FICO users.

A report of any negative item can lower a FICO score quickly and negatively affect the score for a long period of time. For example, a single 30-day late payment could remain on the credit report for up to seven years. However, while destroying a FICO score can happen quickly, improving a FICO score takes a long time. As mentioned at the beginning of this section, credit and reputation are similar in terms of being fragile and needing protection.

How a FICO Score is Determined

Five primary factors determine a person's FICO credit score. These factors include payment history, the amount of credit and the credit utilization, the length of credit history, the mix of credit types, and new credit or new accounts. All of the factors are considered in the determination of the FICO score. According to FICO, the percentages in the chart below are averages for the general population. However, the percentages may vary for particular groups, such as people who have limited credit history. The percentages may also be changed to provide custom credit scores for a particular user.

How a FICO Score Breaks Down

EXHIBIT 9.5

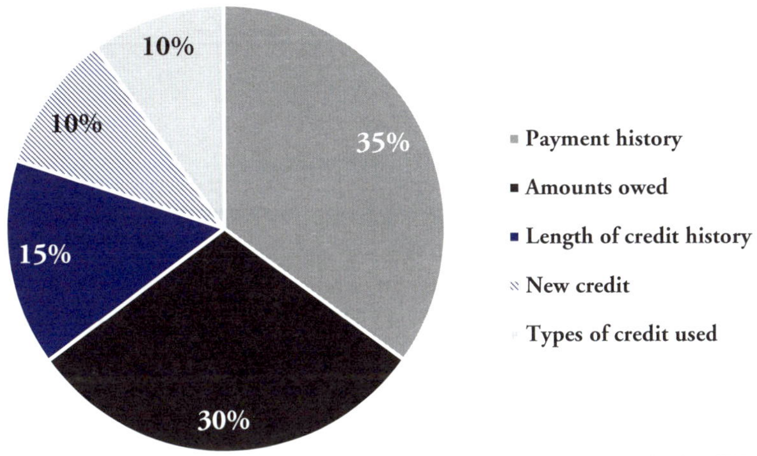

Payment History

Payment history is the most important factor in the determination of a FICO score and accounts for 35 percent of the score. Up to seven years of payment history is included in this category, as well as the presence or absence of derogatory payment information.[1] A few late payments will not destroy a person's credit score. The FICO score also takes into consideration the details of late payments, such as how late and how much was owed.

Amounts Owed

Debt burden and credit utilization is the second most important factor in determining a FICO score and accounts for 30 percent of the score. Included in this category are such items as credit utilization, the number of accounts with balances, the amounts owed over various types of accounts, and the down payments made on installment loans. Borrowers who are close to maximizing their currently available credit are considered a higher risk than those who have a substantial amounts of available credit.

The optimal credit utilization percentage is between 1 and 30 percent of total credit available.

EXAMPLE 9.1

> Gina has five credit cards with a $5,000 limit on each for a total credit available of $25,000. If she owes $2,500, she has a 10% utilization.

1. Derogatory marks are long-lasting negative records on a credit report. Examples include bankruptcy, civil judgments, foreclosures, etc.

EXHIBIT 9.6

Impact of Credit Utilization Percents on Credit Score

Utilization	Negative / Positive	Impact of Score
0%	Negative	<20 Points>
1% - 20%	Positive	0 Points
21% - 30%	Positive	0 Points
31% - 40%	Negative	<30 Points>
51% - 75%	Negative	<75 Points>
76% - 100%	Negative	<100 Points>

**Author Estimates*

Simply closing accounts can have a negative impact on credit score because credit utilization may be affected. In addition, the age of any account that is closed may negatively impact a credit score. If the oldest account is closed, the age of credit history declines, which is a negative factor in determining credit score.

Length of Credit History

The length of credit history is the third factor and accounts for 15 percent of the FICO score. This factor includes the average age of credit accounts and the age of the oldest account, as well as the age of the newest account. It is generally more favorable to have older accounts that have a longer history of favorable credit activity. However, newer accounts may show a requisite amount of activity from which to determine a credit score.

Credit Mix

The mix of credit is the fourth factor and accounts for approximately 10 percent of the total FICO score. Consumers might have credit from a home loan, auto loan, credit cards, school loans, bank, or other lenders. Lenders are generally more impressed if the consumer can manage a mix of credit including credit cards, installment payments, and mortgage payments, rather than simply one type of credit (e.g., credit cards). FICO scores increase as the consumer demonstrates a history of managing different types of credit (i.e., credit cards, bank loans, installment loans). This factor may be more important for consumers with otherwise limited information on their credit report.

Quick Quiz 9.1

1. A credit report includes information about a person's income.
   a. True
   b. False

2. A credit report includes moving vehicle citations.
   a. True
   b. False

3. A credit report can be used to determine the risk of a person filing an automobile insurance claim.
   a. True
   b. False

4. A credit report can be used to determine the risk of a person filing an homeowner's insurance claim.
   a. True
   b. False

False, False, True, True.

New Credit

According to FICO, opening several new lines of credit in a short period of time represents an increase in risk for potential creditors. Recent hard inquiries and new credit represent the fifth factor and account for approximately 10 percent of the FICO score. Hard inquiries that are made by potential creditors for granting of credit remain on the report for two years. However, they only count negatively for 12 months. The impact of one hard inquiry is generally fewer than 5 points on the overall score. However, it is best not to open new accounts too quickly. Otherwise, there may be a negative impact on the FICO score. Requesting a credit report from a credit reporting agency does not impact the credit score. Below is a distribution of various FICO scores for the period 2005-2013.

In April 2015, FICO announced a piloted alternative scoring system to make millions of Americans who currently do not have a FICO score credit worthy. FICO joined with Equifax to use data from cable, cell phone, electric and gas bills to produce a score of credit worthiness for persons who would not have scores otherwise.

EXHIBIT 9.7

Distributions of FICO Scores by Percentages for 2005 - 2013

Percent of Population									
FICO Score	October 2005	October 2006	October 2007	October 2008	October 2009	October 2010	October 2011	October 2012	October 2013
300-499	6.6	6.5	7.1	7.2	7.3	6.9	6.3	6.0	5.8
500-549	8.0	8.0	8.0	8.2	8.7	9.0	8.7	8.5	8.4
550-599	9.0	8.8	8.7	8.7	9.1	9.6	9.9	9.9	9.8
600-649	10.2	10.2	9.7	9.6	9.5	9.5	9.8	10.1	10.2
650-699	12.8	12.5	12.1	12.0	11.9	11.9	12.1	12.2	12.7
700-749	16.4	16.3	16.2	16.0	15.9	15.7	15.5	16.2	16.3
750-799	20.1	19.8	19.8	19.6	19.4	19.5	19.6	18.8	18.4
800-850	16.9	17.9	18.4	18.7	18.2	17.9	18.1	18.4	18.6
Total	100	100	100	100	100	100	100	100	100

Source: http://www.fico.com/en/blogs/risk-compliance/us-credit-qualities-continues-to-inch-forward/

It should be noted that the percentages in each category of the above exhibit remained relatively constant across the time year period 2005-2013. This stability is especially interesting given the economic crisis that occurred during this period.

The median FICO, which is relatively stable, was 723 in 2014. The mean or average FICO score was 640 in 2014 and has been trending downward.

Credit scores are important because they can determine whether a consumer is likely to obtain credit and if so, at what rate of interest. Borrowers with higher credit scores are considered less risky and are generally able to obtain credit at a lower cost, which is reflected in a lower rate of interest. Higher interest rates increase the total cost of ownership, whether that is a home, a car, or other items. This concept is demonstrated in the following exhibit.

EXHIBIT 9.8

Cost of Poor FICO Scores (760-850 vs 620-639)

Impact of Credit Score (FICO)*			
	30-Year Mortgage	**15-Year Home Equity Loan**	**36-Month Auto Loan**
Loan Amount	$250,000	$100,000	$30,000
FICO Score	**Interest Rates**	**Interest Rates**	**Interest Rates**
760-850	3.564%	6.037%	3.189%
620-639	5.153%	10.362%	16.627%
Differential Cost / %	<1.588%>	<4.325%>	<13.438%>
FICO Score	**Monthly Payment**	**Monthly Payment**	**Monthly Payment**
760-850	$1,131.56	$845.86	$874.94
620-639	$1,365.53	$1,096.86	$1,064.02
Differential Cost/ Month ($)	<$233.97>	<$251.00>	<$189.08>
Additional Interest Cost with Poor FICO Score over Term of Loan			
Additional Interest ($)	$84,227.61	$45,180.35	$6,807.01
Additional Interest (%)	21%	30%	22%

As the exhibit above illustrates, consumers with poor FICO scores or credit scores will pay more money for the same good or service than consumers with higher credit scores if they need to obtain credit for the purchase. This same concept is also illustrated in the exhibit below. The exhibit below illustrates the total interest cost for a mortgage, an auto loan, and a credit card over a lifetime, based on various credit ratings.

EXHIBIT 9.9

Interest Impact of Less-Than-Excellent Credit Score on Overall Debt Over a Lifetime (Dollars and Percent)

Cost of Debt (37 Year Old)**		
Assumptions	**Balances and Payments**	
Mortgage	$350,000	
Auto Loan	$30,000 (every 4 years)	
Credit Card	$10,000 (paying $200 month)	
Credit Rating	**Interest over Lifetime (dollars)***	**% Increase from Excellent**
Excellent Credit	$261,495	0%
Good Credit	$293,475	+12.23%
Fair Credit	$353,953	+35.36%
Poor Credit	$470,585	+79.96%
Bad Credit	$580,630	+122.04%

** Calculated using Credit.com calculator.*

*** Assume the 37-year-old has a $350,000 mortgage, purchases an automobile for $30,000 every four years and finances 80%, and has credit cards with a balance of $10,000 paying $200 a month.*

As illustrated above, a lower credit score will cost a consumer more in terms of interest on borrowings. Below are exhibits that depict factors that positively and negatively impact a credit score, the numerical impacts to a credit score for certain negative events, and the time it takes for a credit score to recover.

EXHIBIT 9.10

Factors That Affect Credit Scores

Positively Affects Credit Score	Negatively Affects Credit Score
Consistent, Timely Payments over Time	Late Payments
More History Accounts	Significant Change in Utilization Rate
No 30/60/90 Days Late	Closing Accounts
No Late Charges	Opening New Accounts
Credit Utilization	Liens
No New Hard Inquiries	Judgements
No Recently Closed Accounts	Foreclosures
No Charge-Offs	New Hard Inquiries
No Liens	Bankruptcy
No Judgements	Child Support in Arrearage
No Foreclosures	Wage Garnishments
No Bankruptcy	

EXHIBIT 9.11

Impact to FICO Score*

	Consumer A	Consumer B	Consumer C
Starting FICO Score	680	720	780
FICO score after these independent events:			
30 days late on mortgage	600 - 620	630 - 650	670 - 690
90 days late on mortgage	600 - 620	610 - 630	650 - 670
Short sale / deed-in-lieu /settlement (no deficiency balance)	610 - 630	605 - 625	655 - 675
Short sale (with deficiency balance)	575 - 595	570 - 590	620 - 640
Foreclosure	575 - 595	570 - 590	620 - 640
Bankruptcy	530 - 550	525 - 545	540 - 560

Source: FICO Banking Analytics Blog. 2011 Fair Isaac Corporation.
** These are approximations.*

EXHIBIT 9.12

Estimated Time for a FICO Score to Fully Recover*

	Consumer A	Consumer B	Consumer C
Starting FICO Score	680	720	780
Time for a FICO Score to recover after these independent events:			
30 days late on mortgage	9 months	2.5 years	3 years
90 days late on mortgage	9 months	3 years	7 years
Short sale / deed-in-lieu /settlement (no deficiency balance)	3 years	7 years	7 years
Short sale (with deficiency balance)	3 years	7 years	7 years
Foreclosure	3 years	7 years	7 years
Bankruptcy	5 years	7 - 10 years	7 -10 years

Source: FICO Banking Analytics Blog. 2011 Fair Isaac Corporation.
** These are approximations.*

Note: Estimates assume all else held constant over time (e.g., no new account openings, no new delinquency, similar outstanding debt).

VantageScore

The three major credit bureaus (Equifax, Experian, and TransUnion) joined together to create the VantageScore, which was launched in March of 2006. It weighs payment history more than FICO and now ranges from 300 to 850.[1] The credit agencies' objective in creating VantageScore was to make credit scoring more consistent and accurate across all of the bureaus. VantageScore attempts to remedy this issue by putting more weight on the past 24 months of credit history. Although relatively new, VantageScore is widely used by financial institutions, credit card issuers, and auto lenders.

KEY CONCEPTS

1. Explain a VantageScore.
2. Identify how a VantageScore is different from a FICO score.
3. Recognize if a secured credit card is a good way to establish credit.
4. Identify one of the easiest loans to obtain.

EXHIBIT 9.13

FACTORS THAT INFLUENCE VANTAGESCORE

FACTORS THAT INFLUENCE VantageScore	Recommendations to Improve Score
Extremely Influential: Payment History	Pay credit bills on time
Highly Influential: Age and type of credit	Maintain a mix of types of credit
Highly Influential: Percent of credit limit used	Keep balances low – under 30%
Moderately Influential: Total balances of debt	Reduce the amount of total debt
Less Influential: Recent credit behavior	Do not open too many accounts too rapidly
Less Influential: Available credit	Maintain the amount of credit that is really needed

Other Scores

There are many credit scores other than FICO and Vantage, including credit scores for the automobile insurance industry and the homeowners insurance industry. FICO first introduced insurance scores in 1993. Today, many property and casualty insurers use some form of credit score. According to FICO, there is a direct relationship between the likelihood of an insurance claim and a person's credit score. In other words, a person with a lower credit score is more likely to file an insurance claim than a person with a higher credit score. These scores are used in part to determine a person's insurance premium.

FICO, TransUnion, and LexisNexis are the primary providers of insurance scores. Standard scores and custom scores are used by the insurance industry. Two of the more common scores are the **auto insurance score** and the home owner insurance score.

1. Earlier VantageScores ranged from 501 to 990. However, VantageScore 3.0 now ranges from 300 to 850.

Neither the auto insurance score nor the **home insurance score** require that a person own a car or own a home. These are simply calculated scores based on the information that is included in a person's credit report. Consumers may or may not be able to obtain their insurance scores, depending on which company designed them.

Establishing Credit

If a person has no credit, the easiest way to establish credit is with a secured credit card, a co-signer, a single purpose card (e.g. gas card), or an automobile loan with a substantial down payment.[1] A secured credit card requires the consumer to place a security deposit with the issuer. The issuer then provides a credit card usually with a dollar limit equal to the security deposit. These cards are available to many of those who have little or no credit.

When first establishing credit, the borrower (debtor) should clearly understand the terms of any loan or credit agreement. For example, the fee structure of a credit card. Understanding the agreement will help to prevent borrower mistakes that can be costly, such as not knowing about the annual fee, late fees, penalties, interest rates, rewards, and interest-free financing.

The best kind of credit card to initially establish credit is one that is simple to understand: no annual fee, no penalty interest, no international transactions fees, and waives the first late payment fee or no late fees. It is important to know the statement date, the minimum payment due, and the due date of the payment. It is advisable to set up electronic transfer payments from a bank account to be received by the creditor four to five days before the actual due date of the payment. By making the payment a few days early, a debtor is able to monitor the credit card balance online to make sure that the payment was received on time and posted by the credit card company. If a consumer is carrying credit card debt from month to month, it is considerably advantageous to make payments as soon as possible, well in advance of the due date. The reason for this timing is that most credit cards use the average daily balance method to calculate interest charges, which effectively takes advantage of the fact that most consumers wait until the end of the month to pay.

Quick Quiz 9.2

1. Payment history is the most heavily weighted variable in a FICO score.
   a. True
   b. False

2. Opening new lines of credit in a short period of time can have a negative impact on a credit score.
   a. True
   b. False

3. Credit from a mix of lenders is considered superior to a single source of credit (e.g., credit card) for credit score purposes.
   a. True
   b. False

True, True, True.

1. In Fundamentals of Financial Planning, good debt versus bad debt is discussed in Chapter 3. Automobile loans that extend beyond three to five years and/or have a high rate of interest are generally considered bad debt. Remember that automobiles are depreciating assets and borrowing money for a depreciating asset is not the best use credit.

EXHIBIT 9.14

Credit Card Statement

Capital One

Customer Service 1-800-955-7070
www.capitalone.com

Visa Signature — Account ending in 1234

NEW BALANCE	MINIMUM PAYMENT	DUE DATE
$726.35	$25.00	Mar 28, 2015

PLEASE PAY AT LEAST THIS AMOUNT

Revolving Credit Limit: $30,000.00 — Cash Advance Credit Limit: $15,000.00
Available Revolving Credit: $29,273.65 — Available Credit for Cash Advances: $15,000.00

Feb. 04 - Mar. 03, 2015 — 28 Days in Billing Cycle

MINIMUM PAYMENT WARNING: If you make only the minimum payment each period, you will pay more in interest and it will take you longer to pay off your balance. For example:

Payment Amount Each Period If No Additional Charges Are Made	Approximate Time to Pay Off Statement Balance	Estimated Total Cost
Minimum Payment	3 Years	$890

If you would like information about credit counseling services, call 1-888-326-8055.

LATE PAYMENT WARNING: If we do not receive your minimum payment by your due date, you may have to pay a late fee of up to $35.00 and your APRs may be increased up to the Penalty APR of 29.40%.

Previous Balance		Payments and Credits		Fees and Interest Charged		Transactions		New Balance
$900.06	−	$900.06	+	$0.00	+	$726.35	=	$726.35

At $25 per month, it will take about 36 months to pay off the $726.35 balance

Mr. Smith has a $30,000 revolving credit limit. With a balance of only $726.35, this will help with his credit utilization.

TRANSACTIONS

PAYMENTS, CREDITS & ADJUSTMENTS FOR JOHN SMITH #1234

1	25 FEB	ELECTRONIC PAYMENT	($900.06)

TRANSACTIONS FOR JOHN SMITH #1234

1	03 FEB	WINN-DIXIE #1583LAPLACELA	$60.06
2	06 FEB	PUBLIX #1213ORANGE BEACHAL	$31.46
3	07 FEB	PUBLIX #1296PENSACOLAFL	$52.04
4	09 FEB	WALGREENS #5801LA PLACELA	$13.07
5	10 FEB	CVS/PHARMACY #05442DESTREHANLA	$22.28
6	11 FEB	WINN-DIXIE #1583LAPLACELA	$152.33
7	14 FEB	WINN-DIXIE #1583LAPLACELA	$34.01
8	18 FEB	WINN-DIXIE #1588DESTREHANLA	$24.86
9	21 FEB	WINN-DIXIE #1583LAPLACELA	$24.96
10	21 FEB	DORIGNAC'S FOOD CENMETAIRIELA	$93.40
11	28 FEB	DORIGNAC'S FOOD CENMETAIRIELA	$207.10
12	02 MAR	LA PLACE CLEANERSLA PLACELA	$10.78
		TOTAL FOR JOHN SMITH #1234	**$726.35**

▶ **Total Transactions This Period $726.35**

REWARDS INFORMATION

PREVIOUS AVAILABLE REWARDS BALANCE	14,863
REWARDS EARNED THIS PERIOD (reflects transactions posted during this billing cycle)	1,454
AVAILABLE BALANCE AS OF 03/03/2015	16,317

For up-to-date rewards tracking, visit www.capitalone.com or simply call 1-800-228-3001

No Hassle rewards

INTEREST CHARGE CALCULATION

Your **Annual Percentage Rate (APR)** is the annual interest rate on your account.

Type of Balance	Annual Percentage Rate (APR)	Balance Subject to Interest Rate	Interest Charge
Purchases	13.90% P	$0.00	$0.00
Cash Advances	24.90% P	$0.00	$0.00

P,L,D,F = Variable Rate. See reverse of page 1 for details

Mr. Smith has good credit and his interest rates are extremely high. However, the rates are not imposed if the balance is paid on time.

Another way to establish credit is to buy a car using a car loan. Most people do not know that the credit score used to determine a car loan is called the FICO auto industry option score (auto credit score). This score is different from the auto insurance score and from the regular FICO score. The **auto credit score** is usually calculated by FICO for use by auto lenders to determine loan qualifications, down payments, and interest-rates. About 90 percent of auto lenders base their lending decisions on auto credit scores. The auto credit score is calculated principally on previous auto loan history. Many auto lenders are willing to make auto loans even to those with less desirable auto credit scores. The reason for this is that persons who borrow money on automobiles generally make their payments. Even those with other credit problems tend to make their auto loan payments in order to keep their automobiles. Automobile dealers regularly install GPS systems in cars sold to those with marginal credit. The borrower approves such installation in the financing agreement. The GPS is used to locate the car for purposes of repossession in the event of missed or late payments.

It is generally easier to obtain an auto loan than any other type of loan, and is a great way to begin to build good credit. Once an automobile loan has been made, it is a good idea to pay the loan automatically from a bank on a recurring basis to assure that all payments are made on time.

Reporting housing rental payments is sometimes a good idea for those with no credit histories or insufficient data to have credit scores. Often adding rental history payments to an otherwise incomplete credit report can make the report scoreable. While those with mortgage payments are regularly reported to credit agencies, those who rent have not been reported. All of the major reporting agencies now include rental payments (if reported). However, consumers cannot directly report their own rental payments. The property manager or landlord can report the rental history directly to reporting agency or the lesser (tenant) can sign up with a third-party rent reporter (for example, Rent Reporters).

What is a Good Credit Score

A good credit score is one that permits the borrower to get the very best terms, such as down payment, term of loan, any points, and interest rate for the credit or loan desired. The best score will vary with the type of debt and the lending environment. However, auto loans and credit cards generally require lower minimum FICO scores than mortgages. FICO public relations personnel suggest that a score of 760 will get the best credit rates and terms. For a mortgage, a score of around 700 is needed for conventional loans, and 620 for FHA loans. A car loan will require less.

Even a good credit score may not be approved for credit by a particular lender. Often, a lender will use income, employment, and other criteria in addition to the credit score for purposes of credit approval. The lender obtains such information not from the credit score or credit report but rather from the credit application filled out by the potential borrower.

EXHIBIT 9.15

MANAGING THE BASICS OF CREDIT

Suggestion	Factor
Keep credit balances low but not $0[1]	Credit utilization
Do not close accounts	Credit history
Pay accounts on time	Payment history
Only apply for credit as needed	Hard inquiries
Have a mix of credit (cards, installments, mortgages)	Credit mix
Get free credit reports annually	Monitor

1.This statement does not mean maintain balances on credit cards. Having a balance as of the end of the payment cycle is counted toward utilization. It simply means that having zero debt (that is, not using the credit line at all) does not help a person's credit score, which is an indication of how well the person handles debt.

A wise user of credit, in addition to the suggestions above, will establish and frequently monitor all transactions on ATMs, debit cards, credit cards, bank accounts, and mortgages. It is always a good idea to obtain and read credit reports and obtain credit scores prior to seeking additional credit. Everyone is entitled to receive a free credit from annualcreditreport.com. In addition, there are other providers of free credit reports.

Consumer credit scores are usually updated monthly. However, in cases of frequent creditor reporting, a credit score could be updated almost daily. Some credit agencies will provide a "rescore" for a fee. The usual turnaround time for a rescore is three days.

Avoid Damaging a Credit Score

Once credit is established, it is important to avoid activities that are perceived as negative by the credit reporting agencies. Below are a few examples of activities that are perceived negatively by credit reporting agencies.

Even if paid off every month, accumulating large credit card balances and thus increasing credit utilization can have a negative effect on credit scores. Credit utilization of less than one percent is negative and credit utilization in excess of 30 percent is negative. The best percentage for credit utilization is between one percent and 30 percent utilization. For example, if the total credit available is $10,000 on all cards then utilization per month should not exceed a total of $3,000.

Quick Quiz 9.3

1. A secured credit card requires only 50% of the card limit as security.
   a. True
   b. False

2. An auto loan is one of the easiest loans to obtain.
   a. True
   b. False

3. A good credit score will always assure credit approval.
   a. True
   b. False

False, True, False.

Closing and opening several credit card accounts at once will have a negative impact on credit scores even if the closed accounts have zero balances. This is because closing accounts changes credit utilization percentages and may affect credit history.

Hard credit inquiries negatively affect credit scores and remain in the calculation of the credit score for approximately 12 months. Soft credit inquiries do not negatively affect credit scores.

Other Users of Credit Information

This chapter has illustrated the impact in terms of the cost of maintaining a low credit score. However, there are other users of credit information that make decision based on a consumer's credit scores. Potential employers, life insurance providers, potential landlords, and cell phone companies are examples of other users of credit information.

Employers routinely check credit of applicants who are seeking employment with their organization. Those employers in the financial services industry, such as banks, brokerage houses, and insurance companies, are in the business of helping customers with their financial situation. They cannot afford to have someone who is not responsible with money. Accounting and money management positions also require employees who are financially responsible. Certainly, credit is not the only criteria in these employment decisions. However, it is a fact today that many jobs require the candidate to permit the employer to review their credit history.

Life insurance providers check credit as part of the process of evaluating the risk of an applicant for life insurance. Life insurance companies want to verify that the applicant can afford the amount of life insurance they are requesting. A lower credit score may or may not even impact life insurance premiums.

Landlords often check the credit history of those renting or leasing an apartment or condominium. Landlords want tenants who do not create problems and who pay their rent on time, every month. An applicant with a history of credit problems may be required to pay a higher security deposit than an applicant who has better credit.

Cell phone carriers routinely check credit history for those applying for cellular phone service. This credit history may impact the type of plan a person is eligible for and whether or not a security deposit may be required.

Many people do not realize how important their credit history is in many facets of daily life. Like a person's reputation, credit is hard to build and easy to damage.

DEBIT, CREDIT, AND CHARGE CARDS

DEBIT CARDS VS. CREDIT CARDS

Debit cards and credit cards each have individual benefits and risks. Debit cards are linked directly to a consumer's bank account. Charges are debited from the bank account very rapidly. Many people think that the funds are immediately debited from an account when using a debit card. In actuality, a transaction may clear within 24 hours, but it could take as long as 72 hours or longer. Regardless of the exact time, debit card transactions result in funds being taken from a person's account significantly faster than the required payment for a credit card. Credit cards allow consumers to borrow money from the card issuer, which is essentially a line of credit or loan from the card issuer.

EXHIBIT 9.16

COMPARISON OF DEBIT AND CREDIT CARDS

	Credit Card	Debit Card
Usage	A line of credit loan	A direct deduction from a bank account
Connected to an account	No	Yes, directly linked to a consumer's bank account
Receive monthly bills	Yes	No
Statements available	Yes	Yes
Credit score required	Yes	No
Spending limit	Card limit	Account limit
Interest	Yes generally on any late and/or outstanding balances and usually very high	No
Security	Poor	PIN increases security
Fraud	Relatively low since consumers are generally not held liable for fraudulent activities. Credit card charges are relatively easy to contest. The liability is limited to $50 for fraudulent purchases.	Very high. If someone steals a debit card the money is removed directly from the consumer's bank account. Some debit cards can also have a $50 liability limit if offered by the issuer, but charges must be reported within a few business days.
Other fees	Late payment	Overdraft fees
Credit reporting	Usually monthly to each of three reporting agencies	No reporting

Card skimmers (magnetic strip type readers) are probably the greatest risk to debit and credit cards. Criminals can easily install card skimmers at stores such as gas stations. Restaurants can also be a source of trouble for both credit and debit cards as unscrupulous waiters may bring handheld card skimmers to work and swipe a patron's card information.

It is always a wise idea to use credit cards for significant purchases because of the leverage that the customer has with the credit card provider. In addition, credit cards have warranties that go beyond the manufacturer warranties. This features is a one of the benefits of credit cards. Credit cards also have better limited liability exposure ($50) than debit cards. For online purchases it is always a better idea to use credit cards than debit cards. The fraud protection of credit cards is better than that of debit cards, and hackers cannot overdraft a bank account using a credit card.

Credit card companies charge merchants for processing their customer transactions. When a customer uses a credit card to make a purchase, the credit card company pays the merchant, but charges the merchant a fee. These merchant fees generally range between two percent and five percent of the sales price. As a result, credit card companies offer consumers incentives to use their card over cards from other companies. These incentives often include airline miles, cash back bonuses, as well as other benefits. Consumers can take advantage of these benefits with cards that have a low annual fee or no annual fee.

The credit CARD Act, often referred to as the Credit Cardholders Bill of Rights, was signed into law in May of 2009. The law's two primary purposes are to improve fairness with credit card customers and improve transparency. The law does this by prohibiting certain practices that are unfair or abusive such as hiking up the rate on an existing balance or allowing a consumer to go over their credit limit and then imposing an over limit fee. The law also makes the rates and fees on credit cards more transparent so consumers can understand how much they are paying for their credit card and can better compare different cards.

Charge Cards

Charge cards are different from credit cards because charge card issuers expect payment of the full balance within 30 days. Secondly, charge cards generally charge annual fees. The balance that may be accumulated is not generally limited like a traditional credit card as individual purchases are approved electronically as they are made. American Express is the most well-known charge card issuer at this time.[1] They also have credit cards but have the only charge card currently available. These charge cards are useful for business transactions, but credit cards can be used equally well and with no annual fee.

IDENTITY THEFT AND FRAUD

Criminals have incurred credit card debt, depleted debit cards, obtained home loans, and have purchased weapons in victims' names. Identity theft is a big business, estimated to be $2.1 billion (2012), up from $1.52 billion (2011). Identity theft has affected 12.6 million people in the United States.[2] The rate of increase in the number of victims was approximately 10 percent in 2012. The rate of increase of money lost was approximately 33 percent.

1. American Express does permit certain charges to be paid over time. These charges will incur interest until fully paid.
2. 2013 Identity Fraud Report by Javelin Strategy Research.

EXAMPLE 9.2

On April 11, 2015, the U.S. Attorney for the Southern District of Florida announced the arrest of 42 defendants who used tens of thousands of stolen IDs to try to collect $22 million in tax refunds and other government benefits.

KEY CONCEPTS

1. Understand the steps that should be taken by a victim of identity theft.
2. Identify the sources of identity theft.
3. Explain the acronym SCAM.
4. Differentiate an extended fraud alert from an account freeze

Consumers who suspect that they have been a victim of identity theft should take action immediately. According to the Federal Trade Commission, identity theft made up 18 percent of consumer complaints, and about 85 percent of identity theft incidents involved fraudulent use of credit card information. A person affected should contact the credit card issuer to report suspicious activity or a misplaced credit card. Early reporting improves the chances that fraudulent charges will be refunded. The person affected should contact the credit agencies and report the situation. Credit card information may be used to compromise other types of accounts. Therefore it is essential for consumers to closely monitor all credit and bank accounts.

When businesses ask for Social Security numbers, some consumers simply give it to them. In fact, physician offices generally ask new patients to fill out many forms and a patient's Social Security number is almost always one of the requested items. The best advice is to leave it blank. They do not need it and patients should not give it to them. Another tactic is to ask why someone needs a person's Social Security number. Most of the time, they do not need it.

Many consumers click on random links in emails that ultimately lead to malware, which infects their computers and captures private information. To avoid identity theft consumers should check their credit and bank accounts for a few minutes each day to make sure that all the transactions and accounts are correct. Consumers should take the time to shred sensitive documents such as bills, tax returns, property tax notices, and insurance papers. Also, making sure that all devices, including computers, tablets, and smart phones, are secure. Often times these devices store user names and passwords that allow thieves access to banking and financial accounts. Consumers must take the time to also guard sensitive data from those who would contact them through phone, text, social media, or email. Consumers simply have to jealously guard their privacy or become the victim of identity theft.

EXHIBIT 9.17

Steps that Victims of Identity Theft Should Take

Steps That Victims of Identity Theft SHould Take	
1.	File a report with law enforcement.
2.	File a complaint with the Federal Trade Commission at www.identitytheft.gov or the FTC Identity Theft Hotline at 1-877-438-4338 or TTY 1-866-653-4261.
3.	Place a 'fraud alert' on the all credit records by contacting one of the three major credit bureaus: • Equifax, www.Equifax.com, 1-800-525-6285 • Experian, www.Experian.com, 1-888-397-3742 • TransUnion, www.TransUnion.com, 1-800-680-7289
4.	Contact the victim's financial institutions and close any accounts opened without permission or that have been tampered with.
5.	Check the Social Security Administration earnings statement annually. Accounts can be accessed online at www.ssa.gov.

Consumers with compromised Social Security numbers and victims of tax-related identity theft should also complete IRS Form 14039, Identity Theft Affidavit, continue to pay their taxes and file their tax returns, even if they must do so by paper.

An often overlooked item in identity protection is the mailbox, which presents an opportunity for a thief to steal sensitive documents. A consumer should either secure the mailbox or alternatively set up a mailbox at the post office to receive mail. Consider what arrives in the mailbox: W-2 forms, 1099 forms, and other important documents such as Social Security information, earnings information, account information, banking, and insurance information.

Identity theft and identity fraud are federal crimes. Many people have reported that criminals have taken funds from credit cards, bank accounts, or other financial institutions. In the worst cases, these criminals have taken over entire identities, incurring large debts and committing crimes while using the victim's identity and name. The cost in many cases is not only the direct financial loss, but the cost of restoring the victim's reputation.

Sources of Identity Theft

The identity theft assistance center (ITAC) reports that 72 percent of victims do not know the source of the crime.

SOURCES REPORTED BY IDENTITY THEFT ASSISTANCE CENTER (ITAC)

EXHIBIT 9.18

SOURCES OF FRAUD OR IDENTITY THEFT	
28.0%	Knew source
21.6%	Computer-related identity crime
15.1%	Lost/stolen wallet, purse, checkbook, credit/debit card
11.6%	Corrupt business or employees
4.7%	Breaches of computer data
91.0%	Total accounted for
9.0%	Other
100.0%	Grand Total

Almost one in four consumers who received a data breach letter became a victim of identity fraud. Those with Social Security numbers compromised were five times more likely to become fraud victims than those whose Social Security numbers were not compromised.[1] Personal information lost in data breaches is frequently used to commit identity fraud.

In addition to online fraud or data breaches, 1.5 million consumers were victims of familiar fraud, which means the victim knew the criminal.[2]

Ways Identity Theft or Fraud is Committed

Most people do not realize how easily criminals can obtain personal data. Direct stealing of information, shoulder surfing, dumpster diving, mailbox searching, discarded credit offers, SPAM, phone scams, and card readers are all ways that criminals can obtain personal information.

Shoulder surfing is essentially eavesdropping on those who punch in numbers or verbally give numbers over the phone. **Dumpster diving** is going through the trash while looking for identity information from cancelled checks, bank statements, credit card statements, federal or state tax documents, discarded credit card offers, and phone numbers.

There are scams to get the consumer to voluntarily disclose personal information. As previously mentioned, criminals install electronic card readers in gas pumps and on other devices to record credit or debit card numbers. Employees in the food service industry may also use small hand-held card readers to record a person's credit card information. Sometimes the crime is as unsophisticated as the thief simply writing down credit card and other numbers.

1. 2013 Identity Fraud Report by Javelin Strategy Research.
2. 2013 Identity Fraud Report by Javelin Strategy Research.

Case Study 1

Former Bank Employee and Co-Defendant Sentenced in Identity Theft Tax Fraud Scheme

On Sept. 11, 2014, in Miami, Florida, Tenisha Nkesha Francis, of Lake Worth, was sentenced to 42 months in prison, three years of supervised release and ordered to pay $117,002 in restitution. Ryan Michael Francis, of Riviera Beach, was sentenced to 57 months in prison, three years of supervised release and ordered to pay $202,720 in restitution. The defendants each previously pled guilty to one count of aggravated identity theft and one count of theft of government funds. According to court documents, Tenisha Francis worked as a Financial Services Representative at a bank. Tenisha Francis opened seven fraudulent accounts at the bank with stolen identification information obtained from co-defendant Ryan Francis. She was paid between $200 and $500 to open each fraudulent account. After opening the accounts, Tenisha Francis performed maintenance on these accounts and changed certain identifiers associated with the accounts, such as customers' dates of birth, addresses and telephone numbers. Stolen U.S. Treasury checks were deposited into the accounts, and funds were withdrawn via check card purchases, ATM withdrawals and checks payable to third parties including Ryan Francis, his wife, Vanessa Brown, and Ryan Francis' company, J.A. Kingz Automotive, LLC.

Signs of Identity Theft

There are telltale signs of identity theft. The graphic below identifies some of the more frequent signs of identity theft.

Signs of Identity Theft
Unexplainable bank withdrawals
Failure to receive bills or mail
Merchants refuse checks
Debt collectors call about unknown debt
Unknown accounts appear on credit reports
Receipt of unknown medical bills
IRS notices of multiple tax returns or unknown income reported
Notice of data breach from business with which there is a legitimate account

AVOID BECOMING A VICTIM OF IDENTITY THEFT

SCAM is an acronym from the Justice Department to help avoid identity theft. The S is for stingy about giving out any personal information unless the person or institution is known, identified, and trusted. S could also be for skeptical. Be skeptical of any and all inquiries. Hold mail when traveling. C is for check financial information, such as accounts, balances, and transactions, regularly. Pay particular attention to what should be there and what should not be there, such as addresses, number of accounts, recent transactions, etc. A is for ask for credit reports and review them carefully. M is for maintain careful records. Keep records for at least one year and documents, such as tax returns, for at least three years.

SCAM	
S	Be **S**tingy and skeptical about giving out personal data and information.
C	**C**heck financial information often (alerts, accounts, etc.).
A	**A**sk for credit reports and review them regularly.
M	**M**aintain careful records.

Case Study 2

Return Preparer Sentenced for Tax Fraud and Identity Theft Schemes

On Sept. 12, 2014, in Miami, Florida, Stevens Nore, of Port Saint Lucie, was sentenced to 84 months in prison, three years of supervised release and ordered to pay $2,761,397 in restitution. Nore was previously convicted by a jury of 30 counts, including 21 counts of preparing false tax returns, four counts of filing false individual tax returns, three counts of theft of public money, and two counts of aggravated identity theft. According to court records, from June 11, 2009 through April 2012, Nore owned and operated Fraternity Tax and Services, a tax return preparation business. Nore prepared and submitted Individual Tax Returns (Forms 1040), with accompanying schedules, to the IRS on behalf of taxpayers claiming false deductions and credits for tax years 2009 to 2011. Nore also filed false personal tax returns for 2010 through 2013 by falsely stating the amount of gross receipts and sales on Schedule C forms. Nore stole three tax refunds totaling $26,349 to which he was not entitled, and used the identity of two individuals without their permission.

What to do if You are a Victim of Identity Theft

Victims of identity theft should immediately attempt to minimize the damage by taking actions such as notifying agencies:

- Contact Federal Trade Commissions (FTC) online, by mail, or by phone.
- Contact any other relevant federal agency such as Post Office Inspection Service, Social Security Administration, or Internal Revenue Service.
- Call the fraud units of each of the principal credit reporting agencies and place a fraud alert.
- Contact all creditors and financial institutions.
- Contact police to file a report.

Placing a fraud alert with the credit reporting agencies stays on the credit report for 90 days but can be renewed. A fraud alert provides the victim with a right to one free copy of each credit report. The victim should then order all credit reports, review them carefully, and then monitor progress.

The next step for a victim is to consider placing an extended fraud alert or a credit freeze on the credit file. Such an alert requires that potential creditors verify the identity of the person seeking credit. A freeze stops all access to the credit report. A fraud alert is free and is a federal right. A freeze is dependent on state law and may or may not be free. An extended fraud alert entitles the person to two free credit reports from each credit reporting agency within 12 months. The extended fraud alert lasts for seven years.

Following a credit freeze, the victim will have to request it to be lifted to allow a creditor or potential creditor to review the file. The request can be specific to the creditor, or it can be lifted temporarily or permanently for all inquiries.

Once credit reports have been obtained and examined, the victim of identity theft should dispute the errors on the report resulting from the thief with the credit bureaus and the specific creditor involved. The victim should request that the credit reporting agencies block the disputed information from appearing on his or her credit report.

Radio Frequency Identification Cards (RFID)

There are many **radio frequency identification (RFID) cards** in use today including passports, debit, and credit cards. These cards can be identified by looking for the symbol with four curved lines (waves) or by inquiring of the card service representative. The RFID debit and credit cards permit payment by tapping the card or waving the card near a payment terminal. These cards are susceptible to theft by scanning equipment and thus need protection. These cards may be protected by using an RFID protected wallet or purse. Aluminum foil has been touted as providing protection for RFID cards. However, there is much dispute about aluminum foil's efficacy.

Chip and Pin Technology (EMV)

Magnetic stripe credit cards have been used for years in the United States. However, these magnetic stripes present a serious security flaw. This flaw is the same flaw that was exploited at Target and Neiman Marcus in 2014 to steal millions of credit card numbers. Due to the massive security breaches, credit card companies are moving to a new security technology known as EMV smart card payment system, often referred to as **Chip and Pin**.[1]

This technology, which was created in the mid-1980s, inserts an embedded computer chip in the card, creates a unique number for each transaction, and requires a pin to approve any charge. The microchip in the credit card is referred to as an EMV smart chip. The C and P card is more expensive but far superior to the stripe and sign card. It is used in most of the world outside of the United States. U.S. banks have resisted this technology because of its costs, but they are currently adopting it to reduce fraud.

Quick Quiz 9.4

1. Victims of identify theft should act immediately to protect themselves.
   a. True
   b. False

2. When a doctor or another "official" asks for your Social Security number, you should generally give it to them.
   a. True
   b. False

3. The Justice Department's acronym, SCAM stands for Sensitive, Careful, Alert, Monitor.
   a. True
   b. False

True, False, False.

Case Study 3

Former New York City Police Department Officer Sentenced in Manhattan Federal Court to 28 Months in Prison for Fraud and Identity Theft (source: FBI)

JOHN L. MONTANEZ, a former police officer with the New York City Police Department ("NYPD"), was sentenced February 18, 2015 in Manhattan federal court to 28 months in prison for credit card fraud and identity theft. The sentence was imposed by U.S. District Judge Katherine Polk Failla.

Law enforcement executed a search of his apartment and of his locker at his precinct. The search of the apartment yielded, among other things, identification documents in other names and a device allowing for the swiping of a credit/debit card. The search of the locker yielded 16 identification documents in other names, including driver's licenses, benefits cards, and Social Security cards. The identification documents obtained from the search of the locker appeared to come from arrests that MONTANEZ affected or participated in throughout the course of his career as a police officer.

1. EMV stands for Europay, MasterCard, and Visa. Chip and PIN is actually a brand name for the EMV smart card payment system.

KEY TERMS

AUTO CREDIT SCORE - Score calculated principally based on previous auto loan history.

AUTO INSURANCE SCORE - Using data from the TransUnion credit report, it helps auto insurance companies to assess the risk of insuring a consumer by measuring the probability that an auto insurance claim might be filed.

CHIP AND PIN (EMV TECHNOLOGY) - An embedded computer chip in the card (card is more expensive), creates a unique number for each transaction and requires a pin to approve any charge.

CONSUMER LENDING - Credit cards, home equity loans, home equity lines of credit, auto loans, other recreational vehicle loans, and appliance loans.

CREDIT AGENCIES - Companies that compile and maintain credit information from credit card companies, banks, mortgage companies, and other creditors for the purpose of creating personal in-depth credit reports on individuals. The major credit reporting agencies are Experian, Equifax, and TransUnion.

CREDIT SCORE - A number that summarizes a person's credit risk based on an evaluation of his or her credit report at a particular point in time.

DUMPSTER DIVING - A means of identity theft, that involves going through someone's trash while looking for identity information from cancelled checks, bank statements, credit card statements, federal or state tax documents, discarded credit card offers, and phone numbers.

THE FAIR CREDIT REPORTING ACT OF 1971 - Provides that U.S. citizens have free access to their credit reports and credit scores from each of the three national credit reporting agencies.

FICO SCORE - A credit score developed by FICO (formerly know as Fair Isaac Corporation) that estimates the level of future credit risk for an individual. It is calculated using a formula that evaluates many types of information in the credit report at that credit reporting agency and ranges from 300 to 850.

HARD INQUIRIES - Inquiries made by creditors or potential creditors.

HOME INSURANCE SCORE - Ranges from 150 to 850 and is once again calculated using the TransUnion credit report. It is primarily used by home insurance companies to assess the probability that a homeowner will file a homeowner's insurance claim.

RADIO FREQUENCY IDENTIFICATION (RFID) CARDS - The wireless use of electromagnetic fields to transfer consumer information. This is being adopted by debit and credit card companies to deter identity theft.

SCAM - An acronym from the Justice Department to help avoid identity theft.

KEY TERMS

SHOULDER SURFING - A means of identity theft by the eavesdropping on those who punch in numbers or verbally give numbers over the phone.

SOFT INQUIRIES - Inquiries made by the consumer or by a prospective or current employer.

VANTAGESCORE 3.0 - Ranges from 300-850 and was developed by the three major credit bureau agencies.

DISCUSSION QUESTIONS

1. Why is a credit rating like a reputation?
2. What is the history of consumer lending?
3. What portion of GDP is consumer spending?
4. What are the three credit reporting agencies?
5. What information is included in a credit report?
6. What information is not included in a credit report?
7. Do credit reports ever contain errors?
8. What is a credit score, and why would a lender use a credit score?
9. What is a FICO score?
10. What is a VantageScore?
11. What is the difference between a FICO score and a VantageScore?
12. What impact does a low credit score have on a the terms of a borrower's loan?
13. It is said that "to destroy or seriously negatively impact a credit score only takes a few events but to positively impact a credit score takes a long time." Explain.
14. What are some of the easier ways to obtain initial credit for a person with little or no credit history?
15. Why is an automobile loan a relatively easy loan to obtain?
16. What is a good credit score?
17. Can a person with a good credit score be denied credit? Explain.
18. Explain the differences between credit, debit, and charge cards.
19. How widespread is identity theft and credit fraud?
20. What steps should consumers take if they are a victim of identity theft?
21. What are the sources of fraud or identity theft?

22. What are the signs of identity theft?

23. What is SCAM?

24. Explain the chip and pin credit card security available today.

MULTIPLE-CHOICE PROBLEMS

1. Why are auto loans generally the easiest loans to get?

    a. Due to consumer protection.

    b. There is usually a down payment, and an auto loan is secured.

    c. An auto loan only requires a minimum credit score.

    d. Automobiles are easy to repossess due to GPS being placed in all cars with loans.

2. Which of the following likely has the highest credit score?

    a. Bob has 5 credit cards, credit utilization of 40%, and a perfect payment history for 5 years.

    b. George has 3 credit cards, credit utilization of 29%, an installment loan, a mortgage, and a perfect payment history for 3 years.

    c. Tim has 2 credit cards totalling a $50,000 limit.

    d. Fred has a 30-year mortgage in the 10th year with a perfect payment history and the mortgage is his only debt.

3. All of the following are major credit reporting agencies except:

    a. Equifax.

    b. Pan American.

    c. Experian.

    d. TransUnion.

4. Credit agencies do not collect any of the following information for credit reports except:

    a. Home ownership.

    b. Employment information.

    c. Bank accounts with over withdrawals.

    d. Child support payments in arrears.

5. Credit agencies do not collect any of the following information for credit reports except:

    a. Employment information.

    b. Age of borrower.

    c. Amount of alimony paid.

    d. Tax lien.

6. A creditor makes a hard inquiry to a person's credit report. How long is the hard inquiry reported on the credit report for FICO score purposes?

   a. No effect.
   b. 6 months.
   c. 18 months.
   d. 24 months.

7. A creditor makes a hard inquiry to a persons credit report. How long does the hard inquiry affect the FICO score?

   a. 3 months.
   b. 6 months.
   c. 12 months.
   d. 24 months.

8. The TransUnion automobile insurance score uses all of the following except:

   a. Credit payment history.
   b. Driving record.
   c. Credit utilization percent.
   d. The number of credit accounts.

9. What is the likely effect on the credit score given the following? Assume a 750 score to start.

   - Credit utilization this month 40%.
   - One new hard inquiry this month.
   - One new late payment report this month (30 days)

   a. Down 40 points.
   b. Down 50 points.
   c. Down 60 points.
   d. Down 80 - 82 points.

10. The two most well-known credit scores are?

   a. FICO and Auto.
   b. Auto and Vantage.
   c. Vantage and FICO.
   d. FICO and Rico.

11. The auto credit score is?

    a. The same as the auto insurance score.
    b. Calculated the same way as FICO.
    c. Calculated by FICO.
    d. Only used by 25 - 50% of auto lenders.

12. Credit cards, debit cards, and charge cards are:

    a. All different as to liability exposure.
    b. All different as to required payment period.
    c. All have pre-established limits.
    d. All have annual fees.

13. In most cases of identity theft:

    a. The victim knows the perpetrator.
    b. The most common source is breach of computer data.
    c. The largest source is from shoulder surfing.
    d. Lost or stolen Social Security numbers are the most likely information to lead to fraud.

14. Which of the following is the acronym recommended by the U.S. Justice Department to avoid identity theft?

    a. SCRAM.
    b. SNAG.
    c. SHAKE.
    d. SCAM.

15. An extended fraud alert lasts?

    a. 90 days.
    b. 180 days.
    c. 24 months.
    d. 7 years.

16. Which of the following is incorrect about credit freezes and extended fraud alerts?

    a. A credit freeze stops all access to the credit report.
    b. An extended fraud alert allows the consumer 2 free credit reports within 12 months from each of the reporting agencies.
    c. The extended alert lasts 24 continuous months.
    d. Some states charge a fee for placing a credit freeze.

QUICK QUIZ EXPLANATIONS

Quick Quiz 9.1

1. False. It does not include information on a person's income. A credit report includes a consumer's debt and history of debt payments.
2. False. It does not include information regarding moving violations. A credit report includes a consumer's debt and history of debt payments.
3. True.
4. True.

Quick Quiz 9.2

1. True.
2. True.
3. True.

Quick Quiz 9.3

1. False. A secured credit card requires that funds are deposited before using the card. If a person puts up $500, then he can charge $500. Thus, the card requires 100%, not 50%.
2. True.
3. False. A consumer may be turned down for credit for other reasons than a credit score. Therefore, a good credit score does not assure credit approval.

Quick Quiz 9.4

1. True.
2. False. In most cases, people asking for your Social Security number do not need it and you should not give it to them.
3. False. SCAM stands for Stingy (regarding personal data), Check (financial information often), Ask (for credit reports often), Maintain (careful records).

CHAPTER

10

SOCIAL SECURITY

LEARNING OBJECTIVES

After reading this chapter, you should be able to:

1. Understand the history and purpose of the Social Security program and the conditions under which it was enacted.
2. Provide an overview of the Social Security system, including payroll taxes, benefits, and qualifications.*
3. Identify possible beneficiaries under the Social Security system and the types of benefits they may be entitled to receive.*
4. Explain the computation of the Average Indexed Monthly Earnings (AIME) and the Primary Insurance Amount (PIA) and the impact on benefits relative to historical earnings.*
5. Explain disability benefits, survivor benefits, and maximum family benefits under the Social Security system.
6. Advise clients in choosing the optimal date to begin receiving Social Security benefits, considering the impact of taxation, benefit reductions and credits, as well as life expectancy.*
7. Understand proposed or possible changes to the Social Security system and the possible impact on retirement and other financial planning.
8. Understand and describe the taxation of Social Security benefits.*
9. Provide an overview of the Medicare program, including the payroll taxes and eligibility structure.*
10. Identify the four parts of Medicare coverage, the benefits provided by each, common out-of-pocket costs required for insured individuals, and alternative insurance options to cover the gaps associated with Medicare.*

* CFP Board Resource Document - Student-Centered Learning Objectives based upon CFP Board Principal Topics.

HISTORY

Social Security and other forms of social insurance were born out of changes in economies and in families. For centuries, farming and agriculture provided families with the foundation of their economic security. Farms provided food, shelter, and resources for families to survive. As family members aged, they were cared for on the farms. However, as economies changed as part of the industrial revolution, more and more people became employees working for someone else. This demographic shift continued such that a higher percentage of people began moving from the farms to the cities. As a result, people were less capable of providing for their own welfare as they aged, especially in difficult economic times.

These demographic shifts and the Great Depression set the stage for the Social Security system, which was signed into law by Franklin D. Roosevelt on August 14, 1935. At the signing of the law, President Roosevelt made the following statement:

EXAMPLE 10.1

"Today a hope of many years' standing is in large part fulfilled. The civilization of the past hundred years, with its startling industrial changes, has tended more and more to make life insecure. Young people have come to wonder what would be their lot when they came to old age. The man with a job has wondered how long the job would last.

This Social Security measure gives at least some protection to thirty millions of our citizens who will reap direct benefits through unemployment compensation, through old-age pensions and through increased services for the protection of children and the prevention of ill health.

We can never insure one hundred percent of the population against one hundred percent of the hazards and vicissitudes of life, but we have tried to frame a law which will give some measure of protection to the average citizen and to his family against the loss of a job and against poverty-ridden old age."

Today, the Social Security system is significantly different than what it was envisioned to be almost 80 years ago in terms of the programs offered and the size of the program. The system provides tremendous benefits to millions of Americans, as indicated in Exhibit 10.1. However, the system also has significant fiscal problems that must be addressed and resolved if there is any chance that it continues for generations to come. Two of the primary issues with the program are the number of workers paying into the system relative to the number of retirees and other beneficiaries and the significant increase in the life expectancy of our current and future population.

EXHIBIT 10.1

SOCIAL SECURITY BASIC FACTS[1]

1. In 2014, nearly 59 million Americans received $863 billion in Social Security benefits.
2. An estimated 165 million workers, 94% of all workers, are covered under Social Security.
   - 51% of the workforce has no private pension coverage.
   - 34% of the workforce has no savings set aside specifically for retirement.
3. Social Security is the major source of income for most of the elderly.
   - Nine out of ten individuals age 65 and older receive Social Security benefits.
   - Social Security benefits represent about 38% of the income of the elderly.
   - Among elderly Social Security beneficiaries, 52% of married couples and 74% of unmarried persons receive 50% or more of their income from Social Security.
   - Among elderly Social Security beneficiaries, 22% of married couples and about 47% of unmarried persons rely on Social Security for 90% or more of their income.
4. In 1940, the life expectancy of a 65-year-old was almost 14 years; today it is almost 20 years.
5. By 2033, there will be almost twice as many older Americans as today - from 46.6 million today to 77 million.
6. There are currently 2.8 workers for each Social Security beneficiary. By 2033, there will be 2.1 workers for each beneficiary.

1. Social Security Basic Facts, April 2014.

Know The Numbers (2015)	
Social Security Wage Base	$118,500
Social Security Quarter of Coverage	$1,220
Social Security Bottom Bend Point	$826
Social Security Top Bend Point	$4,980
Social Security Maximum Monthly Benefit	$2,663
Social Security Medicare Part A Deductible Days 1-60	$1,216 per benefit period
Social Security Medicare Part A Deductible Days 61-90	$315 per day
Social Security Medicare Part A Deductible Days 91 and Over	$630 per day
Social Security Medicare Part B Deductible	$147
Social Security Skilled Nursing Care Deductible Days 21-100	$157.50 per day
Social Security Disability Monthly Earnings Limit	$1,090
Social Security Disability Monthly Earnings Limit if Blind	$1,820
Social Security Death Benefit	$255
Social Security Earnings Limitation (under full retirement age)	$15,720
Social Security Earnings Limitation (full retirement age)	$41,880

INTRODUCTION

Social Security benefits were never intended to provide total pre-retirement wage replacement upon retirement. Social Security was created to supplement a covered worker's pension, savings, investments, and other earnings from assets to make up an appropriate wage replacement ratio (e.g., 70 percent). Individuals who retire may need 70 to 80 percent of their pre-retirement income during their retirement to maintain their pre-retirement standard of living.

Low wage earners receive Social Security retirement benefits averaging 60 percent of pre-retirement income. Average wage earners receive an average of 42 percent of pre-retirement income from Social Security benefits, whereas high wage earners receive an average of 26 percent of pre-retirement income (see Exhibit 10.2).

From a financial planning standpoint, it is important to understand Social Security law and the various benefits that are available from Social Security. This chapter provides an overview of the Social Security system and its benefits. The six major categories of benefits administered by the Social Security Administration are:

1. Retirement benefits
2. Disability benefits
3. Family benefits
4. Survivors' benefits
5. Medicare

6. Supplemental Security Income (SSI) benefits. SSI benefits are not funded by Social Security taxes but are funded by general funds from the Treasury.

The **retirement benefit** is the most well-known benefit from Social Security. Full retirement benefits are payable at "full retirement age" (reduced benefits are available as early as age 62) to anyone who has obtained a minimum amount (40 quarters) of Social Security credits. Based on the Social Security law in 1983, the age when full retirement benefits are paid began to rise from age 65 in the year 2000, and increases to age 67 by the year 2027. Workers who delay retirement beyond the full retirement age receive a special scheduled increase (Exhibit 10.14) in benefits for each delayed year extending until age 70.[1]

SOCIAL SECURITY BENEFITS AS A PERCENTAGE OF PRE-RETIREMENT INCOME

EXHIBIT 10.2

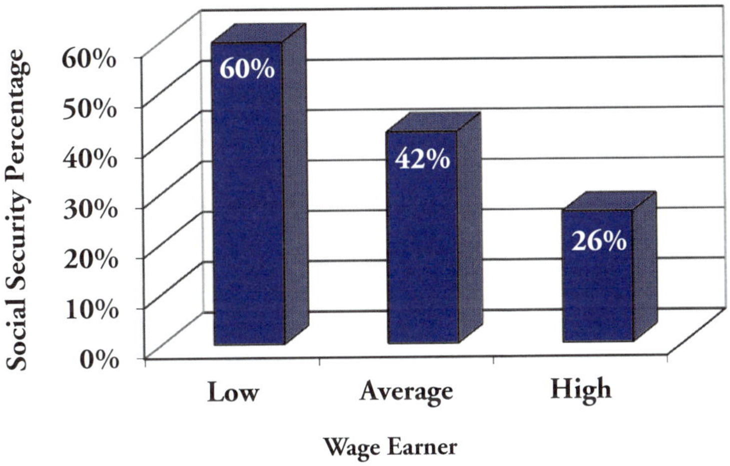

The **disability benefit** is payable at any age to workers who have sufficient credits under the Social Security system to qualify for disability benefits. Recipients must have a severe physical or mental impairment that is expected to prevent them from performing "substantial" work for at least a year or to result in their death. Monthly earnings of $1,090 for 2015 (if the individual is blind, then the amount is increased to $1,820 per month for 2015) or more is considered substantial. The disability insurance program has built-in incentives to smooth the transition back to the workforce including continuation of benefits and health care coverage.

1. The increases are not compounded, and there are no increases for delay past age 70.

EXHIBIT 10.3

SOCIAL SECURITY DISABILITY BENEFITS

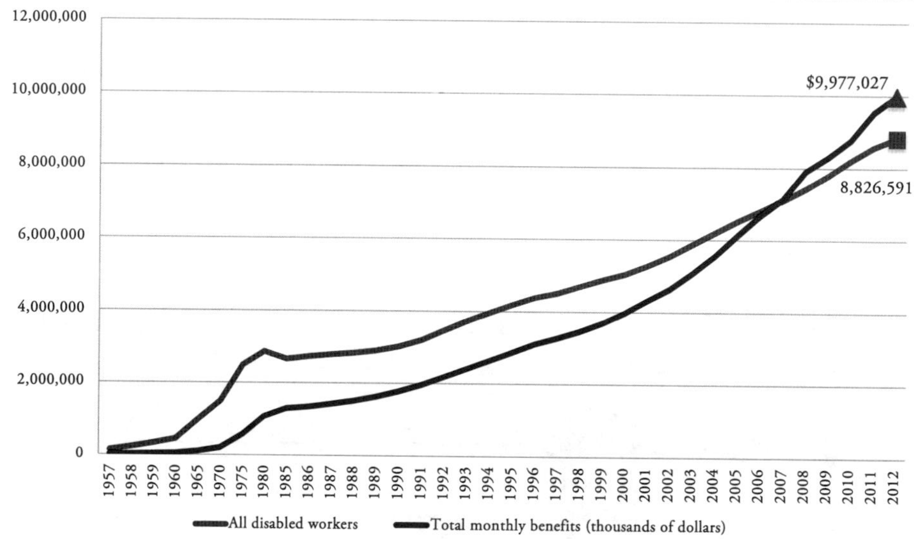

The **family benefit** is provided to certain family members of workers eligible for retirement or disability benefits. Such family members include spouses age 62 or older, spouses under age 62 but caring for a child under age 16, unmarried children under 18, unmarried children under age 19 and full-time students, and unmarried children of any age who were disabled before age 22.

> **KEY CONCEPTS**
>
> 1. What are the six major categories of benefits administered by the Social Security Administration?
> 2. How are funds collected for Social Security?

Survivors' benefits apply to certain members of the deceased worker's family if the worker earned sufficient Social Security credits. Family members entitled to survivors' benefits include those listed for family benefits and may also include the worker's dependant parents if the worker was their primary means of support. A special one-time payment of $255 may be made to the spouse or minor children upon the death of a Social Security covered worker.

Medicare provides hospital and medical insurance. Those who have attained age 65 or those who receive disability benefits for at least two years automatically qualify for Medicare. Others must file an application to become qualified.

Finally, **Supplemental Security Income (SSI)** (funded by general tax revenues and not by Social Security taxes) is another benefit that provides monthly payments to those disabled or at full retirement age who have a low income and few assets. Generally, those who receive SSI also qualify for **Medicaid**, food stamps, and other governmental assistance.

SOCIAL SECURITY TAXES AND CONTRIBUTIONS

Although the Social Security retirement benefits program is thought by many to be one of the most complicated and confusing programs created, the basic concept is quite simple. Employees, employers, and self-employed individuals pay Social Security taxes, known as FICA taxes, during their working years. These payments are pooled in special trust funds. Contributing workers become "covered" workers, meaning that they will fall under the Social Security umbrella of benefits after contributing for approximately 10 years (40 quarters) and will receive retirement benefits based on those contributions and the Social Security benefits formula.

The **Federal Insurance Contributions Act (FICA)** is the law allowing Social Security taxes, including Medicare taxes, to be deducted from paychecks. A portion of these FICA taxes pays part of the Medicare coverage. Both employers and employees pay the taxes for Social Security and Medicare. For the year 2015, an employer and employee each pay 6.2 percent of the employee's gross salary up to a limit of $118,500 for **OASDI (Old Age, Survivor, and Disability Insurance)**.[1] The salary limit rises annually based on annual increases in average wages. Self-employed workers pay 12.4 percent (6.2 percent x 2) of their taxable income up to the same salary limit. The Medicare portion of the Social Security tax is 1.45 percent for both employers and employees and is 2.9 percent for self-employed workers with no limit on the amount of compensation taxed.

EXAMPLE 10.2

If an employee earns a salary of $150,000 in 2015, the first $118,500 of the employee's salary will be subject to a tax of 7.65 (6.2 + 1.45) percent while the remaining $31,500 will be subject to a tax of only 1.45 percent. The employer pays the same amount as the employee.

	Taxable Amount	x	Tax Rate	Total Tax
Employee - Social Security	$118,500		6.20%	$7,347.00
Employee - Medicare	$150,000		1.45%	$2,175.00
Total Tax				$9,522.00

ADDITIONAL MEDICARE TAXES BEGINNING IN 2013

The Affordable care act created two additional Medicare taxes that impact wealthier taxpayers. The first is an additional Medicare tax of 0.9 percent on wages or self-employment income. The second is a 3.8 percent tax on certain amounts of net investment income.

1. The Tax Relief, Unemployment Insurance Reauthorization, and Job Creation Act of 2010 reduced the payroll tax rate for working and self-employed employees during 2011. For 2011, the rate of the old age, survivors, and disability insurance (OASDI) tax on self-employment income was reduced by 2%, to 10.4%. The rate of the employee's OASDI portion of the payroll tax was also reduced by 2%, to 4.2%. The employer's share of OASDI remained at 6.2%. The rate for Medicare taxes was unaffected by this act. The "Payroll Tax Holiday" was further extended until the end of 2012. In 2013, the rate for OASDI returned to 6.2%.

The additional Medicare tax equal to 0.9 percent applies to wages or self-employment income that is above the following threshold amounts:

Married Filing Jointly	$250,000
Married Filing Separately	$125,000
Single	$200,000
Head of Household	$200,000

Employees pay this Medicare tax only. Employers do not pay this tax, but must withhold the tax from wages if the taxpayer has income in excess of $200,000.

EXAMPLE 10.3

Carlos, a single filer, has $130,000 in wages and $145,000 in self-employment income. His wages are not in excess of the $200,000 threshold for single filers, so Carlos is not liable for Additional Medicare Tax on these wages.

Before calculating the Additional Medicare Tax on self-employment income, the $200,000 threshold for single filers is reduced by his $130,000 in wages, resulting in a reduced self-employment income threshold of $70,000. Carlos is liable to pay Additional Medicare Tax on $75,000 of self-employment income ($145,000 in self-employment income minus the reduced threshold of $70,000). Carlos has total earnings of $275,000, which is $75,000 over the $200,000 threshold.

EXAMPLE 10.4

Dave and Dana are married and file jointly. Dave has $150,000 in wages and Dana has $175,000 in self-employment income. Dave's wages are not in excess of the $250,000 threshold for joint filers, so Dave and Dana are not liable for Additional Medicare Tax on Dave's wages.

Before calculating the Additional Medicare Tax on Dana's self-employment income, the $250,000 threshold for joint filers is reduced by Dave's $150,000 in wages resulting in a reduced self-employment income threshold of $100,000. Dave and Dana are liable to pay Additional Medicare Tax on $75,000 of self-employment income ($175,000 in self-employment income minus the reduced threshold of $100,000). Dave and Dana have total earnings of $325,000, which is $75,000 over the $250,000 threshold.

The 3.8 percent Medicare tax is imposed on the lesser of net investment income or modified AGI over the following threshold amounts:

Married Filing Jointly	$250,000
Married Filing Separately	$125,000
Single	$200,000
Head of Household	$200,000

Net investment income is a broadly defined term that includes gross income from interest, dividends, annuities, royalties, and rents other than such income derived from the ordinary course of a trade or business, ***plus*** other trade or business income, for which the entity is a passive activity (or if the entity is trading financial instruments or commodities), ***plus*** net gain attributable to the disposition of property other than property held in a trade or business. It should be noted that net investment income does not include any distribution from a 401(k), 403(b), 457(b) plan or an IRA or Roth IRA. However, such distributions may cause a taxpayer to exceed the threshold amounts.

EXAMPLE 10.5

In 2015, Dan and Mary (MFJ) have $250,000 of dividend income. In this case, they are not subject to the 3.8% surtax.

EXAMPLE 10.6

Same as Example 10.5, but Dan and Mary convert a traditional IRA to a Roth IRA. The taxable amount of the conversion is $100,000. Thus, they will have AGI of $350,000, and $100,000 will hence be subject to the 3.8% surtax.

EXAMPLE 10.7

Same as Example 10.5, but Dan and Mary also take minimum distributions of $50,000. They will be subject to the 3.8% tax on $50,000, which is the lesser of Net Investment Income and the AGI above $250,000.

EXHIBIT 10.4

3.8% Medicare Tax

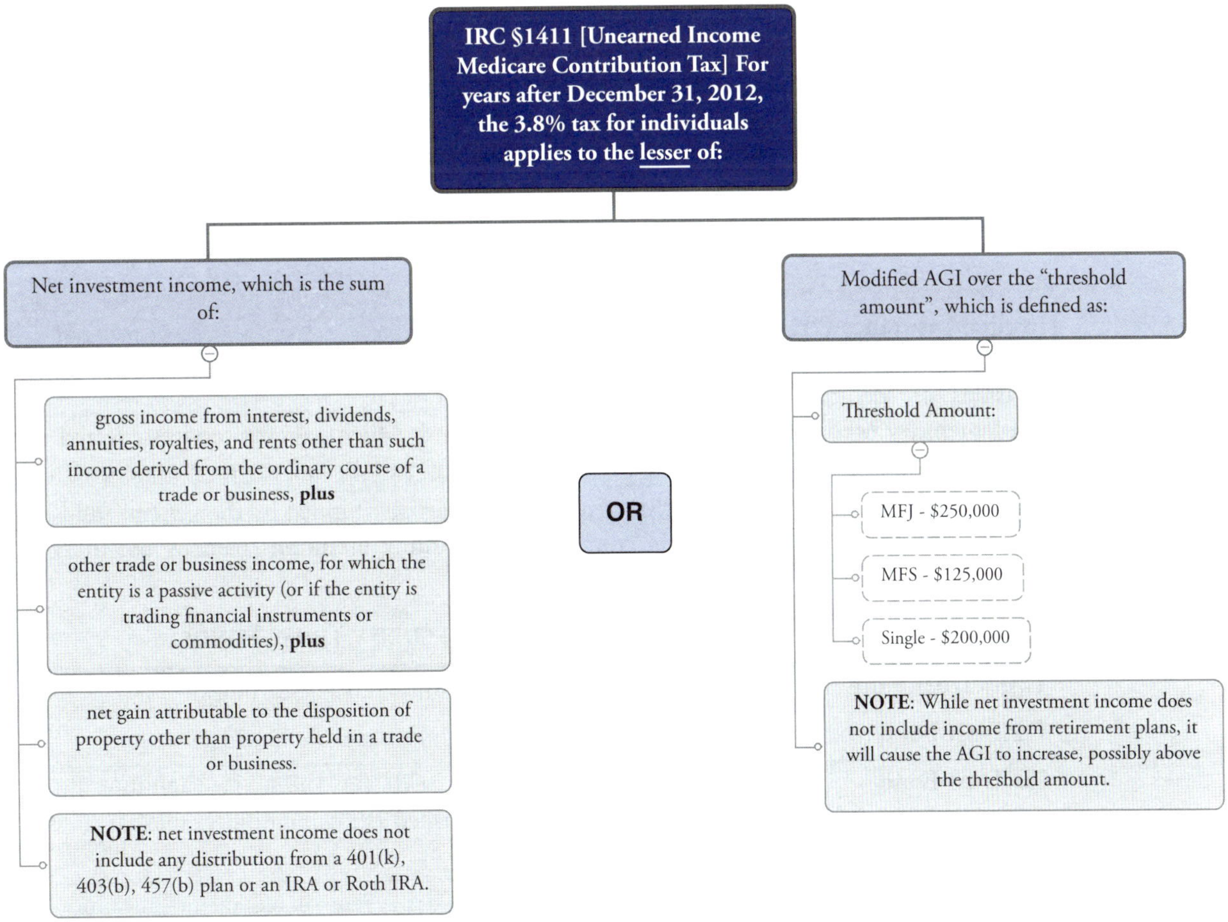

EXAMPLE 10.8

In 2015, Steve and Ashley (MFJ) have $100,000 of dividend income and $100,000 of wages. In this case, they are not subject to the 3.8% surtax because they are not over the $250,000 limit.

EXAMPLE 10.9

Same as Example 10.8, but Steve and Ashley convert a traditional IRA to a Roth IRA. The taxable amount of the conversion is $100,000. Thus, they will have AGI of $300,000. The lesser of $50,000 or $100,000 will be subject to the 3.8% surtax.

EXAMPLE 10.10

Jack and Jill (MFJ) each earn $250,000 and have interest income of $1,000. The $1,000 would be subject to the 3.8% tax.

TRUST FUNDS

The United States Social Security system operates on a "pay-as-you-go" basis. Social Security taxes are collected and divided among several trust funds. The federal **Old Age and Survivors Insurance ("OASI")** Trust Fund pays retirement and survivors' benefits. The OASI Trust Fund receives 5.30 percent of the FICA tax. The federal **Disability Insurance ("DI") Trust Fund** pays benefits to workers with disabilities and their families. The DI Trust Fund receives 0.90 percent of the FICA tax. OASI and DI are the two trust funds used for payment of Social Security benefits (total 6.2 percent).

QUICK QUIZ 10.1

1. Social Security benefits are not payable until an individual reaches full retirement age.
   a. True
   b. False

2. Social Security contributions are placed in the following trust funds: OASI, DI, and SMI.
   a. True
   b. False

False, False.

The two Medicare trust funds are the federal **Hospital Insurance ("HI") Trust Fund**, which pays for services covered under the hospital insurance provisions of Medicare (Part A), and the federal **Supplementary Medical Insurance ("SMI") Trust Fund**, which pays for services covered under the medical insurance provisions of Medicare, known as Part B and the new prescription drug provisions known as Part D.[1] The SMI Trust Fund is partially funded by the general fund of the Treasury with the remaining funding coming from monthly premiums paid by the individuals enrolled in Part B.

EXHIBIT 10.5

SOURCES OF FUNDING TO SOCIAL SECURITY TRUST FUNDS

OASI Trust Fund	5.30 percent (limited to the maximum taxable earnings)
DI Trust Fund	0.90 percent (limited to the maximum taxable earnings)
HI Trust Fund	1.45 percent (all earnings are taxed) (In 1993, the Omnibus Budget Reconciliation Act of 1993 abolished the ceiling on taxable earnings for Medicare.)
SMI Trust Fund	-0- (no FICA taxes used; funded by general federal tax revenues and monthly premiums paid by enrollees)

1. Medicare Prescription Drug. Improvement and Modernization Act of 2003 (PL 108-173).

Case Study 10.1

The case of ***Veterinary Surgical Consultants, P.C. v. C.I.R.***, involved an owner of an S corporation who attempted to avoid FICA and FUTA taxes by declaring his remuneration as a K-1 distribution of corporate net income and not W-2 wages.[1] Dr. Sadanaga performed substantial services for the S corporation, Veterinary Surgical Consultants, P.C. ("VSC"). Dr. Sadanaga worked approximately 33 hours per week for VSC. He was the only individual working for VSC. Tellingly, all of VSC's income was generated from the consulting and surgical services provided by Dr. Sadanaga. As officer and sole shareholder, Dr. Sadanaga declared all remuneration he received on a K-1 form, not on a W-2 form, thus avoiding FICA and FUTA taxes.

VSC claimed that the amounts paid to Dr. Sadanaga were distributions of its corporate net income, rather than wages, and that as an S corporation it passed its net income to Dr. Sadanaga as its sole shareholder. Not surprisingly, the Court disagreed with VSC, i.e., Dr. Sadanaga, and concluded that an S corporation cannot avoid federal FICA and FUTA employment taxes by characterizing compensation paid to its sole director and shareholder as distributions of the S corporation's net income rather than wages. The Court's analysis focused on whether payments represented remuneration for services rendered. To characterize the payments to Dr. Sadanaga as distributions of VSC's net income was "but a subterfuge for reality." The payments constituted remuneration for services performed by Dr. Sadanaga on behalf of VSC. Regardless of how an employer may choose to characterize payments made to its employees, the true analysis is whether the payments represent remuneration for services rendered.[2] Dr. Sadanaga's reporting of the distributions as non-passive income from an S corporation had no bearing on the Federal employment tax treatment of those wages. He was VSC's sole source of income, thereby requiring treatment as an employee.[3] In short, while an S corporation is permitted to pass through items of income in calculating its income tax liability, it may not pass through its tax liability for federal employment taxes.

1. ***Veterinary Surgical Consultants, P.C. v. C.I.R.***, 117 T.C. No. 14, 117 T.C. 141, 2001 WL 1242120 (U.S.Tax Ct.), Tax Ct. Rep. (CCH) 54,527, Tax Ct. Rep. Dec. (RIA) 117.14 (U.S.Tax Ct. 2001).
2. See also ***Spicer Accounting, Inc. v. United States***, 918 F.2d 90 (9th Cir. 1990); ***Joseph Radtke, S.C. v. United States***, 895 F.2d 1196 (7th Cir. 1990).
3. Id., at 94-95.

SOCIAL SECURITY BENEFITS - ELIGIBILITY AND CALCULATIONS

COVERED WORKERS AND INSURED STATUS

To qualify for retirement benefits, a worker must be "**fully insured,**" which means that a worker has earned a certain number of quarters of coverage under the Social Security system. Since 1978, quarters of coverage have been determined based on annual earnings. In other words, earning a designated amount of money, regardless of when it was earned during the year, will credit the worker with a quarter of coverage for that year. In 2015, the designated amount for a quarter of coverage is $1,220. Thus, workers who earn at least $4,880 are credited with four quarters of coverage for 2015. No worker may earn more than four quarters in one year, regardless of earnings. The following is a list of the designated amounts for a quarter of coverage dating back to 1985:

EXHIBIT 10.6

DESIGNATED AMOUNTS FOR A QUARTER OF SOCIAL SECURITY COVERAGE

Year	Amount Needed to Receive a Credit for One Quarter
1986	$440
1987	$460
1988	$470
1989	$500
1990	$520
1991	$540
1992	$570
1993	$590
1994	$620
1995	$630
1996	$640
1997	$670
1998	$700
1999	$740
2000	$780

Year	Amount Needed to Receive a Credit for One Quarter
2001	$830
2002	$870
2003	$890
2004	$900
2005	$920
2006	$970
2007	$1,000
2008	$1,050
2009	$1,090
2010	$1,120
2011	$1,120
2012	$1,130
2013	$1,160
2014	$1,200
2015	$1,220

For most persons, 40 quarters of coverage (10 years of work in employment covered by Social Security) or one quarter per year from age 21 to age 62 will fully insure a worker for life. Fully insured workers are entitled to the benefits under the Social Security system. Some benefits, like survivors' benefits, are available to "currently" (although not necessarily fully) insured individuals. **"Currently" insured workers** are those individuals who have at least six quarters of coverage out of the previous 13 quarters.

KEY CONCEPTS

1. Who are covered workers with regard to Social Security?
2. Who are beneficiaries of Social Security benefits?

EXAMPLE 10.11

In 2015, William earned $10,000 from employment subject to Social Security between January 1 and March 31. He was then unemployed for the remainder of the year. How many quarters of coverage did he earn for Social Security2015?

For 2015, a worker receives one quarter credit for each $1,220 in annual earnings on which Social Security taxes are withheld up to a maximum of four quarters. It is irrelevant that William earned the $10,000 all in the first quarter. William has earned four quarters for the year.

EXAMPLE 10.12

How is a worker's insured status determined under Social Security? It is determined by the number of quarters of coverage received. To achieve currently insured status under Social Security, a worker must have at least six quarters of coverage out of 13 calendar quarters prior to retirement, disability, or death. Any worker with 40 covered quarters is fully insured.

Social Security Beneficiaries

Social Security benefits are paid upon retirement, disability, or death if the eligibility requirements are satisfied. The worker's spouse and children may also be eligible to receive benefits when the worker satisfies eligibility requirements. Generally, monthly Social Security benefits can be paid to:

- A disabled insured worker under age 65.
- A retired insured worker at age 62 or older.
- The spouse of a retired or disabled worker entitled to benefits who:
  - is at least 62 years old, or
  - is caring for a child who is under age 16 or disabled.
- The divorced spouse of a retired or disabled worker entitled to benefits if the divorced spouse is age 62 or older and was married to the worker for at least 10 years.
- The divorced spouse of a fully insured worker who has not yet filed a claim for benefits if both are at least age 62, were married for at least 10 years, and have been finally divorced for at least two continuous years.
- The dependent, unmarried child of a retired or disabled worker entitled to benefits or of a deceased insured worker if the child is:
  - under age 18;
  - under age 19 and a full-time elementary or secondary school student; or
  - age 18 or over but disabled (if the disability began before age 22).
- The surviving spouse (including a surviving divorced spouse) of a deceased insured worker if the widow(er) is age 60 or older.
- The disabled surviving spouse (including a surviving divorced spouse in some cases) of a deceased insured worker if the widow(er) is age 50 or older.
- The surviving spouse (including a surviving divorced spouse) of a deceased insured worker, regardless of age, if caring for an entitled child of the deceased who is either under age 16 or disabled before age 22.
- The dependent parents of a deceased insured worker at age 62 or older.

Quick Quiz 10.2

1. "Fully insured" means that a worker has earned a certain number of quarters (generally 40) of coverage under the Social Security system.
   a. True
   b. False

2. Social Security benefits can be paid to the dependent parents of a deceased insured worker at age 62.
   a. True
   b. False

True, True.

In addition to monthly survivors' benefits, a lump-sum death payment of $255 is payable upon the death of an insured worker. Exhibit 10.7 provides a summary of those eligible for OASDI benefits and the percentages of the worker's primary insurance amount ("PIA") that each beneficiary will receive. The PIA is the retirement benefit that the worker would receive if the worker retires at full retirement age.

EXAMPLE 10.13

Steve, age 38, has just died. He has been credited with the last 35 consecutive quarters of Social Security coverage since he left college. He did not work before leaving college. Which of the following persons are eligible to receive Social Security survivor benefits as a result of Steve's death?

1. Tim, Steve's 16-year-old son
2. Grace, Steve's 18-year-old daughter
3. Olivia, Steve's 38-year-old widow
4. Arline, Steve's 60-year-old dependent mother

Answer: Grace is too old; Olivia does not have a child under 16 and she is too young; and Arline is not eligible because she is too young. Thus, only Tim is eligible.

EXHIBIT 10.7

Summary of Social Security OASDI Benefits (As a Percentage of PIA)

	Assuming Full Retirement Age of the Worker			
	Retirement	Survivorship		Disability[4]
	Fully Insured[2]	Fully Insured[2]	Currently Insured[3]	
Participant	100%	Deceased	Deceased	100%
Child Under 18[6]	50%	75%	75%	50%
Spouse with child under 16[7]	50%	75%	75%	50%
Spouse - Full Age Retirement[1]	50%	100%	0%	50%
Spouse - Age 62[1, 8]	32.5% to 35%	80% to 81%[9]	0%	32.5% to 35%
Spouse - Age 60[1]	N/A	71.5%	0%	N/A
Dependent Parent (age 62)	0%	75/82.5%[5]	0%	0%

1. Includes divorced spouse if married at least 10 years (unless they have remarried). Survivorship benefits are also available to divorced spouse if remarried after age 60.
2. Fully insured is 40 quarters of coverage or one quarter for each year after age 21 but before age 62 (with at least six quarters of coverage).[1]
3. Currently insured is at least six quarters of coverage in the last 13 quarters.
4. Disability insured is based on age as follows:
   - Before age 24 - Must have 6 quarters of coverage in the last 12 quarters.
   - Age 24 through 30 - Must be covered for half of the available quarters after age 21.
   - Age 31 or older - Must be fully insured and have 20 quarters of coverage in the last 40 quarters.
5. Parent benefit is 82.5 percent for one parent and 75 percent for each parent if two parents.
6. Child under age 19 and a full-time student or of any age and disabled before age 22 also qualifies.
7. Spouse with child disabled before age 22 also qualifies.
8. A spouse can choose to retire as early as age 62, but doing so may result in a benefit as little as 32.5 percent of the worker's primary insurance amount. A spousal benefit is reduced 25/36 of one percent for each month before normal retirement age, up to 36 months. If the number of months exceeds 36, then the benefit is further reduced 5/12 of one percent per month.
9. The reduction for a widow(er) is 28.5 percent at age 60. It is prorated for months between full retirement age and age 60.

Note: Notice that when the participant worker is alive (retirement and disability), beneficiaries who qualify for a benefit, qualify for 50% of PIA. When the participant dies, all qualified beneficiaries generally receive 75% of PIA with the exceptions being the spouse who replaces the participant at 100% and any qualified dependent parents. See note 5.

1. 42 U.S.C.414.

EXAMPLE 10.14

Under Social Security (OASDI), what benefits are available to the survivors of a deceased but only currently insured worker?

A $255 lump-sum death benefit, which is generally payable to the insured's spouse, and 75 percent of the worker's PIA is available to a child under 18 or to a surviving spouse with a dependent child under the age of 16.

Social Security Retirement Benefits - A Closer Look

The most well known Social Security benefit is the Retirement Benefit. Until 2000, normal age retirement, the age where full retirement benefits are available to the retiree, was 65 years. The age at which full benefits are paid began to rise in the year 2000. Exhibit 10.8 illustrates the new law, which eventually raises normal age retirement with full benefits to age 67.

Age Full Retirement Benefits Begin (Normal Age Retirement)

EXHIBIT 10.8

Full Retirement Age With Full Benefits	Year Born
65 years	Before 1938
65 years, 2 months	1938
65 years, 4 months	1939
65 years, 6 months	1940
65 years, 8 months	1941
65 years, 10 months	1942
66 years	1943-1954
66 years, 2 months	1955
66 years, 4 months	1956
66 years, 6 months	1957
66 years, 8 months	1958
66 years, 10 months	1959
67 years	1960-present

People who delay receiving Social Security retirement benefits beyond full retirement age receive an increase in their benefit when they do retire. People who take early retirement, currently as early as agc 62, receive an actuarially reduced monthly benefit. (Early and late retirement options are discussed later in this chapter.)

When planning for an individual, it may be appropriate to calculate the individual's expected Social Security retirement benefit or to ask the client to request a Social Security statement and consider the benefit in that individual's retirement plan. Some advisors, however, choose not to consider the estimated retirement benefit in order to be conservative in developing a retirement plan. Others justify the exclusion of Social Security retirement benefits from retirement planning based on the belief that there will be drastic changes to the Social Security system through legislative action or through economically-driven forces.

THE RETIREMENT BENEFIT CALCULATION

KEY CONCEPTS

1. How is a person's Social Security retirement benefit calculated?
2. How does retiring early or retiring late affect Social Security retirement benefits?

Determining a worker's Social Security retirement benefit requires specific, detailed information pertaining to the person's age, actual earnings history that was subject to Social Security taxes, and the worker's retirement date. Social Security benefits are based on earnings averaged over most of a worker's lifetime. Actual earnings, in historical dollars, are first adjusted or "indexed" to current dollars to account for changes in average wages and inflation since the year the earnings were received. Then, the Social Security Administration calculates **average indexed monthly earnings ("AIME")** during the 35 years in which the applicant earned the most. The Social Security Administration applies a formula to these earnings and arrives at a basic benefit, which is referred to as the **primary insurance amount (PIA)**. The Social Security retirement benefit is based on the worker's PIA. The PIA determines the amount the applicant will receive at his full retirement age, but the dollar amount of the benefit depends on the year in which the worker retires. The PIA is indexed to the consumer price index (CPI) annually.

Figuring the Worker's Average Indexed Monthly Earnings (AIME)

To determine a worker's AIME, the worker's actual annual earnings from age 22 to 62 must be converted into current dollars by multiplying the worker's total annual earnings for each year by an indexing factor. The indexing factor is the result of dividing the national average wage for the year in which the worker attains age 60 by the national average wage for the actual year being indexed. Exhibit 10.9 provides national average wages from 1954 to 2013.

EXHIBIT 10.9

NATIONAL AVERAGE WAGE INDEXING SERIES, 1954-2013

Year	Amount	Year	Amount	Year	Amount
1954	$3,155.64	1974	$8,030.76	1994	$23,753.53
1955	$3,301.44	1975	$8,630.92	1995	$24,705.66
1956	$3,532.36	1976	$9,226.48	1996	$25,913.90
1957	$3,641.72	1977	$9,779.44	1997	$27,426.00
1958	$3,673.80	1978	$10,556.03	1998	$28,861.44
1959	$3,855.80	1979	$11,479.46	1999	$30,469.84
1960	$4,007.12	1980	$12,513.46	2000	$32,154.82
1961	$4,086.76	1981	$13,773.10	2001	$32,921.92
1962	$4,291.40	1982	$14,531.34	2002	$33,252.09
1963	$4,396.64	1983	$15,239.24	2003	$34,064.95
1964	$4,576.32	1984	$16,135.07	2004	$35,648.55
1965	$4,658.72	1985	$16,822.51	2005	$36,952.94
1966	$4,938.36	1986	$17,321.82	2006	$38,651.41
1967	$5,213.44	1987	$18,426.51	2007	$40,405.48
1968	$5,571.76	1988	$19,334.04	2008	$41,334.97
1969	$5,893.76	1989	$20,099.55	2009	$40,711.61
1970	$6,186.24	1990	$21,027.98	2010	$41,673.83
1971	$6,497.08	1991	$21,811.60	2011	$42,979.61
1972	$7,133.80	1992	$22,935.42	2012	$44,321.67
1973	$7,580.16	1993	$23,132.67	2013	$44,888.16

Source: Social Security Administration (www.ssa.gov)

EXAMPLE 10.15

For a worker age 62 in 2014, the indexing factor for the year 1980 is determined by dividing the national average wage for 2012 (when the worker attained age 60), which was $44,321.67, by the national average wage for 1980 (the year being indexed), which was $12,513.46, yielding a factor of 3.5419.

		Age 62 in 2014		Age 65 in 2014	
Year	AWI	Age	Factor	Age	Factor
1972	7,133.80	20	6.2129	23	5.7069
1973	7,580.16	21	5.8471	24	5.3708
1974	8,030.76	22	5.5190	25	5.0695
1975	8,630.92	23	5.1352	26	4.7169
1976	9,226.48	24	4.8037	27	4.4125
1977	9,779.44	25	4.5321	28	4.1630
1978	10,556.03	26	4.1987	29	3.8567
1979	11,479.46	27	3.8610	30	3.5465
→ 1980	12,513.46	28	3.5419	31	3.2534
1981	13,773.10	29	3.2180	32	2.9559
1982	14,531.34	30	3.0501	33	2.8016
1983	15,239.24	31	2.9084	34	2.6715
1984	16,135.07	32	2.7469	35	2.5232
1985	16,822.51	33	2.6347	36	2.4201
1986	17,321.82	34	2.5587	37	2.3503
1987	18,426.51	35	2.4053	38	2.2094
1988	19,334.04	36	2.2924	39	2.1057
1989	20,099.55	37	2.2051	40	2.0255
1990	21,027.98	38	2.1077	41	1.9361
1991	21,811.60	39	2.0320	42	1.8665
1992	22,935.42	40	1.9325	43	1.7751
1993	23,132.67	41	1.9160	44	1.7599
1994	23,753.53	42	1.8659	45	1.7139
1995	24,705.66	43	1.7940	46	1.6479
1996	25,913.90	44	1.7103	47	1.5710
1997	27,426.00	45	1.6160	48	1.4844
1998	28,861.44	46	1.5357	49	1.4106
1999	30,469.84	47	1.4546	50	1.3361
2000	32,154.82	48	1.3784	51	1.2661
2001	32,921.92	49	1.3463	52	1.2366
2002	33,252.09	50	1.3329	53	1.2243
2003	34,064.95	51	1.3011	54	1.1951
2004	35,648.55	52	1.2433	55	1.1420
2005	36,952.94	53	1.1994	56	1.1017
2006	38,651.41	54	1.1467	57	1.0533
2007	40,405.48	55	1.0969	58	1.0076
2008	41,334.97	56	1.0723	59	1.0000
2009	40,711.61	57	1.0887	60	1.0000
2010	41,673.83	58	1.0635	61	1.0000
2011	42,979.61	59	1.0312	62	1.0000
→ 2012	44,321.67	60	1.0000	63	1.0000
2013	[redacted]	61	1.0000	64	1.0000
2014	[redacted]	62	1.0000	65	1.0000

Next, each year's annual earnings must be multiplied by its indexing factor to arrive at the indexed earnings for the years from age 22 to 60. Note that the indexing factor will always equal one for the years in which the worker is 60 or older. After all annual earnings are indexed, or converted to current dollar amounts, the highest 35 years of indexed earnings are added together for a total. The sum of the highest 35 years is then divided by 420 (which represents 35 years multiplied by 12 months per year). This calculation yields the average amount of monthly earnings for all indexed years, hence the name Average Indexed Monthly Earnings (AIME). Once the worker's AIME is determined, the next step in determining the worker's retirement benefit is to calculate the primary insurance amount (PIA) for the worker.

EXAMPLE 10.16

Assume Ronnie and Karen both retire in 2014. Ronnie retires at age 62. Karen retires at her normal (or full) retirement age. Assume Karen has covered earnings from 1972 through 2014, as shown in columns labeled "nominal earnings" and Ronnie has covered earnings from 1972 through 2014.

Indexing adjusts nominal earnings to near-current wage levels. For each case, the table shows columns of earnings before and after indexing. Between these columns is a column showing the indexing factors. A factor will always equal one for the year in which the person attains age 60 and all later years. The indexing factor for a prior year Y is the result of dividing the average wage index for the year in which the person attains age 60 by the average wage index for year Y. For example, Ronnie's indexing factor for 1972 (6.2129) is the average wage for 2012 ($44,321.67) divided by the average wage for 1972 ($7,133.80).

The highest 35 years of indexed earnings are used in the benefit computation. The selected indexed amounts are bold. Below the indexed earnings are the sums for the highest 35 years of indexed earnings and the corresponding average monthly amounts of such earnings. (The average is the result of dividing the sum of the 35 highest amounts by the number of months in 35 years.) Such an average is called the "Average Indexed Monthly Earnings" (AIME).

As reflected in the following chart, Ronnie's AIME is $3,027 and Karen's AIME is $4,011.

Year	Ronnie					Karen				
	Age	Nominal earnings	Indexing factor	Indexed earnings	Top 35	Age	Nominal earnings	Indexing factor	Indexed earnings	Top 35
1972	20	$5,167	6.2129	**$32,102**	✓	23	$5,194	5.7069	$29,641	
1973	21	$5,525	5.8471	**$32,305**	✓	24	$5,747	5.3708	$30,866	
1974	22	$5,847	5.5190	**$32,270**	✓	25	$6,262	5.0695	$31,745	
1975	23	$6,140	5.1352	$31,530		26	$6,746	4.7169	$31,821	
1976	24	$6,452	4.8037	$30,994		27	$7,253	4.4125	$32,004	
1977	25	$7,088	4.5321	**$32,124**	✓	28	$8,135	4.1630	**$33,866**	✓
1978	26	$7,535	4.1987	**$31,637**	✓	29	$8,815	3.8567	**$33,997**	✓
1979	27	$7,988	3.8610	$30,841		30	$9,511	3.5465	$33,731	
1980	28	$8,589	3.5419	$30,422		31	$10,396	3.2534	$33,823	
1981	29	$9,186	3.2180	$29,560		32	$11,293	2.9559	$33,381	
1982	30	$9,742	3.0501	$29,714		33	$12,151	2.8016	**$34,043**	✓
1983	31	$10,521	2.9084	$30,599		34	$13,305	2.6715	**$35,544**	✓
1984	32	$11,447	2.7469	$31,444		35	$14,667	2.5232	**$37,007**	✓
1985	33	$12,485	2.6347	**$32,894**	✓	36	$16,197	2.4201	**$39,198**	✓
1986	34	$13,748	2.5587	**$35,177**	✓	37	$18,051	2.3503	**$42,425**	✓
1987	35	$14,513	2.4053	**$34,908**	✓	38	$19,273	2.2094	**$42,582**	✓
1988	36	$15,228	2.2924	**$34,909**	✓	39	$20,445	2.1057	**$43,051**	✓
1989	37	$16,131	2.2051	**$35,571**	✓	40	$21,887	2.0255	**$44,332**	✓
1990	38	$16,827	2.1077	**$35,467**	✓	41	$23,063	1.9361	**$44,652**	✓
1991	39	$17,335	2.0320	**$35,225**	✓	42	$23,994	1.8665	**$44,785**	✓
1992	40	$18,450	1.9325	**$35,654**	✓	43	$25,779	1.7751	**$45,759**	✓
1993	41	$19,369	1.9160	**$37,111**	✓	44	$27,311	1.7599	**$48,065**	✓
1994	42	$20,146	1.8659	**$37,590**	✓	45	$28,659	1.7139	**$49,119**	✓
1995	43	$21,087	1.7940	**$37,830**	✓	46	$30,257	1.6479	**$49,859**	✓
1996	44	$21,884	1.7103	**$37,429**	✓	47	$31,663	1.5710	**$49,744**	✓
1997	45	$23,024	1.6160	**$37,208**	✓	48	$33,582	1.4844	**$49,850**	✓
1998	46	$23,234	1.5357	**$35,680**	✓	49	$34,155	1.4106	**$48,179**	✓
1999	47	$23,869	1.4546	**$34,720**	✓	50	$35,360	1.3361	**$47,245**	✓
2000	48	$24,839	1.3784	**$34,238**	✓	51	$37,071	1.2661	**$46,936**	✓
2001	49	$26,067	1.3463	**$35,093**	✓	52	$39,188	1.2366	**$48,460**	✓
2002	50	$27,602	1.3329	**$36,791**	✓	53	$41,790	1.2243	**$51,165**	✓
2003	51	$29,061	1.3011	**$37,811**	✓	54	$44,305	1.1951	**$52,950**	✓
2004	52	$30,696	1.2433	**$38,164**	✓	55	$47,115	1.1420	**$53,807**	✓
2005	53	$32,410	1.1994	**$38,873**	✓	56	$50,076	1.1017	**$55,169**	✓
2006	54	$33,200	1.1467	**$38,071**	✓	57	$51,629	1.0533	**$54,381**	✓
2007	55	$33,551	1.0969	**$36,803**	✓	58	$52,503	1.0076	**$52,901**	✓
2008	56	$34,388	1.0723	**$36,873**	✓	59	$54,148	1.0000	**$54,148**	✓
2009	57	$36,400	1.0887	**$39,628**	✓	60	$56,092	1.0000	**$56,092**	✓
2010	58	$37,900	1.0635	**$40,308**	✓	61	$56,408	1.0000	**$56,408**	✓
2011	59	$38,113	1.0312	**$39,303**	✓	62	$57,103	1.0000	**$57,103**	✓
2012	60	$39,551	1.0000	**$39,551**	✓	63	$59,955	1.0000	**$59,955**	✓
2013	61	$40,000	1.0000	**$40,000**	✓	64	$60,000	1.0000	**$60,000**	✓
2014	62	$42,000	1.0000	**$42,000**	✓	65	$62,000	1.0000	**$62,000**	✓
			Highest-35 total	$1,271,316				Highest-35 total	$1,684,777	
	Total ¸ 420 Months		AIME	$3,027				AIME	$4,011	

Calculating the Worker's Primary Insurance Amount (PIA)

Generally, the PIA is the actual Social Security retirement benefit for the single retiree who retires at full retirement age. For those who retire early or late and for family or surviving beneficiaries, the PIA is not the actual amount of the benefit but the PIA is used to determine their actual benefit.

The PIA is a result of applying the AIME to the PIA formula. This benefit formula changes the dollar amounts (by CPI), but not the percentages, from year to year and depends on the worker's first year of eligibility, that is, when the worker turns 62, becomes disabled, or dies.

The PIA is the sum of three separate percentages of portions of the AIME. These portions are also known as "bend points." For the year 2015, these portions are the first $826 of AIME, the amount of AIME between $826 and $4,980, and the AIME over $4,980. The bend points for 2015 are thus $826 and $4,980. For individuals who first become eligible for retirement benefits or disability insurance benefits in 2015 or who die in 2015 before becoming eligible for benefits, their PIA will be the sum of:

90 percent of the first $826 of their AIME, *plus*
32 percent of their AIME over $826 up to $4,980, *plus*
15 percent of their AIME that exceeds $4,980.
(Maximum PIA for 2015 is $2,663)

The sum of these three calculations is rounded down to the next lower multiple of $0.10 (if it is not already a multiple of $0.10). For calculations in subsequent years, it is useful to know how to determine a given year's bend points. Exhibit 10.10 shows the established bend points from 1981 through 2015.

EXHIBIT 10.10

BEND POINT TABLE

Dollar Amounts (bend points) in PIA Formula		
Year	First	Second
1981	$211	$1,274
1982	$230	$1,388
1983	$254	$1,528
1984	$267	$1,612
1985	$280	$1,691
1986	$297	$1,790
1987	$310	$1,866
1988	$319	$1,922
1989	$339	$2,044
1990	$356	$2,145
1991	$370	$2,230
1992	$387	$2,333
1993	$401	$2,420
1994	$422	$2,545
1995	$426	$2,567
1996	$437	$2,635
1997	$455	$2,741
1998	$477	$2,875
1999	$505	$3,043
2000	$531	$3,202
2001	$561	$3,381
2002	$592	$3,567
2003	$606	$3,653
2004	$612	$3,689
2005	$627	$3,779
2006	$656	$3,955
2007	$680	$4,100
2008	$711	$4,288
2009	$744	$4,483
2010	$761	$4,586
2011	$749	$4,517
2012	$767	$4,624
2013	$791	$4,768
2014	$816	$4,917
2015	$826	$4,980

Source: Social Security Administration (www.ssa.gov)

These figures for the PIA rise each year based on a cost-of-living adjustment (**COLA**) that is applied to reflect changes in the cost of living. Recent COLAs, which are based on inflation, are shown in Exhibit 10.11.

Cost-of-Living Adjustment (COLA) Per Year*

EXHIBIT 10.11

Year	COLA	Year	COLA	Year	COLA
1991	3.7%	1999	2.5%	2007	2.3%
1992	3.0%	2000	3.5%	2008	5.8%
1993	2.6%	2001	2.6%	2009	0.0%
1994	2.8%	2002	1.4%	2010	0.0%
1995	2.6%	2003	2.1%	2011	3.6%
1996	2.9%	2004	2.7%	2012	1.7%
1997	2.1%	2005	4.1%	2013	1.5%
1998	1.3%	2006	3.3%	2014	1.7%

* *Source: www.ssa.gov/oact/cola/colaseries.html*

As mentioned, the calculation of the Social Security retirement benefit skews benefits toward the low-income worker. This design is evident in the PIA calculation with a 90 percent wage replacement for extremely low income and only a 15 percent wage replacement for higher income. The following exhibit illustrates the wage replacement ratio provided by Social Security at full retirement age based on the annualized income, which is AIME multiplied by 12 months.

Wage Replacement Ratio from Social Security

EXHIBIT 10.12

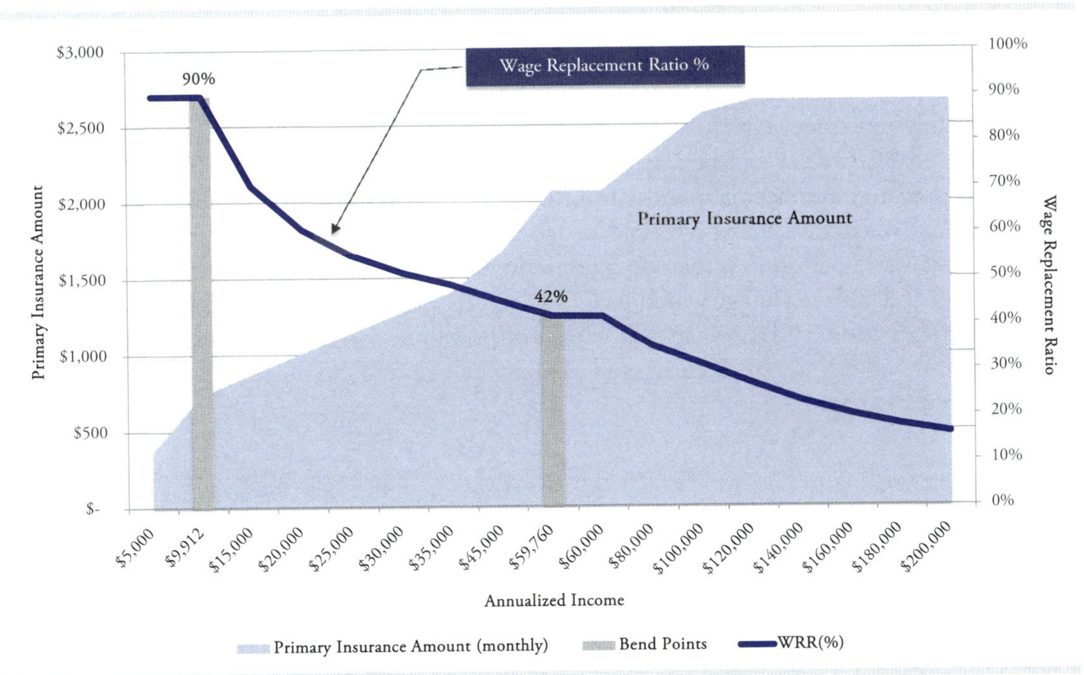

Annual COLA increases are determined by October of each year and go into effect in time so that they first appear on monthly benefit checks received in the following January. In 2015, the maximum monthly retirement benefit for retirees at full retirement age is $2,663, compared to $2,642 in 2014.

Early and Late Retirement Options

Workers entitled to retirement benefits can currently take early retirement benefits as early as age 62. The worker will receive a reduced benefit because he will receive more monthly benefit payments than if the worker had waited and retired at full retirement age. The reduction to one's monthly benefit for early retirement is permanent. Conversely, a delayed or postponed retirement will permanently increase the monthly retirement benefit for a worker.[1]

For each month of early retirement, workers will receive a reduction in their monthly retirement benefit of 5/9 of one percent for up to the first 36 months. For subsequent months of early retirement, the permanent reduction percentage is 5/12 of one percent per month.

EXAMPLE 10.17

Assume Robin begins receiving benefits at the earliest possible age, which is age 62. Then, the benefit amount for Robin is reduced for 48 months of retirement before Robin's normal retirement age, which is 66 years. Assume Robin's PIA before reduction is $1,421.90. The PIA is thus reduced to a monthly benefit of $1,066.43 (rounded to $1066.40).

PIA	$1,421.90
5/9 x 1% x 36 months	Less 20% reduction
5/12 x 1% x 12 months	Less 5% reduction
Monthly Benefit	$1,066.43

Although the full retirement age will increase to age 67, workers will still have the option of taking early retirement at age 62. However, the reduction percentage that is applied to the monthly retirement benefit will increase until 2027. Before 2000, those who retired at age 62 received 80 percent of their retirement benefit, but the increase in full retirement age has increased the number of months from 62 until full retirement age. For instance, in the year 2009, covered workers who retired at age 62 received 75 percent of their monthly retirement benefit, or 25 percent less than their full retirement benefit. By 2027, covered workers retiring at age 62 (full retirement age would be 67) will receive only 70 percent of their monthly retirement benefit. Exhibit 10.13, which was compiled by the Social Security Administration, shows the phase-in of the Social Security full retirement age and accompanying reductions for early retirement at age 62.

1. A spouse can choose to retire as early as age 62, but doing so may result in a benefit as little as 32.5 percent of the worker's primary insurance amount. A spousal benefit is reduced 25/36 of one percent for each month before normal retirement age, up to 36 months. If the number of months exceeds 36, then the benefit is further reduced 5/12 of one percent per month. Source: SSA.gov.

EXHIBIT 10.13

Social Security Full Retirement and Reductions* by Age

Year of Birth	Full Retirement Age	Age 62 Reduction Months	Monthly Percent Reduction	Total Percent Reduction
1937 or earlier	65	36	0.555	20.00
1938	65 & 2 months	38	0.548	20.83
1939	65 & 4 months	40	0.541	21.67
1940	65 & 6 months	42	0.535	22.50
1941	65 & 8 months	44	0.530	23.33
1942	65 & 10 months	46	0.525	24.17
1943-1954	66	48	0.520	25.00
1955	66 & 2 months	50	0.516	25.84
1956	66 & 4 months	52	0.512	26.66
1957	66 & 6 months	54	0.509	27.50
1958	66 & 8 months	56	0.505	28.33
1959	66 & 10 months	58	0.502	29.17
1960 and later	67	60	0.500	30.00

**Percentage monthly and total reductions are approximate due to rounding. The actual reductions are 0.555 or 5/9 of 1 percent per month for the first 36 months and 0.416 or 5/12 of 1 percent for subsequent months.*

Source: Social Security Administration (www.ssa.gov)

No matter what the full retirement age is, a worker may start receiving benefits as early as age 62 and can also retire at any time between age 62 and full retirement age. However, if a worker starts benefits at one of these early ages, the benefits are reduced a fraction of a percent for each month before the full retirement age.

EXAMPLE 10.18

Assume that Josephine, a worker born in 1939, decided to retire on her 62nd birthday. Assume that her full retirement benefit would have been $1,429.20 at age 65 and four months, her full retirement age. If she retires at age 62, what is her monthly retirement benefit?

The answer is $1,119. Josephine retired 40 months early. The monthly retirement benefit reduction percentage is 1/180 (5/9 x 1% = 1/180 = 0.0056) for the first 36 months (1/180 x 36 = 20 percent) and 1/240 (5/12 x 1% = 1/240 = 0.0042) for the 4 subsequent months of early retirement (1/240 x 4 = 1.6668 percent), yielding a total permanent reduction to Josephine's monthly retirement benefit of 21.6667 percent. 21.6667 percent x $1,429.20 = $309.66. $1,429.20 - $309.66 = $1,119.50 (rounded).

EXAMPLE 10.19

What if Josephine retired at age 64 and six months? What is her permanent monthly retirement benefit (subject to COLA increases)? Note she retired 10 months early from normal retirement age.

The answer is $1,349. 1/180 x 10 = 5.5556 percent. 5.5556 percent x $1,429.20 = $79.40. $1,429.20 - $79.40 = $1,349.80 (rounded).

For those covered individuals who take late retirement, or when benefits are lost due to the earnings limitation, the monthly retirement benefit and the benefit paid to the surviving spouse will increase each year (until age 70) as follows:

EXHIBIT 10.14

PERCENTAGE INCREASES FOR DELAYED RETIREMENT

Increase For Year Born	Annual Percentage Increase Each Year Of Late Retirement	After Age
1917-1924	3.0%	65
1925-1926	3.5%	65
1927-1928	4.0%	65
1929-1930	4.5%	65
1931-1932	5.0%	65
1933-1934	5.5%	65
1935-1936	6.0%	65
1937	6.5%	65
1938	6.5%	65 and 2 months
1939	7.0%	65 and 4 months
1940	7.0%	65 and 6 months
1941	7.5%	65 and 8 months
1942	7.5%	65 and 10 months
1943 or later	8.0%	66

EXAMPLE 10.20

Jeanette will turn 66 in 2015 (thus she was born after 1942). She is considering taking Social Security retirement benefits at age 62, 66, or 70. Assume her monthly expected benefit is $1,000 at full retirement age, expected inflation is 4%, and her life expectancy is 90. Calculate the present value of her benefits at ages 62, 66, and 70 (A, B, or C).

Choice A – Begin Benefits at age 62.

PMT	$750	($1,000 less 25% reduction)
N	336	(90-62) x 12
i	0.3333	4/12
FV	0	
$PV_{@62}$	**$151,450.19**	

Choice B – Begin Benefits at age 66.

PMT	$1,000	Full benefit at full retirement age
N	288	(90-66) x 12
i	0.3333	4/12
FV	0	
$PV_{@66}$	$184,948.61	

Discount to age 62 for comparison.

PMT	$0	
N	4	(66-62)
i	4	
FV	$184,948.61	
$PV_{@62}$	**$158,094.84**	

Choice C – Begin Benefits at age 70.

PMT	$1,320	($1,000 plus 8% x 4 years increase)
N	240	(90-70) x 12
i	0.3333	4/12
FV	0	
$PV_{@70}$	$217,828.85	

Discount to age 62 for comparison.

PMT	$0	
N	8	(70-62)
i	4	
FV	$217,828.85	
$PV_{@62}$	**$159,165.41**	

As you can see, even though the benefit is reduced if Jeanette begins her benefit early, the PV of the total benefit at age 62 is not much less than if she took the benefit at age 66. Similarly, if she begins her payments later, her yearly payments will be higher but the PV of the benefit at age 62 is not much more than if she had taken benefits at age 66. The significance here is that all things being equal, the acceleration or delay of benefit generally has little impact on the PV of the benefit at age 62. However, the choice of retirement age is significant when considering the annual income needed to maintain one's standard of living.

Another critical factor in this analysis is the life expectancy of the worker. If the life expectancy is significantly less than what was assumed it might not make sense to delay benefits. Another factor that was not considered is the tax impact of benefits, which is discussed later in this chapter.

Although the calculations explained above can provide estimates of the Social Security benefits a retiring worker may receive, an advisor should have the client obtain his entire Social Security earnings history up to the moment of retirement from the Social Security Administration to get the most accurate benefit estimate.

EXHIBIT 10.15

Social Security Benefits at Different Ages

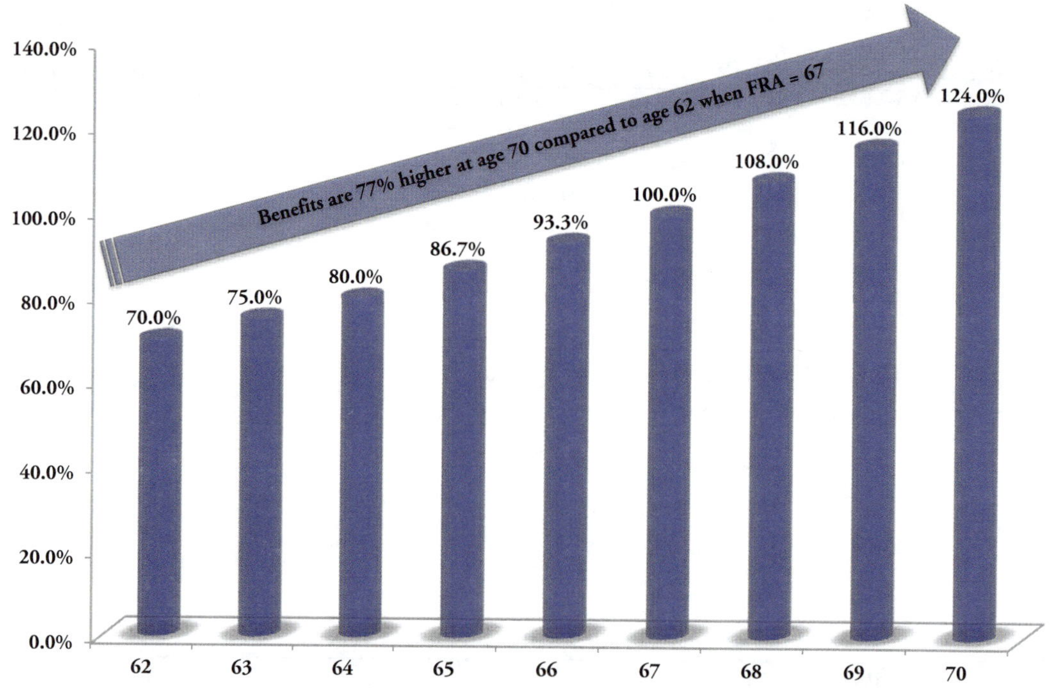

Reduction of Social Security Benefits

Besides early retirement, there are two other situations in which beneficiaries can have benefits reduced. The first instance is a reduction of benefits based on earnings, referred to as the **retirement earnings limitations test**. The other instance is through taxation of Social Security benefits. Both of these measures reduce one's net benefits.

A person may continue to work even though he is considered "retired" under Social Security. For a retiree who receives Social Security retirement benefits before normal retirement age, the earnings received by the beneficiary cannot exceed certain limitations without triggering a reduction in Social Security benefits. Beneficiaries can earn up to the limitation amount and receive all of their benefits, but if their earnings exceed the designated limit for the calendar year, then benefits will be reduced or eliminated. The law provides for earnings limitations of $15,720 for those under the full retirement age for 2015. The Social Security Administration reduces $1 in benefits for each $2 earned by those beneficiaries above $15,720. In the year that the retiree reaches full retirement age, $1 in benefits will be deducted for each $3 earned above the given year's limit but only for earnings before the month the retiree reaches full retirement age. For 2015, the limit for earnings in the year the retiree reaches full retirement age is $41,880. The earnings limitation increases every year as median earnings nationwide increase. Once the retiree reaches normal retirement age, benefits will not be reduced regardless of the earnings limitations.

In the event that a beneficiary, who is younger than normal retirement age, has earnings that exceed the limitation, that beneficiary's benefits will be reduced depending on his or her age. The beneficiary must file an annual report of his earnings to the Social Security Administration by April 15 of the year following the year worked and must provide the exact earnings for that year and an estimate for the current year. The filing of a federal tax return with the IRS does not satisfy the filing requirement with the Social Security Administration. Also, the wages count toward the earnings limitation when they are earned, not when paid, whereas income for the self-employed normally counts when paid, not earned. If other family members receive benefits based on the beneficiary's Social Security record, then the total family benefits may be affected by the beneficiary's earnings that exceed the earnings limitation. In such a case, the Social Security Administration will withhold not only the worker's benefits but will withhold those benefits payable to family members as well.

Quick Quiz 10.3

1. Social Security benefits are based on the average of the three highest paid years for a covered worker.
   a. True
   b. False

2. Full retirement age for Social Security is decreasing because of the trend of individuals retiring early.
   a. True
   b. False

False, False.

EXAMPLE 10.21

Matthew is 64 years old and despite being retired from his occupation as an attorney, earned $20,000 in 2015 while working as a golf instructor at a local golf course. Matthew's monthly retirement benefit from Social Security is normally $1,200, which totals $14,400 for the entire year. Because Matthew exceeded the retirement earnings limitation, how much money will be reduced from Matthew's Social Security retirement benefit for 2015?

Matthew's total earnings in 2015	$20,000
Earnings limitation	($15,720)
Remainder excess	$4,280
One-half deduction	÷ 2
Benefits reduced by:	**$2,140**

The Social Security Administration will reduce Matthew's benefits for the year by $2,140. Matthew will receive $12,260 in retirement benefits ($14,400 annual retirement benefit less $2,140 reduction). Matthew's total income for 2015 will be $32,260, instead of $34,400.

EXAMPLE 10.22

Mike is 67 years old. He has a full-time job working as a masseur. This year (2015) he anticipates earning $22,000 from his job. How much, in dollars, will Mike's Social Security benefits be reduced for the earnings test?

None, because Mike is over normal retirement age.

Generally, only wages and net self-employment income count towards the retirement earnings limitation, whereas income from savings, investments, and insurance does not. The following is a nonexclusive list of sources of income that DO NOT count toward the earnings limitation:

- Pension or retirement income
- 401(k) plan and IRA withdrawals
- Dividends and interest from investments
- Capital gains
- Rental income
- Workers' compensation benefits (generally not payable after a worker has retired)
- Unemployment benefits
- Court-awarded judgments, less components of award that include lost wages
- Contest winnings

REAPPLYING FOR SOCIAL SECURITY BENEFITS

The Social Security Administration will allow a recipient of benefits to increase their benefits by withdrawing and reapplying at a future date. When someone applies for Social Security at age 62, their benefits are reduced. For example, if full retirement age is age 67, then the benefit at age 62 is only 70 percent of what it would be at full retirement age. In addition, it is only about 53 percent of what it would be at age 70.

KEY CONCEPTS

1. How are Social Security benefits taxed?
2. What benefits are available from Social Security other than retirement benefits?
3. What is the maximum family benefit?

The process for withdrawing and reapplying is relatively simple, but requires that all of the Social Security benefits be paid back to the Social Security Administration. To withdraw, the Request for Withdrawal of Application (Form SSA-521) must be completed. Once this form is completed and approved, the person may reapply at a future date.

The Social Security Administration modified the withdrawal rules such that application withdrawals are limited to one per lifetime and the withdrawal must occur within the first 12 months of the first month of enrollment. This change occurred because of the potential abuse from withdrawing and reapplying to receive a higher benefit. Consider the following example, which was permitted prior to December 8, 2010 and is no longer permitted.

EXAMPLE 10.23

Amy's full retirement age is 67 and her expected benefit at age 67 is $1,000. If Amy began receiving benefits at age 62, she would receive $700 per month. If she wanted to withdraw at age 70 and reapply, then she would need to return $67,200 (8 years x months x $700 per month), which represents the benefits she received. Her new benefit would be $1,240 (3 year delay from full retirement age with 8 percent credits per year) per month without considering the impact of inflation and cost-of-living adjustments.

The simple payback period is determined by dividing what she has to return ($67,200) by the increase in her monthly benefit ($540). This calculation equates to approximately 124 months or 10 years and 4 months.

Another way to evaluate this option is to compare the annuity that is generated from the investment to a commercial annuity from a financial services company. Amy can generate an annual annuity of $6,480 ($540 x 12 months) from an investment of $67,200, which equates to 9.64 percent. This amount should be compared to what the market is offering. In addition, the "annuity" from Social Security may also have a positive impact on a surviving spouse who might benefit from a higher annual benefit.

This withdrawal and reapplying process was a technique that had received a large amount of press, which ultimately resulted in the Social Security Administration greatly restricting the rules. Today, withdrawals can be made, but must be done within 12 months. This new limitation eliminates the "interest-free loan" issue, but still allows beneficiaries to change their benefits due to unforeseen circumstances within the first year of applying.

TAXATION OF SOCIAL SECURITY BENEFITS

Apart from the earnings limitation, some beneficiaries may be required to pay income tax on their Social Security benefits. For persons with substantial income in addition to Social Security benefits, up to 85 percent of their annual Social Security benefits may be subject to federal income tax. The Social Security Administration is concerned with a beneficiary's **modified adjusted gross income** (MAGI). For purposes of Social Security, MAGI is equal to the taxpayer's adjusted gross income plus tax exempt interest, including:

- interest earned on savings bonds used for higher education;
- amounts excluded from the taxpayer's income for employer-provided adoption assistance;
- amounts deducted for interest paid for educational loans;
- amounts deducted as qualified tuition expense; and
- income earned in a foreign country, a U.S. possession, or Puerto Rico, that is excluded from income.

EXAMPLE 10.24

Last year Charlie and Eva had adjusted gross income of $40,000. They also had the following items:

- Eva spent 3 months during the year in Mexico visiting her mother. While she was there, she earned $5,000 that has been excluded from their AGI.
- While in Mexico, Eva fell in love with a little orphan girl. Luckily, Charlie's company has an Adoption Assistance Program. The program paid $8,000 towards the adoption and the amount was excluded from Charlie's AGI.
- Charlie has been attending night school for several years and has several student loans. Last year he paid and deducted $200 in student loan interest. He also took a qualified tuition expense deduction for $600 he paid to the school.

- Charlie and Eva had $900 in interest. $400 was from tax-exempt bonds and the remaining $500 was from corporate bonds.

Charlie and Eva's MAGI for last year is:

Adjusted Gross Income (AGI)	$40,000
+ Foreign Income Excluded	$5,000
+ Adoption Assistance Excluded	$8,000
+ Student Loan Interest Deduction	$200
+ Qualified Tuition Expense Deduction	$600
+ Tax-Exempt Bonds Interest	$400
= Modified Adjusted Gross Income (MAGI)	**$54,200**

Note that the $500 of corporate-bond interest has already been included in Charlie and Eva's AGI.

Generally, 50 percent of Social Security benefits may be subject to federal income taxes for beneficiaries who file a federal tax return as an "individual" and have a modified adjusted gross income between $25,000 and $34,000. For those with a modified adjusted gross income plus one-half of Social Security greater than $34,000, up to 85 percent of their Social Security benefits may be subject to federal income taxation. For those beneficiaries that file a joint federal tax return and have a modified adjusted gross income with their spouse between $32,000 and $44,000, 50 percent of their Social Security benefits will be subject to federal income taxes. Finally, if beneficiaries filing a joint tax return have a modified adjusted gross income plus one-half Social Security benefits that exceeds $44,000, 85 percent of their Social Security benefits may be subject to federal income taxation.

In summary, for persons with substantial income in addition to their Social Security benefits, up to 85 percent of their annual benefits may be subject to federal income tax.

EXHIBIT 10.16

Social Security Hurdle Amounts

	Married Filing Jointly	All Others Except MFS = 0
1st Hurdle	$32,000	$25,000
2nd Hurdle	$44,000	$34,000

If MAGI plus one half of Social Security benefits exceeds the first hurdle but not the second, the taxable amount of Social Security benefits is the lesser of:

- 50% Social Security Benefits, or
- 50% [MAGI + 0.50 (Social Security Benefits) - Hurdle 1].

EXAMPLE 10.25

A married couple has interest income of $18,000 and Social Security benefits of $20,000. What amount of their Social Security benefits must be included in their taxable income?

Lesser of:

- 0.50($20,000) = $10,000, or
- 0.50 [$18,000 + 0.50 (20,000) - 32,000] = Negative

They would have $0 inclusion due to a negative result.

EXAMPLE 10.26

A married couple has income of $30,000 and Social Security benefits of $20,000. What amount of their Social Security benefits must be included in their taxable income?

Lesser of:

- 0.50($20,000) = $10,000, or
- 0.50 [30,000 + 0.50 (20,000) - 32,000] = $4,000

They would have $4,000 of Social Security benefits included in taxable income.

If MAGI plus one-half the Social Security benefits exceeds the second hurdle, the taxable amount of Social Security benefits is the lesser of:

- 85% Social Security Benefits, or
- 85% [MAGI + 0.50 (Social Security Benefits) - Hurdle 2], plus the lesser of:
  - $6,000 for MFJ or $4,500 for all other taxpayers, or
  - The taxable amount calculated under the 50% formula and only considering Hurdle 1.

EXAMPLE 10.27

A married couple has income of $60,000 and Social Security benefits of $20,000. What amount of their Social Security benefits must be included in their taxable income?

0.85 ($20,000) = **$17,000**

0.85 [$60,000 + 0.50 ($20,000) - $44,000] =	$22,100
Plus the lesser of:	
• $6,000, or	
• 0.50($20,000) = $10,000, or	
• 0.50[$60,000+0.50($20,000)-$32,000] = $19,000	
	$6,000
	$28,100

Therefore, **$17,000** must be included in their taxable income.

EXAMPLE 10.28

A married couple has income of $45,000 and Social Security benefits of $20,000. What amount of their Social Security benefits must be included in their taxable income?

0.85 ($20,000) = **$17,000**

0.85 [$45,000 + 0.50 ($20,000) - $44,000] =	$9,350
Plus the lesser of:	
• $6,000, or	
• 0.50($20,000) = $10,000, or	
• 0.50[$45,000+0.50($20,000)-$32,000] = $11,500	
	$6,000
	$15,350

Therefore, **$15,350** must be included in their taxable income.

EXAMPLE 10.29

Last year Michelle, a single taxpayer, received $10,400 in Social Security benefits. For the entire year, she had an adjusted gross income of $28,000. How much, if any, of her Social Security benefit is taxable?

First, determine Michelle's modified adjusted gross income. Modified adjusted gross income is the sum of adjusted gross income, nontaxable interest, and foreign-earned income. One-half of Michelle's Social Security benefits must then be added to her MAGI. For Michelle, the equation is as follows: $28,000 + [$10,400 x 0.50] = $33,200. Since Michelle's modified adjusted gross income plus one-half of her Social Security benefits is between the two base amounts for a single individual of $25,000 and $34,000, we can use the following formula to determine her taxable amount. The income tax base will be the lesser of 50% of her Social Security benefits <u>*OR*</u> 50% of the difference between Michelle's modified adjusted gross income plus one-half of her Social Security benefits less the base amount of $25,000. Based on this formula, Michelle will be subject to income tax on $4,100 of her Social Security benefit.

- 0.50($10,400) = $5,200
- 0.50($33,200 - $25,000) = $4,100 (the LESSER amount)

EXAMPLE 10.30

A married couple files jointly and has an adjusted gross income of $38,000, no tax-exempt interest, and $11,000 of Social Security benefits. How much, if any, of their Social Security benefits is included in gross income?

The lesser of the following:

- 0.50 ($11,000) = $5,500, or
- 0.50[$38,000+0.50($11,000)-$32,000]=0.50($11,500) = $5,750

They will include $5,500 in gross income. If the couple's adjusted gross income was $15,000 and their Social Security benefits totaled $5,000, none of the benefits would be taxable since 0.50 [$15,000 + 0.50 ($5,000) - $32,000] is negative.

EXAMPLE 10.31

Frank and Lois, married filing jointly, have tax-free municipal bond interest of $2,000. Assuming that Frank and Lois have differing AGI amounts ranging from $20,000 to $50,000, the Social Security amount includable in taxable income is shown below. Thus, if Frank and Lois have $20,000 in AGI, then only $1,000 of the Social Security benefit is included (4% of the benefit is included), but if they have AGI of $50,000 then $20,400 is includable (85% of the benefit is included). Notice that once an individual is substantially over the second hurdle they can expect to include 85% of the Social Security benefit.

Preliminary AGI	$20,000	$25,000	$30,000	$35,000	$40,000	$45,000	$50,000
Tax free bond interest	$2,000	$2,000	$2,000	$2,000	$2,000	$2,000	$2,000
MAGI	$22,000	$27,000	$32,000	$37,000	$42,000	$47,000	$52,000
50% of Social Security	$12,000	$12,000	$12,000	$12,000	$12,000	$12,000	$12,000
MAGI plus 1/2 Social Security	$34,000	$39,000	$44,000	$49,000	$54,000	$59,000	$64,000
First hurdle	$32,000	$32,000	$32,000	$32,000	$32,000	$32,000	$32,000
Second hurdle	$44,000	$44,000	$44,000	$44,000	$44,000	$44,000	$44,000
Excess of income over first hurdle	$2,000	$7,000	$12,000	$17,000	$22,000	$27,000	$32,000
Excess of income over second hurdle	$0	$0	$0	$5,000	$10,000	$15,000	$20,000
1. 50% of SSB	$12,000	$12,000	$12,000				
2. 50% [MAGI + 0.50 (SSB) - Hurdle 1)	**$1,000**	**$3,500**	**$6,000**				
3. 85% of SSB				$20,400	$20,400	$20,400	**$20,400**
4. [85% [MAGI + 0.5 (SSB)- Hurdle 2]] + 6000				**$10,250**	**$14,500**	**$18,750**	$23,000
5. [85% [MAGI + 0.5 (SSB)- Hurdle 2]] + 50% [MAGI + 0.50 (SSB) - Hurdle 1]				$14,450	$18,700	$22,950	$27,200
6. [85% [MAGI + 0.5 (SSB)- Hurdle 2]] + 50% of SSB				$16,250	$20,500	$24,750	$29,000
Includable portion of Social Security	$1,000	$3,500	$6,000	$10,250	$14,500	$18,750	$20,400
Percent of SS Taxed	4%	15%	25%	43%	60%	78%	85%

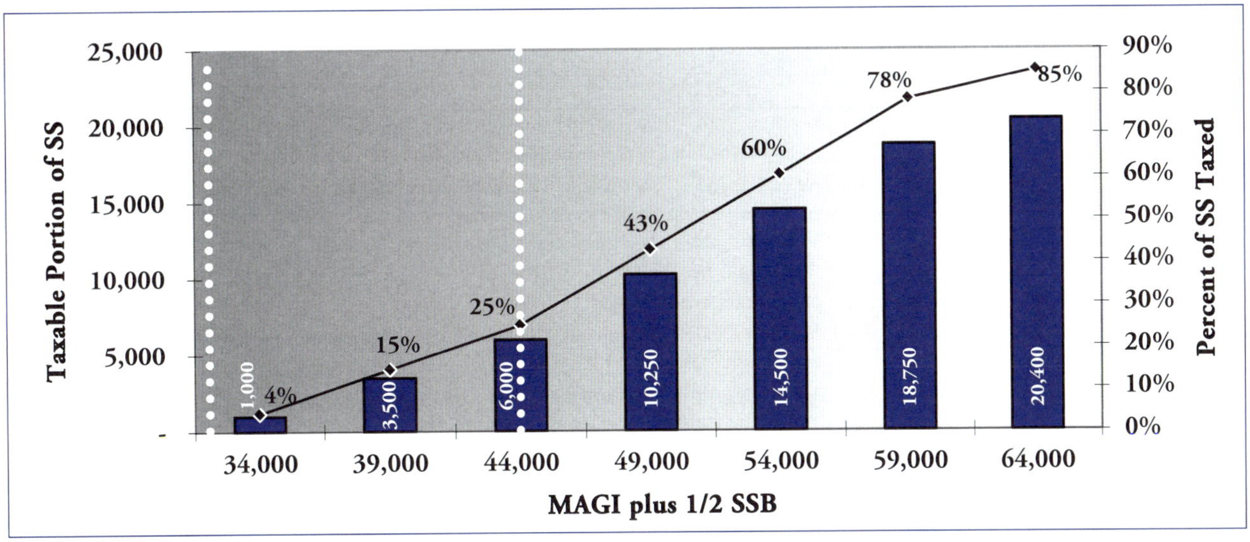

OTHER SOCIAL SECURITY BENEFITS

DISABILITY BENEFITS AND DISABILITY INSURED

Benefits are payable at any age to workers who have enough Social Security credits and who have a severe physical or mental impairment that is expected to prevent them from doing "substantial" work for a year or more or who have a condition that is expected to result in death. Workers are insured for disability if they are fully insured and, except for persons who are blind or disabled at age 31 or older, have a total of at least 20 quarters of coverage during the 40-quarter period ending with the quarter in which the worker became disabled. Workers who are disabled before age 31 must have total quarters of coverage equal to one-half the calendar quarters that have elapsed since the worker reached age 21 ending in the quarter in which the worker became disabled. However, a minimum of six quarters is required.

EXHIBIT 10.17

WORK CREDITS FOR DISABILITY BENEFITS

Born After 1929, Become Disabled at Age:	Number of Credits You Need:
31 through 42	20
44	22
46	24
48	26
50	28
52	30
54	32
56	34
58	36
60	38
62 or older	40

- Before age 24 - The disabled individual may qualify if they have 6 credits earned in the 3-year period ending when the disability starts.
- Age 24 to 31 - The disabled individual may qualify if they have credit for working half the time between age 21 and the time they become disabled. For example, if they become disabled at age 27, they would need credit for 3 years of work (12 credits) out of the past 6 years (between ages 21 and 27).
- Age 31 or older - In general, the disabled individual needs to have the number of work credits shown in the chart. Unless they are blind, they must have earned at least 20 of the credits in the 10 years immediately before they became disabled.

In 2015, earnings of $1,090 or more per month are considered substantial; therefore, a worker earning more than $1,090 per month would not be eligible for Social Security disability benefits. (If the individual is blind, then the amount is increased to $1,820.) The disability program includes incentives to smooth the disabled individual's transition back into the workforce, including continuation of benefits and healthcare coverage. Disability under the Social Security system is defined as an inability to engage in substantial gainful activity by reason of a physical or mental impairment expected to last at least 12 months or result in death. The impairment must be of such severity that the applicant is not only unable to do his previous work but cannot, considering age, education, and work experience, engage in any other kind of substantial gainful work that exists in the national economy.

Family Benefits

If an individual is eligible for retirement or disability benefits, other members of the individual's family might receive benefits as well. Family members who may receive retirement or disability benefits include the following:

- A spouse, if the spouse is 62 years old, caring for a child under age 16, or caring for a child who was disabled before age 22.
- A child, if the child is unmarried and under age 18, under age 19 but still in school, or age 18 or older but disabled.

For those workers who are entitled to retirement or disability benefits, an ex-spouse who was married to the worker for more than 10 years could also be eligible for retirement benefits based on the worker's record.

A child's benefit stops the month before the child reaches 18, unless the child is unmarried and is either disabled or is a full-time elementary or secondary school student. Approximately five months before the child's 18th birthday, the person receiving the child's benefits will get a form explaining how benefits can continue. A child whose benefits stop at 18 can have them started again if the child becomes disabled before reaching 22 or becomes a full-time elementary or secondary school student before reaching 19. If the child continues to receive benefits after age 18 due to a disability, the child also may qualify for SSI disability benefits. When a student's 19th birthday occurs during a school term, benefits can be continued up to two months to allow completion of the school term.

Survivors' Benefits

If a worker earned enough Social Security credits during his lifetime, certain members of the worker's family may be eligible for benefits when the worker dies. The family members of the deceased worker who may be entitled to survivors' benefits include:

- A widow or widower age 60, age 50 if disabled, or any age if caring for a child under age 16 or a disabled child.
- A child of the deceased worker, if the child is unmarried and under age 18, under age 19 but still in school, or age 18 or older but disabled.
- Parents of the deceased worker, if the deceased worker was their primary means of support.

A special one-time payment of $255 may be made to a deceased worker's spouse or minor children upon death. If a spouse was living with the beneficiary at the time of death, the spouse will receive a one-time payment of $255. The payment may be made to a spouse who was not living with the beneficiary at the time of death or an ex-spouse if the spouse or ex-spouse was receiving Social Security benefits based on the deceased's earnings record. If there is no surviving spouse, a child (or children) who is eligible for benefits on the deceased's work record in the month of death may claim the payment.

THE MAXIMUM FAMILY BENEFIT

When a person dies, the deceased's survivors receive a percentage of the worker's Social Security benefits ranging from 75 percent to 100 percent each. There is a limit on the amount of monthly Social Security benefits that may be paid to a family. This limit is called the **maximum family benefit** and it is determined through a formula based on the worker's PIA. While the limit varies, it is equal to roughly 150 to 180 percent of the deceased worker's PIA. If the sum of the family members' benefits exceeds the limit, the family members' benefits are proportionately reduced. For old-age and survivor family benefits, the formula computes the sum of four separate percentages of portions of the worker's PIA. For 2015, these portions are the first $1,056 of PIA, the amount between $1,056 and $1,524, the amount between $1,524 and $1,987 and the amount over $1,987. These are the bend points for the maximum family benefit formula for the year 2015, with the following percentage calculations:

150 percent of the first $1,056 of the worker's PIA, *plus*
272 percent of the worker's PIA over $1,056 through $1,524, *plus*
134 percent of the worker's PIA over $1,524 through $1,987, *plus*
175 percent of the worker's PIA over $1,987.
This number is rounded to the next lower $0.10.

QUICK QUIZ 10.4

1. Up to 85% of an individual's Social Security benefits may be included in their taxable income.
   a. True
   b. False

2. Once divorced, non-working ex-spouses will not receive Social Security benefits.
   a. True
   b. False

3. The maximum family benefit establishes a limit on the benefits that can be received by one family.
   a. True
   b. False

True, False, True.

EXAMPLE 10.32

If an individual has the maximum PIA for 2015, $2,663 per month, this would provide a maximum family benefit of $4,660.30 per month as shown by the calculation below:

$1,056 x 1.50 =	$1,584.00
($1,524 - $1,056) x 2.72 =	$1,272.96
($1,987 - $1,524) x 1.34 =	$620.42
($2,663 - $1,987) x 1.75 =	$1,183.00
	$4,660.38
	Rounded to $4,660.30

EXAMPLE 10.33

Natalie and Brian, both age 50, are married and have two children, Ashley (age 15) and Kayli (age 5). Brian is disabled and has a PIA amount equal to the maximum PIA ($2,663). As seen in the example above, the maximum family benefit is $4,660.30. Because Brian is disabled, Natalie, Ashley, and Kayli are each entitled to receive a benefit equal to 50% of Brian's PIA, subject to the maximum family benefit limit, because the two children are under 18 and Natalie is a spouse/caretaker of a child under 18. Without regard to the maximum family benefit, they would each receive

Brian	$2,663	100% of PIA
Natalie	$1,332	50% of Brian's PIA
Ashley	$1,332	50% of Brian's PIA
Kayli	$1,332	50% of Brian's PIA
Total	$6,658	

Because the benefit exceeds the maximum family benefit, the amounts for Natalie, Ashley, and Kayli must be prorated. Therefore, they will each receive $665.79 [($4,660.38 - $2,663)÷3].

Brian	$2,663.00	100% of PIA
Natalie	$665.79	50% of Brian's PIA subject to maximum family benefit
Ashley	$665.79	50% of Brian's PIA subject to maximum family benefit
Kayli	$665.79	50% of Brian's PIA subject to maximum family benefit
Total	$4,660.38	

Assume instead that Ashley is 19 and no longer eligible to receive benefits under Brian. The maximum family benefit would be calculated as follows:

Brian	$2,663.00	100% of PIA
Natalie	$998.69	50% of Brian's PIA subject to maximum family benefit
Ashley	$0.00	Not eligible
Kayli	$998.69	50% of Brian's PIA subject to maximum family benefit
Total	$4,660.38	

Now assume Ashley is 19 and Kayli is 17. In this case, Natalie is no longer eligible because she is not caring for a child under 16. The family benefit would be calculated as follows:

Brian	$2,663	100% of PIA
Natalie	$0	Not eligible
Ashley	$0	Not eligible
Kayli	$1,332	50% of Brian's PIA
Total	$3,995	

Notice that Kayli is limited to 50% of Brian's PIA, thus they do not reach the maximum family benefit.

CHOOSING WHEN TO BEGIN SOCIAL SECURITY RETIREMENT BENEFITS

There are many issues in deciding when to begin receiving Social Security retirement benefits. As discussed earlier in this chapter, Social Security retirement benefits may be reduced if other income is earned before full retirement age, benefits may or may not be subject to income tax, and benefits may be increased or decreased depending on the start date of benefits relative to full retirement age. In addition to these issues, there are other considerations that may impact the total benefits collected by the worker and the worker's spouse.

Ideally, the present value of the total lifetime benefits for a person with an average life expectancy would be the same whether the beneficiary takes a smaller benefit at age 62 or a larger benefit at 70, as the calculations are actuarially based. However, that is not the case. Decisions that are made by a worker can greatly impact both the present value of benefits and total lifetime benefits collected. In fact, even if a retiree's life span is cut short, delaying retirement benefits past age 62 often makes a lot of sense.

As discussed earlier in the chapter, delaying retirement benefits increases the annual benefit when it is received. However, delaying commencement of receipt of retirement benefits should not be confused with a cost-of-living adjustment (COLA). cost-of-living adjustments are averaging about 1.6 percent or 1.7 percent increases over recent years, but once retirement benefits are being paid to a retiree, those benefits only increase based on the COLA. Nonetheless, by delaying benefits from age 62 to 63, the yet-to-be-received benefit increases approximately seven percent for that one year. Delaying benefits for anyone born in or after 1943 beyond full retirement age increases benefits by eight percent per year. That return is large for what is considered to be a very secure investment. Once the Social Security benefit is adjusted for inflation through application of the COLA, the rate is even more attractive.

KEY CONCEPTS

1. How are retirement benefits impacted by cost-of-living adjustments and by delayed credits?
2. What strategies can be used to potentially increase total lifetime benefits under Social Security?
3. How can a divorced spouse use "file and suspend?"

Is the eight percent increase worth delaying the start of benefits? That question is more complicated than it appears. Some of the important factors in this question are based on an individual's thoughts regarding wealth, cash flow needs, life expectancy, perception of the solvency of the Social Security program, as well as others.

An easy way to estimate a breakeven point for delayed benefits is to consider the benefit that is given up compared to the increase in future benefits. For example, assume a benefit of $1,000 per month or $12,000 per year at full retirement age. If the worker delayed benefits by one year, the benefits would increase by eight percent to $12,960 (without regard to a COLA). Therefore, the benefits that are received are $960 higher, but $12,000 had to be forfeited. Dividing what was given up ($12,000) by the increase ($960) results in a simple breakeven of 12.5 years. This calculation is very simplistic and does not consider the time value of money or other implications, such as taxation of benefits. However, it does provide basic guidance about how long one needs to live to justify giving up current benefits for higher future benefits.

The simplified breakeven analysis can be modified to include a COLA and a discount rate. As the spread between the COLA and the discount rate increases, so does the time it takes for the present value of the delayed benefits to exceed the present value of the benefits commencing immediately. For example, using a discount rate of four percent and a COLA of two percent (a spread of 2 percent) increases the breakeven point from 12.5 years to approximately 14 years. Thus, for someone to delay benefits until age 70 based solely on payback or breakeven, the person would have to live to at least age 82½, without considering the time value of money. However, there are other reasons that delaying benefits may be beneficial to the worker or their family members.

For non-married, lower wage earners who will not qualify for the maximum retirement benefit, it is important to keep in mind that the retirement benefit formula is based on the highest 35 years of work. If a non-married worker had historically lower earnings compared to earnings today, that worker might consider working longer to not only allow the automatic increase or growth of delaying the retirement benefit, but to also serve to increase the 35 year base, which is the basis for determining the retirement benefit. Delaying is especially helpful to those who do not work all 35 years, as that situation tends to have a more noticeable effect on the retirement benefit.

There is much written on the topic of when and how couples should begin collecting Social Security benefits. Below is a basic discussion of some of the relevant strategies. However, before discussing strategies, it is important to understand a few of the rules that impact the amount collected by workers and their spouses:

- Married individuals are entitled (1) to a worker-determined retirement benefit based on their own earnings and/or (2) to a spousal benefit equal to one half of their spouse's benefit claimed at normal retirement age. If a married individual files a claim prior to attaining normal retirement age, the laws governing Social Security deem the individual as claiming both types of benefits.
- In contrast, upon reaching normal retirement age, individuals may choose which benefit to receive, and they are not deemed to be claiming both. As a result, married individuals may claim a spousal benefit at age 66 (currently normal retirement age) and convert to their own retired worker benefit at a later date, allowing receipt of one type of benefit while concomitantly building up delayed retirement credits for a higher worker benefit later.
- When a person's current spouse attains full retirement age and they both apply for retirement benefits and then request to have the payments suspended, it permits the person to receive spouse's benefits. The spouse, who delayed benefits, will continue to earn delayed retirement credits until age 70.
- Spouses who have reached full retirement age and are entitled to receive a spouse's benefit, as well as their own benefit, may choose to receive only the spouse's benefit. This choice allows the spouse to delay applying for their retirement benefits until later while taking advantage of delayed retirement credits.
- Surviving spouses are entitled to 100 percent of the worker's benefit amount after the worker dies.

Many married couples use these rules to increase the amount they receive from Social Security. Once both spouses reach full retirement age, they can both file for benefits and suspend benefits. This strategy, known as "file and suspend," allows for increases in each spouse's benefits. It also

Quick Quiz 10.5

1. Delaying benefits to age 70 may be beneficial even if a person does not live beyond age 80.
   a. True
   b. False

2. A worker, who reaches full retirement age at age 67, can increase their benefit, without regard to a COLA, by 32 percent by delaying benefits until age 70.
   a. True
   b. False

3. The "file and suspend" strategy only works for married spouses and not ex-spouses.
   a. True
   b. False

True, False, False.

allows for one of the spouses, generally the one who has a smaller retirement benefit, to begin collecting the spousal benefit during the same time that the other spouse's benefits are increasing.

EXAMPLE 10.34

In the case of a one-earner couple where the wife, Bella, did not work a minimum of 40 quarters to qualify for a retired worker benefit, she would only be eligible for a spousal benefit. However, for Bella, in this hypothetical, to begin receipt of this spousal benefit, the husband, Thomas, must first have "claimed" his own retirement benefit. The "file and suspend" strategy allows Thomas, upon reaching normal retirement age, to file or claim and immediately suspend benefits, which in turn allows Bella to receive a spousal benefit based on Thomas's earnings record. Thomas is then free to continue working and receive delayed retirement credits, increasing not only Thomas's monthly benefit but also Bella's potential survivor benefit. By using "File and suspend," Bella and Thomas can enhance the value of their lifetime benefits.

EXAMPLE 10.35

Sandra and John are married and have both worked the requisite number of quarters to qualify for retirement benefits. Let's assume that John made more money than Sandra over the last 35 years of their work. Many knowledgeable in this area employ the strategy of having the wife (Sandra) claim early at age 62 and the husband claim late at age 70. The strategy or reasoning is that Sandra is able to receive her relatively lower spousal benefit or her retirement benefit based on her own earnings only over the relatively shorter expected lifespan of John rather than over the relatively longer expected lifespan of the average woman. Accordingly, Sandra could claim early to realize her benefit sooner and receive those paychecks, but her survivor benefit to begin upon her husband's death is based on a maximized survivor benefit that grew because the husband worked as long as possible and received delayed retirement credits.

Assume that Sandra is the same age as John and that her retirement benefit based on her own earnings is greater than her spousal benefit based on John's earnings. When John attains the current normal retirement age of 66, John then "claims" his benefits, permitting Sandra to start collecting her spousal benefit. John can then suspend his own benefit and increase the monthly amount by working until age 70. The latter approach is sometimes referred to as "Claim Now, Claim More Later."

Divorced spouses can also claim benefits based on their ex-spouse's record if they were married ten years or longer. Generally, the divorced spouse can collect based on their ex-spouse's record as long as they are unmarried, they are age 62 or older, and the ex-spouse is entitled to Social Security retirement or disability benefits. If a divorced spouse has reached full retirement age and is eligible for a spouse's benefit, then he or she can choose to receive only the divorced spouse's benefits and delay receiving their own retirement benefits until a later date. If retirement benefits are delayed, a higher benefit may be received at a later date based on the effect of delayed retirement credits. Thus, in effect, the spouse is able to receive a benefit from the ex-spouse's working history and let their own benefit increase until age 70.

EXAMPLE 10.36

Jimmy and Cassie were happily married and raised four wonderful children, who went on to become contributing members of society: a butcher, a baker, a dancer, and a home maker. However, once the children left the home, Jimmy and Cassie grew apart and finally divorced after 25 years of marriage. They both were professionals early in their career and became college professors. As a result, their retirement benefits are comparable. While Jimmy has remarried, Cassie remains single. At full retirement age, Cassie could claim a spouse's benefit and let her retirement benefits increase until she turns age 70.

These types of strategies should be considered when deciding whether to begin commencement of retirement benefits for oneself and that of a spouse. In many instances, total benefits from Social Security can be greatly increased.

MEDICARE BENEFITS

Title XVIII of the Social Security Act, designated "Health Insurance for the Aged and Disabled," is commonly known as Medicare. As part of the Social Security Amendments of 1965, the Medicare legislation established a health insurance program for aged persons to complement the retirement, survivors, and disability insurance benefits under Title II of the Social Security Act.

KEY CONCEPTS

1. What benefits are provided by Medicare?
2. What benefits are provided by Supplemental Security Income?
3. How does marriage or divorce affect Social Security benefits?

When first implemented in 1966, Medicare covered most persons aged 65 or older. In 1973, the following groups also became eligible for Medicare benefits:

- persons entitled to Social Security or Railroad Retirement disability cash benefits for at least 24 months,
- most persons with end-stage renal disease (ESRD), and
- certain otherwise non-covered aged persons who elect to pay a premium for Medicare coverage.

Beginning in July 2001, persons with Amyotrophic Lateral Sclerosis (Lou Gehrig's Disease) are allowed to waive the 24-month waiting period.

Beginning March 30, 2010, individuals in the vicinity of Libby, Montana who are diagnosed with an asbestos-related condition are Medicare-eligible.

Medicare originally consisted of two parts: Hospital Insurance (HI), also known as Part A, and Supplementary Medical Insurance (SMI), which in the past was also known simply as Part B. Part A helps pay for inpatient hospital, home health agency, skilled nursing facility, and hospice care. Part A is provided free of premiums to most eligible people; certain otherwise ineligible people may voluntarily pay a monthly premium for coverage. Part B helps pay for physician, outpatient hospital, home health agency, and other services. To be covered by Part B, all eligible people must pay a monthly premium (or have the premium paid on their behalf).

A third part of Medicare, sometimes known as Part C, is the Medicare Advantage program, which was established as the Medicare+Choice program by the Balanced Budget Act (BBA) of 1997 and subsequently renamed and modified by the Medicare Prescription Drug, Improvement, and Modernization Act (MMA) of 2003. The Medicare Advantage program expands beneficiaries' options for participation in private-sector health care plans.

The MMA also established a fourth part of Medicare, known as Part D, to help pay for prescription drugs not otherwise covered by Part A or Part B. Part D initially provided access to prescription drug discount cards, on a voluntary basis and at limited cost, to all enrollees (except those entitled to Medicaid drug coverage) and, for low-income beneficiaries, transitional limited financial assistance for purchasing prescription drugs and a subsidized enrollment fee for the discount cards. In 2006 and later, Part D provides subsidized access to prescription drug insurance coverage on a voluntary basis for all beneficiaries upon payment of a premium, with premium and cost-sharing subsidies for low-income enrollees.

When Medicare began on July 1, 1966, approximately 19 million people enrolled. In 2014, almost 54 million people are enrolled in one or both of Parts A and B of the Medicare program, and over 16 million of them have chosen to participate in a Medicare Advantage plan.

Generally, individuals who are over age 65 and receive Social Security benefits automatically qualify for Medicare. Also, individuals who have received Social Security disability benefits for at least two years automatically qualify for Medicare. All other individuals must file an application for Medicare.

EXHIBIT 10.18

MEDICARE PARTS

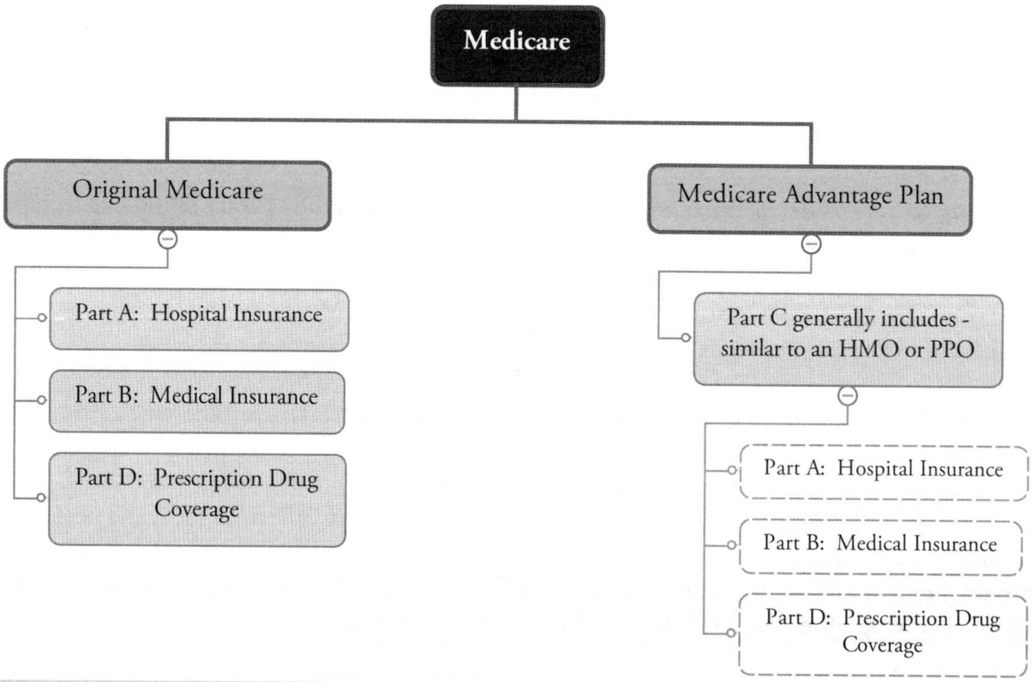

Part A, Hospital Insurance, is paid for by a portion of the Social Security tax. Part A helps pay for necessary medical care furnished by Medicare-certified providers, including inpatient hospital care, skilled nursing care, home health care, hospice care, and other care. The number of days that Medicare covers care in hospitals and skilled nursing facilities is measured in what is termed **benefit periods.** A benefit period begins on the first day a patient receives services in a hospital or skilled nursing facility and ends after 60 consecutive days without further skilled care. There is no limit to the number of benefit periods a beneficiary may have.

Benefit periods are identified because deductibles, coinsurance, and premiums relate to a benefit period instead of a calendar year. For instance, coverage under Medicare Part A for 2015 requires a deductible of $1,260 per benefit period. For the 61st through the 90th day of each benefit period, the insured individual must pay $315 per day in the form of coinsurance. Any days over 90 in a benefit period are considered lifetime reserve days. There are 60 lifetime reserve days available with coinsurance of $630 per day. Lifetime reserve days do not renew with each benefit period. It is important, therefore, to determine the number of days used in each benefit period.

Medicare Time Line

EXHIBIT 10.19

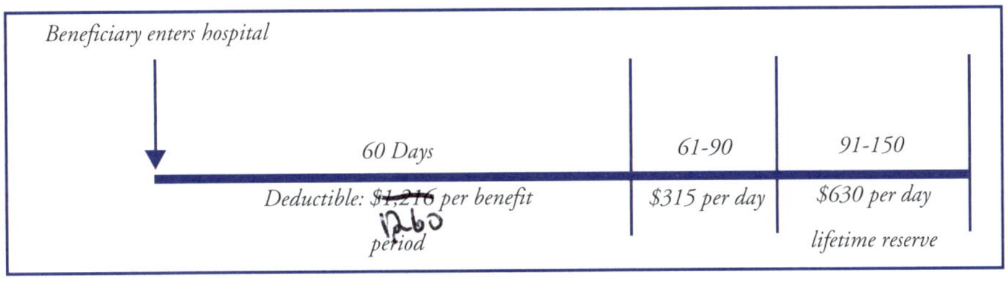

Skilled Nursing Facility Time Line

EXHIBIT 10.20

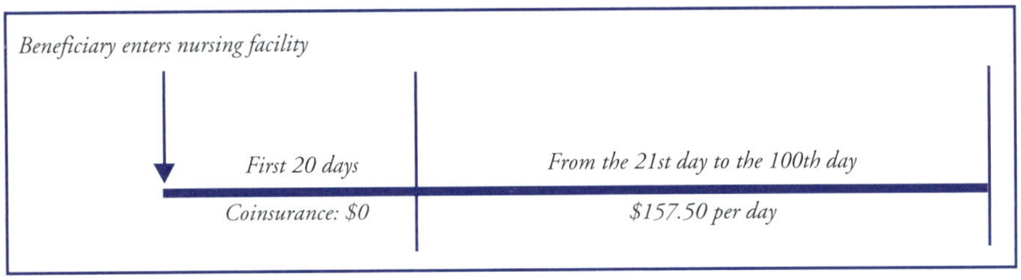

EXHIBIT 10.21 **MEDICARE DEDUCTIBLE, COINSURANCE, AND PREMIUM AMOUNTS (2015)**

Hospital Insurance (Part A)

• **Deductible** - $1,216 per Benefit Period
• **Coinsurance**
  • $315 a day for the 61st through the 90th day
  • $630 a day for the 91st through the 150th day for each lifetime reserve day (total of 60 lifetime reserve days – nonrenewable)
• **Skilled Nursing Facility coinsurance** - $157.50 a day for the 21st through the 100th day per Benefit Period
• **Hospital Insurance Premium** - $407 (reduced from $426 in 2014) per month (Note: This premium is paid only by individuals who are not otherwise eligible for premium-free hospital insurance and have less than 30 quarters of Medicare covered employment.)

Medical Insurance (Part B)
• **Deductible** - $147 per year • **Standard Monthly Premium** - $104.90 for new enrollees. The premium may be higher if income exceeds certain limits.

Source: Social Security Administration (www.ssa.gov)

Medicare Part A helps pay for up to 90 days of inpatient hospital care during each benefit period. Covered services for inpatient hospital care include: semiprivate room and meals, operating and recovery room costs, intensive care, drugs, laboratory tests, x-rays, general nursing services, and any other necessary medical services and supplies. Convenience items such as television and telephones provided by hospitals in private rooms (unless medically necessary) are generally not covered. Medicare does not pay for custodial services for daily living activities such as eating, bathing, and getting dressed. Medicare does, however, pay for skilled nursing facility care for rehabilitation, such as recovery time after a hospital discharge. Part A may help pay for up to 100 days in a participating skilled nursing facility in each benefit period. Medicare pays all approved charges for the first 20 days relating to skilled nursing facility care, and the patient pays a coinsurance amount for days 21 through 100. Medicare may also pay the full, approved cost of covered home healthcare services, which includes part-time or intermittent skilled nursing services prescribed by a physician for treatment or rehabilitation of home-bound patients. Normally, the only cost to the insured for home health care is a 20 percent coinsurance charge for medical equipment, such as wheelchairs and walkers.

Medicare Part B, Medical Insurance, is optional and is subject to a monthly premium. Part B is financed by the monthly premiums paid by those who are enrolled and out of the general revenues from the U.S. Treasury. Medicare Part B is used to pay for doctors' services; ambulance transportation; diagnostic tests; outpatient therapy services; outpatient hospital services, including emergency room visits; X-rays and laboratory services; some preventative care; home healthcare services not covered by Part A; durable medical equipment and supplies; and a variety of other health services.

Medicare Part B pays for 80 percent of approved charges for most covered services. Unless an individual declines Part B medical insurance protection, the premium will automatically be deducted from their Social Security benefits. The 2015 standard premium amount is $104.90 a month. The deductible for Part B is $147 per year. The insured is responsible for paying a $147 deductible per calendar year and the remaining 20 percent of the Medicare-approved charges. Medicare Part B usually does not cover charges for prescription drugs, routine physical examinations, or services unrelated to treatment of injury or illness. Dental care, dentures, cosmetic surgery, hearing aids, and eye examinations are not covered by Part B.

EXHIBIT 10.22

MEDICARE PART B PREMIUMS (2015)

Premium	Filing Status: Single	Filing Status: MFJ
$104.90	$85,000 or less	$170,000 or less
$146.90	$85,001-$107,000	$170,001-$214,000
$209.80	$107,001-$160,000	$214,001-$320,000
$272.70	$160,001-$214,000	$320,001-$428,000
$335.70	Above $214,000	Above $428,000

Various plans under Medicare are available to insureds. The original Medicare Plan is the way most individuals get their Medicare Part A and Part B benefits. This is the traditional payment-per-service arrangement where the individual insured may go to any doctor, specialist, or hospital that accepts Medicare, and Medicare pays its share after services are rendered. Medicare carriers and fiscal intermediaries are private insurance organizations that handle claims under the original Medicare Plan. Carriers handle Part B claims while fiscal intermediaries handle Part A plans. The Social Security Administration does not handle claims for Medicare payments.

Many private insurance companies sell Medicare supplemental insurance policies, such as Medigap and Medicare SELECT. These supplemental policies help bridge the coverage gaps in the original Medicare Plan. These supplemental policies also help pay Medicare's coinsurance amounts and deductibles, as well as other out-of-pocket expenses for health care.

When a worker is first enrolled in Part B at age 65, there is a six-month open enrollment period in Medigap. During the time of open enrollment, the health status of the applicant cannot be used as a reason to refuse a Medigap policy or to charge more than other open enrollment applicants. The insurer may require a six-month waiting period for coverage of pre-existing conditions. If, however, the open enrollment period has expired, the applicant may be denied a policy based on health status or may be charged higher rates.

MEDICARE PART D SUBSIDY

Medicare prescription drug plans, known as the Medicare Part D Subsidy (Part D or Medicare Prescription Drug Plan), became available beginning January 1, 2006, to individuals with Medicare. Part D is intended to save participants money on prescription drug costs and help protect against higher drug costs in the future. Insurance companies and other private companies work with Medicare to offer these drug plans by negotiating discounts on drug prices. These plans are different from the Medicare-approved drug discount cards, which were phased out by the earlier of May 15, 2006 or when an individual's enrollment in a Medicare prescription drug plan took effect.

Medicare prescription drug plans provide insurance coverage for prescription drugs. Part D covers both brand-name and generic prescription drugs at certain pharmacies in a Part D participant's area. If an individual is enrolled in Medicare, then that individual is eligible under Part D regardless of income, assets, health status, or current prescription expenses. Like other insurance, if an individual joins, they pay a monthly premium and pay a share of the cost of their prescriptions. As with Part B, higher income taxpayers will pay higher premiums. In addition, the premiums increase for delayed enrollment into the program by a factor of the "national base beneficiary premium" times the number of full, uncovered months that a senior was eligible but did not join a Medicare drug plan and went without other creditable prescription drug coverage. This premium increase may have to be paid for as long as the Medicare drug plan is maintained.

EXAMPLE 10.37

Mrs. Jones did not join Part D when she was first eligible - by May 15, 2010. She joined a Medicare drug plan with an effective date of January 1, 2015. Since Mrs. Jones did not join when she was first eligible and went without other creditable drug coverage for 55 months (June 2010 to December 2014), she will be charged a monthly penalty of $19.25 in 2015 ($35 x 0.01 = $0.35 x 55 = $19.25) in addition to her plan's monthly premium.[1]

Individuals may enroll in Part D when they first become eligible for Medicare, which is three months before the month the applicant turns age 65 until three months after the applicant turns age 65. If Medicare was available due to a disability, the applicant can join from three months before to three months after the 25th month of cash disability payments. There are two ways to obtain Medicare prescription drug coverage. The individual can either join a Medicare prescription drug plan or join a Medicare Advantage Plan or other Medicare Health Plan that offers drug coverage. Whichever plan is chosen, Medicare drug coverage helps the participant by covering brand name and generic drugs at pharmacies.

Drug plans may vary as to what prescription drugs are covered, how much the individual must pay, and which pharmacies they can use. All drug plans will have to provide at least a standard level of coverage, which Medicare will set. The premium, deductible, co-payment/co-insurance, and coverage may vary from plan to plan. However, some plans might offer more coverage and additional drugs for a higher monthly premium. When an individual joins a drug plan, it is important for them to choose one that meets their prescription drug needs. A list of drugs that a Medicare drug plan covers is called a formulary, which includes generic drugs and brand name drugs. Most prescription drugs used by those with Medicare will be on the given plan formulary, whether it is in brand name or generic form. To insure coverage of an appropriate amount of drugs, a formulary must include at least two drugs in categories and classes of most commonly prescribed drugs to those individuals with Medicare. This helps to insure that people with varying medical conditions can get the medication or treatment they need.

Even individuals who do not use a lot of prescription drugs should consider joining Part D because aging people often need prescription drugs to stay healthy. For a relatively low premium, Medicare prescription drug coverage can protect the individual from unexpected drug expenses in the future.

1. The "national base beneficiary premium" of $35 is assumed for this example. The 2015 premium is actually $33.15.

Part D consists of four phases of coverage: the deductible, the coinsurance phase, the coverage gap, and the catastrophic phase. The deductible must be satisfied prior to any benefits being provided from the plan. In the initial phase, sometimes referred to as the coinsurance phase, beneficiaries pay a portion of the expenses up to an annual limit. The coverage gap is often referred to as "donut hole" because in this phase, beneficiaries pay most of the costs of prescription drugs, but may receive discounts depending on the plan. The catastrophic phase covers all but a small coinsurance amount for the remainder of the year.

Other Medicare Health Plan Choices

Medicare offers alternative methods of obtaining Medicare benefits through other health plan choices. Choices that vary by area include coordinated-care or Medicare managed care plans such as Health Maintenance Organizations (HMOs), HMOs with a point of service option, Provider Sponsored Organizations (PSOs), and Preferred Provider Organizations (PPOs). These plans involve specific groups of doctors, hospitals, and other providers who provide care to the insured as a member of the plan, like many employer-sponsored plans throughout the country. Medicare managed-care plans not only provide the same services that are covered by Part A and Part B, but most Medicare managed plans offer a variety of additional benefits like preventative care, prescription drugs, dental care, eyeglasses, and other items not covered by the original Medicare Plan. The cost of these extra benefits varies among the plans.

For those who receive Medicare and have low income and few resources, states may pay Medicare premiums and, in some cases, other out-of-pocket Medicare expenses, such as deductibles and coinsurance. The respective state decides if individuals qualify. For more general information about Medicare, the Social Security Administration's leaflet *Medicare Savings for Qualified Beneficiaries* (HCFA Publication No. 02184) is helpful, as are the websites *www.ssa.gov* and *www.medicare.gov.*

SUPPLEMENTAL SECURITY INCOME BENEFITS

Supplemental Security Income (SSI) makes monthly payments to individuals with low incomes and few assets. In order to obtain SSI benefits, an individual must be age 65, disabled, or blind. The definition of disability is satisfied when the individual is unable to engage in any substantial gainful activity due to a physical or mental problem expected to last at least a year or expected to result in death. Children as well as adults qualify for SSI disability payments. As its name implies, Supplemental Security Income supplements the beneficiary's income up to various levels depending on where the beneficiary lives. If an otherwise eligible SSI applicant lives in another's household and receives support from that person, the federal SSI benefit is reduced by one-third.

The federal government pays a basic rate. The basic monthly SSI check for 2015 is $733 per month for one person and $1,100 per month for married couples. Some states supply additional funds to qualified individuals. To ascertain the SSI benefit rates in a certain state, the advisor or client can contact a local Social Security office in that state or visit the Social Security Administration's website. Generally, individuals who receive SSI benefits also qualify for Medicaid, food stamps, and other government assistance.

To be eligible for the monthly SSI benefit, the beneficiary must not have assets that exceed $2,000 for one person or $3,000 for married couples. This asset determination does not include the value of the home and some personal belongings, such as one car. If the potential beneficiary does not work, he may be eligible for SSI benefits if monthly income is less than $733 for one person and $1,100 for a couple. If the potential beneficiary works, more monthly income is allowed. SSI benefits are not paid from Social Security trust funds and are not based on past earnings of the beneficiary. Rather, SSI benefits are financed by general tax revenues and assure a minimum monthly income for needy elderly, disabled, or blind persons.

FILING FOR SOCIAL SECURITY CLAIMS

The Social Security Administration reports that many people fail to file claims with the Social Security Administration or fail to do so in a timely fashion. Individuals should file for Social Security or SSI disability benefits as soon they become too disabled to work or for survivors' benefits, when a family breadwinner dies. Social Security benefits do not start automatically. Social Security will not begin payment of benefits until the beneficiary files an application. When filing for benefits, applicants must submit documents that show eligibility, such as a birth certificate for each family member applying for benefits, a marriage certificate if a spouse is applying, and the most recent W-2 forms or tax returns.

To file for benefits, obtain information, or to speak to a Social Security representative, individuals must call the Social Security Administration's toll-free number, 800-772-1213, or visit the Social Security Administration's website. The toll-free number can be used to schedule an appointment at a local Social Security office. The Social Security Administration treats all calls confidentially. Periodically, a second Social Security representative will monitor incoming and outgoing telephone calls to ensure accurate and courteous service.

OTHER ISSUES

Effect of Marriage or Divorce on Benefits

Marriage or divorce may affect one's Social Security benefits, depending on the kind of benefits received. If a worker receives retirement benefits based on his own earnings record, the worker's retirement benefits will continue whether married or divorced. If an individual receives benefits based on his spouse's record, the individual's benefits will cease upon divorce unless the individual is age 62 or older and was married longer than 10 years. Widows and widowers, whether divorced or not, will continue to receive survivors' benefits upon remarriage if the widow or widower is age 60 or older. Disabled widows and widowers, whether divorced or not, will continue to receive survivors' benefits upon remarriage if the disabled widow or widower is age 50 or older.

EXAMPLE 10.38

Larry was married at the following ages and to the following wives. Larry is now 62 and married to Dawn.

	Wife	Current Age	Larry's Age at Marriage	Current Marital Status	Length of Marriage
1	Alice	62	20	Single	10 years, 1 month
2	Betty	63	31	Single	10 years, 1 month
3	Claire	64	42	Single	9 years
4	Dawn	65	53	Married	9 years

Who, among the wives, may be eligible to receive Social Security retirement benefits based upon Larry's earnings if Larry is retired or not retired?

Any divorced spouse, age 62 and married to Larry for 10 years or longer is eligible to receive benefits. If Larry is retired, then his current wife is also eligible to receive benefits. However, she cannot collect benefits if he is not retired.

If Larry is retired: Alice, Betty, and Dawn.

If Larry is not retired: Alice and Betty.

For all other forms of Social Security benefits, benefits will cease upon remarriage, except in special circumstances. When a person marries, it is presumed that at least one person in the marriage can provide adequate support. Likewise, Social Security benefits may recommence based on the previous spouse's benefits if the marriage ends.

Change of Name

If an individual changes their name due to marriage, divorce, or a court order, that individual must notify the Social Security Administration of the name change so the Social Security Administration will be able to show the new name in their records and properly credit that individual for earnings. This notice will ensure that the individual's work history will be accurately recorded and maintained.

Leaving the United States

Beneficiaries who are United States citizens may travel or live in most foreign countries without affecting their eligibility for Social Security benefits. However, there are a few countries where Social Security checks cannot be sent. These countries currently include Cuba, and North Korea.

Also, beneficiaries that go to any of the following countries can receive Social Security benefits only if they meet and agree to certain restricted conditions. These countries are:

- Azerbaijan
- Belarus
- Georgia
- Kazakhstan
- Kyrgyzstan
- Moldova
- Tajikistan
- Turkmenistan
- Ukraine
- Uzbekistan
- Vietnam

Quick Quiz 10.6

1. Medicare Part A generally pays for "Places" while Part B pays for "Services."
   a. True
   b. False

2. In order to obtain Supplemental Social Security benefits, the individual must be 62, disabled, or blind.
   a. True
   b. False

3. Social Security beneficiaries who are United States citizens may live in most foreign countries without affecting their eligibility for Social Security benefits.
   a. True
   b. False

True, False, True.

Beneficiaries should inform the Social Security Administration of their plans to go outside the United States for a trip that lasts 30 days or more. By providing the name of the country or countries to be visited and the expected departure and return dates, the Social Security Administration will send special reporting instructions to the beneficiaries and arrange for the delivery of their checks while they are abroad.

2015 Social Security Fact Sheet

EXHIBIT 10.23

Fact Sheet

SOCIAL SECURITY

2015 SOCIAL SECURITY CHANGES

- **Cost-of-Living Adjustment (COLA):**

  Based on the increase in the Consumer Price Index (CPI-W) from the third quarter of 2013 through the third quarter of 2014, Social Security and Supplemental Security Income (SSI) beneficiaries will receive a 1.7 percent COLA for 2015. Other important 2015 Social Security information is as follows:

	2014	2015
Tax Rate:		
Employee	7.65%	7.65%
Self-Employed	15.30%	15.30%

NOTE: The 7.65% tax rate is the combined rate for Social Security and Medicare. The Social Security portion (OASDI) is 6.20% on earnings up to the applicable taxable maximum amount (see below). The Medicare portion (HI) is 1.45% on all earnings. Also, as of January 2013, individuals with earned income of more than $200,000 ($250,000 for married couples filing jointly) pay an additional 0.9 percent in Medicare taxes. The tax rates shown above do not include the 0.9 percent.

	2014	2015
Maximum Taxable Earnings:		
Social Security (OASDI only)	$117,000	$118,500
Medicare (HI only)	No Limit	
Quarter of Coverage:	$1,200	$1,220
Retirement Earnings Test Exempt Amounts:		
Under full retirement age	$15,480/yr. ($1,290/mo.)	$15,720/yr. ($1,310/mo.)

NOTE: One dollar in benefits will be withheld for every $2 in earnings above the limit.

	2014	2015
The year an individual reaches full retirement age	$41,400/yr. ($3,450/mo.)	$41,880/yr. ($3,490/mo.)

NOTE: Applies only to earnings for months prior to attaining full retirement age. One dollar in benefits will be withheld for every $3 in earnings above the limit.

SSA Press Office 440 Altmeyer Building 6401 Security Blvd. Baltimore, MD 21235 410-965-8904 FAX 410-966-9973

There is no limit on earnings beginning the month an individual attains full retirement age.

- **Social Security Disability Thresholds:**

Substantial Gainful Activity (SGA)		
Non-Blind	$1,070/mo.	$1,090/mo.
Blind	$1,800/mo.	$1,820/mo.
Trial Work Period (TWP)	$ 770/mo.	$ 780/mo.

- **Maximum Social Security Benefit:** Worker Retiring at Full Retirement Age:

	$2,642/mo.	$2,663/mo.

- **SSI Federal Payment Standard:**

Individual	$ 721/mo.	$ 733/mo.
Couple	$1,082/mo.	$1,100/mo.

- **SSI Resources Limits:**

Individual	$2,000	$2,000
Couple	$3,000	$3,000

- **SSI Student Exclusion:**

Monthly limit	$1,750	$1,780
Annual limit	$7,060	$7,180

- **Estimated Average Monthly Social Security Benefits Payable in January 2015:**

	Before 1.7% COLA	**After 1.7% COLA**
All Retired Workers	$1,306	$1,328
Aged Couple, Both Receiving Benefits	$2,140	$2,176
Widowed Mother and Two Children	$2,635	$2,680
Aged Widow(er) Alone	$1,253	$1,274
Disabled Worker, Spouse and One or More Children	$1,943	$1,976
All Disabled Workers	$1,146	$1,165

KEY TERMS

AIME (Average Indexed Monthly Earnings) - A worker's highest 35 years of earnings adjusted for inflation and averaged on a monthly basis. AIME is used as the basis for the PIA calculation.

Benefit Periods - Begins on the first day an individual receives services as a patient in a hospital or skilled nursing facility and ends after 60 consecutive days without further skilled care.

Cost-of-Living Adjustment (COLA) - The cost-of-living adjustments applied to Social Security benefits.

Currently Insured Workers - A worker who has earned at least six quarters of coverage out of the previous 13 quarters for Social Security.

Disability Benefit - A Social Security benefit available to recipients who have a severe physical or mental impairment that is expected to prevent them from performing "substantial" work for at least a year or result in death. To qualify for these benefits, the recipient must have the sufficient amount of Social Security credits.

Disability Insurance (DI) Trust Fund - The trust fund that pays benefits to workers with disabilities and their families. It is funded by 0.90 percent of an individual's taxable earnings up to $118,500 (2015).

Family Benefit - A Social Security benefit available to certain family members of workers eligible for retirement or disability benefits.

FICA (Federal Insurance Contributions Act) - A law allowing Social Security taxes, including Medicare taxes, to be deducted from employee's paychecks.

Fully Insured - A worker who has earned 40 quarters of coverage under the Social Security system.

Hospital Insurance (HI) Trust Fund - The trust fund that pays for services covered under the hospital insurance provisions of Medicare (Part A). It is funded by 1.45 percent of an individual's taxable earnings (no limitation).

Maximum Family Benefit - The limit on the amount of monthly Social Security benefits that may be paid to a family.

Medicaid - Provides medical assistance for persons with low incomes and resources.

Medicare - A federal health insurance plan for those who have attained full retirement age or have been disabled whether retired or still working.

KEY TERMS

Modified Adjusted Gross Income (when calculating taxable Social Security) - The sum of an individual's adjusted gross income plus tax exempt interest, including interest earned on savings bonds used for higher education; amounts excluded from the taxpayer's income for employer provided adoption assistance; amounts deducted for interest paid for educational loans; amounts deducted as qualified tuition expense; and income earned in a foreign country, a U.S. possession, or Puerto Rico that is excluded from income.

Old Age, Survivor, and Disability Insurance (OASDI) - An inclusive title given to the Social Security benefit system.

Old Age and Survivors Insurance (OASI) - The trust fund that pays retirement and survivors' benefits funded by 5.30 percent of an individual's taxable earnings up to $118,500 (2015).

PIA (Primary Insurance Amount) - The amount on which a worker's retirement benefit is based; the PIA determines the amount the applicant will receive at his full retirement age based on the year in which the retiree turns 62. The PIA is indexed to the Consumer Price Index (CPI) annually.

Retirement Benefit - The most familiar Social Security benefit, full retirement benefits are payable at normal retirement age and reduced benefits as early as age 62 to anyone who has obtained at least a minimum (40 quarters) amount of Social Security credits.

Retirement Earnings Limitations Test - A test that may reduce the Social Security benefit paid to an individual based on their other income.

SSI (Supplemental Security Income) - A program administered by the Social Security Administration and funded by the general Treasury that is available to those at full retirement age or the disabled who have a low income and few assets.

Supplementary Medical Insurance (SMI) Trust Fund - The trust fund that pays for services covered under the medical insurance provisions of Medicare, known as Part B. The coverage is funded by general federal tax revenues and monthly medicare premiums paid by enrollees.

Survivors' Benefit - Social Security benefit available to surviving family members of a deceased, eligible worker.

DISCUSSION QUESTIONS

1. List and describe the six major categories of benefits administered by the Social Security Association.

2. How are Social Security funds collected?

3. Which individuals are covered workers under the Social Security system?

4. List the beneficiaries of Social Security benefits.

5. How is a person's Social Security retirement benefit calculated?

6. How does retiring early or retiring late affect the calculation of Social Security benefits?

7. How are Social Security benefits taxed?

8. What other benefits are available from Social Security other than retirement benefits?

9. Discuss the maximum family benefit.

10. What Social Security benefits does Medicare provide?

11. Describe Supplemental Security Income benefits and when they are available.

12. How does marriage or divorce affect Social Security benefits?

MULTIPLE CHOICE PROBLEMS

1. Social Security is funded through all of the following except:

    a. Employee payroll tax.
    b. Employer payroll tax.
    c. Sales tax.
    d. Self-employment tax.

2. Brisco, now deceased, was married for 12 years. He had two dependent children, ages 10 and 12, who are cared for by their mother age 48. His mother, age 75, was his dependent and survived him. At the time of his death, he was currently but not fully insured under Social Security. His dependents are entitled to all of the following benefits except:

    a. A lump-sum death benefit of $255.
    b. A children's benefit equal to 75% of Brisco's PIA.
    c. A caretaker's benefit for the children's mother.
    d. A parent's benefit.

3. Medicare Part A provides hospital coverage. Which of the following persons is not covered under Part A?

    a. A person 62 or older and receiving railroad retirement.
    b. Disabled beneficiaries regardless of age that have received Social Security for two years.
    c. Chronic kidney patients who require dialysis or a renal transplant.
    d. A person 65 or older entitled to a monthly Social Security check.

4. Part B of Medicare is considered to be supplemental insurance and provides additional coverage to participants. Which of the following is true regarding Part B coverage?

    a. The election to participate must be made at the time the insured is eligible for Part A Medicare and at no time after.
    b. The premiums for Part B are paid monthly through withholding from Social Security benefits.
    c. Once a participant elects Part B, he must maintain the coverage until death.
    d. Coverage under Part B does not include deductibles or coinsurance.

5. A person receiving Social Security benefits under the age of 65 can receive earned income up to a maximum threshold without reducing Social Security benefits by the earnings test. Which of the following count against the earnings threshold?

    a. Dividends from stocks.
    b. Rental income.
    c. Pensions and insurance annuities.
    d. Gambling winnings.

6. Betty Sue, age 75, is a widow with no close relatives. She is very ill, unable to walk, and confined to a custodial nursing home. Which of the following programs is likely to pay benefits towards the cost of the nursing home?

    1. Medicare may pay for up to 80 additional days of care after a 20-day deductible.
    2. Medicaid may pay if the client has income and assets below state-mandated thresholds.

    a. 1 only.
    b. 2 only.
    c. Both 1 and 2.
    d. Neither 1 nor 2.

7. Which of the following concerning the Social Security system is correct?

    a. SSI benefits are funded by the Treasury, not Social Security taxes, as are the other benefits.
    b. The Social Security retirement benefit is payable at full retirement age with reduced benefits as early as age 59 to anyone who has obtained at least a minimum amount of Social Security benefits.
    c. The two Medicare trust funds are the federal Medical Insurance Trust Fund for Part A and the Supplementary Hospital Insurance Trust Fund for Part B of Medicare benefits.
    d. Benefits can be paid to the dependent parents of a deceased insured worker at age 59 or over.

8. Which of the following concerning the Social Security system is correct?

   a. Workers entitled to retirement benefits can currently take early retirement benefits as early as age 59.
   b. A worker who takes early retirement benefits will receive a reduced benefit because he will receive more monthly benefit payments as payments commence earlier than if the worker had waited and retired at full retirement age.
   c. Family members of an individual who are eligible for retirement or disability benefits include a spouse if the spouse is at least 59 years old or under 59 but caring for a child under age 16.
   d. Generally, individuals who are over the age of 59 and receive Social Security benefits automatically qualify for Medicare benefits.

9. All of the following statements concerning the Social Security system are correct except:

   a. If a worker receives retirement benefits based on his own earnings record, the worker's retirement benefits will continue whether married or divorced.
   b. Widows and widowers, whether divorced or not, will continue to receive survivors' benefits upon remarriage if the widow or widower is age 60 or older.
   c. By providing the name of a country or countries to be visited and the expected departure and return dates, the Social Security Administration will send special reporting instructions to the beneficiaries and arrange for delivery of checks while abroad.
   d. A special one-time payment of $1,000 may be made to a deceased worker's spouse or minor children upon death.

10. All of the following statements concerning Social Security benefits are correct except:

    a. The maximum family benefit is determined through a formula based on the worker's PIA.
    b. If a worker applies for retirement or survivors' benefits before his 65th birthday, he must also file a separate application for Medicare.
    c. People who are disabled or have permanent kidney failure can get Medicare at any age.
    d. The Social Security Administration is concerned with beneficiaries' combined income, which, on the 1040 federal tax return, includes adjusted gross income and nontaxable interest income.

11. All of the following statements concerning Social Security benefits are correct except:

    a. In order to obtain SSI benefits, an individual must be age 65 or older and must be disabled.
    b. The number of days that Medicare covers care in hospitals and skilled nursing facilities is measured in what is termed benefit periods.
    c. The definition of disability is that the individual is unable to engage in any substantial gainful activity due to a physical or mental problem expected to last at least a year or expected to result in death.
    d. Benefits are payable at any age to workers who have enough Social Security credits and who have a severe physical or mental impairment that is expected to prevent them from doing "substantial" work for a year or more or who have a condition that is expected to result in death.

12. Joyce and Melvin have been married for 30 years. In 2015, they received $22,000 of Social Security benefits and had $12,000 of interest income. What portion of the Social Security benefit is taxable?

    a. $0.
    b. $6,000.
    c. $10,200.
    d. $11,500.

13. Emile is single and received $28,000 of dividend income during the year. He also received $18,000 of Social Security benefits. What portion of his Social Security benefits are taxable?

    a. $0.
    b. $7,050.
    c. $9,000.
    d. $15,300.

14. Antoine immigrated from Italy last century, became a citizen and has worked the better part of his life in the United States, for which he is truly thankful. His full retirement age (normal retirement age) for Social Security benefits is age 66, but after a hard life working he wants to retire at age 63 and travel throughout America and back to his homeland. If his benefit at age 66 is $1,000 per month, how much will he receive in Social Security retirement benefits if he begins receiving benefits at age 63?

    a. $700.00.
    b. $800.00.
    c. $812.50.
    d. $1,000.00. The same benefit, he will simply not receive it for as long.

15. Antoine immigrated from Italy last century, became a citizen and has worked the better part of his life in the United States, for which he is truly thankful. His full retirement age for Social Security benefits is age 66, but after a hard life working he wants to retire at age 63 and travel in America and back to his homeland. After contacting the Social Security administration, they informed him that his benefit at age 63 would be $1,200 per month. Just prior to retiring, he sold his business for $100,000. Which of the following statements is correct?

    a. The sale of the business will not impact the amount of his retirement benefits from Social Security.
    b. The sale of the business will cause his benefits to be reduced by $1 for every $2 over the annual limit.
    c. The sale of the business will definitely increase the portion of his Social Security benefits that are subject to income tax.
    d. The sale of the business may cause him to pay a higher Medicare Part B premium in the year of the sale due to his higher income.

16. Antoine immigrated from Italy last century, became a citizen and has worked the better part of his life in the United States, for which he is truly thankful. His full retirement age for Social Security benefits is age 66, but after a hard life working he wants to retire at age 63 and travel in America and back to his homeland. He sold his restaurant for $150,000 and was retained by the acquiring company as a consultant for a one-year period. His consulting fee this year will be $50,000 and the benefit he expects to receive from Social Security is $2,000 per month. Which of the following statements is correct?

    a. He should delay receiving Social Security retirement benefits until after this year because he will be in a high tax bracket due to the sale of his business.
    b. He should delay receiving Social Security retirement benefits until after this year because there will be such a large reduction in benefits due to his consulting income and the sale of the business.
    c. He should begin receiving Social Security benefits today because although there is a reduction in benefits today, there will be an increase after full retirement age.
    d. He would be better off beginning Social Security benefits next year.

17. Kathryn taught at Fun Academic University for 25 years and is filing for Social Security retirement benefits this year, when she turns age 72. Her PIA is $1,000 per month as adjusted for inflation. How much in benefits will she receive assuming her full retirement age was 66?

    a. $1,320.
    b. $1,360.
    c. $1,480.
    d. $1,587.

18. A worker's AIME:

   a. Must be determined by converting actual earnings into current dollars through an indexing factor.
   b. Is determined from wage information over prior years' work.
   c. Uses the highest 35 years of indexed earnings (for workers that worked at least that long).
   d. Yields an average amount of monthly earnings for all indexed years.
   e. All of the above.

19. Which of the following is a useful strategy to benefit a married couple?

   a. File and defend.
   b. Claim and earn.
   c. Suspend and spend.
   d. File and suspend.

20. Which of the following are correct?

   a. Surviving spouses are entitled to 100 percent of the worker's benefit amount after the worker dies.
   b. Divorced spouses can also claim benefits based on their ex-spouse's record if they were married 8 years or longer.
   c. For someone to delay benefits until age 70 based solely on payback or breakeven, the person would have to live to at least age 92, without considering the time value of money.
   d. All of the above are false.

QUICK QUIZ EXPLANATIONS

Quick Quiz 10.1

1. False. Reduced Social Security benefits can be withdrawn as early as age 62.
2. False. Social Security contributions are placed in the following trust funds: OASI, DI, and HI. The SMI Trust Fund is not funded by Social Security contributions.

Quick Quiz 10.2

1. True.
2. True.

Quick Quiz 10.3

1. False. The Social Security retirement benefit is based on the worker's PIA. A worker's PIA is based on the worker's average indexed monthly earnings during the 35 years in which the worker earned the most.
2. False. Full retirement age for Social Security is increasing because of increasing life expectancies.

Quick Quiz 10.4

1. True.
2. False. Once divorced, a non-working ex-spouse who was married to the worker for more than ten years can still receive Social Security benefits based on the worker's record.
3. True.

Quick Quiz 10.5

1. True.
2. False. The increase equals 8 percent per year times three years, which is a 24 percent increase.
3. False. The strategy actually works for spouses who are married as well as those that were married for at least 10 years.

Quick Quiz 10.6

1. True.
2. False. In order to obtain SSI benefits, an individual must be 65, disabled, or blind.
3. True.

Appendix

A

GLOSSARY

A

ACCELERATED BENEFITS PROVISION - Entitles a qualified insured to receive a pre-death benefit deemed nontaxable.

ACCUMULATION PHASE - The period over which annuity funds are accumulated.

ACTIVITIES OF DAILY LIVING (ADL) - Physical functions that an independent person performs each day, including bathing, dressing, eating, transferring, toileting, and maintaining continence.

ACTUAL CASH VALUE - The depreciated value of personal property.

ADHESION - A take it or leave it contract.

ADULT DAY CARE - Services provided during the day at a community-based center. Programs address the individual needs of functionally or cognitively impaired adults.

ADVERSE SELECTION - The tendency of those that most need insurance to seek it out.

AGENTS - Legal representatives of an insurer and act on behalf of an insurer.

AIME (AVERAGE INDEXED MONTHLY EARNINGS) - A worker's highest 35 years of earnings adjusted for inflation and averaged on a monthly basis. AIME is used as the basis for the PIA calculation.

ALEATORY - A type of insurance contract in which the dollar amounts exchanged are uneven.

ANNUAL RENEWABLE TERM (ART) - Type of term insurance that permits the policyholder to purchase term insurance in subsequent years without evidence of insurability, but premiums on the policy increase each year to reflect the increasing mortality risk being undertaken by the insurer.

ANNUAL RESET METHOD - The index-linked interest crediting rate is determined each year by comparing the index value at the end of the contract year with the index value at the beginning of the contract year. Interest is then added to the annuity each year during the term.

ANNUITANT - The individual upon whose life the contract is dependent. It is generally the life expectancy of the annuitant that affects the timing and amount of payout under the contract.

ANNUITIZATION - The time when annuity funds are exchanged for a stream of income guaranteed for a period of time.

ANNUITIZED - The time when regular, periodic (such as monthly or annual) payments begin for life or for a specified period of time in excess of one year.

ANNUITY - A contract between an individual (annuitant) and an insurance company which promises to pay an income on a regular basis for a specified period of time.

Any Occupation - Type of disability insurance policy that provides benefits to a policy owner if he or she is unable to perform the duties of any occupation for which he or she is suited by education, training, or experience.

Apparent Authority - When the third party believes implied or express authority exists, but no authority actually exists.

Appraised or Agreed Upon Value - Used for hard to value items and where the insured may own property that exceeds standard limits of property insurance policy.

Asset Accumulation Phase - This phase is usually from the early 20s to late 50s when additional cash flow for investing is low and debt to net worth is high.

Assignment - The process of transferring all or part of the policy's ownership rights.

Assisted Living - Senior housing that provides individual apartments, which may or may not have a kitchenette. Facilities offer 24-hour on site staff, congregate dining, and activity programs. Limited nursing services may be provided for an additional fee.

Assumption of Risk - The injured party fully understood and recognized the dangers that were involved in an activity and voluntarily chose to proceed.

Auto Credit Score - Score calculated principally based on previous auto loan history.

Auto Insurance Score - Ranges from 150 to 850 and uses data from the Trans Union credit report. It helps auto insurance companies to assess the risk of insuring a consumer by measuring the probability that an auto insurance claim might be filed.

Automatic Increase Rider - A provision that automatically increases the monthly benefit by a stated percentage each year.

B

Bed Reservation - Some policies will pay to reserve a bed in the nursing home when the insured leaves to go into a hospital. This reservation can last a specified number of days or until the insured returns from the hospital.

Beneficiary - Those persons entitled to the death benefit of the annuity.

Benefit Periods - Begins on the first day an individual receives services as a patient in a hospital or skilled nursing facility and ends after 60 consecutive days without further skilled care.

Brokers - Legal representatives of an insured and act in the best interest of the insured.

Buy-Sell Agreements - Arrangements that require the sale and purchase of securities owned by one individual to another following a specified triggering event, such as the death of a business owner.

C

Cap Rate - Some indexed annuities impose an upper limit on the index-linked interest rate.

Capitalized-Earnings Approach - Method to determine life insurance needs that suggests the death benefits of a client's life insurance should equal an income stream sufficient to meet the family's needs without depleting the capital base.

Cash Refund Annuity - Guarantees that the annuitant or the annuitant's family will receive the premium payments made to purchase the annuity, but instead of continuing to make periodic payments until there is a full recovery of the premium, the balance is paid in cash at the annuitant's death.

Chip and Pin (EMV technology) - An embedded computer chip in the card (card is more expensive), creates a unique number for each transaction and requires a pin to approve any charge.

Chronic Illness - Having a physical or cognitive impairment that prevents the insured individual from performing at least two of the six activities of daily living for at least a 90-day period, or requiring substantial supervision to prevent the insured from posing a danger to himself, herself, or others.

Coinsurance - The percentage of financial responsibility that the insured and the insurer must uphold in order to achieve equity in rating.

COLA Rider - Provides a cost of living adjustment to benefit payments based on increases in inflation.

Collateral Source Rule - Holds that damages assessed against a negligent party should not be reduced simply because the injured party has other sources of recovery available such as insurance or employee benefits (health or disability insurance).

Collision - Auto insurance coverage that protects the insured against upset and collision damages, such as those sustained in an accident involving other vehicles, or those sustained when an auto runs off the road and into a lake.

Comparative Negligence - The amount of damage is adjusted to reflect the injured party's proportion of contribution to the cause of the injury.

Comprehensive (or Other than Collision) - Auto insurance coverage that protects the insured's auto against perils out of the insured's control, such as missiles or falling objects, fire, theft, earthquake, hail, flood, and vandalism.

CONCEALMENT - When the insured is intentionally silent regarding a material fact during the application process.

CONDITIONAL - The insured must abide by all the terms and conditions of the contract, if the insured intends to collect under the policy.

CONSERVATION (RISK MANAGEMENT) PHASE - This phase is from late 20s to early 70s, when cash flow assets and net worth have increased and debt has decreased somewhat. In addition, risk management of events like employment, disability due to illness or accident, and untimely death become a priority.

CONSUMER LENDING - Credit cards, home equity loans, home equity lines of credit, auto loans, other recreational vehicle loans, and appliance loans.

CONTINGENT BENEFICIARIES - Person(s) or organization named to receive the death benefit if the primary beneficiary is not available to receive the policy proceeds.

CONTRIBUTORY NEGLIGENCE - Negligence on the part of the injured party that contributes to the harm and, therefore, the injured has to bear some responsibility for the injury.

CO-PAYMENT - A loss-sharing arrangement whereby the insured pays a percentage of the loss in excess of the deductible.

CORRIDOR TEST - One of two Congress-imposed tests to determine whether a life insurance contract meets the definition of an MEC. This test calls for the policy to be tested using actuarial principles and requires the premiums to represent no more than a specified portion of the death benefit.

COST-OF-LIVING ADJUSTMENT (COLA) - The cost-of-living adjustments applied to Social Security benefits.

CREDIT AGENCIES - Companies that compile and maintain credit information from credit card companies, banks, mortgage companies, and other creditors for the purpose of creating personal in-depth credit reports on individuals. The major credit reporting agencies are Experian, Equifax, and TransUnion.

CREDIT SCORE - A number that summarizes a person's credit risk based on an evaluation of his or her credit report at a particular point in time.

CROSS-PURCHASE BUY-SELL AGREEMENT - An arrangement between individuals who agree to purchase the business interest of a deceased owner.

CURRENTLY INSURED WORKERS - A worker who has earned at least six quarters of coverage out of the previous 13 quarters for Social Security.

Custodial Care - Board, room and other personal assistance services (including assistance with activities of daily living, taking medicine and similar personal needs) that may not include a skilled nursing care component.

D

Declarations Section - The section of an insurance policy that describes exactly what property is being covered.

Decreasing-Term Insurance - Type of term insurance that allows the owner to pay the same premium for the insurance protection each year. The death benefit on the policy will, however, decrease each year to offset the increasing mortality cost due to the passage of time.

Deductible - A specified amount of money the insured is required to pay on a loss before the insurer will make any payments under the policy.

Deferred Annuity - An annuity contract that does not begin payments immediately, but waits until some future time to start payments.

Definition Section - The section of an insurance policy that defines key words, phrases, or terms used throughout the insurance contract.

Description Section - The section of an insurance policy that describes exactly what is being insured.

Disability Benefit - A Social Security benefit available to recipients who have a severe physical or mental impairment that is expected to prevent them from performing "substantial" work for at least a year or result in death. To qualify for these benefits, the recipient must have the sufficient amount of Social Security credits.

Disability Insurance - A type of insurance that provides supplementary income in the event of an illness or accident resulting in a disability that prevents the insured from working at his or her regular employment.

Disability Insurance (DI) Trust Fund - The trust fund that pays benefits to workers with disabilities and their families. It is funded by 0.90 percent of an individual's taxable earnings up to $118,500 (2015).

Distribution (Gifting) Phase - This phase is from the late 40s to end of life and occurs when the individual has high additional cash flow, low debt, and high net worth.

Dumpster Diving - A means of identity theft, that involves going through someone's trash while looking for identity information from cancelled checks, bank statements, credit card statements, federal or state tax documents, discarded credit card offers, and phone numbers.

DWELLING - Residential structure covered under a homeowners insurance policy.

E

ELIMINATION PERIOD - The period of time, beginning upon injury or sickness, that an insured is disabled but is not collecting benefits from the insurer.

ENDORSEMENT - Attachment or addition to an existing insurance policy that changes the original terms.

ENTITY PURCHASE (REDEMPTION) AGREEMENT - Type of buy-sell agreement that obligates the business entity to purchase an owner's interest in the entity upon that owner's death.

EQUITY-INDEXED ANNUITIES - Have characteristics of both fixed and variable annuities, either immediate or deferred, that earn interest or provide benefits that are linked to an external equity reference or an equity index.

ESTOPPEL - The legal process of denying a right you might otherwise be entitled to under the law.

EXCLUSION SECTION - The section of an insurance policy that will exclude certain perils, losses and property.

EXPENSE INCURRED METHOD – this method provides for reimbursement of expense once bills are submitted to the insurance company. The reimbursable amount cannot exceed the benefit amount.

EXPRESS AUTHORITY - Authority given to an agent through a formal written document.

F

FAMILY BENEFIT - A Social Security benefit available to certain family members of workers eligible for retirement or disability benefits.

FICA (FEDERAL INSURANCE CONTRIBUTIONS ACT) - A law allowing Social Security taxes, including Medicare taxes, to be deducted from employee's paychecks.

FICO SCORE - A credit score developed by FICO (formerly know as Fair Isaac Corporation) that estimates the level of future credit risk for an individual. It is calculated using a formula that evaluates many types of information in the credit report at that credit reporting agency and ranges from 300 to 850.

FINANCIAL RISK - A loss of financial value, such as the premature death of a family's primary wage earner.

First-to-Die - Type of joint life insurance policy that covers two individuals, but the death benefit is paid upon the death of the first individual.

Fixed Annuity - The most conservative type of annuity that earns a minimum guaranteed rate of return.

Fixed Deferred Annuity - Accumulates interest at a stated rate that is commonly adjusted on an annual basis, subject to a minimum interest rate guarantee.

Flexible Premium Annuity - Allows the insured the option to vary premium deposits.

Flexible Spending Account (FSA) - Employer-sponsored plan that permits employees to defer pre-tax income into an account to pay for health care expenses. FSAs require the employee to either use the contributed amounts for medical expenses by the end of the year, or forfeit the unused amounts to the company.

Floor Crediting Rate - An indexed annuity is the minimum index-linked interest rate that will be credited to the contract in a given period.

Fully Insured - A worker who has earned 40 quarters of coverage under the Social Security system.

Fundamental Risk - A risk that can impact a large number of individuals at one time (earthquake or flood).

Future Increase Option Rider - A provision that permits the insured to increase benefit coverage as they get older.

G

Grace Period - A provision in most insurance policies which allows payment to be received for a certain period of time after the actual due date without a default or cancellation of the policy.

Group Health Insurance - Health plans offered to a group of individuals by an employer, association, union, or other entity.

Group Term Insurance - A type of life insurance coverage offered to a group of people (often a component of an employee benefit package) that provides benefits to the beneficiaries if the covered individual dies during the defined covered period.

Guarantee Funds - Run by the state insurance commission, they act as the payor of last resort in the case of an insurance company failure.

Guaranteed Purchase Option - Allows the insured to increase the benefits by a stated percentage periodically.

Guaranteed Renewable - A provision that requires the insurance company to renew the policy for a specified period of time or until the insured attains a certain age.

H

Hard Inquiries - Inquiries made by creditors or potential creditors.

Hazards - A specific condition that increases the potential or likelihood of a loss occurring.

Health Maintenance Organizations (HMOs) - A form of managed care in which participants receive all of their care from participating providers. Physicians are employed by the HMO directly, or may be physicians in private practice who have chosen to participate in the HMO network. The independent physicians are paid a fixed amount for each HMO member that uses them as a primary care physician.

Health Savings Accounts (HSA) - A plan that permits employees or individuals to save for health care costs on a tax-advantaged basis. Contributions made to the HSA by the plan participant are tax-deductible as an adjustment to gross income (above the line), and distributions from the HSA to pay for medical expenses are excluded from income.

High Deductible Health Insurance Plans - Plans with a deductible of at least $1,300 for individual coverage and $2,600 for family coverage in 2015, with a maximum out-of-pocket stop loss amount of $6,450 for single coverage and $12,900 for family coverage in 2015.

High Watermark Approach - Determining index-linked interest is accomplished by comparing the value of the index at various points during the term (usually on anniversary dates).

Home Health Care - Limited part-time or intermittent skilled nursing care and home health aide services, physical therapy, occupational therapy, speech-language pathology services, medical social services, durable medical equipment (such as wheelchairs, hospital beds, oxygen, and walkers), medical supplies, and other services provided in the patient's home.

Home Insurance Score - Ranges from 150 to 850 and is once again calculated using the TransUnion credit report. It is primarily used by home insurance companies to assess the probability that a homeowner will file a homeowner's insurance claim.

Homeowners Insurance - A package insurance policy that provides both property and liability coverage for the insured's dwelling, other structures, personal property, and loss of use.

Hospice Care - Offers a special way of caring for people who are terminally ill, typically utilizing a team-oriented approach to address medical, physical, social, emotional, and spiritual needs.

HOSPITAL INSURANCE (HI) TRUST FUND - The trust fund that pays for services covered under the hospital insurance provisions of Medicare (Part A). It is funded by 1.45 percent of an individual's taxable earnings (no limitation).

HUMAN-LIFE VALUE APPROACH - Method to determine life insurance needs that suggests the death benefit of a client's life insurance should equal to the economic value of the client's future earnings stream.

I

IMMEDIATE ANNUITY - An instrument created when the contract owner trades a sum of money in return for a stream of income that begins immediately.

IMPLIED AUTHORITY - The authority that a third party relies upon when dealing with an agent based upon the position held by the agent.

INCONTESTABILITY CLAUSE - Clause in a health insurance policy that prevents the insurer from challenging the validity of the health insurance contract after it has been in force for a specified period of time unless the insured fraudulently obtained coverage in the beginning of the policy.

INDEMNITY HEALTH INSURANCE - Traditional, fee-for-service health insurance that does not limit where a covered individual can get care.

INDEX TERM - The period over which index-linked interest is calculated for equity-indexed annuities.

INDEXING METHOD - The approach used to measure the amount of change, if any, in the index. Some common indexing methods include: (1) the annual reset (ratcheting) approach, (2) the high watermark approach, and (3) the point-to-point approach.

INDIVIDUAL MAJOR MEDICAL PLANS - Major medical insurance coverage purchased independently from an insurance company (not as part of a group).

INFLATION - The increase in the general price level, and is often measured by the Consumer Price Index (CPI).

INFLATION PROTECTION - Helps the insured to maintain the purchasing power of the original contract benefit.

INITIAL RATE - The first rate of interest that is earned under a fixed annuities contract and is guaranteed for a specified period of time.

Installment Refund Annuity - A special type of term certain annuity whereby the insurer promises to continue periodic annuity payments after the annuitant has died until the sum of all annuity payments made equals the purchase price of the annuity.

Insured - The person whose life is insured by the policy.

Intentional Interference - Intentional act committed against another that causes injury.

Intermediate-Care Nursing Facility - A licensed facility with the primary purpose of providing health or rehabilitative services. Typically provides custodial care along with intermittent, as opposed to daily, medical care.

IRD Assets - Assets that have a deferred income tax liability that was not paid prior to the date of the owner's death.

J

Joint and Survivor Annuity - Promises to make payments over the lives of two or more annuitants, and annuity payments are made until the last annuitant dies. This is, commonly used to fund the retirement cash-flow needs of married couples.

L

Lacking Sound Mind - The state of not having the capacity to understand the purpose and terms of the contract, therefore the contract lacks a meeting of the minds or mutual consent.

Last Clear Chance Rule - This rule states that a claimant who is endangered by his own negligence may recover if the defendant has a "last clear chance" to avoid the accident and failed to do so.

Law of Large Numbers - A principle that states the more similar events or exposures, the more likely the actual results will equal the probability expected.

Level Premium Term Insurance - Type of term insurance that charges a fixed premium each year over a specified period of years, so the premium does not increase over that period.

Libel - A written statement that causes harm to another.

Life Annuity Contracts - Protect clients from outliving their assets by providing a series of periodic payments to the annuitant, typically made for as long as the annuitant lives.

Limited-Pay Policies - Type of whole life policy with a payment schedule (typically 10 or 20 years). At the end of the payment period, the policy is considered to be paid-up, at which time no additional premium payments are due.

LONG-TERM CARE INSURANCE - Coverage that pays for all or part of the cost of home health care services or care in a nursing home or assisted living facility.

LONG-TERM CARE SERVICES - Medical and non-medical care for people with chronic illnesses or disabilities that assists people with Activities of Daily Living, such as dressing, bathing, and using the bathroom. Long-term care can be provided at home, in the community, or in a facility.

LONG-TERM DISABILITY - Provides coverage for specified term, until specified age, or until death.

LONGEVITY INSURANCE - A sophisticated name for a deferred annuity purchased by an individual at or before retirement that will not begin to make payments until that person reaches an advanced age.

LOSS OF USE - Under homeowners insurance coverage, loss of use is a combination of additional living expenses and loss of rental income.

M

MANAGED CARE INSURANCE - Health-care delivery systems that integrate the financing and delivery of health care. Managed care plans feature a network of physicians, hospitals, and other providers who participate in the plan. Managed care includes HMOs, PPOs, and POS plans.

MAXIMUM FAMILY BENEFIT - The limit on the amount of monthly Social Security benefits that may be paid to a family.

MAXIMUM LIFETIME BENEFIT - the total amount of money that could be paid under the LTC policy for charges incurred for covered services.

MEDICAID - A state and federal assistance program that pays for medical care and most long-term care expenses for eligible persons with low incomes and limited assets.

MEDICAL PAYMENTS - A no-fault, first-party insurance coverage designed to pay for bodily injuries sustained in an auto accident.

MEDICARE - A federal program that pays for healthcare for persons over age 65 and for people under age 65 with disabilities.

MENTAL AND NERVOUS DISORDERS - Long-term care insurance policies can exclude coverage of some mental and nervous disorders, but the policy must cover serious biologically-based mental illnesses and other diseases, such as schizophrenia, major depression disorders, Alzheimer's disease, and other age-related disorders. However, a long-term care insurer may refuse to sell a policy to someone already suffering from these otherwise covered exclusions.

Minors - In most states, a minor is under the age of 18. If a minor enters into a contract, the minor can void the contract at any time.

Modified Adjusted Gross Income (when calculating taxable Social Security) - The sum of an individual's adjusted gross income plus tax exempt interest, including interest earned on savings bonds used for higher education; amounts excluded from the taxpayer's income for employer provided adoption assistance; amounts deducted for interest paid for educational loans; amounts deducted as qualified tuition expense; and income earned in a foreign country, a U.S. possession, or Puerto Rico that is excluded from income.

Modified Endowment Contract (MEC) - A cash value life insurance policy that has been funded too quickly. Under an MEC, the death benefit payable to the beneficiary is not subject to income tax, but policy loans or cash value withdrawals are taxable.

Modified Whole Life Policies - Type of whole life policy with lower premiums than a regular policy for an initial policy period (often 3 to 5 years), which increase to a higher-level premium at the end of the initial period.

Moral Hazard - The potential loss occurring because of the moral character of the insured, and the filing of a false claim with their insurance company.

Morale Hazard - The indifference to a loss created because the insured has insurance.

Mortality Cost - Equals the probability of dying within the year times the face value of the policy.

Mortality Risk - The risk that an individual will die within the year.

Mutual Consent - Common understanding and agreement between parties to a contract regarding what the contract covers and the terms of the contract.

N

Needs Approach - Method to determine life insurance needs that suggests the death benefits of a client's life insurance should equal the cash needs that the family will require at death plus income replacement needs.

Negligence - Harm caused by failure to use reasonable care.

Non-Cancelable - A provision that prevents the insurance company from cancelling the policy for any reason provided the policy premium is paid.

Non-Forfeiture Benefit - The insurer must guarantee that the insured will receive some of the benefits paid for even upon cancellation or lapsed coverage.

NON-QUALIFIED ANNUITIES - Annuity contracts purchased with funds outside of qualified retirement plans or IRAs (for example, from investment accounts or private savings).

NONFINANCIAL RISK - A risk that would result in a loss, other than a monetary loss.

O

OBJECTIVE RISK - The variation of actual amount of losses that occur over a period of time compared to the expected amount of losses.

OFFER AND ACCEPTANCE - Consists of one party making an offer to purchase a good or service, and the acceptance is when consideration is received.

OLD AGE AND SURVIVORS INSURANCE (OASI) - The trust fund that pays retirement and survivors' benefits funded by 5.30 percent of an individual's taxable earnings up to $118,500 (2015).

OLD AGE, SURVIVOR, AND DISABILITY INSURANCE (OASDI) - An inclusive title given to the Social Security benefit system.

OPEN PERILS - All-risk coverage for personal property that provides for a much broader and more comprehensive protection program than named-perils coverage.

ORDINARY (OR STRAIGHT) LIFE - Type of whole life policy that requires the owner to pay a specified level premium every year until death (or age 100).

OTHER STRUCTURES - Small detached structures on the insured's property in addition to the main house, such as garages, greenhouses, or storage buildings.

OWN OCCUPATION - Type of disability insurance policy that provides benefits to a policyholder if he is unable to perform the duties of their occupation. This type of policy is more expensive than an any occupation policy.

OWNER - Person, trust, or company that owns the annuity contract and names the annuitant and beneficiaries. The owner could also be the annuitant and/or the beneficiary.

P

PAROL EVIDENCE RULE - States that "what is written prevails." Oral agreements that are not reflected in the written contract are not valid.

PARTIAL DISABILITY - A provision that provides payments that are less than those paid for a total disability.

PARTICIPATION RATE - Determines how much of the increase in the index will be used to calculate the index-linked interest.

PARTICULAR RISK - A risk that can impact a particular individual, such as death or the inability to work because of a sickness or accident.

PARTIES TO ANNUITY CONTRACT - The annuitant, the beneficiary, the owner, and the insurance company.

PERILS - The immediate cause and reason for a loss occurring.

PERSONAL AUTOMOBILE POLICY - Insurance policy that covers liability for injuries and damages to persons inside and outside the vehicle and covers the cost to repair/replace a damaged or stolen vehicle.

PERSONAL LIABILITY UMBRELLA POLICY - Coverage designed to provide a catastrophic layer of liability coverage on top of the individual's homeowners and automobile insurance policies.

PERSONAL PROPERTY - Valuable items owned by the insured that are covered under homeowners insurance.

PHYSICAL HAZARD - A physical condition that increases the likelihood of a loss occurring.

PIA (PRIMARY INSURANCE AMOUNT) - The amount on which a worker's retirement benefit is based; the PIA determines the amount the applicant will receive at his full retirement age based on the year in which the retiree turns 62. The PIA is indexed to the Consumer Price Index (CPI) annually.

POINT-TO-POINT INDEX-LINKED CREDITING METHOD - Based on the difference between an index value at the end of the term compared with the index value at the start of the term.

POINT OF SERVICE PLAN (POS) - A form of managed care that is considered a managed care/ indemnity plan hybrid, as it mixes aspects of HMOs, PPOs, and indemnity plans for greater patient choice. A primary care physician coordinates patient care, but there is more flexibility in choosing doctors and hospitals than in an HMO.

POOLING OF RISK - The spreading of risk among a large number of similar contributors to the pool. Protection is provided to the entire pool of contributors. With annuities, the risk that is being spread is the risk of outliving retirement funds, or superannuation.

PRE-EXISTING CONDITIONS - A pre-existing condition is an illness or disability for which an insured has received previous medical advice or treatment usually within six months prior to the application for long-term care coverage.

Preferred Provider Organization - A form of managed care in which participants have more flexibility in choosing physicians and other providers than in an HMO. The arrangement between insurance companies and health care providers permits participants to obtain discounted health care services from the preferred providers within the network.

Premium - The amount participants pay to belong to a health plan.

Presumptive Total Disability Coverage - A provision that automatically considers certain conditions to be totally disabling, such as loss of sight in both eyes, hearing in both ears, the use of both hands, the use of both feet, or the use of one foot and one hand.

Primary Beneficiary - Person(s) (may be a group designation) or organization to receive the death benefit upon the death of the insured.

Primary Care Physician - A physician that is designated as a participant's first point of contact with the health care system, particularly in managed care plans.

Principle of Indemnity - Asserts that an insurer will only compensate the insured to the extent the insured has suffered an actual financial loss.

Principle of Insurable Interest - Asserts that an insured must suffer a financial loss if a covered peril occurs, otherwise no insurance can be offered.

Pure Risk - The chance of loss or no loss occurring.

Q

Qualified Annuities - Annuity contracts purchased with funds in a qualified retirement plan or IRA.

R

Radio Frequency Identification (RFID) Cards - The wireless use of electromagnetic fields to transfer consumer information. This is being adopted by debit and credit card companies to deter identity theft.

Refund of Premium - The company will refund some or all of the insured's premiums minus any claims paid under the policy if the policy is canceled. The insured's beneficiary will receive such refund if the insured dies.

Reinsurance - A means by which an insurance company transfers some or all of its risk to another insurance company.

Replacement Cost - Represents the amount of money necessary to repair or replace property, without any deduction for depreciation.

Representation - A statement made by the applicant during the insurance application process.

Residual Benefits Provision - A provision that will provide continuing benefits for an insured who returns to work but suffers a reduction of income due to a disability.

Res ispa loquitur - A doctrine of the law of negligence that is concerned with the circumstances and the types of accidents, which affords reasonable evidence if a specific explanation of negligence is not available.

Restoration of Benefits - Some policies restore benefits to the original maximum amounts if the insured no longer needs long-term care services, usually after 180 days.

Retirement Benefit - The most familiar Social Security benefit, full retirement benefits are payable at normal retirement age and reduced benefits as early as age 62 to anyone who has obtained at least a minimum (40 quarters) amount of Social Security credits.

Retirement Earnings Limitations Test - A test that may reduce the Social Security benefit paid to an individual based on their other income.

Retirement Life Expectancy - The period between retirement and death.

Rider - A modification or change to a life or health insurance policy.

Risk - The chance of loss, uncertainty associated with loss, or the possibility of a loss.

Risk Avoidance - A risk management technique used for any risks that are high in frequency and high in severity.

Risk-Based Capital - The investment risk assessment undertaken by the insurance company in investing the money backing up the annuity pool.

Risk Reduction - The process of reducing the likelihood of a pure risk that is high in frequency and low in severity.

Risk Retention - Accepting some or all of the potential loss exposure for risk that are low in frequency and low in severity.

Risk Transfer - The process of transferring a low frequency and high severity risk to a third party, such as an insurance company.

S

SCAM - An acronym from the Justice Department to help avoid identity theft.

SCHEDULE - Attachment or addition to an existing insurance policy that lists individual items.

SECOND-TO-DIE - Type of joint life insurance policy that is often used in estate planning to provide liquidity at the death of the second spouse. A second-to-die policy names two insureds and pays the death benefit only when the second insured dies.

SECONDARY MARKET ANNUITIES - Called pre-owned annuities or in-force annuities. These annuities can be purchased from the original owner at a discount or from a third party, wherein which the stream of income is assigned to the purchaser. These; typically offer a rate of return or yield that is well above the yield available on standard fixed annuities, immediate annuities, or even bonds of a similar credit quality.

SELF-INSURED RETENTION - A payment similar to a deductible that an insured is usually required to pay for each loss under a personal umbrella policy.

7-PAY TEST - One of two Congress-imposed tests to determine whether a life insurance contract meets the definition of an MEC. This test states that if the cumulative premium payments made on the policy are in excess of the net level premium for the policy during the first seven years (or following a material change to the policy), the life insurance contract will be deemed an MEC.

SHORT-TERM DISABILITY - Provides coverage for up to two years, and typically has a 5 to 30 day elimination period (the period an insured must wait before receiving benefits).

SHOULDER SURFING - A means of identity theft by the eavesdropping on those who punch in numbers or verbally give numbers over the phone.

SIMULTANEOUS DEATH PROVISION - Provision in a life insurance policy for situations in which the insured and the beneficiary die within a short time of one another and it is not possible to determine who died first, Generally the policy death benefit is distributed as if the beneficiary had predeceased the insured.

SINGLE LIFE ANNUITY - Also known as a straight life annuity, provides a stream of income to the annuitant for life.

SINGLE PREMIUM ANNUITY - An annuity purchased with a single lump sum.

SINGLE PREMIUM POLICY - Type of whole life policy that requires the owner to pay a lump sum in return for insurance protection that will extend throughout the insured's lifetime. These policies will always be a MECs.

SINKING FUND - A sinking fund is a fund established by a company to pay for future expenses or to retire debt. It is created by setting aside income over a period of time (generally years).

SKILLED CARE FACILITY - Provides the highest level of service combining both daily medical and custodial care.

SKILLED NURSING CARE FACILITY - 24-hour nursing care for chronically-ill or short-term rehabilitative residents of all ages. It provides the highest level of service, and combines daily medical and custodial care.

SLANDER - Verbal statement that causes harm to another.

SOFT INQUIRIES - Inquiries made by the consumer or by a prospective or current employer.

SPECIAL NEEDS TRUST - A specific type of trust that is used to provide benefits to persons or beneficiaries with special needs. They are designed to protect eligibility for government assistance programs.

SPECULATIVE RISK - The chance of loss, no loss, or a profit.

SPLIT DEFINITION - Type of disability policy where an insured is covered against the risk of not performing his or her own occupation for a period of time, and after that period expires, an any-occupation definition of disability is used.

SPLIT LIMITS - Three separate liability coverage limits covering bodily injury (per person and per occurrence) and property damage.

SSI (SUPPLEMENTAL SECURITY INCOME) - A program administered by the Social Security Administration and funded by the general Treasury that is available to those at full retirement age or the disabled who have a low income and few assets.

STRAIGHT OR PURE LIFE ANNUITY - An annuity that provides a stream of income to the annuitant for life.

STRICT AND ABSOLUTE LIABILITY - Liability resulting from law. Strict liability allows for defense, absolute liability does not.

SUBJECTIVE RISK - The risk an individual perceives based on their prior experiences and the severity of those experiences.

SUBROGATION CLAUSE - A clause in an insurance policy that requires that the insured relinquish a claim against a negligent third party, if the insurer has already indemnified the insured.

SUICIDE CLAUSE - Provision in a life insurance policy specifying that the insurance company will not pay the benefit if the insured attempts or commits suicide within a specified period from the beginning of the coverage. The clause is designed to hedge against the risk that individuals with suicidal thoughts will purchase life insurance and commit suicide shortly thereafter.

Supplementary Medical Insurance (SMI) Trust Fund - The trust fund that pays for services covered under the medical insurance provisions of Medicare, known as Part B. The coverage is funded by general federal tax revenues and monthly Medicare premiums paid by enrollees.

Surrender Charge - A fee levied on a life insurance policyholder upon cancellation of the policy to cover the up-front costs of issuing the policy.

Survivors' Benefit - Social Security benefit available to surviving family members of a deceased, eligible worker.

Survivorship Clause - Provision in a life insurance policy specifying that the death benefit will only be paid to the beneficiary if the beneficiary survives the insured by a specific number of days.

T

Term Certain Annuity - Acts as a hedge against the mortality risk retained when an individual purchases a single life annuity by preserving some or all of the capital for distribution to the annuitant's heirs, but this hedge comes at a cost.

Term Insurance - Life insurance policy that states that if the premium has been paid and the insured dies during the term of the policy, the insurance company will pay the specified death benefit.

Terminal Illness - Having a life expectancy of less than 24 months, which must be certified by a qualified health professional.

The Fair Credit Reporting Act of 1971 - Provides that U.S. citizens have free access to their credit reports and credit scores from each of the three national credit reporting agencies.

Total Plan Benefit – The total amount of money that could be paid under the LTC policy for charges incurred for covered services.

Traditional Medical Care - Attempts to treat or cure illnesses.

U

Underwriting - The process of classifying applicants into a risk pools, selecting insureds, and assigning a premium.

Unilateral - There is only one promise made; and in the case of an insurance contract, it's made by the insurer to pay in the event of a loss.

UNINSURED / UNDERINSURED MOTORIST - Motorist without liability coverage or whose insurer can/will not pay claim, hit-and-run driver, or motorist with insufficient liability coverage according to state law.

UNIVERSAL LIFE INSURANCE - Type of term insurance with a cash-value accumulation feature allowing individuals to make premium contributions in excess of the term-insurance premium. The excess premiums are deposited into an account with various investment options.

V

VANTAGESCORE 3.0 - Ranges from 300-850 and was developed by the three major credit bureau agencies.

VARIABLE ANNUITIES - Provide consumers with an opportunity to individually tailor the types of investments backing up the annuity contract to their unique needs, and equity-indexed annuities provide returns linked to market-based indexes.

VARIABLE LIFE INSURANCE - Type of life insurance policy that permits the owner of the life insurance policy to direct the investment of the policy's cash value. Variable policies typically offer a series of investment options that often include investment funds managed by the insurer and outside investment managers.

VARIABLE UNIVERSAL LIFE INSURANCE POLICIES (VULS) - Type of life insurance policy that combines variable and universal life insurance and gives the policyholders the option to invest as well as alter insurance coverage.

VARIABLE WHOLE LIFE POLICIES - Type of life insurance that provides for a fixed premium payment and permits the cash value of the policy to be professionally managed by the insurance company or an outside investment manager.

VIATICAL SETTLEMENT - An arrangement in which a policyholder sells their life insurance policy to a third party.

VICARIOUS LIABILITY - One person may become legally liable for the torts of another (e.g., parent / child, employer where the employee is acting in the scope of employment).

W

WAIVER - The relinquishment a known legal right.

WAIVER OF PREMIUM - Allows the insured to stop paying premiums during the period in which he or she is receiving policy benefits. However, this provision may only apply to certain benefits, for example, nursing home or home healthcare.

Warranty - A promise made by the insured that is part of the insurance contract.

Whole Life Insurance - Type of life insurance that provides guarantees from the insurer that are not found in term insurance and universal life insurance policies.

Appendix

B

INDEX

D

E

F

G

H

I

J

L

M

N

O

P

R

S

T

U

V

W